P9-DWO-775

## DATE DUE

| | | | |
|---|---|---|---|
| MY 5 '95 | | | |
| DE 8 '95 | | | |
| AP 19 '96 | | | |
| NO 4 '96 | | | |
| DE 5 '96 | | | |
| DE 20 '96 | | | |
| RENEW | | | |
| MY 29 '97 | | | |
| OC 20 '9 | | | |
| MY 19 '9 | | | |
| DE 1 '99 | | | |
| OC 11 '0 | | | |
| | | | |
| NO 15 '01 | | | |
| | | | |
| DE 6 '01 | | | |
| | | | |
| | | | |

DEMCO 38-296

# THE MAKING OF TERRORISM

# THE MAKING OF TERRORISM

## MICHEL WIEVIORKA
Translated by DAVID GORDON WHITE

THE UNIVERSITY OF CHICAGO PRESS    Chicago and London

Riverside Community College
Library
4800 Magnolia Avenue
Riverside, California 92506

FEB    '95

HV6431 .W5313 1993
Wieviorka, Michel.
The making of terrorism

es Hautes Etudes en Sciences
iers *Internationaux de*
*Workers' Movement* (with
Alain Touraine and François Dubet, 1987).

Originally published as *Sociétés et terrorisme,* by Michel Wieviorka.
© Librairie Arthème Fayard, 1988.

The University of Chicago Press, Chicago 60637
The University of Chicago Press, Ltd., London
© *1993 by The University of Chicago*
*All rights reserved. Published 1993*
*Printed in the United States of America*

·02 01 00 99 98 97 96 95 94 93     1 2 3 4 5

ISBN: 0-226-89650-1 (cloth)    0-226-89652-8 (paper)

Library of Congress Cataloging-in-Publication Data

Wieviorka, Michel.
   [Sociétés et terrorisme. English]
   The making of terrorism / Michel Wieviorka ; translated by David
Gordon White.
      p.   cm.
   Includes bibliographical references (p.     ) and index.
   1. Terrorism.   2. International relations.   I. Title.
HV6431.W53   1993                                        93-13633
363.3'2—dc20                                             CIP

♾ The paper used in this publication meets the minimum requirements of
the American National Standard for Information Sciences—Permanence of
Paper for Printed Library Materials, ANSI Z39.48-1984.

# Contents

# Foreword

Terrorism is fear and radical disengagement. It creates or confirms the existence of a nearly unbridgeable gulf. It is the expression of a communication failure between those who resort to it and those who are its victims. As soon, however, as some kind of link is forged and an informed knowledge of terrorist actors becomes available, the phenomenon loses its fundamental attributes, its mysterious, shocking, and dramatic character, at times to the point of seeming to melt away.

The terror that terrorism awakens in us is directly proportional to our ignorance of terrorist actors. These powers of darkness lose their fascination and interest as soon as they are exposed to the light, whether through arrest, imprisonment, repression, or simple exhaustion. At such times, they can quite commonly become pitiful laughingstocks. A terrorist movement at its height operates like a magnet, drawing attention to itself well beyond its terrorist acts per se. Overheating in the media, panic in the corridors of power, empty-handedness in the police and intelligence services, miscarriages in the halls of justice, and the human drama of victims and their families all combine to reinforce the image of the terrorist as an all-powerful figure. Conversely, disinterest reigns as soon as an incident has passed, and our memories are hardly jogged when we see these same terrorist actors, now portrayed as miserable figures, at the conclusion of an escapade. Terrorism seems to be a matter of feast or famine: we get too much of it when it is dished up hot, and too little when the action has cooled down.

While it is the case that terrorism consists of a set of more-or-less circumscribable practices, it can also be whatever we choose to call it as our passions and interests rise and fall from one moment to the next. On those occasions in which there is general consensus in the denunciation of terrorism, the phenomenon itself will always be defined from a strictly subjective viewpoint, whence the highly apposite formula which states that one man's terrorist is another man's freedom fighter.

Here, the researcher is faced with a delicate choice.[1] On the one hand, he may align himself with prevailing opinions and adopt a subjective outlook. In this case, terrorism basically becomes a more-or-less irrational and wholly intolerable threat to be interpreted in terms of its implications for the society it threatens: the flouting of values, the endangering of institutions, and the breaking of the bonds that hold society together. Carried to its limits, such a perspective not only serves to describe the failure of reason, the perversion of the democratic ideal, or the insanity or barbarity of the terrorists themselves. It can be taken much further, to serve in an investigation of those social conditions which give rise to the very notion of terrorism. In this light, terrorism becomes a matter of packaging, a category whose explication and utilization have less to do with the phenomenon itself than with certain characteristics of the society which it impacts. These may include crises in social institutions, general feelings of economic decline, an inability to formulate a coherent foreign policy, silence on the part of intellectuals, a climate of insecurity, and the existence of ethnic or religious groups linked to terrorism, groups which may either wish to discuss or to minimize the phenomenon, etc.

On the other hand, the researcher may attempt to take an opposite tack. Of course, this does not mean that he will presume to take up the viewpoint of the terrorist actors themselves, but rather that he will attempt to study them in and of themselves. So, for example, he will analyze those political and intellectual splinter groups through which these persons are brought together, or those same persons' gradual loss of touch with reality. Terrorism that had been highly subjective now becomes much more objective—perhaps too much so, given that explanation and justification often go hand in hand.

While each of these two approaches has its advantages and disadvantages, it is nevertheless appropriate that we rank them.

The transition to terrorism is a choice, a set of more-or-less deliberate decisions in which terrorists take the initiative through their acts. If the notion of terrorism is a compelling one for a given society, there has to be some concrete ground for it beyond that society's own self-production: the ground in this case is an eruption of extreme violence.

This violence, both real and palpable, also has its own specificity, inasmuch as it is distinct from political violence.

It is for this reason that this study, even as it remains attentive to the social portrayal or packaging of terrorism, must opt resolutely for a perspective that highlights the actors themselves. This standpoint does not reject the notion of a sharp break between them, the terrorists, and us, the people whom they subjugate. At a much deeper level, however, it adds what we may qualify, in the literal sense of the term, as our thesis: pure terrorism is a highly subjective rationale of action, which has adopted an entirely skewed relationship with the phenomenon it uses as its point of reference. More than simply being a sharp break between those who use it and those whom it targets, it is also primarily a relationship—between its perpetrators and some collective entity, i.e. the people, class, or nation it claims to be representing—that has been rendered unrealistic or artificial.

This perspective clashes with general public opinion, which begins by contrasting terrorism with democracy. Yet ours is paradoxically the more radical perspective of the two, underscoring as it does the fact that the truly terrorist actor has become cut off from the sole ground on which he might have legitimated his action. This is the legitimacy conferred by a population group that recognizes itself in his violent action.

# Acknowledgments

Before becoming my attentive, generous, and demanding research advisor, Alain Touraine taught me the skills and gave me the practical experience that have made the present study particularly rewarding for me. The debt I owe him is so great that a mere expression of my thanks is, to say the least, inappropriate and inadequate. It is my hope that he who provided me with my professional training and guided me in my research will find some merit in the work that will be presented here.

Alain Geismar was the first to draw me into the study of terrorism, and to truly put my feet in the stirrups. His friendly support was both practical and intellectual; and it was with him that I had my most probing discussions on the subject. He helped me to avoid a number of wrong turns, and introduced me to a body of literature the breadth of which I had previously been unaware. He also put me in touch with the first protagonists I encountered in my fieldwork.

This fieldwork was divided into three principal phases. For the first of these, a sociological intervention with two groups of former Italian terrorists, I put together a research team consisting of Carla Bertolo, Suzanne Famery, and myself. A study of violence in Euskadi led me to form a second team, in which I participated together with Jacques Garat and Francis Jaureguiberry. These fellow researchers enriched the fieldwork with their historical, sociological, and linguistic expertise; and often bore more than their share of the kinds of thankless tasks that this sort of research entails. Mireille Matthys, who had the extenuating job of transcribing and translating the proceedings of our meetings, also made exceptional contributions to the numerous discussions that we held concerning the underlying principles of our research.

A sociological intervention is based on discussions held with groups of approximately ten actors, who interact with a series of co-discussants who have some connection to their movement. Using such a method to study violent action, it was imperative that we adhere to strict rules of ethics, so as to insure, above all else, the strict anonymity of all who participated in our research. In numerical terms, these were approximately a hundred persons, consisting of former protagonists or active sympathizers in armed insurgency, as well as co-discussants whom we invited to various meetings. In nearly every case, they are designated by pseudonyms in the present work.

It is my hope that the members of these groups, former terrorists or present-day active supporters of armed insurgency, will acknowledge— regardless of the nature of their past actions—that this work has remained faithful to the content of the discussions they held with us. The raw documents generated by our common research (the reports of our meetings), which are as much their property as my own, have been handed over to them alone. The co-discussants who came to meet them, often from very far away, showed themselves to be possessed, in every case, of a rare intellectual courage. Without these persons—political and economic authorities, professors, teachers, churchmen, journalists, militants from new social movements, mothers of prisoners, etc., our research could never have been completed.

It is with a heavy heart that I now come to the third phase of my research, for which the preliminary planning was carried out in Lebanon, together with Michel Seurat. I shared a few weeks of his life during which time he was most kind in taking me along on his own fieldwork. All I can do here is to honor the memory of a friend who was a conscientious, understanding, and remarkably well-informed researcher.

François Dubet, Suzanne Famery, Jacques Garat, Alain Geismar, Francis Jaureguiberry, Gilles Kepel, Henri Mamarbachi, Krzysztof Pomian, François Zabbal, as well as Fabrizio and Antonio, each read portions or the whole of a first draft of this book. Their remarks and criticisms, together with those of Alain Touraine, led me to reformulate my arguments, a task which took nearly two years, which should give some idea of the debt I owe them.

Claire Lusson and Jacqueline Longérinas, as well as Jacqueline Blayac, had the immense task of organizing and typing this work, and I am fully recognizant of the great demands I placed on them.

The University of Paris—Dauphine has, through its amenability, always facilitated my research.

The members of Centre d'Analyse et d'Intervention Sociologiques and my students at Ecole des Hautes Etudes en Sciences Sociales have been lively and stimulating discussion partners.

A number of institutions and their directors, starting with the EHESS and François Furet, have lent me their financial and moral support. I thank the Education Ministry's Direction du Financement de la Recherche, the Fondation Saint-Simon, the Fondation pour les Etudes de Défense Nationale, the autonomous Basque government, and the Law Faculty of the University of San Sebastián for their financial and material support; and Admiral Chabaud and Louis Joinet for their encouragement.

Last, my thanks to the periodicals which agreed to publish my first writing on this subject: *Passé-Présent, Connexions, Esprit, Etudes polémologiques,* and *Sociologie du travail.* And, last but not least, my thanks to Eric Vigne, who indefatigably and amicably helped me to render accessible, this time in a reasonable format, the far too voluminous manuscript of my *thèse d'Etat* (published by Fayard),[1] and to Douglas Mitchell, who encouraged me to prepare an abridged, and perhaps more rigorous, version of it for publication in English.

# Part One

## A SOCIOLOGICAL ANALYSIS OF TERRORISM

# 1

# Social Movement, Antimovement, and Terrorism

There can be, at the inception of a terrorist movement and regardless of the ideals it expresses, currents of sympathy and some measure of understanding on the part of the public, which recognizes a certain legitimacy and common sense to its use of violence. Then, sooner or later, these more-or-less benevolent feelings sour as terrorist violence becomes increasingly lethal and indiscriminate. Terrorism comes to manifest itself on a massive scale and, more importantly, its perpetrators, seeing that they have taken matters too far, drift into irrational patterns of behavior. Moral condemnation goes hand in hand with a blanket dismissal of violence as so much absurdity and madness. These two in turn become the principal categories in a description of violence, which is somehow supposed to take the place of an explanation. How else is one to make sense, for example, of the behavior of those German terrorists who, originally indignant at their fathers' passivity and complicity with regard to nazism, ended up—in a show of support for the Palestinian cause—isolating Jews from the other passengers on the flight they hijacked over Entebbe,[1] with the idea of reserving a special fate for them? Are we not in the presence of *utter madness, total absurdity, and barbarism?*

These are everyday, rather than sociological, categories. Widely reinforced by a media-based orchestration, in which the machinery of repression plays an appreciable role, these are the categories of the man on the street. As such, they disclose a general refusal to accept as well as an inability to comprehend the language and actions to which a given group has fallen prey. Our task here is not to condemn such phenomena, but

3

rather to bring to light the underlying nature of certain patterns of behavior on the basis of their overt manifestations. In its most extreme forms, terrorism is heavily weighed down with a separatist baggage that cuts off all communication between the meanings it claims for itself and the meaninginglessness that others impute to it. On the one hand, there are the perpetrators of violence who, overcharged with meaning, see themselves as the very embodiment of History, Truth, Justice, the Nation, or the Proletariat; on the other, there are the bystanders, the people it is victimizing who, in the blaze of gunfire, see nothing in it but murderous obscenity and a loss of reason.

Once it has been consummated, this break raises problems for one who would analyze the phenomenon from a sociological perspective. Where there once had been a social relationship, there now is a state of war, and where there had once been people occupying the social or political stage, there are now only obscure power bases. The rapport or relationship needed to ground a sociological analysis has been dissolved. For the terrorist, all meaning has been tipped to one side of the scale while, for those who are outside his circle, said meaning has become entirely divorced from the acts he perpetrates. This surplus of meaning is more than a mere negation of social or political connectedness. The outcome of processes which had drawn the terrorist into a rising spiral of violence, it now bears witness to this actor's inability to shed those original and evanescent ideals which first inspired him to move into action. Instead, he has clung to them, in an increasingly ideological fashion, endowing them with a coherence and cohesiveness that finds its expression in the use of weapons and a flood of rhetorical discourse. These he has processed in a way all his own, a way which, incomprehensible when viewed from without, proves much more rational and logical when viewed from within. He has twisted and kneaded them, but most importantly, he has fused them into a single whole. Before we return to the intellectual processes behind such an endeavor, let us begin by first concentrating on their final result.[2]

Here, our approach will be based on a limited number of cases in which terrorism, originally arising out of social causes, comes to be transformed into spinoffs linked to leftist extremist ideologies. In the end, however, we will show that our hypotheses may be extended to cover other orders of terrorist action.

At no time do leftist extremist actors ever stop championing the idealized notion—whether it be of proletarian labor or the peasantry—of the social movement. Even when it becomes linked to other demands, the social movement remains the central justification for armed resistance, whether such be taken up in order to replace a social movement, to awaken it, or to provide it with the political preconditions necessary for actions of its own. In its extreme forms, however, armed insurgency—thrusting itself in directions which have nothing to do with the image these movements have of themselves—loses all touch with these social movements. The transfigured image that the former may give of the latter may become so far removed from reality as to become antithetical to it. It is for this reason that we will, following the lead of Alain Touraine, take the notion of *social antimovement* as our starting point, in order to subsequently examine the battered and inverted image of the social movement which terrorism chooses to bear as its standard. In and of itself, this notion cannot suffice to define terrorism sociologically, but it does put us on the right track: terrorism is the most extreme and distorted form an antimovement can take.

## The Concept of Social Antimovement

We will begin by taking a number of categories from the sociology of action as our basis for study.[3] A *social movement* is characterized by three fundamental dimensions—the principles of identity, opposition, and totality—which it is capable of articulating at a highly theoretical level. A *social antimovement* begins by inverting these three dimensions. Then, rather than combining them, it fuses them together into a single whole.

The *principle of identity,* which defines the actor and the people in whose name he speaks, ceases to be a reference to any social entity—to producers or workers, for example, in the paradigmatic case of the labor movement—and rather champions some mythic or abstract entity, essence, or symbol. Deified or naturalized, the social entity is thus made out to be either meta- or infrasocial. Here, the armed insurgent expresses himself in the name of such principles as justice, morality, and freedom more often than in that of any real social entity; and he defines himself through his adherence to a community rather than in terms of his insertion into a social relationship, as he would have previously done. When social and national movements band together, the people in whose name the activist speaks become reduced, in his discourse, to a sort of essence or a pure construct, or become defined solely in terms of obstacles to their proper existence. In certain historical instances, this has given rise to the championing of a purity and homogeneity which, inseparable from the fear that can give rise to a refusal of the otherness of the other, may take the forms of racism, anti-semitism, xenophobia, etc.

The *principle of opposition* that defines the social adversary here becomes transformed into a martial image. No longer is there a rival to be challenged for his monopolization of material or cultural resources, but rather a threatening enemy. Taken a step further, this enemy becomes the epitome of a hostile environment in which the whole of society, law and order, and thereby the state—indeed, the entire geopolitical system defined, for example, as being enslaved by imperialism—are fused together into a single menacing mass. Inside and outside are severed from one another, with war or radical disengagement becoming lowest common denominators. In the most extreme cases, the enemy is not only perceived as being on the outside, but is also seen as having infiltrated to the very midst of the people in the name of which one is speaking, and sometimes into the very workings of one's own organization. This leads to a search for and the elimination of scapegoats, traitors, and spies, and gives the impression of a paranoia that knows no bounds.

The *principle of totality*, which defines the field of historicity that a social movement and a given leader are vying to control, ceases to be a common reference to a given cause, and no longer fuels new future-directed actions. Where there had once been a common ground on which differences could be resolved, now all that remains is a need to overthrow the present system. Rather than seeking to steer the society in which one finds oneself, one instead looks to catapult it into an at times elaborately described future order. Often, this transformation of the principle of totality takes the form of so many pipe dreams of communal utopias, or of myths that combine, at some imaginary level, elements which are in fact irreconcilable. In the most extreme cases, it is the championing of absolutes, of a do-or-die attitude, and of a destruction of the existing order, that predominates. Apparent intermediary or negotiated solutions, state opposition, and the machinery of repression will, in such cases, aggravate rather than palliate such demands for radical disengagement.

A social antimovement—constituted as it is by its reference to an identity defined outside of a properly social relationship, the transformation of adversaries into enemies and the call to radical disengagement—not only inverts the categories of the social movement, but also tends to reduce itself to an ideologically coherent whole. The concept of social antimovement is close to that of totalitarianism, as such was developed by Hannah Arendt and Claude Lefort.[4] As Alain Touraine has noted, it can also be applied to religious sects.[5]

The formation of an antimovement does not necessarily imply that violence, whether defensive or counteroffensive, must come into play.

In a single crisis situation, the degeneration of social movements into antimovements may take complementary yet divergent forms, in which a number of participants become radicalized and take up violent activities, while others enter onto a sectarian path as a community turns in on itself. So for example, the Black Panthers appeared on the American scene at the same time as Martin Luther King was becoming a charismatic figure. In the 1980s, the general trend of the American counterculture groups of the 1960s was toward the formation of communes, a certain number of which transformed themselves into religious sects. Others broke up, some fell into self-destructive violence (the "suicide," in the forests of Guyana, of the nine hundred members of the People's Temple sect), while still others drifted into terrorism (the Weathermen). Similarly, as we will show in the final portion of this book, the Islamic movements have long alternated between exemplary community participation and outward-directed violence, combining two orientations which are, in and of themselves, expressions of one and the same urge towards radical disengagement.

An antimovement can constitute the basis for the formation of a terrorist action. The violence specifically associated with such an action does not, however, merit this qualification, at least from the perspective we have adopted, even if it can at times put on a terrorist face. So long, however, as it is carried out by individuals who enjoy real community backing and whom the community recognizes as the more-or-less legitimate spokespersons for its own aspirations, and so long as it is the expression of a radical disengagement the community has undergone or wishes to undergo, such an act does not fall within the purview of a rationale of terrorist action. This is why we will later draw a sharp distinction between pure terrorism and the communal unrest of certain Lebanese Shiite groups.

## Terrorism and Social Antimovements

The violence that may stem from a social antimovement is always possessed of a concrete point of reference, from which it more or less directly proceeds. Rationales for terrorist action—which speak, to be sure, in the name of some movement, albeit in an artificial fashion—proceed in a different manner.

Terrorist actors exhibit the three defining principles of a social antimovement, combining the three in a way that can readily be defined as fusion rather than integration. In their case, however, these principles have, on the one hand, deteriorated even further, and on the other have come, in a sense, to feed on themselves. Here it takes the form of a course of violence which, possessed of a rationale all its own, propagates itself without its perpetrators having to verify their words or deeds with the people in whose name they claim to be acting.

Here, the inversion of the principle of identity results in an aggravated *subjectivism* in which the terrorist, incapable of bringing his own social identity to the fore, defines himself primarily through his total commitment to the cause. He can no longer speak without identifying his personal experience with that of the cause for which he is the self-proclaimed vanguard. This is further facilitated when he takes some given personal experience to be his original point of reference, even before taking up a course of violence. Such was the case, as we will see, in the Italian movement of 1977. An even more striking example was that of the German Red Army Faction whose primary criterion was that of the individual's total commitment to its cause, with an absolute and existential personal break with the system being equated with self-emancipation—whence the constant references, on the part of these terrorists, to the Frankfurt school and, most especially, to Marcuse. Substituting himself in a unilateral if not fanatic manner for a social entity whose existence is an impossibility, or promoting himself as the necessary catalyst for the awakening of a dormant class, the terrorist makes himself out to be the consciousness of all who have been alienated, deprived of the ability to act, or who remain unconscious of the historical role they have to play. In the most extreme of cases, and less often than one may think, he internalizes—sometimes to the point of nihilism and self-destruction—the inability of a social movement to assert itself.

In a complementary fashion, the opposition principle is characterized by a veritable *objectivization* of the enemy. No longer a threat to be parried or turf to be controlled, he is transformed into a concrete target to attack, properties to destroy, a person to physically eliminate, or a system to annihilate.

Lastly, the principle of totality becomes wholly dissolved, as it were, in a radical disengagement that is at once cast as a life-and-death combat. Gone is nearly every image of a future utopia, description of the society for which one is fighting, or mythic depiction of a new order. The ends of one's acts become confused with their means, with all sense of vision being reduced to plans for the destruction of all that stands in the way of the actor's subjectivity. It is no longer the creation of a new society that is most important, but rather the destruction of the existing order. Unlike revolutionary militants, terrorists speak but rarely of taking over the power of the state, and much more often in terms of striking a blow against the "system." This is why terrorists often give the impression of being pure fanatics. It is also why the only way a terrorist movement can seemingly be brought to a halt is through its forceful defeat and annihilation, by internal collapse, or by the realization of its goals. In this it resembles, in a certain sense, the great totalitarian regimes of this century. The reference to an essence, the subjective identification with history, the struggle against objectivized enemies, and the call to radical disengagement are so many modes for inverting the categories of the social movement, diverging from those of the antimovement, and reducing all one says and does into an ideologically coherent whole. In a terrorist ideology, nothing is out of place. There is hardly a single historical incident it cannot interpret, or into which it cannot, as Hannah Arendt has stated so clearly with regard to totalitarianism, "inject a secret meaning."[6] Its version of events becomes an autonomous system, the evolution of which is generally driven by an internal dialectic. "Once it has established its premise, its point of departure, experiences no longer interfere with ideological thinking, nor can it be taught by reality"[7]—which does not mean, as we will see, that the terrorist is insensitive to the world around him.

It is in this sense that terrorism is an extreme, degenerate, and highly particularized variety of social antimovement. Not only is it irreducible to the latter's patterns of behavior, but it is also incapable of defining itself without lifting, from the movement it takes as its point of reference, categories which it reproduces on a wholly artificial register and which it totally transfigures.

The transition to terrorism constitutes an ideological endeavor which passes—sometimes quickly, or even by short-circuiting it, and sometimes through a series of long and complex processes—through an antimovement phase. Following this, a revised version of the original movement is generated which, in spite of its claims to constitute a return to the original movement, is in fact a further departure from it. "Bommi" Baumann, one of the founders of the Second of June movement in Germany, describes the stages through which he and a number of militants made their decision to move from the antimovement within which they had theretofore been active into an armed resistance front. "Our former group," he relates, "like the whole of the hash-smoking rebel milieu, was no longer interested in anything but getting high, the Hare Krishnas, and other such foolishness. We couldn't do a thing with those people. The only time they interacted with the outside world was when they passed themselves off as apostles of health foods or as Hare Krishna monks . . . So we started hanging out with the apprentices and young workers at Kreuzberg . . . and then we set about reorganizing our infra- structure."[8]

A number of features distinguish terrorism from social antimovements. Like religious sects, terrorist groups are characterized by a cleavage be- tween inside and outside. Here, however, the community does not turn in on itself, but rather takes an opposite tack, engaging in an activism whose every ounce of strength is consecrated to the destruction of the system "outside." Here, violence is intimately linked to the idea of resis- tance. This is not, however, a defensive resistance as is the case with antimovements, which may be defined in terms of a rejection of their social identity. It rather sees itself as counteroffensive in nature. Terror- ism is unique inasmuch as it is possessed of a dual specificity: on the one hand, it necessarily associates ideology with practice, and its self-image with the bearing of arms; on the other, it is perpetrated by groups which are always relatively external to the movement of which it is the inverted image—and to the antimovement, of which it is a destructured form.

All the things that terrorism has to say—its reference to a mythic actor, its martial opposition to its enemies, and its demand for radical disengagement—can perhaps, in the final analysis, be said through the language of bombs and shellfire. Such do in fact constitute the concrete essence of the terrorist's understanding of the meaning of his action. However impoverished and reduced it may be, there always is an ideol- ogy underlying a terrorist action. It may be garrulous or wordy, as in the majority of leftist extremist cases where great effort is made to claim responsibility and provide commentary for an action, in which cases communiqués, for example, become so many wartime news bulletins. It may be taciturn, as is most often the case with the present-day far right, which has no intentions of divulging its ideology to the public. Another characteristic of pure terrorism is that it never seems capable of coming to an end. To borrow a distinction defended with great brio by Daniel Vidal on the subject of the eighteenth-century Calvinists of Languedoc, it functions in a mode which, more prophetic than sectarian, is a labor of loss. "The prophet," writes Vidal, "is an agent of change, a man of toil, a transitional figure. Transitional because he is, once words and bodies have been crucified, the death of the social relationship."[9] The prophets studied by Daniel Vidal were so many expressions of the sup- pression of a movement that had become anathema, and impossible to maintain. In no way were these either antimovements or terrorist movements. To the extent, however, that it is a process in constant motion, terrorism is more closely related to the prophetic enterprise than to any sectarian phenomenon. It too is "a constant process of dissociation, a breaking of social ties and a rending of the social fabric."

When a terrorist phenomenon is stopped short, ideology and practice may be divorced from one another. The use of weapons is abandoned, leaving nothing—as we will have the occasion to see in the case of a group of former Italian terrorists—but the ideological side of the movement, a side that can only be shored up if the group turns in on itself, via a kind of sectarian discourse. Within such a closed system, the group's theoretical unity can come to be restored in such a way that its rationale for action, now introverted, may be directly applied in the form of concrete actions. It is for this reason that separating the level of discourse from that of practice is not the way to understanding terrorism. When terrorist practice is stopped by the forces of repression for example, and its perpetrators are fortunate enough to escape death or imprisonment, its ideologies generally tend to splinter or break down. It is only through a self-isolation of the sort practiced by sects that such ideologies can be maintained. But whereas the formation of a sect assumes the hardened features of an antimovement, terrorism wears the antimovement's destructured, dissociated and prophetic face.

This process is easy to observe after the fact, when an armed resistance group has failed or has been plunged into turmoil. It is more common, however, before the fact, at such times when political groups, operating in a sectarian mode, generate a robust ideological system which effectively blocks all temptation to take up the course of armed resistance. Thus, in the early 1970s, a good number of militants belonging to the Trotskyist wing of the French Left were members of doctrinarian and sectarian organizations for which all forms of terrorism were prohibited, whereas French Maoism, more prophetic in nature, put itself on the road to civil war.

Terrorism is constantly operating at two levels. As Jean-Pierre Charnay has noted so well, it "fights the established order both as a political philosophy and as a strategic and tactical mode of action."[10] Its dissolution of any cause or goal other than that of destruction, the highly subjective definition of its protagonist's identity, as well as the equally objective definition of its antagonist—all of these factors funnel into two corollaries. On the one hand, they commit the terrorist to combative patterns of behavior, as well as to alliances that entail planning and strategy. On the other, these plans and strategies presume a situation of total war, and simultaneously champion unlimited violence and a standard of action which, carried to its furthest extremes, can result in martyrdom and self-destruction. Reducing the world to a power struggle between opposing forces, presuming to at once *relate* and *dictate* history, the terrorist champions an ethic of total resistance. In the jungle that constitutes for him the system in which he lives and moves, this ethic can only take a martial—and thereby planned and strategic—form.

A moment ago, we differentiated between social movement, social antimovement, and terrorism; and shortly we will be looking at those processes through which certain groups move back and forth between the three, as well as the agents specific to these processes. For the moment, however, let us pose the following specific question: can a social movement itself give rise, through the interplay of its internal changes—and through the production of an antimovement—to a terrorist phenomenon? We will approach this matter via the example of the labor movement.

## The Case of the Labor Movement

It goes without saying that every social movement has its bright side, which makes it the bearer of an alternative plan for society as well as the offensive actor in a battle waged, in the name of its own contribution to it, against those presently in charge. But every social movement also has its dark and defensive side, one that is more deprived than dispossessed, more excluded than dominated, and more enraged than inspired by any vision of a better society. On a practical level, these two sides may very well appear to be disunited. So for example, the spirit of the labor movement was long quickened, on the one hand, by the pride of its master craftsmen who had a trade, and on the other by the proletarian consciousness of its manual and unskilled workers, who had no positive principle—no trade or skill—to inspire them. Whereas a person who takes pride in his work will be inclined towards negotiation or even corporatism, the proletarian mind tends more toward radical disengagement and rioting. Whereas the former address their demands directly to their employers, who are also the people who control the labor market, the latter have a less distinct image of their adversary which, more distant, is only known to them through those of its agents with whom they are brought into closest contact, the floor bosses and foremen. In a collective work,[11] we showed that it is only in a Taylorized factory that these two sides of labor consciousness actually meet and stand shoulder to shoulder in forging a class consciousness and a social movement. If such a movement lacks an angry and enraged proletarian component, it loses its separatist tendencies, and becomes sidetracked into autonomous activities which bar it from speaking in the name of universal social emancipation.

Both of these two sides of the labor movement can express themselves through violence. Many are the professional tradesmen who have taken part in anarchistic movements that preached action as the highest form of propaganda, and many are the unskilled workers who have revolted. It should be recalled here that violence is never wholly absent from social movements, nor is it the exclusive feature of their defensive side, which contains elements that border on those of the social antimovement. Is it possible, for all this, to argue that at the heart of every labor movement there is an antimovement, or that the deterioration of labor patterns of behavior can lead, in some circumstances, beyond antimovement into pure terrorism?

Historical and sociological literature has often stressed the immaturity of those labor resistance groups that turned to violence. A labor movement, as the argument goes, can only be engineered after its actors have ceased their destructive activities. This idea lies at the heart of a number of works by the great historian Eric Hobsbawm, who maintains that revolt and certain forms of violence constitute a prepolitical form of action, prior to the conscientization and self-organization of a labor movement.[12] Let us, however, speak here in more precise terms. There is a wide gulf between the smashing of machines and the beginnings of organized terrorism, of which the most famous examples are to be found in Luddism, the riots of manual laborers incapable of organizing a strike, and the policy of direct action preached by French revolutionary syndicationists at the end of the last century. One can, in each case, speak of social violence. But can one speak in terms of social antimovement?

Let us first go into the factory or workshop, where violence—in the form of disguised or undisguised sabotage, intimidation, and the smashing of machines—operates at the level of labor action. Pierre Dubois's work on the subject clearly shows that such patterns of behavior are linked to the relations of production.[13] Like the labor slowdown, the violence of sabotage—and even violence directed against real people, whether concretely or in the form of threats—is most often a defensive move on the part of labor, in response to or in expectation of changes in the workplace. Taylor was clearly aware of this. As a defensive form of behavior, it erupts with even greater severity when institutional structures for the treatment of worker's demands are absent or inoperative, i.e. where unions are prohibited or powerless. As a counteroffensive form of behavior, it expects immediate results of the same order as those realized through direct action. We may see the formulation of such an attitude in the vigorous language used by Emile Pouget in his *Père Peinard:* it is a way of getting even, of taking revenge, and of holding one's own against management exploitation. It furthermore has the long-term benefit of educating workers, because it teaches them how to fight. Here, violence is an instrumental means for exerting pressure, and even a bargaining tool that is especially useful in supporting wage demands or a campaign for greater worker control over hiring policies. It can also be used as a tool against deskilling or increased organization in the workplace. Nothing here has anything of the social antimovement about it: the violence that is internal to working relations is but one of a number of—often collective and sometimes programmed—forms of labor behavior. It is a general indication of a crisis in the relations of production, of an absence of structures for dealing with conflict, or of the difficulties of coping with social inequality in any other way.

It is especially when relations of production appear to be the most threatened that unrest tends to spread beyond the limits of a given firm into a labor-organized defense of a community fighting for its existence. Thus, the violence that erupted in the Lorraine region of France when closings of industrial plants were announced was linked to the rallying of the entire community—and not the workers alone—around the labor cause.[14] Here, opposition was not directed against a social adversary— the employers—but rather against those decisions which, by eliminating the steel plants, destroyed a social relationship which these people wanted to maintain.

Let us now turn to the industrial riot, which has been brilliantly analyzed by Michèle Perrot.[15] This is an act of the frustrated masses who, unskilled and preoccupied with economic troubles, are eager for radical disengagement and committed to the prospect of long-term violence. The industrial riot is a volatile explosion of rage which, at times directed against foreigners, is dictated by hunger, exclusion from the labor market, or by hatred pure and simple. Here, violence is not instrumental but—to return to a classic distinction—rather expressive. It is more a statement of the privation, rejection, and misery one has suffered than an attempt to realize some goal. Here, Michèle Perrot is correct when she underscores the fact that, unlike the strikes carried out by skilled workers in the period she studies (late nineteenth century) which were crowned with a 62 percent rate of success, those of the unskilled worker, which were much more violent and closer to riots, resulted in massive failure rate of 67 percent.[16] But here too, it would be out of place to speak in terms of a social antimovement. The violence that manifested itself in the protests of manual workers or, closer to home, in the resistance of French unskilled workers in the early 1970s, was primarily and intrinsically an expression of the hopelessness of their action. Rather than defining patterns of behavior that distance its perpetrators from relationships in which they are more subjugated than subordinated, violence rather bears witness to the intolerable situation of victimization, violence, and oppressive living conditions those same perpetrators suffer.

It is already difficult, then, for us to find any trace of antimovement in labor violence, the only context in which such an impression might hold up being that of the community movements that arise and proliferate in times of crisis or when massive layoffs are in the offing. It is even more difficult to speak of labor terrorism.

Have there not been at least a few historic cases in which a shift occurred—from a sudden, expressive outbreak of violence nonetheless circumscribed by labor relations or the defense of a threatened community—to more organized forms of violence that turned terrorist? This is the impression one has with Luddism, which spread through the eastern Midlands and Yorkshire regions of Great Britain in the early 1800s or, in France, with the Bande Noire which left a lasting mark on the history of Montceau-les-Mines between 1882 and 1885. Both appear to be labor movements that turned terrorist, with the Luddites smashing machines and terrorizing their owners, and the Bande Noire attacking symbols of Catholicism as much as they did any economic power; both carried out reigns of terror from below while maintaining a certain link with the labor action per se. It suffices, however, to merely look at the facts themselves to reject the notion of a terrorism arising out of a social movement. In the case of the Luddites, the work of the British school of social history, and most especially that of Thompson and Hobsbawm, have taught us to avoid overly simplistic ideas. Geographically widespread and giving the impression of a rebellion at times, Luddism was at once a backlash and a defensive action, which sought to maintain the old system of relations of production; and counteroffensive, which rather looked to impose a set of rules favorable to its own interests in the face of new technologies. In this, it was a precursor of Chartism. Theirs could not be called a campaign of indiscriminate violence, because it spared those owners who respected the old system, and thereby the independence and favorable wages of those skilled workers who were threatened by job loss, de-skilling, pay cuts, or a loss of autonomy through the trend toward greater mechanization. The case of the Bande Noire is aptly described by R. Beaubernard as a secret organization which first began by attacking crosses and statues, followed by a chapel, some priests, and some monks, and then assaulted a variety of people (two mining bosses, an engineer, a miner, a grocer, etc.) with guns and dynamite. Here, we are basically in the presence of a group of anarchists who, politicizing "a protest, a savage revolt against management and church oppression" (these are Louise Michel's terms), cut themselves off from local public opinion and imperiled the weak and vulnerable miners' unions of the time. "Using the Bande Noire as an excuse," exclaimed Millerand, one of the three defense lawyers of the anarchists, who might have been indicted after the police had infiltrated their group, "they seized papers from the union halls."[17]

The fact that gangs of this sort carried out reigns of terror—and we find a similar case in the United States, in the Molly Maguires—should not lead us to jump to false conclusions.[18] In an overexploited labor environment, and at a highly unstable political juncture, unrest can seemingly rise to a political level, and move in the direction of becoming a terrorist phenomenon. The truth is that these episodes reflect a clash—as we have seen with the Luddites—between labor pride and a variety of social threats, which the former attempts to thrust aside before adapting to them. Alternatively, they can be reduced to the attraction, by a core of external political agents (who probably came from Lyon, in the case of the Bande Noire), of a limited population group which, more used to brawling than to working, was therefore well removed from conflicts rooted in the workplace or relations of production.

The terrorist or preterrorist initiatives of the radical Left in the 1970s were, too, quite often triggered by angry workers. Some of these were highly skilled, and veterans of earlier social and political conflicts: we most often find such persons in Italy or in the most hard-line and potentially violent elements of the Gauche Prolétarienne (Proletarian Left) in France. These militants defined themselves more in terms of their political fundamentalism—together with the feeling that the Communist party had abandoned its historic mission as a revolutionary force—than through any properly social action. The majority of these, however, were young unskilled workers (whose poor social integration has often been noted), uprooted persons from the Mezzogiorno who came to work in the urban industrial centers of northern Italy, overly qualified students reduced to working on assembly lines, and young North African immigrants to France. While the anger and rage felt by these workers often inclined them towards organized violence, it also quickly alienated them from the sphere of organized labor fronts. Neglected by the traditional labor organizations, these individuals, capable of moving directly from catatonia to excess, and attracted to absolutist positions as well as more circumscribed economic demands, were generally heteronomous, and thereby willing to join the ranks of those political organizations which knew how to channel their rage. This confirms what was merely implied by the case of the Bande Noire of Montceau-les-Mines: the transition to terror can mobilize social actors to the extent that they are prepared to adapt themselves to the mediation of political or intellectual agents. This most commonly occurs on the dark side of social movements, in which a social labor action, lacking any positive principle (such as a skill or trade) with which to commend itself, is more inclined to turn into an antimovement, or fall into a situation of political dependence or heteronomy. Terrorism can also arise in the wake of prolonged social agitation, when a conflict spills outside the factory gates and the sphere of labor relations to establish itself at a political level. The labor movement in itself can, by dissociating this dark side from its bright side, provide the basic elements for a working-class fundamentalism, or for a workers' rage, which political agents are capable of transforming into terrorist violence. It is impossible, however, for those elements of an antimovement that a labor movement, especially on its darker side, can sometimes incorporate (however much it may be discontinuous, fragmented, egalitarian, or attracted, when left to its own devices, by the promise of a unified world and an all-embracing universality), to spontaneously detach themselves from the movement and veer off into terrorism. At no time is it possible to effect a direct changeover from labor violence to terrorist violence. Just because there exists, at the heart of the labor movement, various elements of an antimovement does not mean that it can transform itself, of its own accord, into terrorism. Such a transformation is an exogenous process, set in motion by the intervention of specific actors who are foreign to the labor movement as a whole, as well as to those of its sectors which are the most sensitive to the categories of the antimovement.

Can this statement also hold for those much more striking historical incidents which we may qualify as revolutionary? It would be cavalier of us to answer this question in the space of a few lines or even a few pages. Let us simply note that this question is most often answered even before it is posed by a historiography which, in the perspective of Lenin's

*What Is to Be Done?*, subordinates its analysis of the labor movement to that of revolutionary political fronts in the same way that Leninist practice subordinates union action to political action. From this standpoint, revolutionary violence is viewed as a well-reasoned initiative taken by a vanguard that is capable of channeling the social energy of working masses unconscious of their historical role. Rare is the study which distinguishes, in its discussion of revolutionary situations, between social movements and political powers. Still rarer is one that analyzes the labor movement on its own terms and in its specific relationship to violence. The suggestions made by Victoria Bonnell seem to correspond well to the lessons that may be learned from the limited instances of leftist extremist terrorism, i.e. that revolutionary violence can take the form of a political entity capable of stirring up the labor movement's most desperate or least integrated actors.[19] Such an entity is, however, much more a party interested in controlling these human resources than it is an expression of the rise and transformation, at a level other than its own, of a social movement.

We must now ask whether our approach can be applied, in complementary fashion, to rightist extremist terrorism, the analysis of which is best carried out in terms of the mythic or artificial relationship that obtains between its perpetrators and social actors in leadership positions.

Rightist extremist terrorism is most often carried out in the name of order and the nation, with its ideological inspiration deriving only marginally from a given social or socioeconomic focus, with such being guided by nationalist references. However—as may be observed, for example, in its German manifestations or its faint rumblings in pre–Second World War Poland—on those rare occasions in which it mentions the middle class or the nation's economic elites, it does so in order to underscore their weakness and impotence, and even their propensity to betray the national cause and its basic interests. Such a movement can originally arise out of a desire to bring together the worlds of labor and money, for example through the corporatist models developed at one time by the Action Française group; elsewhere it can take shape in a climate in which a number of its ideologues borrow certain concepts from union action. But the bottom line here is the feeling that the dominant class has failed in its mission, either because it has refused to secure the country's economic development, or because it has done so without identifying itself with the nation.

So it was that pre-nazi terrorism reached its height, in June 1922, with the assassination of Walther Rathenau, who was not only a statesman but also a powerful captain of industry—he was the owner of AEG (Allgemeine Elektrische Gesellschaft), a veritable trust—and a Jew besides, whom the nationalists hated for his internationalist economic ideas. A similar case is that of Poland, where the anti-Semitic violence which became more and more terrorist in nature as the Second World War approached, owed much to the nationalist far right. This group was strongly convinced that the Polish elites were not ensuring growth in the industrial and commercial sectors—that is, in two sectors in which Jewish (and German) predominance was striking.[20]

Rightist extremist terrorism works, albeit much more indirectly than that of the far left, from a relationship with a mythic or weak social entity. Its relationship to social elites is however of the same order as that which obtains between leftist extremist terrorism and the proletariat. Much more than an armed extension of a form of social hegemony, it is either a radical disengagement from those who support said hegemony in ways it deems unacceptable—whence certain features of pre–Second World War German and Polish anti-Semitism—or a substitution for a developmental action which it deems insufficient.

## Communal Movements and Social Antimovements

Social violence, the violence linked to an antimovement, and a rationale of terrorist action are different in nature, even if their boundaries appear to be hazy or uncertain. Such forms of violence may either be conjoined and thereby mutually reinforcing, or succeed one another chronologically. It can happen that a terrorist organization will succeed in mobilizing an antimovement symbolized, for example, by a peasant community. Much less frequent is the case in which a political actor engaged in armed resistance actually returns to the social movement from which he started. Most common is the phenomenon of a social movement that becomes transformed into an antimovement, and thence into terrorism.

As we have seen, the hallmark of a social antimovement is that it transfers its actor from a prior relationship of social domination into a situation of estrangement or disengagement, in which concentration on a community goes hand in hand with opposition to an adversary who has now been made into an enemy. From this standpoint, *the social antimovement can in many ways resemble communal movements, and most especially national liberation movements,* which are themselves also dominated by a reference to a given community and a call to radical disengagement, to separatism.

Such a realization may incline us to looking at the ways in which these movements took shape, and to searching for their potential social origins. Rather than taking such a perilous road we will instead limit ourselves to noting this resemblance, and to applying it as a means to broadening the scope of our observations which have, to this point, been essentially limited to leftist extremist domestic terrorism.

By assimilating the notions of antimovement and community to one another (both being grounded in the notion of the *unity* of a social body over and against its broader context), it becomes possible to apply our preceding analyses to both terrorism of a directly communal inspiration and, more importantly, to nationalist and religious brands of terrorism. It is in this way that we shall be able to mark the distinction, regarding such groups, between strategies for terrorist action on the one hand, and rationales for terrorist action on the other.

The violence that can at times arise from a social antimovement does not constitute, in and of itself, a rationale of terrorist action. It is even less a rationale of community action. It only becomes such when an armed group, in the absence of any direct or concrete relationship to it, declares itself to be the spokesperson for a communal reference group. This dissociation may herald the formation of a communal conscious-ness, and decrease in direct proportion to the strengthening or broaden-ing of the latter.

Similarly, the birth or certain difficult junctures in the existence of a national liberation movement can result in the adoption of terrorist methods, which may in turn yield, in times of expansion, to other sorts of practices.

In this perspective, terrorism as a rationale of action constitutes a tangent along which groups may break away from the community in whose name they claim to be acting—whether defined in religious or national terms, or in terms of a social antimovement—before attempting, through vigilantist actions, to radicalize the conflict.

## Three Registers

If terrorism is primarily a deviation or spinoff from a locus of meaning, a rift between a bearer of weapons and his movement of reference, it is also favored, in its emergence and development, by conditions obtaining at other levels as well.

The most complex of present-day terrorist phenomena follow a rising spiral in which—working from references to such social or communal symbolic entities as the blue-collar worker, the peasantry, or the nation as a whole—a perpetrator of political violence begins by attacking the state (which makes him an authentic terrorist), before entering onto an international scene in which he becomes the heteronomous agent of a power having little in common with his original insurgency. Here we find, beyond the social system, three levels consisting of the political system, the State, and the international scene (even if certain less complex cases do not bring all three levels into play).

### The Political Level

A political system can—through a crisis situation, its own self-isolation, its total submission to a single regime or, on the contrary, its deterioration into a pluralism in which anything goes—very easily create conditions favorable to the emergence of patterns of violent behavior liable to degenerate into pure terrorism.

Thus the political successes, in the early 1970s, of the leftist political parties in Europe owe much to the institutionalization of the labor movement and to the room that opened up on the left with the gradual disengagement of powerful left-wing parties from the labor movement—if we are to maintain a strictly sociological definition of the latter.

Here we have a common, strictly political, and quite incomplete explanation for the upsurge not only of real political violence, but also of leftist extremist terrorism, as appeared in several Western democracies in the late 1960s. It was the result of a crisis in political representation which—itself impelled by the crisis, fall, and institutionalization of the labor movement—was ushered in by the previolent phase of the leftist movement. This explanation is only valid for the far left. Violence from the far right can also stem from comparable phenomena, most particularly from a crisis on the right.

Often, a political system can authorize the treatment of certain demands while rejecting others, in accordance with the strategic interests of the powers backing it. Its inner workings determine its criteria for its acceptance or rejection of demands. These criteria therefore have an impact not only on properly social issues, but also upon those political or intellectual agents who speak in the name of said issues. The more a system closes in on itself in this way, the more neglected social actors and marginalized political and intellectual agents, finding no institutional channels through which to voice their opposition in word and deed, become discouraged. This discouragement can in turn translate, within these groups, into a limited sense of self, self-absorption, sectarian isolation, and even separatist violence and the beginnings of armed resistance. Here we have a functionalist or Durkheimian explanation for the political violence that can sometimes spill over into terrorism: it is a response to an institutional system that has closed in on itself, and to that system's refusal or inability to deal with social demands.

The hallmark of political violence is its *instability* and its hypersensitivity to changing events. This instability stems for the most part from the mediating role of the political system as a changing house between the levels of society and state. This is why political violence—whether it be provoked by a crisis in representation or participation, or generated by a perceived divergence from a model or some organized power base (with the two phenomena often being linked)—always has the tendency to raise itself up from the level of politics to that of open confrontation with the state. At this point, it can veer wildly into purely terrorist activities, or deteriorate into such infrapolitical forms of violence as delinquence, criminality, or random violence—with the whole being clothed, as we will see was the case in Italy, in the garb of political discourse on "proletarian rehabilitation."

It is at the level of politics that certain individuals, often intellectuals, may begin to enter into violent patterns of behavior which can later veer off into terrorism. It is only rarely that such terrorism occurs in the political sphere.

### The State

When a government becomes strongly repressive, counterviolence takes on a certain legitimacy and, in a democracy, gains in strength as the ranks of its followers and sympathizers swell. When it manifests an attitude of openness and understanding, its acts can come to be interpreted on the one hand as signs of weakness, which thereby encourage armed insurgents to keep up their pressure; and on the other lead more moderate and sensible activists to a more open stance, in which they lay down their arms. This in turn isolates hard-line elements who, relieved by the departure of the moderates of a counterweight to their own extremism, fall into patterns of increased violence.

This observation leads one to suggest that the state, through its interventions which are themselves governed by the nature of its interface with society, bears as much responsibility for the origins of domestic terrorism as it does for its proliferation. It is impossible, however, to construct a single all-purpose explanation or to develop specific all-encompassing laws in this regard. Every case is different, and that which holds for one incident does not necessarily hold for another.

While the state may lay down the conditions in which violence will or will not develop, it is only indirectly involved in its origins. It is, however, at the level of the state that violence that has become terrorist in nature first rears its ugly head. From here on in, the researcher becomes forced to anaylze interactions of a police or military order, as these come to replace now-dismantled or subordinate political relations.

The level of the state is a fundamental one inasmuch as it constitutes the sphere in which terrorists carry out their activities. It is less so when the matter at hand is one of grasping the ways in which a terrorist action comes into being, in which case all three levels—those of state, society, and the political system—enter into play. The level of the state primarily constitutes a threshold to which actors who have become terrorists must raise themselves, and a vector within which political or ideological spin-offs tend to occur. Here, the state is not so much a locus of power to be conquered as it is an enemy to be brought down and destroyed.

### The International Scene

It is one thing to explain the origins of international terrorism; to define what is at play and what is at stake on the international scene is quite another. While specialized literature on the subject often tends to conflate the two registers of this problem, anyone who intends to analyze must begin by separating them.

There are two (potentially complementary) interpretations which, working from the overall state of the present-day international scene or from certain of its component parts, seek to explain the proliferation of international terrorism. The first of these looks at the sum total of relationships between the countries of the world, and considers terrorism to be the result of an unstable world order which classical forms of war and diplomacy are incapable of regulating.[21] The second places special emphasis on particular centers of power, beginning (down to the mid-1980s, in any case) with Moscow.[22]

Both of these interpretive models prove to be terribly weak in the total lack of interest that they show for those processes by which certain actors enter into the service of certain states. If we are to understand international terrorism, we must be able to show how and why it is that some states and not others are able to *simultaneously* resort both to this highly unusual type of action and to agents who are so many orphans of lost national, social, and political causes. We shall also have to explain these orphans' standards—and deviations from those standards—by starting from the beginning and following the rising spiral that can lead certain groups to fall in with the governmental or paragovernmental networks which direct or administer their activities.

With this, it becomes possible to delineate the two approaches our research must follow on the subject of international terrorism. The first consists of an analysis of terrorist regimes, and the plotting of their position vis-à-vis both their own societies and other regimes. The second complementary approach, and that approach to which we will give preference in this work, will concentrate not only on terrorist states, but also on the actual perpetrators of violence, for whom international terrorism constitutes a culminating level of violence, the final endpoint of a militant trajectory. From this standpoint, the shift to the level of the international scene introduces two basic features of its own.

On the one hand, it shows that the actor has diverged at least one time from a movement for which he continues to see himself, often in a highly ideological or artificial way, as the highest expression. On the other hand, and correlative to the first point, it implies a powerful heteronomy, of both a practical and ideological order: practical because the actor, in order to act, needs certain material support (money, weapons, logistic bases of operation, training camps, forged documents, etc.), the distribution of which is tightly controlled; and ideological because he is brought to link the cause with which he identifies himself with the aims of a power possessed of its own particular ideas, aspirations, and interests.

# 2

# Intellectuals and Terrorism

Historically, it is the exception rather than the rule that social violence—an urban riot, peasant revolt, or an explosion of working-class rage—should give rise to organized patterns of behavior. Political violence, and terrorism in particular, are inconceivable without the practical and ideological intervention of specific agents. Such interventions, which may at times prolong a popular dispute, or else be the result of the same, provide it with its concrete and instrumental framework, and provide it its political import. Whether it be set in motion by prophets (such as the millennialist fanatics of the Apocalypse discussed by Norman Cohn)[1] or a modern political party, this act of violence, once it proves itself capable of securing a political implementation of a social action, cannot be qualified as terrorist violence.

From the outset, such an act is contemplated at a different level than are the various forms of social behavior, and the relatively autonomous character of its elaboration will only increase in cases of actual terrorism. The ideas and political culture through which models of armed insurgency are shaped do not stem directly from social or communal resistance itself. They only come into their own when a particular well-defined group of social figures endeavors to delineate the meaning of a given conflict and, in some cases, to give it practical direction.

As rigid and doctrinaire as they may at times appear, these models for violent action are neither external nor indifferent to developments external to the groups that generate them or adapt them to their needs. The history of their transformations, concretized through the various splits and realignments of these groups, cannot be reduced to a mere history of ideas or of intellectuals: the recourse to terrorism, if it in fact puts theory into practice, is first and foremost the result of an analysis which political actors, unable to find an alternative means to reconciling their ideas with a situation beyond their control, carry out in their own interests. It is for this reason that we must distinguish between the theme of philosophies of violence (and therefore references to theories of violence) on the one hand and, on the other, that of the role of intellectuals, when these are defined as persons who ensure that terrorist activity be organized, unified, and guided. Such organization must always be complex since it proceeds, *simultaneously,* from models or matrices that are often syncretic, and from a processing, carried out on the basis of these models, of the social and political—if not geopolitical—reality within which these actors operate. This can of course move them to modify the original model or matrix in any number of ways.[2]

The perspective we have adopted here does not exclude another viewpoint, which consists of defining these persons through their special interests—or, more exactly, through their relationship to state power—rather than through the signifying roles they presume to embody. We will first take up this latter viewpoint in order to point out its utility as well as its limitations. Next, we will examine the important questions that are brought to the fore, from the viewpoint of an analysis of terrorism, by those persons whom the ideologues single out as the inspirational or organizational personifications of the highest aspirations of resistance movements that are more often mythic than concrete. How may these persons be depicted?

Appearing as it did in the contemptuous writings of Maurice Barrès against the defenders of Dreyfus, the term *intellectual* is somewhat anachronistic. It is, moreover, ethnocentric (to understand this, it suffices to consider the discomfort we feel in applying it to the revolutionary *ulamās* of the pro-Islamic movements). It can also happen that those who organize violent action have much less of the ideologue than they do of the strategist about them. Here, we may take the example of the Organisation de l'Armée Secrète, whose ranks were composed of military men or Algerians of European origin (doctors, café owners, merchants, small-scale industrialists, etc.)—persons who, with the possible exception of Susini, maintained a rather distant relationship to the world of ideas and abstraction. Might it not be better to use Julien Benda's term *clercs* for those particular individuals who endow such actions with their deepest and broadest meanings?[3] Whatever the case, we will retain for the sake of simplicity the term *intellectual,* without going into the interminable (even if they are legitimate) semantic discussions it may provoke.

## Intellectuals and Power

Let us begin by adopting a rather unromantic viewpoint and allow that intellectuals, by virtue of the position they occupy in society, have their own vested interests, both individual and collective, and that they constitute one or several well-defined social groups in constant struggle to improve their relative status if not to take power into their own hands. This idea has been carried to its most radical conclusions by Konrad and Szelenyi,[4] for whom the intelligentsia may even constitute a class in its own right. Such a notion, when applied to political violence and terrorism, implies that these actors' relations with actual resistance groups, their questioning of widely held cultural values, their championing of a universal or sacred order, and their criticism of all forms of domination associated with the use of violence are so much window-dressing for the categorical strategies and the particular, even manipulative, interests of these figures who enjoy a nearly total monopoly over the use and power of speech. From this perspective, the recourse to violence as formulated by intellectuals devolves from this group's relative position, either within society or vis-à-vis state power.

It was Tocqueville who provided this argument with its *lettres de noblesse.* Examining the role of writers in France and England in the eighteenth century, he noted: "In England, writers on the theory of government and those who actually governed co-operated with each other, the former setting forth their new theories, the latter amending or circumscribing these in the light of practical experience. In France, however. precept and practice were kept quite distinct and remained in the hands of two quite independent groups. One of these carried on the actual administration while the other set forth the abstract principles on which good government should, they said, be based; one took the routine measures appropriate to the needs of the moment, the other propounded general laws without a thought for their practical application; one group shaped the course of public affairs, the other that of public opinion."[5]

Let us broaden the scope of this remark: the intelligentsia proffers its abstract representations, its championing of absolute principles, and its call to overthrow the established order in direct proportion to its isolation from the workings of state government, an isolation which allows it to formulate such ideas without the slightest care for prevailing conditions or possibilities for reform. This places us at some considerable distance from those approaches which define such persons through their relationships to leading figures in their society or community. Here, the primary emphasis is on the relationship to power, the proximity to or distance from the real world—which, for all intents and purposes, is tantamount to the state. The fevered thirst for an absolutist stance—for a do-or-die attitude, radical disengagement, and thereby terrorism—would thus be the hallmark of only the most marginalized of intellectuals. Here too, ideology would be determined by relative proximity to power.

One can quite easily move from such a line of reasoning to a functionalist approach based upon frustration, resentment, or failed efforts. So it is that Raymond Aron can contend that "in the twentieth century, revolutionary situations will always crop up wherever there are frustrated, unemployed ex-students . . . Even the industrial societies of the West are imperilled when disgruntled experts in search of practical action and soured *literati* in search of an Idea unite against a régime which is guilty of failing to inspire either patriotic pride or the inward satisfaction of sharing in a great collective enterprise."[6] More concretely, Lewis Coser,[7] studying, like many before him, the leading figures of the Reign of Terror, notes that the twelve members who made up the Committee for Public Safety were, overall, more-or-less failed individuals: Saint-Just, in revolt against the courtiers and the aristocracy; Jean Bon Saint-André, a Protestant pastor cut off by his religion from public affairs; Billaud-Varenne, a lawyer whose practice had failed; Carnot, a sterling military man at a dead end in his career; Collot d'Herbois, a person hurt by the fact of not being treated as a peer by nobles or the bourgeoisie, etc. "It should be clear that most of these men had experienced circumstances that alienated them from the basic values of their society . . . they were all deviants, at least in terms of ideas, from the currently dominant values." He applies the same concept to the bolsheviks, heirs to an intelligentsia that had been stripped of its status in Russian society, and which refused to take things lying down. Similarly, historical and sociological literature continues to portray terrorists—such as Nechaev, a mediocre student whom Confino describes as having been at once fascinated by and ill at ease within the university[8]—as failed, frustrated, and unsung intellectuals. The image of the self-assured terrorist, living the wild life and surrounded by beautiful women, is but the other side of the same coin: for what, apart from his cold-bloodedness, is the notorious Carlos, if not a hyperconformist who appreciates luxury and a way of life which corresponds to the legitimate values that lie at the heart of a functionalist image of society?

Disappointment, frustrated or unrealizable upward mobility—these are sociological categories from which one may quite effortlessly drift into psychological approaches to political violence and terrorism. Are the members of the learned class who formulate modes of terror and violence not preselected by personal, or even biological, characteristics which marginalize them from a very early age onwards? Is the feeling that one has split off from the forward march of society not more often based on subjective rather than objective criteria? Is it not possible to explain commitment to a cause in terms of paranoid tendencies or of narcissistic wounds received in infancy? Such questions quickly bring us to the subject of the terrorist personality type, concerning which no research worthy of the name has ever been carried out.

In a number of historical cases concerning a number of armed insurgency groups, the intelligentsia or some of its members have enjoyed a direct, if not familial, access to the powers of state government, broadly participating in the cultural life of a society for which they nevertheless stood out as the leaders of violent protest. This is particularly the case with a number of revolutionary movements in Latin America. In other cases (those of a good number of revolutionary leaders in Eastern and Western Europe), there can be no doubt that the thirst for action that one encounters is due to some degree of self-identification with progress or some other universal principle, a self-identification which itself follows from a certain condition of exclusion. But, as we shall see even in the most extreme of cases, the radicalization of the intelligentsia and the role of its members in the concrete and ideological organization of violence can never be explained without relating it in some way, however tenuous, to those struggles or movements that have aroused or have been capable of arousing either their own society or community, or their society or community of reference. It is for this reason that any concrete analysis of the role played by the intelligentsia must necessarily start from a sociology of the processing of meaning, which may be verified, without prior judgment, through hypotheses drawn from the sociology of exclusion and frustration.

## Influence and Responsibility

Does there not exist an immediate bond—i.e. of influence—between intellectuals and terrorism? Whenever the intellectual appeals to or affirms the legitimacy or necessity of violence, is he not responsible for acts which do not involve his physical participation as such?

When it is combined with a real or mythic cause, the notion of taking up armed resistance can sometimes become tantamount to a philosophy of violence, which has left its mark on the works of Georges Sorel, Frantz Fanon, and especially Jean-Paul Sartre, whose attraction to extremist behavior has often been noted.[9] But here too, we must be cautious: while we may in the early 1970s have seen a figure like Sartre supporting— even in their terrorist tendencies—the "Maos" of the Gauche Proléta- rienne ("Maintain a manifestly illegal organization that is able at all times to launch illegal and violent activities"),[10] we also know for a fact, through the statements of a number of the organization's former lead- ers, that the very existence of a rigorous dialogue with such great intel- lectuals as Sartre contributed in great part to a certain restraint, and the subsequent self-dissolution of the movement—which barred the way to the very great leap into armed confrontation it had been con- templating.[11]

What holds for the left holds for the right as well, and what holds for the most important figures also holds for many other persons of lesser importance. "We must be intellectual and violent," declared Charles Maurras at the turn of the century; and one need only consult *Candide*, *L'Insurgé*, or *Je suis partout* to see that some thirty years later the cham- pioning of order and the French nation went hand in hand with a hatred and violence of such an order as to fill the pages of the right-wing press with veritable incitements to commit murder.[12]

In certain historical circumstances, the question of responsibility on the part of intellectuals is not merely theoretical or moral: it is posed, on a wholly practical level, when a state judicial system begins to attack ideologues whose hands may well be clean. This we saw in post–Second World War France with regard to Drieu La Rochelle, Brasillach, and Charles Maurras; we have also seen it in Italy, within the context of the war on terrorism, in the case of Toni Negri. The issue, obfuscated in this case by the incredible negligence of the Italian justice system, can lead—as Bernard-Henri Lévy has noted—to a choice between two quite unsatisfactory options: one can either turn a given intellectual into a scapegoat, or else send him away to live with his own conscience.[13] Negri's case is, however, more extraordinary than it is exemplary, lo- cated as it is at the rarely trod crossroads of the two paths. More often than not, the intellectuals are either far removed from the political prac- tice that their ideas directly found, or else they are, on the contrary—at least as soon as terrorism comes into the picture—not only its ideologues but also its strategists. With this, we open onto a new set of problems.

## The Intellectual Roots of Terrorism

The French philosophers of the Enlightenment laid the foundations for the French Revolution. In the words of Raymond Aron, they "neither heralded nor desired the apocalyptic collapse of the old world . . . the men who conceive [revolutions] are not those who carry them out."[14] While we may be putting the matter too bluntly here, let these words serve to alert us to the following: the escalation of violence, especially when it rises to the fever pitch of terrorism, is inseparable from the progress of ideas; the latter is, however, of such an order of complexity that one often learns more by looking at its blind alleys and roadblocks than at its main thoroughfares.

When they talk—which is not always the case—terrorist groups produce bodies of discourse, which may be analyzed through an approach whose goal it is to detect the presence, more or less at a distance, of a traceable genealogy of ideologies. By availing itself of extant documents, such research may untangle the web that terrorist discourse weaves, and so, by tracing connections between theory and practice, work its way back to their ideological roots. It is in this way that Philippe Raynaud, in an analysis that owes much to the thought of Alain Besançon, indicates the syncretic nature of German Red Army Faction (RAF) ideology, which is a blend of Marxist-Leninist orthodoxy of Komintern inspiration and various elements borrowed from the Frankfurt school.[15] Also inspired by Hannah Arendt's analyses of totalitarianism, this approach sees terrorism, in the final analysis, as a purely ideological phenomenon, as the pursuit or rationale of an idea which, in the end, wholly emancipates its exponent from any relationship to the real world. From this perspective, terrorism may be likened to a missile that, cut off from any social guidance system, has veered out of control. Carrying in its payload the germs of a historically recurring disease of the spirit—an ideology—and stopping for fuel at certain intellectual staging points, it returns to earth whenever conditions are most favorable—i.e. whenever totalitarianism arises—to the propagation of said disease. "The history of ideology," writes Alain Besançon, "may be compared to the different successive *phases* through which certain parasites pass in a cycle that, while apparently arbitrary, is nonetheless necessary to their full development."[16]

When applied to a terrorist phenomenon, such an approach may be criticized from two standpoints. The first of these is of a methodological order: the texts upon which it is based are, of necessity, given equal weight, without any care given to examining the conditions of their production. As such one may attribute equal importance to documents produced at different moments in the life cycle of a terrorist movement or even prior to the formation of the movement, and which either address a wide range of strategic concerns (internal debates, appeals to public sympathy, preparation of a legal defense, etc.), or are the products of highly specific situations (detention, for example). The major limitation to this approach is, however, of a theoretical order, which must be taken up on two counts.

First, in its definition of terrorist ideology, it favors doctrinarian and theoretical principles over presentations of the same which are made in response to the concrete situations in which they are applied. Returning to our earlier example, is it possible to understand the terrorism of the German far left without a thorough investigation of its intellectual roots as well as the ever-changing nature of the relationship between its perpetrators and a highly institutionalized labor movement, the student and urban protests of the 1960s and 1970s, the ecology movement, the pacifists, etc.? The answer is no—and the testimony of Hans Joachim Klein, who describes the series of failures that first drew him toward and later drove him away from various social and cultural movements before plunging him into terrorism, is clear proof of this.[17]

Secondly, and of equal importance for us, is the fact that this kind of approach bases itself on an assumption that there are certain constants that are internal to any ideology, or even that there is some sort of historical continuity to ideology. Differences in ideological content are thus seen as secondary in relation to the monolithic phenomenon constituted by the inner logic of an idea. What is it that we actually find? *In every case* in which a terrorist initiative has been launched, it has always entailed a *disengagement* from and a *reversal,* on the part of its militants, of their position with regard to the intellectual matrix from which they had proceeded prior to moving from nonviolent resistance to armed confrontation, or from limited violence to all-out terrorism. Who were the masked *cagoulard*s and prime movers behind the underground and paraterrorist groups that poisoned France on the eve of the Second World War? Nearly all were "men who had left the right-wing leagues at one time or another, disgusted by their unwillingness or inability to act effectively,"[18] activists who had broken, most notably, with the intellectualism of Action Française. Who were the founders of the Basque ETA? Students who had separated from the Basque Nationalist party (PNV) to form a new bloc founded on the coexistence of a renewed nationalism and revolutionary Marxist-Leninist themes, the likes of which were inconceivable within the PNV. Who were the German terrorists? Militants who took class warfare to be their focus before taking up an anti-imperialist position which entirely annulled all reference to the proletariat of their own society. And so on. We may summarize these remarks by affirming that the transition to terrorism or the aggravation thereof takes place much more readily at critical junctures than through the broadening of preexisting ideologies. We should note, in particular, that this conclusion adapts itself perfectly to the major phenomenon of the past twenty years: the great reversal, throughout the entire world, of those revolutionary models which had followed the Marxist-Leninist line.

Before we begin examining this phenomenon, let us add a supplementary note to what has been said above. Could we not apply such an approach—which, in the final analysis, sees an internal logic of ideas rather than one of actions behind indiscriminate acts of terrorism—to the religious roots of violence? Here, we might underscore the fact that apart from any violence overtly wreaked in the name of religion (the existence of which various Islamic movements remind us daily), there are a good number of armed insurgents who act in the name of the religious faith upon which their actions are founded, and who would thereby appear to reinforce the position of those who insist on the continuity of ideas that lead into terrorism. But what is it that we actually find? In a great number of modern-day instances, the most striking phenomenon we notice is that of a disengagement from one's religious background or training, a secularization of activities organized by leaders who, having passed through a religious phase, have deserted religion or at least abandoned it as the guiding principle of their struggle. One finds militants of Christian background in the most radical wings of the Palestinian movement, as well as among those who have broken with it; one also finds them, by the thousands, among Italian terrorists who define themselves not so much in terms of their keeping of the faith as those of their disengagement from and break with the Church. Better yet, the renouncing of one's terrorist engagements can coincide with a return to religion. This we see today in Italy, where a number of prisoners, sometimes the very same persons who had been the greatest exponents of unlimited violence, are repenting and simultaneously returning, ardently, to the Church's fold. Religious faith often underlies communal violence when it is bound up in the daily life of a threatened or expanding group. Its role seems to become all the more pivotal—as we will see with regard to the Lebanese Shiites—when a movement has become transformed into an antimovement. Religious faith can serve to justify a situational return to terrorist methods; but even when faith is present, it is not necessarily central to rationales for terrorist action, which can proceed from the abandonment of a religious reference as often as from applications thereof.

## The Great Reversal

Classical Marxism and Leninism have almost never favored terrorism. They are not hostile to violence, the midwife of history, but allow that it can only have meaning in a revolutionary situation which—as Lenin explained it in terms bordering on the canonical—one must know how to exploit. The communist tradition has constantly denied "petit bourgeois" adventurism, Blanquism, leftist movements, and anything that has, in any way, shape or form, betrayed an error in judgment regarding the revolutionary ripeness of a situation. So it is that, throughout the world, entire generations of communist militants have been taught to be vigilant against all deviations into terrorism, and to resist being carried away by a subjective desire for revolution.

This model, which has hollowed out within its mould a special niche for the committed intellectual, is quite the opposite of one that would cast the intellectual as a free and dispassionate individual who identifies himself with values that transcend any particular social or political issue. This latter model is one which corresponds to that blocked out by Julien Benda, who denounced the subordination of the spiritual to the temporal, or of ideal values (Reason, Justice, Truth) to the pursuit of practical ends, which could only backfire on the intelligentsia. One finds nothing of the sort in the communist tradition. The role of the intellectual, as Gramsci explains, cannot be anything but "organic," bending to the prevailing structures of order and domination; Benedetto Croce, for example, who thought himself to be external to any class struggle, was never anything but an ideologue working in the service of the ruling class—or else that of the working class; i.e., of the "Party."[19] The subscription of French intellectuals to the French Communist party was a phenomenon of massive proportions in France down to the end of the 1960s. For some, this was, above all else, a political choice. "In a world brutally divided into masters and servants," exclaimed Paul Nizan, "the time has at last come either to acknowledge a long-hidden alliance with the masters or else to champion the cause of the servants. There can be no grey area of class impartiality."[20] For others, this was a means by which to channel literary or poetic furor into the revolutionary cause: expressions of this may be found, for example, in the writings of certain surrealists.[21] Above all else, this choice was one that implied a total submission which, as far as we are concerned, relieved the intellectual of all direct responsibility for potential violence. The intellectual could attempt, as did Sartre, to maintain a certain distance and assume the rather uncomfortable role of fellow traveller. The meaning of the intellectual's intervention had, however, always to be defined through his relationship to the Party, and he always had, in one way or another, to yield to the Party[22]—an axiom which rendered anathema both the adventurism and estheticism of a Malraux and the moralism of a Camus.

In France, this model first came to be shaken by personal or concrete commitments, during the Resistance or, more importantly, at the time of the Algerian War and the *porteurs de valises*. This tendency gathered momentum, in Western societies, with the cultural changes of the 1960s and 1970s. The communist movement, even if it always preached a form of populist and proletarian art and literature, remained positivist in its attitude toward the universal culture—showing a marked preference for that of the Enlightenment—to which it was heir. This movement, in whose service the intellectuals were presumably working, claimed "great" literature, classical music, and philosophy to be integral parts of its heritage, while looking upon the sciences with a favorable eye.

The leftist movement of the 1960s, the first decisive step in a process that would lead a number of persons to the brink of terrorism, is inseparable from the general climate of disengagement from cultural norms which crystallized in the events of May 1968—the "breach," as Lefort, Morin, and Castoriadis have termed it. Science was subjected to doubt, the values of the industrial society were rejected, and calls were sounded, from every quarter, to rule-breaking, to sexual liberation, as well as to a "do-or-die" attitude. Whether they did so out of an intention to express it in some revolutionary mode, or rather to react against the old in some fundamentalist way, those who crossed the line to engage in armed resistance were placing themselves squarely in the heart of the new value system. No longer the zealous servant of some party, the intellectual activist had become filled with a boundless subjectivity which drove him to act directly, in his own name. He became, or once again became, an acting subject. The German terrorists of the Second of June movement were motivated by a libertarian inspiration which was also fueled by the theory and practice of antipsychiatry. Influenced by the ideas of Marcuse, the terrorists of the RAF defined the revolutionary subject as "anyone who frees himself from these constraints (of alienation) and refuses to participate in the crimes of the system."[23] In Italy, the terrorist phenomenon was never so widespread and spectacular as in the 1977 movement which, fired by a culture critique based on real life and real human needs, eventually collapsed, with its former adherents coming to swell the ranks of various combatant organizations. In all of these movements, the classic image of the committed intellectual was broken down, with the members of the intelligentsia either becoming so many ideological references external to the movement's actions, or else active revolutionary subjects, the mappers and planners of armed confrontation. The only vehicle these movements could find for their revolutionary subjectivism were greatly overhauled (at least in comparison to classic models) Marxist-Leninist formulas.

These classic models had ruled out any separation of the action of the vanguard and the action of the masses, of political consciousness from social consciousness, or of the cult of the Party from the cult of the masses. Now, with a number of national liberation movements as well as the Maoist experience showing that the Bolshevik Revolution was not the only way to change the world, the old formulas were eroded even further, and major schisms with the USSR began to form. The concept of revolution became complemented by that of guerrilla struggle, with people beginning to believe it possible to create a revolutionary situation by leaping over all classic political and organizational intermediaries, by simply bearing arms in the name of the people—even without the people themselves. *Foquisma* became a reality in Latin America, and came to serve as a showroom of sorts for all the variations on the classic Leninist models that that part of the world could produce; it in turn became a powerful example for a number of armed insurgencies throughout the world. In cases where it had previously been necessary to await the maturation of the revolutionary process, immediacy became the order of the day; in cases in which the Party was supposed to be the political vanguard and even a strategist of violence, now it was the military branch of the organization that was leading the way. These transformations nonetheless retained the core Leninist doctrines and their model of a vanguard which identified itself with the march of history and the consciousness of its oppressed actors. So long as this vanguard remained active and involved in the struggle, violence remained limited, more verbal and theoretical than practical. It is when the vanguard, divested of its social base, became involved in a meaningless action, whose success could only be measured in terms of its ability to mobilize the masses, that indiscriminate terrorism began to rear its ugly head.

For Western societies, then, terrorism of the German, Italian, and Japanese—and later French (Action Directe) and Belgian (Communist Combatant Cells [CCC])—varieties appeared as the product of the cultural innovations of the 1960s and the crisis within traditional Marxism-Leninism. This does not imply, however, that it did not continue to exist here and there, often grafted onto a libertarian focus. Such was the case, for example with the German Second of June movement and the French Action Directe.

In other societies, and most especially in a number of Arab nations, the reversal we have been tracing has followed other rules. There, Marxism—as Maxime Rodinson has so aptly described it[24]—has not only been an imported commodity connected since 1917 with Soviet propaganda, Komintern slogans, and the emergence of organizations imitative of the great European communist parties. It has also borrowed a great deal from Europe, especially through the medium of (notably French) universities, which are attended by students who go on to become revolutionary militants in their own countries. It has also stemmed, however, from internal stimuli, with its most promising ideologies being those which have been able to answer to the dual concern of simultaneously effecting national liberation and modernization. Down to the late 1970s, the role of the revolutionary intellectual was to ensure that society gain back lost historical ground. "The further a society falls behind other societies," as Abdallah Laroui explained in 1974, "the deeper and wider the aims of the Revolution; the more the intellectual is conscious of this lag, the greater his responsibilities become . . . the Arab intellectual is heir to every freedom movement—individual, communal and national— movements which the bourgeoisie of the nation-state has, in every case, failed to see through to their end."[25]

Middle Eastern terrorism has no role to play either in the promoting of these ideas, or in the growth of the various forms of revolutionary nationalism which, together with the Ba'ath party and Nasserism, indeed with the most central elements of the Palestinian movement, give voice— in the words of Maxime Rodinson—to "a general desire for modernization and a better standard of living within the framework of national independence."[26] It has no role to play in the attempts by intellectuals to reduce the gulf "between the demands of modern life requiring alignment on the European-American model, and nationalist feelings coming

basically from those same demands of modern life."²⁷ Its locus is rather
to be found in the abandonment of such attempts, in those transformations in which the championing of a religious or communal separatism
has replaced the will to modernize, and in which war against the West
has supplanted the struggle for national independence. What little remains of Marxism-Leninism and Arab nationalism has become rigidified
and diminished, stripped of any social base, and constantly frustrated by
rifts between opposing regimes. Such ideologies motivate none but a few
splinter groups, who have become little more than playthings in the
hands of terrorist states.

## The University

The ideological crises that can provoke a fall into terrorism can take the
form of long, chaotic processes during which modifications may occur
in the ways intellectuals present themselves and interact with others.
They can also occur within sharply defined temporal and spatial limits,
and come into play, in the beginning, at specific arenas of intellectual
ferment, where the exchange of ideas can issue into currents of thought
capable of inspiring militant activities with a potential for violence. Institutions exist, or can be created, in which the work of the intelligentsia
follows a relatively autonomous analytical mode. Intellectuals may also
be defined on the basis of their frequentation of specific, at times structured and organized, milieus in which they find, as Lewis Coser has
noted, "an audience, a circle of people to whom they can address themselves and who can bestow recognition."²⁸ Ought we not, if we are to
grasp the role played by intellectuals, to take interest in these milieus
and, as Coser suggests for the eighteenth century, study the salons, the
cafés, the learned societies, the literary marketplace, etc.? From our perspective, i.e. that of the emergence or the shaping of terrorism, such a
procedure leads us directly into a vortex out of which violence has often
erupted: the university. We can understand nothing of leftist extremist
terrorism if we fail to address the Italian, German, and Japanese student
movements of the 1960s, nor can we properly grasp the appearance
of Russian popular resistance and its terrorist transformations without
looking at nineteenth-century Russian student life. More generally, we
note that violence quite regularly proliferates from within the university,
as may also be seen in the case of Sendero Luminoso, which was formed
at the University of Ayacucho; as well as in that of fundamentalist Islam
which, after becoming a veritable mass movement on Egyptian cam-

puses, resulted (according to Gilles Kepel's excellent analysis) in the assassination of President Sadat.[29]

Here, we must draw an analytical distinction between two separate processes which can at times become combined in historical practice.

On the one hand, the university produces intellectuals. It ensures the formation and circulation of ideas, places bearers of knowledge in contact with educated youth, provides for an intermingling of people capable of bringing together cultures and ways of thinking that would otherwise have been unaware of one another, and allows for the introduction of ideas from beyond the local or national horizon. On the other hand, it is the headquarters of student movements, with the relative autonomy these enjoy. In the first case, the students it brings together constitute an intelligentsia; in the second, these same students place themselves squarely in a student-oriented sphere of activities. The first of these two definitions implies that the university is an arena for the formation of political and intellectual elites, elites that will go on to join or form organized groups, or even enter the ranks of future armed resistance movements having no direct connection with their student status. The second implies that the university is a springboard for movements that challenge the organization of the production and spread of knowledge, and this at a level that is sociologically lower than the students' own living and working conditions. In certain historical cases, terrorism proliferates out of a student movement that has drifted into patterns of behavior which no longer have anything to do with their original founding principles. Such was the case, for example, with the Russian popular leaders. "It was the student movement that would provide the popular front with its human raw materials and its first rank and file," writes Venturi.[30] This movement, once politicized, became an opposition party, encountered severe repression, gave birth to underground movements, and most especially called on these to join the people, and to leave the university without hesitation. What if the government closed the universities? "Let them close," wrote Ogarev in *Kolokol* in 1862, ". . . one cannot become a free man without first becoming one of the people."[31] When the meaning of one's acts loses its student orientation and is now found outside the university, there then begins a process which leads, via popular fronts, to what will culminate in the fullness of time in a terrorist action.

An analogous process began to emerge in France where, in the backwash of the May 1968 student movement, and in some cases even before—as early as 1966–67—some of the most active militants left the university to "set themselves up" as action groups, involving themselves in labor and political causes in which several had brushes with terrorism. This clearly developed in Italy where the 1968 movement gave rise to the first stirrings of armed resistance (Renato Curcio, founder of the Red Brigades, was a student at Trent), and where, especially in 1976–77, the university became a massive fermenting vat within which the leftist movements of the 1960s and the 1975–76 autonomy movement were broken down.

The same was the case—even if this instance was more exceptional than exemplary in the context of Islamicist movements—with the violence of the Muslim Brotherhood in Sadat's Egypt. Highly politicized and overshadowed until the end of the 1960s by an often Nasserist Marxist left, a large portion of the student movement in Egypt became converted to an active Islamicist cause. The group's primary complaints were with the overcrowding and intolerable shortages endemic to Egyptian university life: lack of seating in lecture halls and classrooms, the excessive indirect costs of an education, overpopulated housing, etc. Starting in 1972–73, there developed a pro-Islamic movement that was capable of dealing with these problems, a movement that bore the stamp of its student orientation. The *jama'at islamiyya*—Islamic student associations—gained a foothold, as Gilles Kepel has noted, "by elaborating a strategy to transform campus life" by persuading "students that it was through them that they could take their own destiny in hand here and now, and not by parroting official slogans and governmental projects which were in any case fated to sink without a trace beneath the weight of mismanagement and corruption."[32] They succeeded in promoting causes that incorporated student demands within a body of classic themes. So, for example, they set up student minibus services, thanks to which they no longer had to be bothered by passengers who piled into the overcrowded public buses, and in which they were permitted to travel by adopting the Islamic dress more or less required of them. As they became progressively politicized, the jama'at—now powerful and subject to strong repression—followed a classic trajectory into a populist movement that moved the students out of the university and onto a path of violence which, originating from within the university, escalated outward. The university, no longer the heart of social conflict, had rather become a headquarters from which political action could be organized.

In the same way, the Sendero Luminoso in Peru only took up armed resistance at the end of a long process in which a student movement that had challenged the university administration became inverted before launching into intense political activity within the university. Its action later spread beyond the university walls, and finally abandoned it entirely.

The few cases we have reviewed here confirm, each in its own way, that terrorism arises out of crises and splits which affect those very people whose vocation it is to give meaning to their action. In the university, the crisis often stems from the fallout of a student movement, which frees up a group of politicized agents who have revitalized past political theory, incorporated new elements into the same and, most especially, learned how to use to their own advantage the momentum of intellectual movements. It is such a group which, very often, comes to constitute the beginnings of a move toward terrorism. In Cairo, the students moved from Nasserism to a revolutionary Marxism and, most importantly, to an Islamic fundamentalism. In Ayacucho in Peru, as in Russia a century before, students moved from a dispute within the university to a popular or leftist movement, and from these, to terrorism, etc. In broader terms, what is unique to the persons who ensure the ideological processing of the meaning of terrorist action, and who later become both its directors and conductors, is their ability to cut and paste movements and ideologies. So it is that they are able to model and remodel conceptual frameworks in which it is possible to recognize, at a single glance, both their deviations from prior or classic models, which one finds twisted or turned upside down, and their unilateral effort to speak, on the basis of some personal experience, of social or national struggles with which they (no longer) have any relation whatsoever, save for a mythic one. These deviations, this unilateralism, are not the only track the intellectuals can follow once they have begun to pull back, for whatever reason, from the real struggles—struggles which themselves can, all too easily, be stopped short or made to do an about-face. The choice that leads them into terrorism is in fact more often the exception than the rule. Every time we see it being made, however, it is safe to hypothesize that behind it there lies a much deeper crisis, a crisis affecting the intelligentsia in the ways it thinks and the ways it relates to social and political life.

# 3

# The Media and Terrorism

A widely held theory, to which we have already alluded, views the connection between the media and terrorism as a symbiotic one. In this perspective, contemporary terrorism dates from the late 1960s—or, more exactly, from the first airline hijackings organized by the Popular Front for the Liberation of Palestine (PFLP)—and may be explained in terms of the reactions that the media, led by television, supposedly provoke in response to acts which are, intrinsically, of limited immediate impact.

This theory is founded upon the notion of reciprocal interest. Terrorists provide the media with the sort of public spectacle they need to satisfy their audience—a highly compelling performance that combines the elements of bloodshed and mystery, human interest and politics, heroes and villains—while the media, for their part, supply the terrorists with an immediate audience, available at a low price, on a potentially planetary scale.

A number of authors have vied with one another in expanding on such widely held commonsensical ideas.[1] The classical theory we have just evoked maintains that there is a discontinuity between contemporary terrorism and its antecedents, which arose in societies lacking modern means of communication. It seems to imply that unless the modern world does away with or places strict regulations upon these means, it cannot hope to avoid the terrorism that is consubstantial with them. It postulates a kind of expectation of terrorism on the part of media spectators, listeners, or readers that in turn gives rise to a popular demand for violence which, denatured and experienced, as if by proxy, at a level of fantasy, would somehow help to compensate for the absence of powerful personal experiences.[2] Clearly, none of these postulates is admissable as it stands. In many ways, Russian terrorists of the late nineteenth century resembled the terrorists of today, while certain countries have no experience of terrorism in spite of the important role played by their mass media; and here we may note that domestic terrorism has ceased to exist in the United States since the liquidation of the Weathermen and the Symbionese Liberation Army in the 1970s.

However, while arguments of this order may challenge such immediate, ahistorical theorizing, they cannot undercut it entirely. Only a systematic examination of each of the partners in the media-terrorism duo and, beyond this, a questioning of the very image this duo presents can permit us to delineate the specific role played by the media in the production of terrorism.

## Terrorists and the Media

From the viewpoint of the terrorists themselves, there exists no single relationship between terrorists and the media. Rather, there are four—at least if one limits one's analysis, as we will here, to the media in democratic societies.

The first of these relationships is simply one of *pure indifference*. Here, the terrorists neither seek to frighten a given population group beyond their intended victims nor to realize a propaganda coup through their acts. There is no expectation of any mediation whatsoever on the part of the press. This first mode is unusual, since terrorism most often aims at arousing a widespread reign of terror, or at widely publicizing explanations of its struggle, if not both.

This kind of relationship may nonetheless be found in domestic terrorism and, more specifically, in the phases of preterrorist violence that can develop within a society or a sector of society relatively uninvolved with the mass media. So, for example, in Peru, the Sendero Luminoso long remained quite uncommunicative and seemingly uninterested both in the wider media and in creating an underground press through which to broadcast its ideology on a media level.

The second relational mode is that of *relative indifference*. We observe this mainly in cases in which perpetrators of violence remain indifferent about making the headlines not out of disinterest with regard to the most powerful media, but because there already exist channels of communication through which to discuss and explain their positions. Sufficient means may be furnished by a legal and relatively free press from either the far right or the far left, radio transmitters located in safe zones, centers for free expression such as universities, churches, or mosques, or places in which communication occurs and in which ideas concerning violence can be questioned and legitimated. Here, violence is not necessarily media-oriented: its aim is neither to put on a show nor to capture the attention of the mass media. This second mode corresponds, primarily, to preterrorist actors who are well on their way to, but still far from becoming truly engaged in, clandestine activity or indiscriminate and unchecked violence.

A third relational mode is that of the *media-oriented strategy*. Here, the actors not only anticipate that the media will expand upon their words and deeds, but go much further in a calculated manipulation of what they know of media operations. Their communiqués are carefully refined and their activities programmed to account for characteristics proper to the various media they mean to provoke into action.

In this sort of relationship, it is easy to move from the idea of strategy to one of tactics. Throughout a terrorist incident, especially when it lasts for several weeks or more, the aim is to progressively raise the tension level, to play on the nerves of the public or the government in question, and possibly induce it to commit an error or leave itself open to ridicule.

A prime feature of these media-oriented strategies is their respect for the press's independence. They may use it, at times in remarkable ways—as was visibly the case throughout the 1978 Aldo Moro kidnapping in Italy, or during certain incidents that occurred in Lebanon—but in no way do they seek to destroy or threaten it as such. Terrorists are generally contemptuous of the free press, even as it informs them and even helps them on occasion to evaluate the progress of the powers of repression. But so long as they are engaged in an instrumental relationship with the media, they do not question the existence of an autonomous system of news reporting.

The fourth relational mode, by contrast, presents a *total break* with the broader community. Hereafter, the press ceases to be a medium to be cynically manipulated, an Achilles' heel of democracy, but rather comes to be viewed as a collaborator in the system to be destroyed. Journalists become enemies for the same reasons as do the other actors involved—the owners, judges, teachers, businessmen, diplomats, etc. Although not the primary targets of terrorist movements, it is often the reporters who are placed in the greatest danger, and the list is long of those who have disappeared in full-blown terrorist situations, such as those which erupted in Turkey or Argentina at the end of the 1970s. Reporters also make extraordinary hostages, since their kidnappers know well that professional solidarity has a broad ripple effect whenever it is a member of the press who is kidnapped.

Without always resorting to hostage-taking or assassination, terrorist groups that have broken off completely with the outside cannot brook the notion of an independent media, and thereby cannot accept the principle of any measure of press neutrality. They reproach it for being dishonest and, further, for collaborating with their enemies. They expect it to remain silent if it refuses to report their activities in a favorable light, and they attempt to intimidate it or to oblige it by force to serve as a mouthpiece for their positions.

■

The four relational modes we have just described can be used to characterize a number of terrorist movements. But, they can also be revelatory of an evolution within any one of them. It is common, for example, for political organizations to move from a preterrorist phase defined by relative indifference to a rationale of terrorist action that begins by being highly strategic, but in which a radical disengagement with the outside comes to predominate.

This evolution is not a surprising one. The changeover to terrorism can be linked to the isolation of its actors, and thus to their relative estrangement from those occasions for discussion that had previously rendered their violence preterrorist, and often purely verbal in nature. Similarly, the phase of media-oriented strategy involves conditions that are so specific as to render it a relatively rare and always unstable phase. It implies great irresponsibility on the part of the media, general panic on the part of the authorities, and prodigious self-control as well as a concrete knowledge of the press on the part of the terrorists. It further requires the unbroken attention of public opinion, and therefore a constant increase in suspense and entertainment value that it is hardly possible to maintain for very long. If the press regains its self-control, if the authorities show a minimum of efficiency, or if public interest flags or changes sides, terrorists will find it difficult to go against such a flow, and will tend to attack the press more or less actively.

Whatever the relational mode may be, it is difficult to speak in terms of communication with regard to terrorists who, rather than seeking to establish some kind of genuine relationship, are more interested in simply spreading terror or broadcasting their propaganda. At no time is it their intention to enter into and even less to initiate a dialogue: the press, when it is not wholly ignored or attacked, is for them a permanent tool for driving the public to panic and for destabilizing governments; their contempt for journalists and the public is total. It is therefore not astonishing that terrorist discourse—independent of terrorist actions—is often expressed in a language so obscure and wooden as to be intended for the exclusive comprehension of but a few initiates, in the event that they should care to take an interest in it.

### Does the Media Amplify or Merely Program the News?

The classical theory of symbiotic relationship suggests that the media bear partial responsibility for terrorism since they amplify acts of violence by affording the ripple effect the terrorists desire. As we have just seen, however, terrorists are not always anxious to see the press expand upon their words and deeds; the expanding can also be effected by other participants. Media exposure need not be the result of a direct, linear relationship between those who take up the terrorist cause and the journalists, who propagate terrorism by simply doing their job.

Here we must distinguish between at least three ideal types. The first is one in which the authors of a terrorist operation do in fact look for media repercussions, and in which the media fulfill their expectations and their hopes. The most spectacular example of this was undoubtedly that of the Munich Olympic Games (1972), in which television broadcast, to hundreds of millions of spectators, live footage of the events connected with the activities of the Palestinian Black September commando that had forced its way into the living quarters of the Israeli athletes and made its demands known.

A second ideal type is one in which a terrorist incident is produced and directed not so much by the terrorists themselves as by reporters who, cast in the role of media vehicles, become the leading artists in the production of events. An impressive example of this was offered by the fantastic and often surreal chain of events that followed the hijacking of a TWA Boeing jet at the Beirut airport in June 1985. The press, mainly through live broadcasts, reported on events that came to take on an air of farce more than of terrorism, often paying a high price to shoot footage of relaxed hostages, or of their hijackers who had no aura of the forces of darkness about them.

Lastly, a third ideal type, much more common, is one in which media expansion owes much to a third party made up of neither terrorists nor journalists. This is the case when the behavior of public authorities—of the police or of justice—reawakens interest that would otherwise tend to lose its edge and fade; when a lawyer causes a scandal; when intermediaries in a hostage incident seek to make the most of the situation; and especially when the families of the victims organize to increase public awareness, even when such does not particularly serve the purposes of the terrorists themselves.

We must therefore, from the outset, reject the idea of a single, linear process that would render reporters middlemen and mouthpieces for news stories generated by the terrorists alone. We must then go one step further and recognize the fact that the media, as a system which produces news on terrorism, enjoy a relative autonomy.

Beyond such commonsensical remarks on the competition (between press organizations and among journalists) or the complementarity of news bureaus, the print media, television and radio, it is of capital importance to observe, before all else, the role the media play in simply determining what constitutes an event. Such need not correspond to the expectations of the terrorists themselves, who have limited impact on the decision to qualify or not qualify an act as terrorist in nature, and even less in decisions bearing on a story's place in the news or amount of coverage it will be given. Who on the editorial staff keeps the files, and in what way? Are tabs or a regular "watch" kept on a given group (a costly proposition given the limited likelihood that a terrorist event might occur)? How are such stories dovetailed with regular lead columns, or the reporting of the general news, news from the courts, on foreign policy, etc.? The answers to these questions, as I came to observe with Dominique Wolton, show that, for editorial staffs, the terrorist file is a sensitive one. It can force them into decisions, negotiations, or difficult positions—sometimes, given the urgency of moving on a story, without the time to place matters in a broader perspective—as was the case, for example, with the French television network Antenne 2 in the way it reported on French hostages in Lebanon in its news programs. More than this and contrary to prevailing opinion, terrorism does not sell—not as well, at any rate, as sex or money. In short, it gives the media headaches, and the way in which they deal with terrorism prohibits them from playing to the passive and irresponsible role of mere mouthpiece.

These remarks lead us to consider the media not so much from the standpoint of the production of terrorism—for which they are, in our opinion, hardly responsible—as from that of producing stories that are linked to terrorism.

Terrorism is generally magnified by the press during a group's or movement's period of expansion and, contrariwise, oversimplified in its initial and terminal phases. It is primarily the images of terrorist actors that the media generate, and in this they are capable of portraying the same figures, within a period of a few months, first as all-powerful heroes linked through mysterious bonds to dread power bases and endowed with impressive powers of imagination and financial backing; and later as wretched conscripts of terror, isolated and bereft of either mental or material resources.

The media do not always help the public to see things clearly and, beyond their proliferation of images and words, have a general tendency to greatly oversimplify matters of terrorism. Most particularly, they present terrorism as a homogeneous phenomenon in situations where notable differences do in fact exist, for example when several different groups are engaged in armed resistance. As the few available investigations on the subject have shown, they make unfounded suggestions and mix groups together.[3]

The considerable role played by programming in the presentation of terrorism goes well beyond the terrorist actors themselves. It also concerns the societies from which they come, the regimes that aid them, the religions or general ideologies they claim to be speaking for, as well as the different participants in counterterrorist activities: the political powers, the justice system, the police, special services, etc.[4] In its production of a wide array of images, the media contribute to the evolution of a terrorist phenomenon. For example, a group the press has begun to talk about is led, in order to maintain an image that is a condition for its credibility, to carry out increasingly murderous acts.[5]

But while there can be a ricochet effect to depictions of the phenomenon itself, and thereby some indirect media responsibility for terrorism, one should nevertheless be careful not to reverse roles here, or lose sight of the fact that the initiative remains in the hands of the terrorist actors themselves. The fact that the media have an impact on terrorist developments and that they are capable of contributing to their acceleration—in the direction, for example, of the indiscriminate and unchecked violence that has been the prelude to the collapse of a good number of terrorist groups—does not mean that they bring them into being.

In the last chapter, we evoked the role played by intellectuals. These persons, too, generate images that terrorists may well take to heart. But what is it that we find? Every time the notion of terrorism commands society's attention, there arises a broad public consensus which, however, translates into a silence on the part of intellectuals, who have nothing more to add to commonsense discussion than their disagreement, and thereby their self-marginalization.[6] Under such conditions, journalists bear an immense responsibility. They are in fact the only persons who are able to offer a conceptual framework and a body of representations within which to interpret raw information. Yet for all of this, we cannot suspect them, a priori, of wishing to influence our understanding of the facts in sympathy with partisan, police, or any other interest.

## The Government and the Media

If we are to understand the role that the news plays with regard to terrorism, we must do more than simply underscore the complexity of the media and its news programming. Reporters, in this field more than in many others, are dependent, especially in the heat of a crisis, upon leads from the police or other such groups, which alone are capable of providing any details on the nature of an event, the message it carries, the alleged guilty parties, etc. In a much broader perspective, and even when the principle of the freedom of information is in no way restricted or placed in question, the context within which they present and comment on events is decided for the most part by a third party composed neither of terrorists nor of journalists. This is the aggregate that we call the powers that be, which include the executive—which also encompasses the national police and the secret services—the legislative, and the judicial.

This ensemble functions differently from one country to the next, and from one type of terrorism to another. It is always more-or-less destabilized by terrorism, which triggers or aggravates all manner of problems within it.

These problems occasionally concern one or another of the subgroups that constitute the executive, the judiciary, or the legislative; so it is, for example, that the press in France regularly brings the theme of conflict between its various police organizations into its reporting on terrorism. Problems that arise can sometimes take on a strained air of conflict, especially between two of these subgroups. Here, let us compare the American experience with the French experience. In the United States, the treatment of international terrorism has translated, over the past few years, into a constant chiding of the executive—the White House with its National Security Council, the Central Intelligence Agency and the State Department—by Congress. Congress, through its hearings, places strict controls on the executive and orients foreign policy; more than this, it is constantly pointing out the abuses and double-talk of the executive branch, and can contribute to its destabilization, as we saw happen in the case of Irangate. In France, the tensest situations have generally brought about a confrontation between the powers of the executive and the judiciary, most especially in matters of international terrorism. It is often the case—for geopolitical reasons or, more simply, in order to avoid terrorist reprisals—that the political powers have more or less flouted the justice system by deporting, without trial or in a summary manner, international terrorists who should have been judged and would very likely have been sentenced. This theme, of judges being stripped of their powers in the name of higher interests and of the raison d'état, forms the core of the book written by Charles Villeneuve and Jean-Pierre Péret.[7]

As far as our interests are concerned, there is no need to further elaborate on these images of a power forced by terrorism into defensive positions, which are so many tests or challenges to its ability to function.[8] What is essential here is that the press's work is largely conditioned by the attitude of the public powers towards the terrorist threat. It would be too easy to say that it is a mirror reflection of this attitude. In fact, the media do not operate within the same time frame as do each of the subgroups we have just mentioned. They need to be consulted in the heat of a crisis when, for example, judicial police officials cannot make their information public until their investigation has been completed or when, likewise, the political powers themselves take an interest in maintaining secrecy. Furthermore, everyone addresses the public in a different way, with the press being the sole group for whom the task at hand is, simply and with no ulterior motives, to inform.

There is no unified, coherent system within which the various actors meet to communicate with one another, but rather a fragmented, disjointed aggregate in which the attitudes of this or that group are unstable, and in which everything—the pace, the calendar, the time frame—tends either towards public openness or towards secrecy. Yet, it is clear that the media react to terrorism as a function of the way in which power comports itself. When the latter manages to avoid incoherence, internal conflicts and unbridled dramatization, when it is capable of establishing some level of dialogue with the press—most especially in crisis situations in which human lives are at stake—the media do not go overboard in magnifying terrorist acts, at least not in the way their perpetrators would have them do. When the powers that be are overwhelmed, the press can become carried away, occasionally in the direction the terrorists would have wished. When public authorities feel they can wriggle out of their difficulties through double-talk and actions that do not fit their words, as is often the case in international matters, the media, working mainly from leaks, unveil their hypocrisy and pretense without necessarily playing into the hands of the terrorists.

In every case, the treatment of news is so greatly determined, from the outset, by the attitudes of the authorities, by the more-or-less incoherent interplay of their relations, that we can affirm, yet again, the superficial character of the classic theory of a symbiotic relationship.

The media are well deserving of criticism, and the journalistic treatment of terrorism is not without its weaknesses or failings: its overexploitation of events, lack of perspective, and absence of self-criticism whenever serious errors are the press's own, etc. But it is entirely improper to make a scapegoat of them, or to lay the blame for terrorism at their feet. A consideration of the media sometimes aids in understanding certain events or certain particular modalities of their action, but it most certainly does not allow for an analysis of the emergence and development of terrorist activity.

# 4

## Live Terrorism

There exists an intimate link between the actual experience of terrorism and its proliferation. Belonging to an underground group engaged in armed struggle places a number of constraints on one's life, defines one's cultural life and simultaneously contributes to what is often portrayed as a spiral of violence leading towards the extreme and highly particularized patterns of behavior proper to pure terrorism. It is for this reason that an examination of the actual experience of terrorism is for us a vital step to understanding the workings of this phenomenon, as it arises and evolves.

There are presently two major theories on the subject. The first stresses the notion that violence is possessed of its own subjective rationality and that the terrorist syndrome is therefore a self-perpetuating one. The second rather emphasizes the combative relationship that obtains between actors in the process of becoming terrorists and those persons whose job it is to repress them.

### Self-Perpetuating Processes

For those who practice it collectively, violence gives rise to processes that are consubstantial with and intrinsic to itself: it has its own rules, its own rationale.[1] This theory, which suggests that the actor is overwhelmed by the processes he has set in motion, is often central to the explanations that veterans of previous armed struggles give when they seek to account, in political and moral terms abhorrent to violence, for their earlier activities. From this perspective, membership in a most unusual kind of organization—that of an armed resistance group—implies and entails, in and of itself, types of behavior which can only escalate into a rising spiral of violence. In this way, one can understand why acts that appear to be wholly irrational do in fact follow a kind of logic.

This is, first and foremost, a norm or logic of secrecy. Going underground means breaking one's professional, personal, and family ties to enter into a universe with a rhythm all its own. "Apart from cases of 'total immersion,'" notes Jean-Paul Charnay, "the terrorist lives in a state of perpetual anticipation. Set to an alternating rhythm, time becomes stretched out for him. On the one hand, it is fragmented, because he most often divides it between two types of activity, the one visible, quotidian, commonplace, and the other secret, related to his struggle; on the other hand, it is speeded up, in his terrorist missions which simultaneously inspire fear, fascination, and release in him."[2] When the terrorist initiative becomes massive in scale and duration, it forces persons into lifestyles that, while prestigious for some, are appalling for the great majority. The terrorist is only very rarely a hero or a master of evil; more often, he is reduced to a wretched existence as a low-level agent of death. For every Carlos, there are thousands of Giorgios (that Italian terrorist who so wonderfully described the miserable life of a *brigatista*—his own).[3] The experience of living underground, which isolates a participant within his group, trapping him in structures that dictate all that he does, down to his most personal and intimate acts, shapes attitudes and enhances certain personality traits while stunting others. It creates behavior habits which, entirely concentrated on safety and efficiency, are also founded, quite often, on suspicion. In certain cases, it encourages one to adopt a double life, with a legal side that is as neutral and tranquil as possible, as well as an underground side. Most often, however, it involves practices which can only lead to an escalation of violence. The more a group feels the need to maintain secrecy, the less likely it is to allow its organization, driven even further underground, to maintain or develop relations with social or political figures and officials; and the more it will, as a consequence, shy away from turning towards high-visibility organizations for support and assistance. In order to function, in order to act, it is necessary to possess resources no longer procurable through the traditional channels of militancy. Money, housing, hideouts, and means of transport are obtained through illegal and underground means; and when the first weapons arrive, they trigger an armed action which, more often than not, resorts to their use out of a basic need for supplies. Next come the first incidents—sometimes no more than accidents that can occur when a victim panics, or when an activist is clumsy—and then follows the string of events which repression and secrecy cannot but accelerate.

Here, we have presented the workings of this process in isolation, as it were. It is in fact considerably reinforced by other processes, mainly of an ideological order, which afford a political legitimacy to the bearing of arms, as well as by the pressures inherent to any group closed in on itself. Shedding blood is, for example, a transgression that binds together those who participate in it. As soon as it takes place, it becomes a collective requirement which serves to ensure a group's cohesiveness and to provide safeguards for and against those who have taken part in it.

Once its violence spreads, an organization can no longer be satisfied with a handful of salvaged weapons. Here too, a subjective rationale seems to drive it into a sort of vicious circle through which it throws in its lot with arms dealers who are capable, in turn, of suggesting mutual exchanges and initiatives and who, in the end, can transform the terrorist into a mercenary in a cause not originally his own. One finds such heteronomy, for example, with the German and Japanese terrorists who began working in the service of Palestinian movements, or with those Palestinians who placed themselves in the service of a state. This spiral always begins with an attempt to secure some means of exchange or payment—at times in the form of cash—for such services. Finally, there can at times be a pure and simple takeover of a group by the state that controls the territory on which it has its base of operations. It is also for this reason that terrorism, international crime, and drug trafficking can at times join forces.

In the case of terrorism, the arena of violence is not necessarily occupied by a single organization, and every organization is subject to interpersonal and political disagreements and tensions. A chain reaction of violence can in such cases arise from inter- or intra-organizational rivalries which are wholly incomprehensible when viewed from the outside. An organization launches an operation to assert its superiority over a competitor, to inspire budding activists to join its group rather than another, or to bring its existence to the attention of a "sponsor" state; a subgroup commits an act of violence in order to draw its own organization into an arena into which it had hesitated to enter, etc. More than this, a group can at times become so caught up in the plethora of preparations that go into a terrorist action that it will launch it even after external events have rendered it useless, politically unwarranted, but nevertheless militarily necessary. So it was that the combat wing of the Russian

Revolutionary Socialist party explicitly anticipated, in 1904, the eventuality of carrying out its program of action even if the party were to decide to cease its terrorist struggle.

Problems of recruitment can also at times translate into an uncontrolled upsurge of violence. The further a group broadens its armed struggle, the greater its tendency either to recruit gun- and explosive-wielding fanatics, or to allow them a scope or freedom of action that works to the detriment of more politically oriented militants. One also often finds, in organizations that were highly ideological at their inception, individuals for whom all that matters is the use of weapons, or even true sadists, wild adventurers, or maniacs whose uncontrollable activities can implicate the entire organization.

One can thus generate the notion—with innumerable variants deriving from the specific history of each group—of an independent process in which violence irrevocably feeds on itself and proliferates into ever higher levels and more powerful manifestations, until such time as one of its actors, overwhelmed by the process he has set in motion, is utterly destroyed. It is for this reason that this notion is never so powerful as when it is applied to that most extreme form of violence that was the Reign of Terror, portrayed by such eyewitnesses as Laurent Dispot, as a machine possessed of its own subjective rationale and criteria for efficiency.[4] The concept of self-perpetuating mechanisms approaches the perspective of the sociology of terrorist culture. It throws ample light on a number of facets of terrorism and particularly explains, at least partially, the fact that a terrorist cause always advances through a series of spinoffs which gradually lead to levels of aggravated violence. In the final analysis, however, it ignores the ideological and political dimensions that lie at the heart of these processes. It is for this reason that we ought not to automatically assume that the appearance of an underground movement necessarily entails a logic or rationale of terrorist action. When, on December 13, 1981, Solidarność was outlawed in Poland, the long-term underground movement that took shape at no time fell into potentially terrorist patterns of behavior.

## The System of Warfare

The notion of subjective rationale centers on the individual. To this we may adjoin (rather than contrast) a system of action, at one pole of which is located the relatively autonomous armed insurgent. At the other pole, and of equal autonomy of action, is the state against which he is fighting—a state which is itself defined by its repressive activities, carried out against actions within (domestic terrorism) or outside (international terrorism) of its borders. At this level, all may be reduced to a war or a guerrilla action in which damage inflicted and damage taken are nearly all that matter. The state represses and seeks to isolate and smash the terrorist cause, deploying a wide panoply of techniques which have been set forth systematically by Richard Clutterbuck:[5] infiltration, centralization of intelligence, an updated filing system, international coordination, security measures and, at times, strong-arm interrogation techniques, the encouragement of informers, special statutes and courts, etc. In a symmetrical fashion, the terrorist group organizes operations, mobilizes resources, gathers intelligence, and stockpiles weapons and explosives. Both sides often employ the same techniques. The police have no monopoly on keeping files, as has been proven by the voluminous records amassed by certain Italian groups, beginning with the Red Brigades. Nor is infiltration a one-sided affair: a state apparatus can be penetrated just as easily as a terrorist organization. More than a few domestic terrorist operations, lauched from the far left as well as from the far right, could not have been carried out were it not for the informers they had placed at the very heart of the state system, or for their links with certain secret services. More than a few of the international terrorist acts that have been perpetrated have required intelligence and resources generally associated with espionage techniques and practices of the secret services. Terrorists and police or intelligence services, even when they do not come to know one another, at least end up mutually internalizing the behavior patterns of the enemy. On both sides, one finds oneself in a world of experts and professionals who operate within the same temporality, at a rhythm that is their own and not that of the societies that surround them. This symmetry, defining as it does a combat relationship proper to warfare, can result in ambivalent types of behavior of much greater complexity than those of the traitor or double agent. This we find when we look at Russian populism, in the context of which a mutual fascination between police and terrorists produced figures who were fascinating in themselves (about whom Solzhenitsyn speaks, with regard to Russian terrorism),[6] and gave rise to a situation in which the individual, at once a terrorist and an agent working in the service of repression, no longer knew for sure just who he was.

In this perspective, armed struggle and repression oppose one another at every turn, such that any analysis of the two basically becomes a study in strategies, with the idea, as Gérard Chaliand has phrased it, that violence and terrorism are "the choice of the weak who oppose the strong."[7] According to this argument, the weaker a protagonist in a struggle becomes and the less support he has, the more his violence becomes terrorist in nature and the harsher its counterviolence or repression becomes. This sort of explanation assumes that power relationships are the immediate driving forces behind extreme forms of violence. Such an argument is often backed up by remarks concerning the role of the media in our societies. The great weakness of a group of armed militants will incite it to acts whose positive effects, from its standpoint, will be magnified by the publicity they receive. Each strike must therefore hit harder than the last one and each action be more lethal than its predecessor if one is to benefit from the spectacular effects of media interest.

As far as the proliferation of violence is concerned, the wartime relationship that obtains between a state and a terrorist organization can, at least in certain instances, be completely decisive. The more a state represses and isolates its enemy, the further it drives it underground and into last-ditch and rearguard actions. The brutality of its reactions can, moreover, reawaken the support of certain segments of the population, and revitalize the armed struggle.

Apart from findings of this order, however, the strategic analysis of violence is a limited one. The limits of such an approach are the same as those of explanations based on a subjective rationale: it essentially derives from a semiautomatic or linear treatment of violence, which ignores the ideological groundwork of the actor, and fails to deal with those changes which can render it meaningless. Strategic analyses weigh questions of resources and power relationships and reconstitute the strategic interactions of opposing parties, as if the principles underlying their actions had been established once and for all, and as if the effects of violence were predictable and measurable. Even if this type of approach does make it possible to evaluate a number of organizational planning strategies, it is nonetheless quite inadequate and unadaptable to the phenomena that concern us, i.e. those cases in which violence, even under the effects of repression, comes to follow the dictates of principles that, while sometimes innovated upon, are more often inverted in relation to their original import. Like the idea of a perpetual motion machine, this idea of a war game for two or more players—in which a violent player becomes drawn into a strategy of terrorism buildup—needs to be complemented by something that lies at the very heart of terrorist activity: the processes of *inversion* through which a collective action loses touch with its original guiding principles.

Before we examine these processes in the next chapter, however, it is appropriate that we mention a sphere of primary importance to the actual life of the terrorist—prison.

## Prison

No sociology of terrorism can pass over an analysis of that locus, paradoxically of major importance, constituted by the prison. Apart from the fact that the imprisonment of its members does not necessarily mark the end of an armed struggle, the prison proves to be, quite often, the very context in which violent action is pondered, produced, and planned out, most often with a marked tendency towards inversion.

First of all, detention, even in the most repressive conditions (social isolation, sensory deprivation), can never entirely cut off communication with the outside, and can encourage reflection and ideological output. More than a few manifestos of armed resistance organizations have been drawn up in prison; similarly, detainees have contributed to important discussions, both public and intra-organizational, from their cells. This is one of the reasons for which an approach that seeks to comprehend terrorism on the basis of its ideological output alone can, from the outset, be so very skewed: the documents it uses are generated by the a posteriori rationalizations of prisoners who, seeking to legitimate themselves and their cause, defend, through an ideological raising of the stakes, positions internal to the organization from which they are now cut off by prison walls. More often than accounting for their acts, they cast their failure in theoretical terms, or draw up strategies with which to confront the justice system.

Imprisonment can result in the breakdown of an actor who, in one way or another, gives up the fight. Often, however, it brings about a hardening of his resistance, and a continuation of insurgent activities. Prison is an arena for recruitment where armed insurgents, mingling with nonpolitical detainees, weave new networks and steer rebellious criminals into political activities. Thus Sante Notarnicola's fascinating account emphasizes the contacts made in prison as soon as political prisoners and common-law detainees dispense with their division into two categories—even if such breaks a hard-and-fast communist, if not revolutionary, commandment.[8] For those organizations that take advantage of such reconciliations, new recruits can be brought in whose past feelings and experiences incline them more toward an increase in violence than toward greater moderation.

Prison is also that enclosed space within which the most hard-line positions win out, by force if need be, over more cautious positions, indeed, over the attempts of certain detainees to disengage themselves from the cause of armed struggle. Moral and physical oppression maintain a climate of radical opposition to the state, sometimes at the price of a veritable reign of terror. In Italy, one no longer counts the excesses committed by the "hard-liners" against the "dissociates" or the "repenters," excesses that have been carried to the point of barbarous killings in which, for example, a member suspected of treason is put to death with a spike, with the entire body of detainees being forced to participate in the murder so as to seal with blood a mafia-type solidarity. In Peru, the Sendero Luminoso militants have transformed the prisons in which they are incarcerated into indoctrination and radicalization centers. The prison can also be a place in which syncretic ideologies, tending towards armed resistance, are generated. Thus Basque revolutionary nationalism owes much to the coming together, in Franco's prisons, of communists and nationalists.

The prison is also a vortex around which strategies are formulated for reawakening public support. Here one enters into the sphere of practices whose aim it is to demonstrate the inhuman nature of the state as a means to relaunching a movement that has long since lost its social and political base, or to broadening that base.

The hallmark of these strategies is to make a denunciation of state-sponsored barbarism their central focus, and to subsequently graft a number of the ideals of their own movement upon it. By drawing the sympathy of persons indignant at the conditions of their imprisonment, a group gains the means by which to reenter the political arena and recruit new militants. From this standpoint, the German experience is exemplary: once the prisons could be portrayed, quite rightly, as places in which "clean torture" was practiced, prisoner-support committees could be set up and developed to serve as relay-stations for public opinion, as well as nurseries for future activists.[9] And, when public opinion appeared to be insufficiently sensitized, it seems that Red Army Faction strategy could be carried to rather extreme ends, to the point (as maintained by Hans Joachim Klein and others) that it ordered persons to commit suicide in order to "exert moral pressure on the country's left" with corpses.[10] Here, imprisonment leads to a veritable reversal: the struggle, disconnected from its every social power base, becomes nothing but a standoff with the state. In this case, it is hoped that it may serve to reconstruct a power base that, no longer able to define itself on the grounds of social or political ideals, may perhaps do so on the basis of indignation in the face of the barbarism of a power that has been driven to betray its "true" nature.

So it is that one can easily move from a description of actual experience to the image of a terrorist spiral or frenzy, or indeed that of a reversal of the order of that just described. Notions of self-perpetuating processes or of wartime relations are, however, insufficient if one is to accurately trace the paths that lead from a garden-variety political cause to an underground movement and, especially, into terrorism. The notion of *inversion,* which we will now introduce, is much more relevant.

# 5

# Inversion

We will now consider terrorist groups at such times as their terrorist acts are carried to their greatest extremes. Here, all signs point to a negation of the principles and ideals that inspired their very inception. Whereas one had previously suffered on behalf of a humankind mistreated by the system, now one behaves like a barbarian, not only outside of one's organization but also within it. Suspicion, violence, and self-destruction reign at its very heart, as was spectacularly evidenced in Japan in 1971–72.[1] Whereas one had previously championed political action, political control of one's own organization now proves impossible, as it falls into the hands of those who, through their use of arms, impose a military order upon it and raise the ante through bombings and murder. Whereas one had previously denounced the anti-Semitism of the older generation, one now promulgates a hatred of Jews that goes well beyond the already criminal confusion between Judaism and Zionism. Here, the testimony of Hans Joachim Klein is indicative of just how far such hatred, via a number of peculiar twists and turns, can be carried.[2] Whereas one had previously sought to awaken a dormant labor movement or to create conditions favorable to such an awakening, now one asserts its nonexistence and its end as a historical force, claiming to replace it with one's own movement. Whereas one had previously maintained that the masses were the sole repository of truth, now one ignores or scorns them; and whereas one had previously exalted them, one now flatters their basest instincts—their bloodthirstiness and mob justice. Whereas one had once claimed to oppose the drug epidemic as a corrupting and demobilizing force among youth, now one allies oneself with drug traffickers in order to better resist police repression, or to gain support from a peasant base that lives through its cultivation. Whereas one had previously admired and demanded theoretical rigor, one now embraces a military activism which rejects all critical thought and turns its back on all intellectual effort, and so on.

Such is the final product of an action—which had once called itself liberating and emancipating, and which now manifests itself in dread forms of behavior and ideologies that are as sinister when viewed from within as from without—when it is the product of the process we will call inversion. Inversion is an ideological and practical endeavor by means of which actors remove themselves from the concrete experience of those in whose name they are acting, plunge into terrorism, and become heteronomous figures in struggles that are either not their own, or which are only theirs in some accessory fashion.

We must not underestimate the importance of planning and strategy in the evolution of armed resistance fronts, nor should we belittle that of a subjective rationale of violence. But here we do nothing more than to superficially acknowledge the existence of changes—changes we tend to reduce summarily to automatic or purely organizational processes, whereas terrorism, as a political action, is always meaningful and eminently symbolic for those who practice it.

The intellectual effort to justify the choice of arms most often proceeds from the analysis, carried out from a given ideological standpoint—Marxist-Leninist, religious, nationalist, or other—of data relative to the social and political context in which the actor has evolved. The task of processing meaning is—as has been stressed by those who have traced the complex genealogy of the intellectual roots of terrorism—the formulation of an "ideological policy,"[3] to borrow an expression from Philippe Raynaud. It is primarily defined, however, in its relationship to the social and political context out of which violence arises. Terrorist phenomena emerge out of particular situations—crises, the decline or slow emergence of social or national movements, or political impasses, to give but a few examples. As the perpetrators of violence—in their roles of self-proclaimed arbiters of the ideals of actual resistance struggles—become progressively estranged from the struggles themselves, they come to drift, through a series of processes, into an alienation from the meanings of their actions.

These processes, while they do not necessarily produce terrorist violence, always play a defining role in it. We now turn to these processes, which fieldwork and document-based research have allowed us to identify.

## Direct Inversion through Alienation from One's Social Movement of Reference

Sociologically, the simplest, most elementary process is that by means of which a gulf appears and widens between a social movement and a political actor who claims to be speaking on its behalf. This process does not necessarily refer to difficulties of expression that an oppressed social movement may experience in a difficult political situation. The terrorism of the Russian populists, to paraphrase Camus, was often the action of just persons seeking to create the necessary political conditions for an outlawed social action. Such a process has little in common with the concept of social antimovement or the process of inversion. On the other hand, a variety of typical cases do derive from this process, in which a political actor slides into terrorism as he drifts away from the social movement whose views he claims to be voicing. In Daniel Pécaut's parlance, terrorist violence is an *excessive* form of action which appears when social actors are *lacking*.[4]

There exist two possible modes of access (which may be combined) to such a process. The former is effected through an increasingly unilateral and fundamentalist proclamation of some great and lofty vision of society which no longer corresponds to the aspirations of its social actors. The latter comes about through a takeover, of the dark side of a social movement, i.e. of that component which is the least integrated into its institutional structures, the most inclined to break away, and therefore the closest to an antimovement.

The political or intellectual agents who organize the changeover into violence are sometimes deeply immersed in the social group for which they claim to be speaking. Like the Russian populist leaders, they go to the people, or else "set themselves up" in factories, as did a number of French Maoists a century later. But the peasants they wish to mobilize reject them, the workers whose consciousness they seek to raise follow them but once if at all. Sometimes, the illusion does not fade immediately, as for example when workers applaud the first manifestations of preterrorist violence, when intimidation, physical threats and the carrying out of those threats are encouraged if not anticipated, and when violence seems to correspond to the fondest hopes of the blue-collar masses. But this kind of situation never lasts, and violence always parts ways with social movements. For the militants, the choice now becomes crystal clear: either admit their own defeat and impotence, or commit acts of violence which have less and less to do with the social relations they claim to be challenging. Hereafter, there no longer exists an authentic relationship between themselves and their social base, and everything becomes possible and legitimate, because the political participant has taken out a monopoly on ideals. This process of direct inversion varies according as the social movement in the name of which one is acting is already in crisis and is the process of collapsing into an antimovement, or rather is institutionalized to the point of having given up any vision for the transformation of society at large. When there is a crisis, as was the case in Italy throughout the 1970s, inversion may occur through an active participation, on the part of future terrorists, in a social agitation which gives the illusory impression of having a high capacity for action and great expectations. So it was that sociologists began to speak in terms of a resurgence of class warfare in the period of (mainly Italian) labor struggles that erupted in this period.[5] Here, violence began by accompanying crisis behaviors, before becoming political and terrorist in nature, and before replacing the labor movements and their struggles with their own war against the state. When, furthermore, there occurs a concomitant institutionalization of the social movement, the inversion is further sped up, since the political agent begins in such cases from a position that is external to all grassroots activity. This was the case in Japan,[6] and even more so in Germany, where the majority of the terrorists had not only never taken part in a labor-based action, but had moreover developed a strong subjectivity which, bearing witness to a genuine contempt for the German working classes, was also characterized by an unreal identification with the masses of the Third World.

Inversion basically concerns political agents. The more these have the occasion to participate in the conflicts of the movements they claim to represent, the longer the duration of their commitment and the slower and more chaotic the inversion, when it occurs. Contrariwise, the more this commitment plays itself out itself at a political level, without reaching down into or rooting itself in social conflicts, the more abrupt the inversion.

The preceding remarks primarily refer to the experience of industrial societies and to the inversion of the labor movement. They may be expanded so as to include other societal types and other social movements. Inversion as a gradual loss of meaning and estrangement from concrete social relations, to which the activist only refers in mythic or ideological terms, is a characteristic feature of a number of nonlabor movements.

We find it in the dizzying fall of the student—and later urban and feminist—movements of the early 1970s, as well as in the failure of Italian *autonomia* and, on a much reduced level, its French and German counterparts. The trajectory of certain actors comes to take on the appearance of a series of failures, in which we see them being bounced from one insurgency to another before sinking irremediably into terrorism: we see them moving from the university and its student conflicts to the neighborhood or the city and its urban battles for housing or quality of life, and on to interactions with squatters and participation in cultural freedom movements—until at last, after failure upon failure, they enter into an armed underground action.

"Nothing is harder," writes a Colombian guerrillero in his notebook, "than being cut off from the masses and pursued by the enemy."[7] In the context of the Latin American revolutionary movements, processes of inversion were taking place throughout the 1960s, as was clearly grasped by Régis Debray from the moment he began his critique of arms.[8] While the notion of inversion may be applied to a number of national liberation fronts, the question here becomes far more delicate: even in their worst excesses, when they resort to indiscriminate terrorism and to violence against their own people, do these armed nationalist fighters not remain in direct touch with the national consciousness and thereby national ideals? Moral and political judgment cannot take the place of analysis here. The fact that a resistance front uses barbarous or repugnant tactics does not mean that it derives, sociologically, from a process of inversion. The sole criterion for evaluation lies, as we have already stated, in the nature of the observable relationship between its practices and the population group in whose name they are carried out. If the latter refuses to recognize itself in certain acts, if it rejects the terrorists who claim to defend its cause, then and only then may one speak of inversion. Palestinian terrorism, which we will examine at length later in this study, often— but not always—derives from a process of inversion, one which has manifested itself, most especially, in the assassination of moderate PLO leaders. The example of ASALA is similarly an illustrative one.[9] Its first violent actions, aimed at the Turkish state, "roused the diaspora out of its lethargy."[10] When, however, in 1979, this group became terrorist on every front, allying its fighters to other revolutionary movements that were themselves terrorist, promoting a pro-Soviet ideology and political line, worrying the public opinion of democratic societies, and ceasing to direct its attacks against a clear enemy—the Turkish state—this gave rise to a process of rejection, creating a distance between Armenian communities and ASALA terrorists. In this case as well, one may speak in terms of inversion.

## Inversion before the Fact

The idea of direct inversion primarily refers to the notion of a decline or profound crisis within a social or communal movement. When such a movement weakens or falls apart, crisis modes of behavior arise, and the words and deeds of political figures and intellectuals become so intractable as to eventually lead into terrorism. We must, however, expand on this idea so as to include in our discussion a process, of the same order, which does not begin after the fact of a movement's fall, institutionalization, or decay, but rather before the fact, at a time when the actor is trying, without success, to find himself. Here, our analysis is based on the notion of an unrealizable or unworkable movement, of an actor who exists only through his absence, as a negativity.

Such an analysis may appear audacious and indemonstrable, if not teleological. It apparently introduces a metasocial authority as well as a dubious explanatory principle, and seeks to account for a form of behavior—here, that of terrorism—on the basis of social relations that only fall into place after the fact.

Our reference to a movement as a negativity is only meaningful when a number of various and sundry elements herald its formation. Its actors bursting of a sudden upon the social scene, and its actions coalescing via a slow and complex process in which a variety of components, even if they are combined in the end, may well remain dissociated, or even represent antagonistic interests and ideals over a long period of time. So for example the labor movement took shape in the course of a history in which workers' consciousness only truly became a class consciousness after the Taylorization and "scientific" organization of the workplace.[11] Prior to this, as we have already noted, the labor movement was composed of the distinct and often conflicting elements of the prideful attitude of its skilled craftsmen, and the proletarian consciousness of its unskilled laborers, with these two sides of the movement ignoring or fighting with one another more often than they stood together or complemented one another.

It is in the context of such a situation that it may be useful to introduce the notion of an *inversion before the fact* which, exemplified in the anarchist terrorism in the years 1892–94, appeared at a historical juncture in which the labor movement had yet to solidify. The movement did exist, but was still in a weak and faltering state, quite incapable of giving concrete and coherent voice to those conflicts and struggles which, while they were the heralds of an industrial society, were still not yet central to it.

The terrorist flare-up that occurred in France in 1892–94 (comparable phenomena may be studied in other countries, Spain in particular) cannot be reduced to an absence of social ideals or their presence as a negativity. It owes much more to a political tilt on the part of anarchism and, in a wider context, to the makeup of the French state and its political system in that period. But these phenomena, in and of themselves, were mainly impelled by the state of social relations and by the rise of still rather poorly unified labor movements.

The "age of bombings"—as Jean Maitron, the great authority on the subject, has called it[12]—was a relatively short interlude marked by a series of unrelated actions: the explosions on Boulevard St. Germain (March 11, 1892), at the Lobau barracks (March 15), in Rue des Bons-Enfants (November 8, 1893, five dead), and the crime of Léauthier (November 13); the explosions at Palais-Bourbon (December 9), at Hôtel Terminus (February 12, 1894, one dead), in Rue St. Martin (February 20), at La Madeleine (March 15, in which Pauwels was killed by his own bomb), and at the Foyot restaurant (April 4); and the assassination of President Carnot at Lyon (June 24). Ravachol (July 11, 1892), Vaillant (February 5, 1893), Emile Henry (May 21, 1894) and Caserio (August 15, 1894) were executed, and numerous prison terms and deportations handed down.

This phenomenon was a short-lived one, and there are no major incidents, either before or after, that can be linked to it. It was, primarily, a phenomenon that was stopped short at a most particular historical juncture. The way in which this "epidemic" was so abruptly halted brings us back to our discussion of inversion after the fact. It is when we turn to the development, in tandem, of political and social movements in France that we can best grasp the nature of anarchist terrorism, which ceased in 1894. This development is essentially characterized by a reconciliation between anarchism and trade unionism.

All who have studied this period note that it was in the early 1890s that there emerged in France a trade unionism capable of organizing— beyond mutualism or cooperatism—a united front possessed of a common cause, which recognized the need to unite the separate worlds of the highly professional skilled craftsman and the unskilled manual laborer. It was in this period that a shift occurred, from a skeletal and heteronomous union movement which accepted the Guesdian principle of subor-

dinating the economic cause to the political cause, to one which—even
as it was radicalizing—endeavored to take charge over all labor issues,
from industrial riots to economic demands. This was the rise of revolutionary syndicalism and of the trade union halls, in which such powerful
figures as Fernand Pelloutier predominated.[13]

This rise cannot be dissociated from the penetration, into trade unionism, of both anarchist ideas and militants. To be sure, not every anarchist
took this path, and there were in fact many who maintained positions
comparable to those of propagandists of a given political creed, if not
of libertarian individualism, whose vindication of unlawful action had
no connection whatsoever to an insertion into the labor movement. But
the two predominant positions both moved in the direction of a reconciliation with and a participation in the unionization of labor. For some,
anarchism was the end and trade unionism, fertile ground for the sowing
of revolutionary propaganda, the means to that end. For others—men
like Emile Pouget or Fernand Pelloutier, whose influence and role were
decisive[14]—the idea of using the union movement to one's ends was
unacceptable. What was important was the construction of what may
be called an all-purpose labor movement, capable of extending from the
workplace or construction site up to the state, a synthesis that came to be
termed revolutionary syndicalism, anarcho-syndicalism, or direct-action
syndicalism.

The debate between these two positions brought a breath of fresh air
to the anarchist movement, which clearly abandoned, in any case, its
individualist ideologies, and which came to see its revolutionary future
in terms of an alliance with union actions. At the same time, it distanced
itself from its prior positions which had been more or less in favor of
terrorist violence, and more generally from any violence which was not
immediately social or labor-related, or centered on the relations of production and work.

The return to social actions—which were themselves on the rise—did
not necessarily rule out social violence or direct action. Nor did it rule
out the call to revolution, which would thereafter be limited to the form
of the general strike. But violence could no longer be equated with political terrorism. Instead, it became split into grassroots violence—of a social order, and restricted to relations with management—and a mythic
revolutionary violence. In this context, the negative or at best circum-
spect reactions, some twenty years later, to the activities of the Bonnot
gang, show just how far one had moved away from the terrorism of
1892–94. Even when their perpetrators' motives were good, revolution-

ary syndicalism distanced itself from individual acts of violence. It simultaneously rejected the romance of violence and carried out an attack on
crime, which it said could only lead to greater repression and to a retrac-
tion of reforms already won or in the course of being enacted.[15]

The anarchist terrorism of the end of the last century was not only a
manifestation of a rebellion against law and order. It also owes its existence to an absence of meaning and to the lack of social actions. The
terrorists who rushed in to fill this vacuum bore the mark of this negativity, even as they were aware of the central role that social actions would
come to play. It came to an end when this vacuum was filled by the
positive notion of a labor movement which, through the myth of the
general strike and the booming expansion of union halls, asserted itself
as the champion of all hope for a new and just society. It is in this way
that anarchism derived from a process of inversion before the fact, a
process that is comparable to processes of inversion after the fact, of
those instances in which leftist extremist terrorism emerged within societies where the labor movement was in decline or becoming institutionalized.

If there is a sociological distinction here, it would perhaps have to be
made on the basis of the form it takes and the abruptness of its appearance and disappearance. As Roland Gaucher has clearly shown, this
distinction is essentially born out of anarchism's total absence of organization, which was itself inseparable from the libertarian doctrines with
which it justified its existence. Independent of any organization capable
of structuring his action either ideologically or logistically, the anarchist
terrorist "was responsible to no one but himself." Group pressure was
no obstacle to an ideological and, especially, practical abandonment of
the cause, "since he did not have to justify himself before the court
of his comrades."[16] This is why anarchist violence so quickly became
exhausted, and its activities so disjointed; it is also why it never produced
spinoffs, as has modern Marxism-Leninism.

## Fusion

Terrorist phenomena can rarely be reduced to the simple principle of
inversion through estrangement from a social movement, nor even to the
more complex notion (nevertheless based on the same principle) of a
syndrome of failure in mobilizing diverse elements of society. What char-
acterizes groups that come to take up armed resistance is that they nearly
always develop a syncretic discourse which incorporates all manner of
social, cultural, and political meanings into a whole whose inner coher-

ence is generally tentative in nature. We will speak of fusion, somewhat after the fashion of Sartre, to designate the moment in which there occurs a totalization, within a group, that is the necessary but not sufficient condition for that group's present or future violence. This is a common phase which consists of condensing, from social and political practice, elements whose meanings are either contradictory or have previously remained disconnected, into a unified body of discourse and practice. Prophetic and messianic movements, whether or not they be violent, often seek to at once defend an endangered community and to reappropriate for themselves all changes that may have occurred. As Alain Touraine has stated so clearly, populist liberation movements are carried forward by the dream that they can "manage somehow to remain more and more the same while undergoing transformation."[17] Nazism, as its name indicates, wished to speak in the name of socialism and nationalism at the same time. The leftist movement, which was a formative phase in the careers of a number of leftist extremist terrorists, combined revolutionary action and a body of disparate resistance struggles (social, cultural, etc.) into a single concept.

In all the various and sundry forms in which it appears, ideological fusion need not be violent. Often, however, such forms can constitute the necessary transition that opens the way to the use of weapons. This is because syncretism or fusion does not always mean unification. When one attempts to remain the same at the same time as one is changing oneself, when one speaks in the name of a class (i.e. of an actor in social conflict with another actor) while identifying oneself with the nation (as a collectivity defined as independent of any class affiliation), when one welds a variety of projects into a single master plan, one can run into contradictions. One may avoid such contradictions by taking up the path of violence, which elevates the various issues and aspirations one claims to be fighting for to a different level than that upon which they had previously defined themselves. This level of synthesis or of transcending contradictions generally leads to the formulation, in the mind of the actor, of the notion of a single adversary, who often takes the form of an objectivized order—that of the state for domestic terrorists, and that of Western imperialism for certain international terrorists.

The analysis of these processes of fusion becomes especially useful when one looks at situations in which a terrorist actor speaks in terms that are simultaneously social and communal, in terms of class and nation, for example. A practical means for combining these two tendencies within the agenda of a single movement is that of violence, which is itself consequent to the formulation of an ideology, especially one of a populist or leftist order. This we have demonstrated *a contrario* in a study carried out under the direction of Alain Touraine. When the Occitanist movement sought to link together a socioeconomic focus—in which a movement of Languedoc winegrowers predominated—with a nationalist one, it fell apart following its refusal to take up the path of armed insurgency against the state, of which the Montredon-Corbières shooting might have constituted the first shot.[18] We find it as well, with the poles reversed, in the abbreviated career of the Front de Libération du Québec,[19] in the much more long-term and wide-ranging campaigns of the IRA (in Northern Ireland) or of ETA (in the Basque regions of Spain), as well as in those of certain sectors of the Palestinian movement or ASALA. Violence escalates and becomes terrorist violence in direct proportion as it attempts to give simultaneous voice to both sociopolitical and nationalist principles. When these elements are processed separately, the degree of violence changes and (in instances such as these, at least) diminishes. This we will clearly see in our analysis of the Basque movement, whose armed resistance is neither the result of a pure nationalism nor of a pure Marxism-Leninism superimposed upon social themes, but is rather that of a difficult marriage of the two.

Fusion is neither a systematic nor an automatic process, as has been demonstrated in David Apter and Nagayo Sawa's in-depth analysis of the Japanese Sanrijuka movement.[20] In France, farmers (later joined by the New Left) who militated, in the years following 1965, against a governmental project for the construction of an international airport, carried out an often violent-defensive campaign, in which all sorts of themes were blended together. These included a peasant defense initiative similar to that of the Larzac farmers, an anti-imperialist focus, a critique of political intransigency, the voicing of ecological concerns, etc. In the same period there developed in Japan several leftist extremist terrorist organizations (Proletarian Revolution, Japan Committee, United Red Army) who sought to tap into the movement against the Narita airport. They were thrown out of the movement by other militants who, in favor of communal and defensive forms of violence, were opposed to the use of weapons. This communal violence itself became radicalized in the course of the airport's construction and, in its final phase, could have veered into terrorism. A number of tentative contacts were made with the PLO in the early 1980s, and there was talk of internationalizing the struggle; these attempts, however, led nowhere.

Fusion, when it feeds into terrorism, always tends to dissolve the disparate components that lend meaning to an action, and to reduce these, in the final analysis, to a pure subjectivism. The individual himself comes to embody every resistance struggle, and himself becomes the necessary condition for emancipation in its every form. His radical disengagement, realized through the use of weapons, is at once an existential and political one, and resolves in a single stroke a wide array of problems with which he had personally identified himself. It is for this reason that one is tempted to draw a parallel between a sociological approach, based on the notions of fusion or syncretism, and a psychological or sociopsychological analysis, founded on the theory of cognitive dissonance as was developed and used by Leon Festinger and his colleagues.[21] This theory maintains that "the simultaneous existence of cognitives which in one way or another do not fit together (dissonance) leads to effort on the part of the person to somehow make them fit better (dissonance reduction)."[22]

When an individual is in a position in which he has to make a choice which—because it entails the rejection of options which are, from his standpoint, at least partially positive and the embracing of others in which he perceives negative elements—is rendered difficult; similarly, when he has to deal with a contradictory situation, he can attempt to modify either reality, his own opinions, or both. For Festinger, the matter at hand is not so much one of evaluating a situation, or even the reactions it might provoke—frustration, fear, aggressivity, retreat—as it is one of indicating that a decision-making process has been set in motion. This process lies at the core of the theory of cognitive dissonance, which is interested in "what the person is doing during the time it takes to make a decision that enables him to make the decision and determines what the decision is . . ."[23] Describing as it does an individual psychological process, the theory of cognitive dissonance takes but a limited interest in the specific meanings of those cognitive elements which can cause a person, for example, to take up the path of violence. It is even less prepared to offer so much as a schematic rendering of collective action, since that is not its object. It does, however, have the immense virtues of reminding one that human behavior makes sense; of recognizing the actor in his acts; and of accenting the complexity of the cognitive elements with which an individual has to deal. It is compatible with a sociology of action, recording at its own level psychological processes which it certainly describes better than do those other approaches which would attempt to reduce acts of violence to a projection of individual personality or to psychological confusion, or which simply behavioralize individual or collective violence into so many manifestations of instinct or aggressivity.

## Internal Divisions and the Factionalization of the Arena of Violence

Viewed from a distance, a terrorist group, especially if it is only known through its violent acts, projects an image of high ideological cohesiveness. Nothing could be further from the truth. As homogeneous as it might appear, even an armed resistance organization that is limited to a handful of individuals is forever caught up in the discussions and conflicts proper to its political nature. The responses a political power makes to the terrorism that assails or threatens it, the reactions of a population group, as well as the simple evolution of a given social, political, or international situation force the actor to interpret his actions. Such can in turn give rise to a divergence of opinion, which in turn gives rise to differing strategies or positions. Let us take the example of domestic violence. When working-class struggles are on the wane, ought one to wait for better days or to unilaterally launch operations that must lead directly to violence? When student movements are falling apart, is it better to view them as so many incubators out of which militants will eventually enter into the organization, or should one rather maintain an active presence within the milieu? When feminism becomes an active presence within the organization itself, when women contest its sexual division of labor and dominant male chauvinism, should women yield to the primacy of strictly political imperatives, take up internal resistance, or consider splitting off from the group? The same holds for international terrorism which is ever sensitive to geopolitical changes and constantly forced—if only on a strategic level—to revise its positions and to change its course of action.

The processes that lead a community to take up the path of violence, first in theory and then in practice are, from this standpoint, comparable to those which stir up groups already engaged in conflict. In these cases, internal dissension and conflict, which is resolved through self- or forced exile, can result, in a variety of ways, in the disintegration of the group's former ideological and political structure, with its members recombining in a dislocated fashion. Most often, certain of these radicalize, while others conversely give up the path of violence. Whether it be located prior to the emergence of armed resistance—in leftist, popular or nationalist movements, for example—or at the very heart of such an emergence, there exists an ongoing process of division and recombination, which is a reflection of its actors' own self-criticism. This process can result in a fragmentation, out of which several organizations may come to share the arena of armed insurgency. It is through the different ways in which these groups make sense of their actions' various meanings, the primacy they give to one or another of these meanings, and especially their location relative to the inversion process (i.e. before or after) that these groups distinguish themselves from one another. We will illustrate these phenomena in a number of ways; for the moment, however, we will simply give an indication of their diversity through a few examples borrowed from the chronicle of domestic terrorist operations launched by leftist extremists.

In those cases in which an organization is the first to greatly intensify its terrorism, a number of intermediate groups may emerge. Certain of these will primarily be manifestations of social disorganization and serve as so many attempts to politicize various forms of marginal or delinquent behavior, such as those studied by François Dubet.[24] Others will endeavor to maintain certain ties with social movements, or even to effect a return to their social base, alternating between what they claim to be an instrumental violence, bearing arms in the direct implementation of social demands on the one hand, and a form of terrorism approaching that of the front-line organization, itself the most advanced in its tendency toward inversion, on the other. In Italy, both Prima Linea and a dusting of tiny groups thus shared a field dominated, from the top, by the Red Brigades. In those cases in which an original organization constructs an ideological foundation capable of resisting radical inversion, one sees the emergence of groups that somehow spill over to enter into, for example, a process in which a loss of meaning leads into total heteronomy and international terrorism. So it was in Germany that even though the Red Army Faction of Baader and his cohorts constituted the most durable and, in the end, the most stable core of the armed insurgency, it was overtaken, along the road to inversion, by the Revolutionary Cells and the Second of June movement which, although they appeared at a later time, were quicker in placing themselves in a relationship of dependence vis-à-vis the Palestinian terrorist movements.[25]

If the field of violent action is occupied by but a single organization, a rare occurrence in itself, such can only remain the case for a short time. Such a situation can open up the field for armed insurgencies which, through the interplay of fragmentation and the emergence of new groups, become splintered into a wide array of more-or-less original amalgamations of social and political normative standards for action. Otherwise, an armed struggle can—having weathered its first temptations toward and experiences of violence—also effect a return to prior standards, which may take one of two forms: either a return to activities proper to social movements, which implies that these have a certain element of reality to them, or a disintegration or self-dissolution. This latter alternative, which demands long and patient effort on the part of its leaders, was successfully realized by the French Maoists, but failed in the case of the Italian Lotta Continua. If a single organization holds a given arena of political violence and terrorism, it is possible for it to dissolve itself. If the field is shared by a number of groups, self-dissolution can only abet the proliferation of violence, by freeing up activists and "orphans" whom other groups, outside the bounds of that organization, will not hesitate to take under their wing.

## "Military" and Political Factions

The notion of the fine-tuned terrorist organization as a self-governing group capable of articulating political ideologies and strategies for armed struggle is, for the most part, a mythical one. The bearing of arms has always had a tendency to slip out of the politico-ideological grasp of those who first chose it as an alternative and who would attempt to organize it. This tendency does not solely stem from a subjective rationale or the specific demands of military action per se. It also arises from a variety of lags which manifest themselves, within a group or organization, between such technical demands and the demands of the political if not social combat. These lags themselves have a number of sources, which basically stem from an organization's original form.

In those cases in which militarization proceeds from a split between political or mass action and underground action, this lag is a quasi-structural one. Military action imposes precautions, rhythms, and modes of operation that are so peculiar to itself that it quickly enters into contradiction with any legal activity. In cases in which the original organization is also a broad-based one, involved in a great number of localized situations, armed action is likely to give rise to subgroups—difficult to fit into a master plan—which escape central control and carry out wide-ranging and scattered terrorist actions or even a general terror campaign which can veer out of control and into radical inversion. So it is that leaders are constantly called upon to take responsibility for acts they had neither foreseen nor desired. When they fail to do so, they are quickly repudiated by this or that subgroup, thus losing all credibility. When they do claim responsibility, sometimes in spite of themselves, they second behavior which can often alienate them from public opinion, and thereby diminish public sympathy for their cause and bring about its deterioration. This was a particularly sensitive problem for the Russian Revolutionary Socialist party, as evinced in statements made by its leader, Gershuni, at its Second Congress (1907).[26]

Internal tensions between the "military" and "political" wings of an organization can, at the outset, be inconsequential or minimal. However, initiatives that have been blunted by concrete difficulties, arising from repression or the unfolding of a crisis situation, can undergo transformations. Here, a division can arise between those who wish to continue the operation, within the parameters of instrumental violence, and those who would either abandon violence altogether or initiate actions of unbridled and even more lethal violence. This last subgroup, even if it represents a small minority, nearly always exerts a decisive influence on the entire group, drawing it—sometimes at the expense of its more moderate elements who withdraw or leave the organization—onto the path to increasingly irrevocable inversion.

It is not a linear sequence of events, but rather a general tendency or body of variables, which leads a military command to assert its autonomy and comes to constitute the moving force behind an armed liberation front. This tendency can itself become aggravated through successes of a properly military order, which can in turn attract into the organization in question a body of activists whose lowest common denominator is their thirst for violent action—wild adventurers, alienated youth, and uprooted persons who are angry or who want nothing more than to cradle "comrade P 38" (the favorite weapon of the Italian autonomists) or explosives in their arms. This brings about a reinforcement of the military, and internal pressures towards an increase of violence and a corresponding weakening in the role of the "political" wing.

Such alliances, internal divisions, and tensions between "military" and "political" factions point to the fact that the field of terrorism is a protean and ever-changing one, which can never be defined in a constant way. This is a fact that is but rarely acknowledged by the founders of antiterrorist initiatives, who more often ground their actions in repression and intelligence than they do in a policy that would seek to reduce violence by pressuring that which is fluid and heterogeneous in it. It should be noted, however, that the governments are themselves torn between demands for a police and military response to terrorism and calls for a diplomatic or political handling of the same, the latter always being more delicate and often unprofitable in the short term.

■

At the turn of the century, Georg Simmel remarked that it was very easy for action to become transformed into unchecked violence, in which engagement became a self-contained end in itself. He stopped short, however, at an infrasocial interpretation, explaining extreme acts in terms of compulsion, subjective feeling, inner energies, and human aggressivity.[27] Even in the most extreme cases, one cannot accept an explanation that merely behavioralizes patterns of comportment. The sociologist's task thus becomes one of delineating those processes—of a loss of meaning—which seem to underlie any apparent absence of meaning. Here, the concept of inversion is a useful one.

# 6

# Conclusion to Part One

The time has come to apply—and thereby test in a more systematic fashion—the body of analytic schema we now have at our disposal. This endeavor, which will take up the balance of this work, should render intelligible a number of historical phenomena of terrorism.

The sociological tools we have presented are analytical tools, which should allow us to break down that which terrorism has fused together, to reconstruct the trajectories, deviations, and discontinuities proper to its movements, and to recover those of its meanings that have been lost or distorted through the ideological and practical efforts of its armed insurgents. The historian, too, may seek to analytically differentiate between those elements which history tends to combine into a single whole; but his analytical categories will not necessarily be those of the sociologist. "History is synthesis," exclaims Fernand Braudel, "and the historian an orchestra conductor"[1]—but do our tools correspond to the diversity of musical scores that Braudel's conductor must seek to harmonize?

In truth, the very notion of historical synthesis nearly always refers to the search for causes and contributing factors of history. Carried to extremes, a procedure which thus consists of moving from causes to synthesis implies that each and every cause is a valid one since, as Seignobos claimed, the absence of but one cause was tantamount to a veto. Synthesis is only possible when the researcher has enumerated, without omission, the body of factors whose convergence has been decisive to a historical phenomenon. Does it thereby oblige us to endeavor to draw up an exhaustive list of causes to explain, in this or that instance, the emergence or development of a terrorist process? Such a practice can only lead to confusion, bringing together as it would have to distinct or even contradictory intellectual approaches or levels of analysis. To juxtapose a series of contributing factors is to accumulate partial interpretations proper to this or that discipline or field of inquiry, prior to arbitrarily postulating their coherence. The patterns of behavior thus treated find their unity in themselves, in the historical totalization they constitute, with explanation being reduced, in the final analysis, to the notion of a convergence, at a given time, of disparate elements—with each element deriving from a distinct analytical process having nothing to do with those processes proper to every other element. Let us take the example of Italian terrorism. To explain this phenomenon through the simultaneous effects of a governmental crisis, the problems of a generation alienated from a *catto-communista* culture, the radical leftist spinoffs of the 1960s, as well as through the establishment of a subjective rationale and an automatic cycle of violence, is tantamount to suggesting an analytic synthesis of which each component analysis—however relevant it may be—treats of a distinct historical, political, sociological, or psychological problem. To do so also leads, quite often, to a confusion between genesis and structure, change and function, and to a blending of interpretations centered on the actor with others centered on the system, without ever having done so much as to sketch out even the most summary synthetic theory.

The analytical categories we have presented here cannot be reduced to a motley catalogue of causes or factors which may or may not have contributed to this or that case of violence. They are rather circumscribed within an all-encompassing whole which requires that one study, instead of causes or factors, the ideological and practical organization of ideals, which are themselves rooted in social or political relationships. The particular difficulty in this case is that these relationships become lost or distorted in direct proportion to any tailspin into violence and to the separation of the actor from the system—whence his great subjectivity, which goes hand in hand with the objective manner in which he defines the system that has become his enemy.

# Part Two

## SOCIAL MOVEMENTS AND MARXISM-LENINISM: THE ITALIAN PHENOMENON OF LEFTIST EXTREMIST TERRORISM

Black terror, red terror: the history of Italian terrorism begins in 1969 with the explosion of a bomb in the Piazza Fontana office of the Banca dell'Agricoltura in Milan. In subsequent years, it would follow a blind and erratic trajectory on the far right, during which time leftist extremist terrorism, equally lethal, would increase without interruption until its peak in 1980–81.

One is tempted to associate the two phenomena within a single analytical process, to underscore the odd symmetry of their relationship, and to recall that the emergence of leftist armed insurgency took place in the historical context of the rightist "strategy of tension," of that blend of creeping fascism and "golpism" which did not truly disappear until 1973 or 1974. Here, however, we will limit ourselves to examining the formation, successive incarnations, growth, and lastly the decline of leftist extremist terrorism.

A few figures—cruel figures in the words of Donatella Della Porta and Maurizio Rossi[1]—will help to indicate the considerable magnitude of this phenomenon. Between 1970 and 1982, radical leftist terrorists claimed responsibility for 2,188 offenses, of which 272 resulted in deaths; 360 persons were killed or wounded, of which 161 were killed or wounded by the Red Brigades; and a total of 537 organizational acronyms, belonging to groups possessed of some measure of continuity, were counted (even if the Red Brigades were the sole group to remain active throughout the entire period). Most of these acronyms corresponded to spontaneously assembled, unstable, or ephemeral clusters of persons who, having claimed responsibility for a single operation (at most), generally disappeared from the political scene. Several thousand persons were incarcerated in connection with this historical phenomenon alone. Their victims hailed from a variety of backgrounds: judges, journalists, executives, police, constables (the *carabinieri*), political leaders, university professors, students, doctors, bureaucrats, one communist union member and, at the bitter end, "penitents" or comrades in arms suspected of turning traitor. To these must be added those persons who were killed by error or through clumsiness, as well as those who died in the settling of internal scores.

Thanks to the fact that a great number of terrorists—including some leading figures—"talked," we have at our disposal a great wealth of documentation on this phenomenon. Legislative measures taken in favor of "penitence" resulted in a multitude of confessions which, corroborated by other sources, allow for the reconstruction, albeit with a number of dark areas remaining, of the complex of trajectories that marked the history of leftist extremist terrorism in Italy.

A number of works have appeared on the subject, works that have become progressively better informed, and less scandal-mongering or sensationalist in nature, and more analytical over time. Some of these are journalistic, such as the synthesis offered by Giorgio Bocca, the study prepared by the Milanese Barbone group and edited in the form of a "thriller" by Fabrizio Calvi, or the monograph written by Corrado Stajano on the subject of Marco Donat-Cattin, the son of one of the country's most important political figures. Others are more sociological, most particularly the excellent anthology of texts brought together by Donatella Della Porta.[2]

The militants have themselves been responsible for an impressive literary output, which dates from both the time of their terrorist activity and from the subsequent years in which they played the roles of "penitents" or deserters. The "super-penitent" Patrizio Peci signed his name to a long autobiographical account which drew great attention, while at the rock bottom of the Red Brigades hierarchy a certain Giorgio described the miserable existence of the basic *brigatista*.[3] Political parties, union organizations and innumerable intellectuals, both analysts and actors themselves, have also taken the field to give their reading of the question.

A historical reconstruction will thus not run up against the walls of secrecy and mystery that characterize so many other similar phenomena.

# 7

## Fifteen Years of Armed Insurgency

### The Birth of the Red Brigades

The history of the Red Brigades (BR) begins in Milan, where its future leaders, Renato Curcio and Mara Cagol, who had come there from the University of Trent in the fall of 1969, met, among others, a number of "comrades" from Reggio nell'Emilia who had split off from the Italian Communist party (PCI) there. These were the days of the Metropolitan Political Collective (CPM), a group whose pioneers hailed from the great urban industrial centers, and in which the discussion of opportunities for armed resistance was the order of the day. This was especially the case at a meeting, organized at Chiavari in December 1969, which has come to constitute, in the annals of "brigadology," the birthdate of the BR. The truth is, in fact, of a more complex order: a number of statements show that this was more of a process than a clear-cut decision.[1] The CPM, perhaps influenced by the Maoist phenomenon in France, became the Sinistra Proletaria (Proletarian Left), as a number of militants prepared to go underground and take up armed resistance. Following this, the BR acronym came to be attached, for the first time, to an act of violence when a Sit-Siemens director's car was set ablaze.

The founding fathers of the Red Brigades were a group of well-schooled militants whose seriousness, force of conviction, and need for radical change which at times led to their martyrdom and total commitment to the cause—linked in some cases to a Catholic education—has been noted by many. Their political line consisted of making their presence felt within labor struggles as a means to radicalizing them, in "gaining proletarian sympathy and support for the communist revolution . . . in laying bare the hidden structures of power, and exposing instances of collusion . . . between apparently distinct power groups and institutions."[2]

Their policy was thus one of attaching themselves to actual cases of social conflict, of generating an alternative form of power in the factories, if not in working-class neighborhoods, by means of a practice they called *armed propaganda*. This practice was the sole means by which to speed up both the consciousness-raising process and contribute to the formation of an elite that would later give birth to a truly combatant communist party. Committed to a long-term struggle, the Red Brigades defined themselves more as a vanguard than as a political party. In the "councilist" atmosphere of the beginning of the decade, their militants were indeed present at a number of protests and meetings, with their underground character remaining strictly limited, and their first violent acts bloodless. Their activists entered into the agitated milieu of the factories with the greatest of ease, and may well have felt themselves to have been borne forward on the wings of history.

It was thus out of the deep-rooted but controlled violence endemic to labor unrest in this period that they took their first steps. Starting in 1972, these were followed by other, still nonlethal acts. They briefly took a Sit-Siemens director (one who was, moreover, accused of being a fascist) captive; later, in 1973, and this time in Turin, they held a fascist union organizer named Bruno Labate, as well as a number of other persons. Although the workers hardly showed the slightest enthusiasm for these acts, either turning their backs on or remaining unaware of them, the brigatistes seemed not to have been affected by this indifference. They did, however, participate in the internal debates of the radical left, most particularly those of the Potere Operaio (PO) militants.[3] Their association with this group lies at the heart of the "Calogero theorem," named after a Paduan judge who considered there to be an ideological and practical unity between the Red Brigades, Potere Operaio, and other persons and groups who later appeared on the terrorist scene.[4] It is an undeniable fact that the radical left, including the PO, constituted a breeding ground for the Red Brigades and a changing house for future brigatistes. To assert on this basis, however, that there existed a concrete BR-PO alliance would be a dangerous step.

## From the Factories to the State

Early on, the Red Brigades set themselves up in a number of factories, where they began to develop their sociopolitical strategy. In this, they were closer to a number of extraparliamentary groups—from whom they may be essentially distinguished on the basis of their activism—than they were to another terrorist phenomenon, the short-lived Partisan Action Groups (GAP) of Giangiacomo Feltrinelli.

The great social and political transformations that occurred between 1973 and 1976 had a major impact on the evolution of the Red Brigades. The most important of these was the crisis in the labor movement, which came to radicalize a number of its members. Between workers who felt themselves abandoned by a trade unionism that was becoming increasingly politicized, young unskilled laborers who had left the unions, communist fundamentalists, and victims of partial unemployment, there was no lack of enthusiasm for taking up a course of armed resistance. The experience of the Red Brigades was, however, of a somewhat more complex order. At the same time as they were enjoying real growth and setting themselves up in new factories they began to encounter, in 1972–73, disillusionment and disenchantment from within the radicalized wings of the various labor movements. At the Fiat plant in Turin, they managed to set up four brigades, while in Milan, they maintained a continued presence at the Sit-Siemens factory. Here, emerging out of a "study group" formed in 1968, employees and technicians had come to spearhead a number of hard-line actions. It was also here that they kidnapped an engineer named Mecchiorini from the Alfa-Romeo plant, in 1973. But 1973–74 was also the period in which the Red Brigades came to know failure (as described by Patrizio Peci, with special regard to Turin), in the form of a rejection, by the workers, of their militant stance.[5]

It was at this point that a veritable upheaval began to occur, which would later be confirmed. This upheaval may be viewed from the three complementary standpoints of ideology, organization, and practice.

Formerly, the Red Brigades had focused their political considerations on the factory and on the altogether concrete demands of its workers, for which they had wished to be the armed (albeit more symbolic than violent) mouthpiece. Now, even as they retained the proletariat—of which they considered themselves to be the historical epitome—as their point of reference, they would come to increasingly concentrate their analysis on the state, and would posit their notion of the multinationals' imperialist state, or SIM (stato imperialista delle multinazionali). The idea had a magical effect: "With the SIM," said Morucci, who would become a pivotal figure in the BR, "the subversive movements, and the Red Brigades in particular, had at last found the means to tie together all that had previously been unrelated or lacking in direct links."[6] Conflict in the workplace could only be comprehensible through a reference to the factory, the factory to the city, the city to the region, and the region to the Italian state—which was itself subject to American imperialism, through the multinationals and the Christian Democrats, the organizational heart of reactionism.

This ideological innovation went hand in hand with an organizational restructuring that would reach peak efficiency between 1976 and 1978. At the base of this structure were the logistics brigades (forged documents, apartments and hideouts, medical help for the wounded) and the main body of the brigades (set up at a local level, in factory neighborhoods). Each brigade belonged to a column, which supervised a geographical area (Turin, Genoa, Rome, Milan, and the region around Venice). Each column leader belonged to one of the two branches (logistics or main body) at the national level, within which their major actions were evaluated. At the top was the executive committee, made up of the four or five organizational leaders, who took decisions and managed international relations. Lastly, there was a strategic leadership, which theoretically only met once or twice a year, and defined the group's general political line.[7] This model was implemented between 1974 and 1976. In the beginning, it gave greater freedom to its various subgroups than they would enjoy in 1977–78, with the original power of the executive being less powerful than it would become by the 1978 kidnapping of Aldo Moro. As the period of semiclandestine activities came to an end, the organization became more rigid in its structure. Increasingly isolated from or vulnerable within the factories, the brigadistes were driven into militarization and isolation.

Finally, the Red Brigades' targets were gradually changing. To be sure, a continuity with the earlier period remained, and the firebombing of cars belonging to corporation executives and fascist trade unionists went on unabated. An important turning point came, however, with the April 1974 kidnapping, in Genoa, of Judge Sossi. What was changing was the scope of terrorist actions which, moving away from genuine social demands, began to concentrate more on the "multinationals' imperialist state." Blood was shed for the first time, in June 1974, with the murders of two fascists in Padua; it would flow again in October, in a deadly shootout with the carabinieri, who had discovered one of their hideouts. One may easily link this qualitative change with the perception that the Red Brigades' strength was actually on the increase. They were now recruiting and reinforcing their organization, even as they were embarking on a cycle of operations that would thenceforth keep them in the media limelight. From here on in, their actions would be carried out in all of the northern metropolitan areas, and no longer in Milan and Turin alone. At the same time, however, the BR had fallen on hard times in the factories, and were beginning to run up against an organized repression of their activities. Using a number of techniques, the carabinieri were able—largely through the activities of an individual known as "Brother Machine-Gun" (Frate Mitra)—to infiltrate the organization all the way up to Renato Curcio, and to arrest and jail the Red Brigades' founding fathers: Franceschini, Ognibene, Ferrari, Gallinari, Curcio, and others. To be sure, these arrests weakened the organization considerably. They were also, however, the occasion for a number of internal changes, and for a move to a more structured and centralized organization. A new generation of leaders took the founders' places, although not without resistance from the latter, regardless of whether they were in prison.

Two contradictory images from 1976 may help us to evaluate the situation in which the Red Brigades found themselves in this period. On the one hand, they had their backs to the wall, were greatly weakened, and had been reduced, according to a number of estimates made after the fact, to some fifteen "regular members." On the other, they had put together a model for covert organization and developed an ideology which afforded them the theoretical and practical underpinnings needed to see them through a difficult time. And, beginning in 1976, the times were improving.

This new matrix blended Marxist-Leninist orthodoxy with Maoism. It borrowed Lenin's principal theses on the concept of history while updating his analyses of imperialism. It denounced the USSR as social-imperialistic, the Italian Communist party as revisionist, and the extra-parliamentary leftist organizations as being petit-bourgeois in their tendencies. Here one finds, as Philippe Raynaud has put it, a concern to rehabilitate Marxism-Leninism, as well as theses very close to those of the Komintern.[8] Beyond this, the Red Brigades postulated, in their essential borrowings from Maoism, that the organization of labor power was of a piece with the organization of armed resistance. This was a reversal of the classical Leninism one finds in a number of armed resistance groups from the same period, for whom violence was not so much a matter of resolving "contradictions" as it was one of provoking them, and for whom war was not the continuation of a process of politicization but rather its propaideutic.[9]

Let us conclude here by adding that, at the same time as the Red Brigades were transforming themselves from within and thereby securing their historical continuity, another group was failing in its attempt to do the same. This was the Armed Proletarian Nuclei (NAP), which failed as a movement when it tried to replace the proletariat as the social base for its revolutionary struggle with a subproletariat composed of jailed prisoners and attempted—without developing a structure for administration or policy development—to move directly from a revolt on the part of marginals and social pariahs to an armed revolution.

## The Height of Red Brigade Power

The rise of a form of social violence which called itself autonomist and which gained a high profile with the student and broader sociocultural protest movements of 1977 was an encouraging development for the Red Brigades. While they could acknowledge that autonomia had the same objective—the revolution—as they did, they were somewhat concerned over its "spontaneist" tendencies, its subjectivism, and its "immoral" practices. The rise of this group placed some pressure on the Red Brigades, given that a large number of young people, independently or in groups, had but one dream—to join their organization. The BR were prudent in the use they made of their expanded pool of candidates, carrying out long and meticulous investigations of those who came knocking at their door, assuring themselves of their political abilities, and rejecting those persons who had been drawn to them out of a pure thirst for immediate, violent action. This recruitment, as Della Porta and Caselli have indicated,[10] did not yet imply the slightest interface between the two worlds of autonomia and the Red Brigades. The one did not simply feed into the other. At that point in time, those who entered the BR were, in the main, much more often well-trained militants and active members of the labor force than they were enraged marginals.

The forces of repression, overwhelmed by the violence that was breaking out on every front, lacked the stature needed to take on a phenomenon they had thought to have cut off at the source one or two years earlier. Meanwhile, the ranks of the Red Brigades were rapidly filling up and gaining in strength as they organized themselves into a highly efficient working group. As a means to ensuring secrecy, their leaders—

Moretti, Bonisoli, Azzolini, Balzarani, etc.—imposed strict regulations, drawing the distinction between "regular" and "irregular" members, and concentrating power in the hands of an executive committee. This growing concern for organization resulted in a minutely regulated, and in many ways bureacratic, organizational existence: accounts were scrupulously kept, salaries paid, and paid vacations granted, to the extent that it became possible to think of the organization in terms of a career. Conformity reigned, as Marcelle Padovani has clearly shown,[11] and for anyone not located near the top of the organization, life became reduced to the miserable existence of a petty bureaucrat of terrorism, as Giorgio has chronicled.[12] This was a life of exile from one's family and friends, a life of sexual deprivation, a painful lack of interpersonal relations, and of interminable time spent in shadowing people or keeping files on them. One existed in a state of cultural impoverishment, in a micromanaged environment in which attention to detail and organization prevailed.

Thereafter, the BR's potential targets became legion. Now, any government or political leader, any person with responsibility in the industrial sector, or any journalist became a potential victim of an action whose policy it was to wage war against the SIM and the Christian Democrats. On June 8, 1976, they assassinated Francesco Coco, the chief prosecutor, before kidnapping the industrialist Pietro Costa, whom they freed for a ransom of one-and-a-half billion lira. In Turin, where they had managed to infiltrate the factories much further than in Genoa, they could count to their credit, for the year 1977 alone, three dead and a dozen wounded. They were, moreover, able to keep the trial of their founding fathers from taking place when on April 28, they assassinated Fulvio Croce, the president of the Turin Bar Association. The jurors, terrorized, refused to render a verdict. Meanwhile in Rome, which had now become the focus for their activities, the BR patiently laid the groundwork for the greatest operation of their career.

March 16, 1978 had been a long-awaited date, since it was on that day that a government of national unity was to have been presented to the Parliament, thereby sealing the "historic compromise" between the Italian Communist party (PCI) and the Christian Democrats. On that very day, a shocked Italy learned that the Red Brigades had kidnapped Aldo Moro, the president of the Christian Democrat party. This spectacular operation, carried out in Via Fani, in the very heart of Rome, was the work of a highly organized core of crack terrorists who unflinchingly massacred their target's five bodyguards. Now began a long period punctuated by a series of communiqués on the part of the kidnappers and by a refusal to negotiate on the part of the Christian Democrats, who were supported in their intransigence by the Italian Communist party. Cast adrift by his own people, Aldo Moro was assassinated on May 9, with the Red Brigades carrying their political refinement to the point of provocation when they left the body exactly halfway between the headquarters of the Christian Democrats and that of the PCI.[13]

## The Decline

If we let numbers do all the talking, the years between 1979 and 1981 showed a rise in Red Brigade strength. Terrorist actions were on the increase, each deadlier than the last, directed against an ever-broadening range of targets, and culminating in the slaying, in Genoa, of a militant trade unionist who was a member of the Italian Communist party. Membership was on the rise, reaching a total, according to Patrizio Peci's estimate, of some five hundred brigatistes by the fall of 1981. But this expansion was but a sign of weakness, and the first stage of the Red Brigades' decline. With the distinction between themselves and autonomia becoming increasingly blurred, it was no longer possible for the BR to maintain their unity. At the same time, the state apparatus was becoming increasingly capable of taking them head-on while the violence they had been promoting in the factories was now declining under the combined onslaught of repression, union and PCI intervention, and a general rejection on the part of labor.

### Autonomia, the Red Brigades and Prima Linea

The Moro affair had a magnetic effect upon many of Italy's youth who wanted nothing more than to get in on the action. Unrest was still rampant both in the universities and on the dark side of the labor movement, where radical councilism was still the order of the day. In the Venice area, and even more so in Padua, agitation was at its height with an enormous number of groups forming and a great amount of information circulating, if only through the media of a pirate radio station—Radio Sherwood—and the periodical *Autonomia*. In a broader context, a lively debate had been taken up between autonomia and intellectuals on the one hand, and the Red Brigades on the other. The bearing of arms had come to be viewed as legitimate by all concerned parties, with the BR being criticized, however, by the former for their vanguardism and their estrangement from concrete social conflicts. The BR, in turn, criticized autonomia for their "spontaneist" tendencies. In such an environment, was reconciliation possible?

It was not so much an ideological meeting of the minds that in fact occurred, but rather an infiltration, much stronger this time, of the Red Brigades by autonomia. This pressure on the part of autonomia, now very strong indeed, threw the organization into a veritable frenzy of terrorist activity. The BR were finding themselves less and less capable of controlling their members and respecting their own rules of conduct, and the administrative organization was beginning to fall apart at the seams as rash acts and blunders multiplied. Their terrorist strikes were becoming bloodier by the day, and what had been excluded a few years before—that a military operation might involve losses by their own forces—was now being allowed. But more than any of these factors, the BR were seemingly being overtaken in this intensification by Prima Linea, an organization which had previously been less bold in its activities.

## In the Factories

It is difficult to generate a precise image of labor reactions to the kidnapping and later execution of Aldo Moro. Statements on the subject are contradictory, in all likelihood because the facts were of the same order. In some cases, there was indignation, spontaneous work stoppages and wide-scale demonstrations. Elsewhere, the workers only followed the union line because it corresponded to a decision on the part of management to briefly halt production. In still other cases, and this was apparently the most common scenario, indifference reigned together with the feeling of being estranged from some distant political event, which was far removed from day-to-day problems of existence.[14]

What really happened, however, was that the Moro affair—and especially the renewed spread of social unrest inside the factories—forced the union and political leadership to take strong interventionary measures. So it was that after much vacillation, these leaders attempted to mount a forceful reaction, principally through an association with the leftist members of the bench and their union, the Magistratura Democratica. An initiative was taken to mobilize workers against terrorism and the call sounded for them to take up actions which combined their platforms with a defense of democratic institutions. The proceedings of conferences organized by the FML and the provincial federations of the CGIL, the CISL, and the UIL of Turin in 1979 and 1982 bear witness to this endeavor.[15]

More and more often, however, discouragement was winning out over rage, and factory violence, further repressed by an unflinching use of force on the part of management, was on the decrease. So, for example, in October 1979, Fiat laid off sixty-one factory workers accused of terrorism. Even as the unions were denouncing management's tendency to confuse labor protests with terrorism, they were finding themselves increasingly incapable of maintaining their control over a number of labor sectors that had more or less actively gone over to the camp of armed resistance.[16] In this situation, they were obliged to further distance themselves from such groups. Their resolve was strengthened when in January 1979 the Red Brigades assassinated Guido Rossa, a union delegate from the Italsider plant and member of the Italian Communist party, in Genoa. This militant had uncovered the identity of a brigatiste in his factory and had had the courage to not turn a blind eye to him. The BR's vengeance, which was to have been limited to mere injury, turned into a blunder which the CGIL and the Italian Communist party were able to use to their advantage. Violence decreased markedly after 1980, without there being a gain in either union or PCI strength.

### The Crisis within the Red Brigades

The kidnapping of Aldo Moro had opened the police as well as the state to ridicule. It forced state agencies to better organize themselves, and their repression of terrorism to become more efficient. The carabinieri, under the direction of General Dalla Chiesa, proved capable of dealing with a terrorist phenomenon they had thought to have nearly snuffed out in 1975. Starting in 1979, they began to make significant advances, discovering a number of hideouts and carrying out a number of arrests. It was especially after 1980, however, that the repression of terrorism began to score decisive victories, in particular with the arrest of Patrizio Peci, who lost no time in "repenting" and in "turning in" not only the Turin column, but also that of Genoa, as well as in divulging enough information to seriously weaken the Red Brigades' leadership in Rome.

Drawing on the considerable powers they had newly acquired through the 1975 Reale Law, followed by the 1977 Cossiga Law, the police forces carried out one successful operation after another as the prisons filled with detainees who could now be held in preventive detention for several years.[17]

After 1980, the forces of law and order took on an image of increasing efficiency, due in no small part to the use of emergency measures. To these would be added, following the arrest of General Dozier's kidnappers, the use of torture so vigorously denounced by Giorgio Bocca.[18] The state had thus empowered itself in the name of a threatened democracy. Whether such a reinforcement of its arsenal of repression, which considerably undermined individual rights and freedoms, was truly necessary remains an open question. More than a mere occasion for state institutions to respond to a situation calling for emergency measures, a terrorist crisis can also have the effect of putting such institutions back on their feet again, over the body as it were of a phenomenon already in a state of decomposition.

Listing more and more visibly, the Red Brigades' ship began to truly take on water with the announcement of the execution of Aldo Moro. Simultaneous with the heightened level of state repression was the arrival within the BR of less well-trained activists whose all-consuming desire was to carry guns. The first difficulties were of a logistic order. Hideouts and money were running short, and the rules of conduct which had regulated their activities were becoming increasingly ignored.

More than merely organizational, the crisis was essentially an ideological one. Throughout the captivity of Aldo Moro, the brigatistes had interrogated their prisoner, and it was in so doing that they became aware of the weaknesses of their own positions, and the political bankruptcy of their theory of the SIM. The testimonies of Moretti, Bonisoli, and Morucci, as cited by Giorgio Bocca,[19] are very clear on this point. The ideological crisis was of such an order that the BR leadership entrusted its imprisoned comrades—and thus the founding fathers from whom they had theretofore kept their distance—with the task of drawing up a strategic resolution for the spring 1978 "campaign." Beyond its organizational and ideological components, the crisis was also political. In the end, the state had not caved into the demands of the BR, which had expected to win some kind of recognition from it. More than this, their social base and the currents of sympathy and solidarity they had enjoyed in the past were crumbling away with every passing day. Internal tensions were growing, and their rationales of action were showing themselves to be increasingly incoherent.

Two tendencies would come to undermine their organizational structure. The first of these, generally qualified as movementalist, appeared to constitute a return to the original Red Brigades tradition, that of Curcio. It was clearly infiltrated by ideologies which, however denatured they may have become, owed much to the 1977 movement as well as to that blend of "spontaneist" tendencies and references to actual experience generally associated with autonomia. The movementalist wing of the BR was not only more exalted and less prudent than its forebear, it was also more bloodthirsty and in an advanced enough state of disintegration to fall into heteronomous alliances.

In the same period a second, labor-based tendency went autonomous, further destabilizing the organization. So it was that the highly autonomist "Walter Alasia column" came into existence in Milan and, calling for a return to the factories, forcefully implanted itself at the Alfa-Romeo plant. This return to a radicalized working-class base went hand in hand with a program of armed trade unionism. They denounced union leadership as "petit bourgeois"; these replied by accusing the Milanese group of usurping the BR's name for themselves. Mario Moretti, the major BR leader throughout the preceding period, had already been greatly weakened by the rise of the movementalists. Now under pressure from the Milanese labor-based column, he went to that city to reestablish an authentic BR nucleus. This figure, once the leader of hundreds of "regulars," now found himself isolated. The police had no trouble in arresting him, using a simple infiltration technique to work their way up through the ranks and thereby nab him.

Politically, the Red Brigades were beaten. Bereft of their guiding principles—which, having already been ideologically inverted and torn apart, were now taking on a life of their own, a life devoid of any coherent political vision—they were falling apart into an aggregate of dislocated actions.

Nearly as soon as they were arrested, a number of BR members "repented," relieved as it were, so long had it been since they had mentally resigned from and given up all faith and conviction in the organization. Others became "hard core," bringing a reign of terror to the prisons to prevent others from repenting, and settling old scores in ways that had all the trappings of vendetta. So it was that Patrizio Peci's brother, one of the first "penitents," was kidnapped and later killed. Still others were using their weapons in a veritable frenzy of bloodletting, taking so few precautions as to appear to be participating in a self-destructive nihilism. In 1982, the Red Brigades, politically liquidated, had been reduced to nothing more than a nebulous aggregate whose dissociated fragments, reduced to tiny groups, nevertheless remained highly lethal. Finally, even this scattered violence and low-level terrorism receded. At the same time, the political landscape was changing, with the notion of historical compromise having been completely abandoned by those who had promoted it. As for the Italian state, it emerged from this long episode greatly strengthened, politically and militarily victorious.

# 8

# The Social, Political, and Intellectual Roots of Armed Insurgency

Studies of leftist extremist terrorism in Italy generally focus on the notion of *crisis*, which constitutes a pivotal concept in a great number of explanatory models, both sociological and journalistic: the state in crisis, the political system in crisis, a crisis of values, the cultural and social crisis.[1] It would be absurd to minimize the importance of the state, political, and other forms of crisis. At the same time, it would also be shortsighted to dismiss as irrelevant and meaningless the language employed by actors who never ceased to champion the proletariat, the working class and, more broadly, all forms of social conflict. It is therefore appropriate here that we introduce a second perspective, in which terrorism is treated as the outcome of an inversion, effected by the Marxist-Leninist vanguards of a number of social movements.

While one ought not to contrast these two perspectives in an overly systematic way, it would also be wrong to treat them equally, and to simply juxtapose the factors that might have contributed to each. While a state or political crisis cannot be the sole grounds for a terrorist phenomenon, it can in fact constitute a highly favorable environment for a process of inversion. It was just such a process that overturned and chipped away at the constituent elements of the Italian labor movement as well, perhaps, as of the new social movements that had begun to coalesce in the conflicts of 1977—a point to which we will return.

This argument holds for the Italian activist strategy as well as for its ideological formulation. It can also be applied to the debates that fired the Italian intellectual imagination, given that such authors as Alberto

*95*

Melucci and Gianfranco Pasquino have intimated a connection between the rise of terrorism and the revival of various social movements.[2] These studies open up new avenues for analysis and formulate a number of hypotheses, but never truly prove their points. In this light, the argument we are putting forward here should especially serve to open up a fundamental debate concerning the inversion that lies at the core of the terrorist phenomenon.

Here, one might hesitate in choosing between two hypotheses regarding the essential import of the changeover to terrorism. The first of these consists in postulating that the Italian experience was a unified one whose various manifestations were but so many fragmented expressions of the decline of a social movement, i.e. the labor movement. In this perspective, the groundwork laid by the Red Brigades as early as 1970–71 and the autonomia flareups of 1976–77 both derive from the same experience, that of the accelerated disintegration of ideologies claiming a special relationship to labor. Also from this perspective, it is possible to see two tendencies at work within terrorism, with each corresponding to a classic component of the labor movement. The distinction between armed party (BR) and armed movement (autonomia) corresponds to two tendencies which Luigi Ferrajoli has masterfully described in an oft-cited article.[3] On the one hand, one finds the BR's "politico-Jacobin" violence, following in the footsteps of the bolshevik communist tradition. This was a rigorous and rationalized violence, structured by a vanguard which identified itself with History or the Revolution itself. On the other hand, there one finds the "politico-activist" violence of autonomia, a violence that was direct rather than instrumental, more an end than a means to an end, more esthetic than ethical, more influenced by Sorel and anarchism than by Marx and Lenin.

A contrary hypothesis implies that one ought to see in the Italian experience a two-pronged phenomenon of inversion. The first of these would have proceeded from the decline of the labor movement, while the second would have been associated with the rise and fall of the 1977 insurgencies, with both being viewed as so many aborted manifestations of new social movements. In this perspective, the foundation upon which terrorism was built was that of the ruins the labor movement. It did not fly out of control until 1977–78, at which time autonomia subjectivism, with its championing of a new cultural perspective—often closely related to those of the new social movements—found violence to be its sole outlet.

The idea of inversion relates the actor to a particular situation, and accounts for the ideological and concrete processing of an aggregate of social and politicized conflicts. In detailing our hypotheses, we will therefore be led to analyze those conflicts in relationship to which the terrorist actors oriented and invented themselves, and to introduce those ideological norms in the light of which their struggles were interpreted.

## Social Unrest (1968–76)

In France, the 1968 movement was a relatively punctual phenomenon, to the point of being associated, in popular memory, with the month of May alone. Even if the student movement triggered the worker's strike, the two phenomena were more juxtaposed than truly interrelated. Furthermore, the leftist politics that prevailed in the years that followed did not greatly penetrate the labor force. In Italy, the student movement, launched in Turin in 1967, endured for a longer time before it inverted and fell apart. Labor unrest seemed to follow a cycle—between 1968 and 1972—with the infiltration of political ideas and actors into the factories and universities much more pronounced and prolonged than in France.

### The "Negative University"

"It is the history of the School of Sociology at Trent that one must examine if one wishes to know the roots of Renato Curcio and the Red Brigades."[4] For Alessandro Silj, as for most observers, everything begins in the high command of the student movement that was the University of Trent. Yet what a paradox this is! The first Italian university of social sciences was born, in 1964, out of the overt political desire, voiced by a Christian Democrat-controlled provincial council, to develop its region by training an elite adapted to the demands of modern culture and economics. This was a technocratic project, in which the social sciences were to constitute an instrument, adapted to the most advanced scientific and management technology, through which to open the region up to the outside world. Within a few years of its inception, however, it had become the focal point of a controversy that, though limited and corporatist at first, became increasingly politicized.

In January 1966, the students decided to occupy the university in protest against a decision by the authorities to transform its degree in sociology into a degree in "political and social sciences, from a predominantly sociological perspective." Further demands followed, some of which, specifically student-oriented, included participation, at the same level as their professors, in university administration. Other complaints were more general in nature, taking issue with the local population's general reservedness toward or outright refusal of any dialogue with them—students from all over Italy, who had come there to attack fascism and denounce imperialism and the Vietnam War. Thereafter, the life of this university, not unlike the universities of Pisa, Naples, Turin, Venice, Bari, etc., would be highly politicized, with the same question being asked everywhere: was it possible to maintain a democratic university in a capitalist society? Ought one to fight for the university or against it?

The year 1967–68 saw the birth of a "counteruniversity" in Trent, with its own classes, assemblies and debates. Their enthusiasm running high, the students undertook labor investigations of Maoist inspiration, and attempted, by adopting a populist stance, to join in labor resistance movements. At the same time, their actions were moving from a critical to a negative orientation. There appeared a "Movement for a Negative University," which was pioneered by the founders of a review entitled *Lavoro politico,* which contrasted capitalist and socialist uses of science, and which eschewed corporatist and specifically student-oriented demands in favor of broader, more politicized and revolutionary orientations. The concerned Christian Democrat founders considered closing the university that was running counter, in so many ways, to their original ambitions. The more progressive members of their group succeeded however in keeping it afloat. These same persons also had the idea of handing over the direction of the university to the sociologist Francesco Alberoni. Once installed, Alberoni—in the words of a Trent professor cited by Silj—rather than riding the tiger of the controversy, quickly emerged as the tiger itself. The situation had become highly politicized and, in spite of Alberoni's every effort to maintain a dialogue between students and his institution, the administrative council decided to suspend enrollments for the 1970–71 academic year.

At Trent, as in every Italian university, the student movement had rapidly become inverted. It had taken issue with the running of the university, and then broadened its scope to include the social production and transmission of knowledge, before tailing off into an extreme politicization which so forbade all specifically student-related activities as to become the negation of the student movement. This was a classic case of inversion, which gave rise to the formation of a group of political and revolutionary professionals among whom were numbered Renato Curcio and his friend Margherita Cagol, the founders of the Red Brigades.

## Labor Unrest: The 1968–72 Cycle

The cycle of labor unrest which began in the spring of 1968 and ended in 1972 constitutes an impressive process, a process which, beginning in a handful of large northern factories, gained momentum in an "upwardly spiraling" month of May before culminating in the "hot autumn" of 1969. In the process, it shook to their very foundations the basic structures and dynamics of the system of industrial relations. A rich body of literature, led by Alessandro Pizzorno's wide-ranging investigation,[5] emphasizes the innovative nature of these conflicts which occurred at the conjunction of an expansion in the labor market and a change within Italian trade unionism, which had previously been quite dependent upon political parties and poorly established in the factories. This was a period in which an untold number of conflicts provoked direct worker involvement, without any initial impulse or mediation being offered by the union organizations. At the forefront of these disputes were egalitarian demands for reductions in wage and skill differentials, coupled with denunciations of the organization of the workplace, production schedules, and methods of factory management. These were rank-and-file protests, which devised or rediscovered forms of action that had theretofore either been absent from union practice, or had been lost since the time of the workers' assemblies of 1919–20.

Theirs was a radicalized resistance that resorted to rotating strikes and organized work slowdowns as means to lowering production at minimum worker expense. Protest marches more often moved through the factories than through the cities. With arbitration no longer being a strictly union prerogative, open-door bargaining sessions were becoming quite common. It was as if the labor force had invented a new activist model according to which councilism and trade unionism stood on an equal footing. At the base of this model, pyramidal in form, was a body of elected union or non-union delegates, as well as a system of workers' councils or assemblies. Overall, such a model appeared to strengthen the unions by affording them a greater negotiating capacity at the top. Because the trade unionists could work from the basis of social demands, they were able to enjoy greater autonomy than that of the political parties. At the same time, they were moved to join themselves into federations or confederations.

The standard image of these conflicts is that of the "mass-worker," the unskilled laborer who had moved up from southern Italy into the northern urban centers. Yet, Pizzorno's and other careful studies indicate that these actions were less often initiated by southerners who, poorly integrated into the industrial labor market, had become "spontaneitized" or radicalized, than they were the handiwork of workers who already had a history of militant, political, or union activity behind them, who were often skilled, and who were able, at least in the first phase of this cycle, to play a leading role in these actions.

Is it possible, for all this, to posit as a general rule this complementarity between councilism and trade unionism, or between the situationalist and radical tendencies of unskilled laborers from the south and the bargaining strategies more often formulated by skilled workers? To be sure, trade unionism was growing in strength and going through great changes throughout the period between 1968 and 1972, with collective bargaining on the rise: 3,870 negotiated agreements in 1968 against 7,567 in 1972.[6] It was often the case, however, that councilism and trade unionism were at loggerheads with one another, with the revolutionary side of the movement, hostile to reformist positions, constantly denouncing the dead ends into which it claimed union strategy—especially that of the CGIL, itself connected to the Italian Communist party—was leading them. The first steps taken by the Red Brigades in the direction of the factories had nothing to do with a process of inversion in the labor movement, since this had not yet begun to decline in 1969–70. They rather infiltrated those radicalized sectors of the movement in which rank-and-file groups or councilism, rather than backing a renewed and reinvigorated trade unionism, had rejected the "reformist" line. Such could only—as the Red Brigades themselves put it in their first "self-interview," held in 1971—lead to social stabilization, to the greater profit of the middle class and imperialism.

## The Breakup of the Labor Movement

The fact that the great cycle of unrest which began in 1968 ended in 1972 in no way implies that this was followed by a period of social calm. Councilism continued to thrive for several years, the factories were still greatly agitated, and the system of elected delegates was expanding considerably. Marino Regini counts 8,101 factory councils for the year 1972, compared with 32,021 for 1977; and 82,923 elected delegates in 1972, compared with 206,336 in 1977.[7] But the labor movement, which had until 1972 been capable of holding together a rank-and-file action—strongly inclined towards radical disengagement from existing institutions—with a renewed and actively bargaining trade unionism, was now faced with an increasingly aggravated split between these two tendencies.

This dissociation was brought about by a number of factors. The world economic crisis was felt very early in Italy, as early as the end of 1973 in Turin, where Fiat began taking measures to cushion a sudden drop in sales. By 1974, Italy was subject to runaway inflation and massive unemployment, and there was talk of the state going bankrupt (successive devaluations of the lira, deep budget deficits, etc.). Well ahead of countries like France, Italy had launched into industrial restructuring projects carried out in the name of austerity and technological change. The image of the mass-worker was on the decline and trade unionism, increasingly disunited, was falling increasingly under the influence of the political parties. As such, union leaders were entering into concrete negotiations toward the implementation of industrial policies, thereby aggravating tensions between the rank-and-file workers and leadership initiatives. It was not easy, for example, to ask northern workers to accept a number of austerity measures in exchange for their support for a policy to bolster industrial employment in the southern part of the country.

The more the trade unions sought to influence economic policy, the more the rank and file raised their voices in protest over the issue of wages and, beyond this, against what they considered to be a widening gulf between workers' demands and union strategy. This crisis, masked for some time by the growth in union membership which peaked at 59.8 percent in 1977, was nevertheless a real one. Protests were being heard within the unions themselves, with a rising friction between the workers' councils and the trade unions being felt, and a weakening councilism either radicalizing or functioning with increasing difficulty. As for the delegates, they found themselves in the contradictory position of simultaneously being spokespersons for the rank and file and co-discussants with factory management. The institutionalization of the labor movement was beginning to give rise to scattered signs of anger, and even moments of violence. Very quickly, however, the great majority of workers turned away from those persons to whom it had been their wont to turn for armed intervention. In the years following 1973, Red Brigade activities were doing more to isolate the group from labor protests than to involve it, no matter how radicalized these protests had become.

## The Illusion of the Urban Protests

In the years following 1968, "operaism" and the student movement, as well as organizations from the extraparliamentary Left, began to support insurgencies whose aim it was to broaden labor action to a pan-urban level, with the notion of "taking the city" giving rise to a number of urban struggles, especially over the issue of housing. These conflicts broadened between 1973 and 1974, often taking the form of such illegal activities as squatting, self-legislated reductions on charges for utilities, rentals, urban transport, telephones, etc. Whether these did in fact mark, as many believed, an expansion of the labor movement and of its ability to intercede beyond the limits of the factory and its relations of production, is open to question. An investigation, even though comprehensive and carried out in the midst of these events, shows that these protests, gradually jettisoned by the PCI and later by the unions, speak more to a crisis in the Italian state than to the origins of a social movement.[8] Over the years, these disintegrated to the point of becoming little more than so many forms of delinquent behavior (mainly consisting in the looting of department stores), which were termed as "proletarian rehabilitation" in the political jargon of the day.

Fabrizio Calvi perhaps plays his journalistic hand a bit too strongly and disregards a number of unspectacular facets of Milan's political life (meetings, strikes, etc.) when he paints the following sensationalist picture of the city: everywhere, the neighborhood-based actions alternated between the petty criminal acts of the many gangs who invaded movie houses or "expropriated" merchants' stocks without paying them, and a more politicized activity, steeped in the rage of a more-or-less marginalized youth desirous of gaining access to the consumer society that displayed itself before them. A general air of violence descended upon the city, to the point that "when fifty teenagers attacked a Milan supermarket in 1976, no one paid them much attention."[9] Street demonstrations were frequent, often massively attended, increasingly violent—and increasingly confused, often bringing together as they did the "working classes" who were being throttled by austerity and restructuring programs, the "dangerous classes" whom the security forces of the extraparliamentary organizations were unable to keep in line, wage earners for whom institutionalized protest was not enough, and a young underclass looking for a fight. Matters came to a head on December 7, 1976, when thousands of youth, from every part of the city but most especially from Milan's sprawling suburbs, invaded the city in answer to a call from the "workers' clubs" to disrupt the opening-night gala to La Scala's musical season. This was a movement of angry youth, outraged at the sight of high society buying tickets for 150,000 lira while they had to wallow in a life of unemployment and poverty. But was this not simply symptomatic of a disintegration of the fabric of Italian society, an increasingly tumultuous society that had become isolated from those new social movements—the ecologists, antinuclear protesters, feminists, etc.—which were firing the imagination of their neighbors?

It is only the feminists, whose first demonstrations date from 1969 (when they publicly declared that they had had abortions, and thereby purposefully provoked judicial proceedings), who offer a contrasting image to that of the crisis, rage, and violence that erupted in Milan and other urban areas in this period.

There was no direct interface between this random violence and the terrorism whose foundations had been laid in the preceding years. Even those authors who, like Ferrarotti or Acquaviva,[10] have wished to discuss, in the same analytical breath, the upsurge in delinquence and the increasing strength of the terrorists, show caution here. The rage of these generally unemployed and financially insecure youth put a certain amount of pressure, often via leftist extremist political organizations, on those persons who were mapping out the next wave of armed resistance. This rage created a climate of crisis that favored insurrectional or revolutionary ideas which, while they gave rise to a number of words and deeds, had little or nothing in common with the rage itself.

## The Rise and Fall of the Extraparliamentary Left

### On the Left Fringe of the Communist Party

The birth and decay of a student movement, coupled with the rapid rise and later crisis of a labor movement whose rank and file occasionally resisted all "reformist" attempts, cannot explain, in and of itself, the emergence of the revolutionary discourse of armed insurgency. This phenomenon was also, indeed fundamentally, a political one, orchestrated at the time by a spinoff group working on the left fringe of the PCI. Underground in the years prior to the war, the PCI still had armed units at its disposal in 1948. Since that time, it had come to act more and more as a defender of institutions, and had thus shown itself to be increasingly incapable of supporting more radical programs initiated to the left of itself. This opened the way not only to a radicalism which criticized both the party and the unions for their common commitment to reform, but also to a communist fundamentalism for which revolutionary action on the part of a vanguard was the sole path to social change. The first signs of crisis, which appeared in the early 1960s, were linked on the one hand to changes in the world communist movement (the Khrushchev Report, the Sino-Soviet split) and on the other, to internal changes within the PCI itself. Here, its "reformist" turn, by means of which it had come to realize a number of political successes and became further integrated into the institutionalized political system, was most important.

It was at this time that "operaism"—the theoretical blueprint for which was presented in the *Quaderni rossi* (the first issue of which was published in October 1961), the *Quaderni piacentini* (1962), and the *Classe operaia* (1964: this was the product of a schism, in which such intellectuals as Tronti, Asor Rosa, Negri, and Cacciari left the *Quaderni rossi*)—first emerged. At the core of operaism, one finds the notion that it is labor action that must inspire the party to take action, and not the other way around. With this came the correlative notion of labor authenticity, for which the party was to be the mouthpiece, rather than the manipulator or the negation. The labor unrest of 1968 and 1969 strengthened the PSIUP (created in 1964 out of a split within the Socialist party) and fostered a number of other extraparliamentary organizations. Lotta Continua (the Battle Continues) and Potere Operaio (PO: Labor Power) emerged out of a split within the Pisan Potere Operaio organization, following that group's implantation in the Turin Fiat plant. A short time later, Avanguardia Operaia (Labor Vanguard) appeared in Milan. In 1969, the Manifesto group was thrown out of the PCI.

These groups were of operaist inspiration, but also took their lead from a Leninism which the Italian movements, however sensitive they may have been toward the specifically social autonomy of the individual, were nevertheless unable to shed. Angelo Ventura, in a work with which one may take issue on a number of points,[11] felicitously shows how these two trends—operaism's labor autonomy and Leninism—were constantly interacting on the Italian far left, with their many variant forms linking, each in its own way, the championing of spontaneity on the one hand with calls to labor authenticity and vanguardism on the other. It also reminds us, most appositely, that the gap that opened on the fringes of the Italian far left was not the result of political inflexibility but rather of an openness from which issued a number of victories for trade unionism.

In the great northern urban areas, the formation of the radical left was a relatively slow and protracted process, which evolved through a number of stages and dialogues. In other areas, the break was a sharper one. In Reggio nell'Emilia, this took the form of pronounced dissent within the FGCI (Federation of Italian Communist Youth) which had attempted, in 1968, to open up a forum for debating leftist extremist themes. In 1969, however, this same group underwent a process of "restoration," which resulted in the departure of a group of about twenty of its militants. This was in fact an event of major importance. In this city, anything that was not Christian Democrat was organized by the communists ("everything is PCI," writes Silj, "politics, culture, sports, restaurants, and cafés"),[12] and the PCI had been remarkably effective in absorbing the student movement. The departure of Alberto Franceschini and his cohorts to form a "political collective of workers and students" was a veritable bolt from the blue which, even ten years later, could only be talked about "ungraciously and with the greatest of prudence."[13] At Trent, it was in the context of an exceptionally widely followed student movement and ongoing debates led by an already diversified and organized body of leftist extremists that Renato Curcio, Mara Cagol and a number of other persons formed their ideas. At Reggio nell'Emilia, it was a painful disengagement from the PCI that brought about the formation of another group, a number of whose members (Alberto Franceschini, Prospero Gallinari and other less well-known figures) would figure among the core founding fathers of the Red Brigades.

## Turmoil on the Far Left

In 1972–73, the PCI began taking up a new political line which would eventually lead it to assert its independence vis-à-vis both Moscow and Eurocommunism, and lead it to undertake its historic compromise with the Christian Democrats. In June 1974, it gave its tacit support to the Carli Plan, whose goals basically involved simultaneously restructuring the machinery of production and reducing public expenses, most particularly those emanating from the welfare state. Taking votes away from the socialist voting bloc as well as from the radical left in the 1976 elections, the PCI was looking more and more like a ruling party. Its successes did not, however, lead to any new openings on the far left. On the contrary, the radical left began in 1973 to undergo a process of disintegration, which culminated in 1976 with the breakup of Lotta Continua. Out of the ashes of Potere Operaio, which fell apart in 1973, there arose Autonomia Operaia—an ill-defined group about which it is still difficult to know the extent of organization—and a number of collectives. There also arose a handful of publications—*Rosso, Metropoli,*

*Senza Tregua*—in which certain PO intellectuals and others sought to make sense of the new Italian political landscape.

The extraparliamentary Left was torn apart, from the outset, by an insurmountable tension between its desire to constitute a force to be reckoned with on the institutional level and its ambition to be the mouthpiece for social demands which, in the context of the historic compromise, had no realistic political outlet. It was also having enormous difficulty in its political handling of protests that were looking more and more like crisis behavior, if not delinquence, by the day, and with which a broad anticapitalist rhetoric could not easily be combined. Finally, it was destabilized by the rise of feminism, which denounced the generally male-chauvinist environment of the left, rejected the primacy of class warfare and Leninist methods, and threw into turmoil those methods of organization and militancy that had prevailed since 1968.

The collapse of the extraparliamentary Left had immediate consequences for the armed struggle. On the one hand, it freed up or strengthened a great number of radicalized collectives, at the same time as it left orphans whom the armed organizations took it upon themselves to adopt. On the other hand, it opened up an ideological vacuum, and was tantamount to an admission of political failure. From now on, there would no longer be an institutional outlet for the anger, rage, and popular demands that had been aggravated by the national crisis. Now, the radical nature of popular expectations, like that of random violence, led a number of individuals with no other way to react to turn towards the sole remaining activist alternative: the combatant organizations.

### Standing Leninism on Its Head

The time has come to treat these matters with greater precision, for just as we can understand nothing of Italian terrorism without looking at its real social and political struggles, so we also cannot comprehend it without referring to the ideological foundations that legitimated armed insurgency and provided it with its logical coherency.

We may approach this ideological matrix from either of two directions. First of all, it has a history: it emerged and took shape in the late 1960s, and remained intact even as it underwent a number of permutations throughout the duration of the terrorist experience. We should also note that the terrorist ideologies developed through the course of a series of repositionings that occurred, from one crisis or split to the next, on the left fringe of the PCI. In the beginning, at least, these leftists showed great respect for a party that had been able to distance itself from Moscow, and had its own long underground tradition. Furthermore, unlike leftists in France, the Italian leftists had no Trotskyist model which, hearkening back to a lost purity, could stand as a fundamentalist shield against their drift towards armed insurgency. One might also bring external influences into the picture, and especially note the frequency of references to the Maoism of the Long March and the Cultural Revolution. In broader terms, the blueprint for terrorism was drawn within a general climate in which the championing of radical disengagement, transgression, and absolutism were neatly summed up in the title of Ballestrini's widely read work, *Vogliamo tutto* (We want everything).

Second, this ideological matrix is possessed of a structure whose key features can be isolated regardless of the transformations that altered them over time. *Here, terrorism was grounded in a reformulation of Leninism which, while it retained a number of its canons, truly stood its orthodox line on its head.*

Italian terrorist ideologies were at first very classical. They began with its actors' self-identification as a vanguard which, as such, embodied the meanings of their struggles, whether social or national, limited to Italian soil or extending beyond its boundaries. None but the vanguard could decipher the internal contradictions of the system, whose laws of development it had scientifically comprehended and mastered.

This vanguard *was* the proletariat, not in the way in which the latter constituted itself in this or that particular struggle, but rather as a historical vision and as an actor for revolutionary change. Alongside this basic postulate, which authorized practices for the emancipation "of thought from experience," as Hannah Arendt has stated on the subject of totalitarianism, a number of other elements, themselves very closely tied to an often "profoundly dogmatic" orthodoxy, were brought into play.[14] These included the notion that revolution, because it was possible and necessary, was therefore inevitable; and that this process, at once social and political, thereby demanded a certain ability on the part of the working masses to play an active role. No less classically, the writings of armed resistance organizations drew a distinction between the proletariat on the one hand, and skilled workers sensitive to revisionism, as well as the labor aristocracy, on the other. At the same time, they put forward an analysis of imperialism that was essentially an updating of Lenin's theses. Lenin himself had delineated those conditions which cause a revolutionary situation to culminate in revolution: a crisis within the state and between its leaders, as well as an ability on the part of the masses to take the initiative in a historic action. The ideologues of armed insurgency wished to remain faithful to these principles, the strategic formulation of which was reaffirmed by the Third International.[15]

If, then, the history of armed resistance in Italy appears to correspond, point for point, with the errors which Lenin and the Third International specifically stigmatized, this was not because its promulgators were not familiar with the foundational texts. It was rather because these theoreticians, directly inspired by the Maoist experience, had broken with these classic ideas. Here, let us follow Nando Della Chiesa, who helpfully plots out the political ideology of terrorism.[16] Working from the axiom that ideology precedes political knowledge, it invokes the immediacy of revolution, describes Italian democracy as formal, offers an anthropomorphic vision of capital, the state, and its repressive machinery, and wholly divorces policy from ethics, before generating a mystique of violence.

On all of these points, the ideologues broke, in one way or another, with the Leninism of the founding fathers. This syncretic ideology drew on a number of sources. However, its principal feature, which it shared in common with a number of similar experiments in terrorism, lay in the fact that it *reversed the poles in the relationship between violence and politics.* The former, no longer a necessary instrument prudently administered by the party under particular historical conditions, had now become a means to expressing class consciousness and had come to constitute but the first phase in the building of a party. This reversal manifested itself in a number of different ways throughout the history and expansion of Italian terrorism. The Red Brigades, whose intention it first was to promote armed propaganda, later altered their position and began speaking in terms of forming an armed party and engaging in revolutionary civil war; from the outset, Prima Linea had wished to constitute a military echelon placed in the service of the masses.

There is a temptation to reduce terrorism to the various tendencies sketched out by its intellectual sources, and to see in it the pursuit of an idea which, entirely disconnected from social reality, becomes transformed into an infernal machine which, spinning wildly, can only be brought to a halt either by the powers of repression or by losing all control and self-destructing. But what is it that we find in Italy throughout the decade of the 1970s? Its ideological groundwork was first laid by the Red Brigades. After 1976, this became exposed to competition from another model, put forward by Prima Linea, which was closer to classical Leninism. After this, the movement snowballed, terrorism intensified, and the orthodox Leninist line became increasingly abandoned with the development near the end of this period, for example, of the idea of the party as guerrilla movement. These developments were inseparable from a more-or-less constant effort to maintain some measure of contact with the leaders of social and especially labor resistance movements. In these cases, it was more proper to speak of political violence than of terrorism. Violent activity thus had became a subject of political debate, in which the perpetrators of violence were active participants, in the hope that it would gain them sympathy and attribute a certain legitimacy to their acts. There was a relationship between what was happening in Italy's political and social life and the groundwork of the insurgent groups, work that was, on the one hand ideological (within a Leninist framework that was becoming distorted), and on the other military (in the practice of armed resistance).

The fracture that thus occurred within Italian Marxism-Leninism constituted, just as it did in a number of other cases throughout the world, a phenomenon of considerable historical and theoretical importance. Prior to this time, what set Marxism-Leninism apart was its ability to combine a unified theory which concentrated on an actor of reference— the blue-collar worker, the labor movement—with a critique of the system and its internal contradictions. The vanguard was the repository of the meanings of actions because it alone was truly conscious of the proletariat's historic mission. In this context, showing the slightest contempt with regard to the masses or engaging in reckless activities were entirely out of the question.

The move to terrorism in fact marked the dismantling of all that Marxism-Leninism had previously tried to combine. This breakup was driven by changes in the actor of reference himself, in this case the blue-collar worker, proletarian labor. The workers' movement was becoming less and less a social movement, and less and less a symbol of protest capable of challenging prevailing trends in the nation's social and cultural life. This being the case, those who continued to speak in the proletariat's name could only engage in terrorism by distancing themselves from classic Marxism-Leninism in one of two ways.

The first of these consisted in denying the importance of any actual link with the proletariat. Here, a sharp break was made with the cult of the masses, with interest turning away from actual actors and—apart from a dreamlike self-identification with the proletariat—towards the issue of contradictions. In a certain sense, the vanguard no longer believed in anything but itself. As such, it gave itself the mission of exploiting, aggravating, and exploding the system's internal contradictions. This implied a strong subjectivism since, when it came to making the revolution, the armed insurgent could no longer believe in anyone but himself. Feltrinelli's Partisan Action Groups (GAP) are an illustration of this procedure, which was doomed to rapid failure.

The second path leading to terrorism consisted, conversely, in a search for some actual figure to substitute for a faltering proletariat, and to charge this figure with a historical mission. So it was that the Armed Proletarian Nuclei (NAP) of the mid-1970s attributed a central role to the detainees of the Italian prison system. This approach too failed quickly.

The originality of the Italian case lies in the fact that it threaded its way between these two paths, in the progressive and chaotic course of its development. It long sought to maintain its contacts with blue-collar workers, and held out, until its loss of control in the late 1970s, against pure subjectivism, striving instead to reinvent a social figure who retained a labor profile—the "social worker" of Toni Negri, for example. GAP and NAP were two ephemeral formulas, each representing one of the radical paths which the BR and even Prima Linea avoided taking in favor of a slower, more circuitous trajectory.

■

We may now summarize these preliminary remarks. By 1975–76, the student movement had long since broken up entirely. The crisis in the labor movement was evident, and while urban unrest had for a time fueled the idea of extending the former into the cities, the failure and disintegration of both were by now obvious. At the political level, the PCI was advancing on its long march towards the historic compromise, and the extraparliamentary Left had fallen apart as rapidly as it had appeared. The coincidence of these two phenomena created an institutional void for the processing of social demands, which were themselves held in thrall by the crisis. The social insurgencies which protesting political actors had been able to use as reference points were losing their punch. Defensive and broken, with their possibilities for any institutional treatment of social demands having been greatly reduced, they had become more like antimovements than social movements. If we combine these elements with what we already know of the structural weakness of the Italian state and, for this period, the kinds of worries that foster fascism and golpism, then we hold all the keys to understanding how and why the process of armed resistance arose and developed.

The student movement had opened onto a fantastic extension of Marxist-Leninist ideas, which took root in the gap left open on the left fringe of the PCI. In the torrid political climate of the early 1970s, these ideologies thrived. At the same time, labor, urban, social, and political actions, catalyzed by institutional inflexibility and state weakness, appeared to be feeding into a revolutionary process. Then came the crisis in leftist politics, whose Marxist-Leninist ideologies, having become rigidified, were dismantled. More importantly, the political left's social actors were either slipping away (with the decline and institutionalization of the labor movement), falling apart (the urban protests), or asserting themselves in relatively independent ways (the feminists).

In 1977, violence and terrorism gained a new lease on life which, as we have seen, owed much to the changes that were taking place in the factories. This reinvigoration was, however, indissociable from the emergence and the subsequent rapid decay of a movement whose focus, often labor-oriented, became encompassed by a new form of cultural protest. This developed, for the most part, on the outside of the labor movement, within a young segment of the population which felt itself to be far removed from Italy's classic political debates and excluded from Italian society, in a protest that was characterized, from the outset, by a powerful subjectivism and an overwhelming desire for radical disengagement. Its starting point was, once again, a student movement or, more exactly, in crisis behavior provoked by a university reform proposal.

## The End of Leftist Politics

In the early 1970s, it was immigrants from the south of Italy who had come to work in the northern factories that were the most angry sector of society. Always brought into their firms at the bottom rung, their radical stance could be explained in terms of a shift, from south to north, and from rural to urban areas. Following 1975–76, however, this rage had rather become the prerogative of educated and much more urbanized young people who, more concerned with spending money than with working for it, were often unattached to any particular firm or to the labor force in general.

Compared to earlier times, this blue-collar youth had much in common with young students for whom school and especially the university had become an absurd existence.[17] This was a group that saw its own ideas mirrored in the nebulous and relatively unstructured principle of autonomia, which called itself a movement and not a party, and whose discourse was primarily an expression of the disintegration of leftist politics. Nowhere was it more clearly visible than in the university which had become, according to a common expression, a "social parking lot." There, according to the situation, one could encounter patterns of behavior indicating a withdrawal from or total rejection of society, as well as communal practices and forms of rhetoric entirely divorced from the reality its spokespersons claimed to be describing.[18] The university was not only democratized, it was given over to the masses, and the students who found themselves there—thereby postponing their entrance into a shrinking labor market—were more often underprivileged than members of a future elite. Titles and diplomas continued to be valued, but they no longer implied any kind of social benefit. The teaching profession was greatly impacted by the crisis as well, with eighty-five thousand of its *precari* (untenured instructors) living without hope or illusion, and mired in financial troubles, job instability, and quite often a real inability to fulfill their teaching or research functions. Exams were becoming the stuff of fiction, with students seeking to impose "political controls" on grades and the distribution of scholarships, and courses more and more frequently taking the confused form of "self-administered seminars."

Precari, students in crisis, and young blue-collar youth alien to the values of industrial society could no longer be inspired by just any vision. With the very notion of socialism having collapsed, the sole feasible model that remained to them was a communism located at opposite poles from that of the PCI. If they were going to take up the fight, it would more likely be to have *tout et tout de suite* than to create a new world order. Their patterns of social behavior were closer to those of an antimovement than to those of a movement. There did, however, exist a continuum between the two worlds of the factory and the university. This was their common protest—dictated by the crisis—which consisted of a rejection of trade unionism and classic political organizations, a refusal to work, and a championing of basic needs and real life experience. But this continuum extended even further, into the urban neighborhoods and working-class suburbs, where delinquence was growing at a spectacular rate and where, even more than before, idle and penniless young people oscillated between delinquence, drug abuse, and more political forms of behavior characterized by the desire to come to blows and to handle "comrade P 38."

By 1976–77, it was no longer possible for students and precari to speak in the name of the labor movement and demand that it be freed from its chains. No longer speaking in terms of knowledge or the meaning of history, they were having more and more difficulty in behaving like members of an intelligentsia. Their political activism was beginning to take on an artificial air, becoming hyperideological and far removed from the preoccupations of the university community. They were living the end of leftist politics, in a much more spectacular way than their French homologues of the same period.[19]

## The Events of 1977

The student mobilization that began in the south (Palermo and Naples) in December 1976 was originally motivated by two major concerns. On the one hand, it was an antifascist struggle and on the other, an opposition to the university reform proposed by Malfatti, the then education minister.

In the universities, meetings of the entire student body were becoming more and more frequent. The buildings were being occupied, often on the initiative of the precari, who were the first to denounce the Malfatti reform, accusing it of resolving nothing on the structural level, of increasing selectivity, and of rendering even less probable their chances of ever gaining job security and the decent salaries they had long been demanding. An alternative reform proposal, introduced by the PCI, was also rejected by the students who were generally becoming increasingly intolerant of communist interference in university affairs.

By mid-February, the entire student population had become mobilized, and was hostile to the PCI and to all "vertical" political organizations. Demonstrations were on the rise, with the movement asserting its "autonomy," choosing to highlight unemployment and other cultural themes (boredom, festivity, etc.) without formulating counterproposals or university-related demands.

On February 18, Luciano Lama, general secretary of Italy's most powerful labor union, the CGIL, came to the University of Rome, surrounded by a large security force. From atop a truck, he criticized "those students who refuse to accept the guidance of the workers' movement." A hail of insults followed, together with slogans chanted by the "metropolitan Indians," all of which treated Lama, the PCI, and the CGIL with irony and derision. Then came a violent attack, in spite of a decision taken two nights before in an open meeting. The trade unionist and his cohorts left their truck and fled the university, which the police evacuated that very evening.

"Tanks in Chile, unions in Italy"—the break between the student movement and the labor organizations was expressed in the form of the "metropolitan Indians" ironic slogans as well as the violence perpetrated by groups who claimed, in Rome, to be acting in the interests of labor autonomy. In the days that followed, there were a series of demonstrations that were hostile not only to the government, but also to the unions and the PCI, which was gradually realizing the magnitude of the problems raised by the student movement. The communist press reported the proceedings of closed meetings in which the PCI tended to separate the wheat from the chaff, i.e. the "metropolitan Indians" whose demands were judged to be consequential, from autonomia, which they portrayed as dangerous or fascistic, and which they criticized in scornful and highly virulent terms.

The movement's first national meeting was held in Rome on February 26 and 27. Nothing emerged from the meeting, which was torn apart by the combined pressure of the feminists and the "metropolitan Indians." In the days that followed, demonstrations were held in a number of cities. On March 4, Panzieri, accused of the murder of a fascist, was sentenced to nine years in prison. This sentence, which many found unjustifiable, gave rise to a resurgence of antifascist and antigovernment activity. The FML made a gesture towards reconciliation when it invited student delegates to its March 8 convention in Florence.

On March 11, Lo Russo, a militant medical student, was killed during a demonstration held in Bologna, by a bullet fired during a brutal police intervention provoked by a confrontation between Communion and Liberation fundamentalists and students. On March 12, demonstrations were held all over Italy. Most impressive was that held in Rome which, hostile to the Christian Democrats and even more so to the PCI, turned violent: firearms were used by a number of student extremists, and an armory pillaged. The autonomia following appeared to be growing stronger in the University of Rome. On March 16, a demonstration, called by the PCI together with the Christian Democrats and the Italian Socialist party (PSI) to protest against violence and terrorism and rally in favor of the democratic and republican order, was widely attended in Bologna. The students demonstrated as well, with the boundary between the two demonstrations being somewhat hazy, and the security forces of the PCI remaining inactive. At the same time, the central committee of the PCI was debating over the issue of Italy's youth, with some (Amendola) emphasizing their extremism and violence and others (Pajetta) underscoring the necessity of dealing constructively with student aspirations rather than opposing them.

On March 18, throughout Italy with the exception of Rome, and on March 23 in Rome, both workers and students took part in strikes and demonstrations without ever addressing the matter of reconciliation. In the course of an important meeting held in Bologna, the students responded to union leader Bruno Trentin with the words "Together, yes, but against the Christian Democrats." In Rome, where no agreement could be reached between the students and the unions, the two groups marched separately, with some two hundred thousand workers on the one hand, and fifteen or twenty thousand students on the other. These latter demonstrated without attempting to confront the union marchers, their procession taking on a festive air. On the following day, the Lotta Continua headlined: "The PCI and Lama face off against the irony of 25,000 comrades."

The mobilization continued after the Easter break, but was less widely followed than it had been in the preceding months. Was this a student movement? Not in the least. At most, this was crisis behavior manifesting itself on university precincts. Its participants were not students, but blue-collar (and under) youth who had been left out in the cold by austerity policies to which the PCI and to a lesser extent the unions had assented. Their rage was further increased by the acceptance, on the part of the Left, of measures for the strengthening of police powers. There were rumblings of anger against the PCI in a number of factories as well, as evinced in a meeting, held in Milan on April 4 at the demand of 260 factory councils. Here, the order of the day was nothing less than the resignation of the entire CGIL, CISL, and UIL leadership, and the convocation of a meeting of rank-and-file delegates to debate the union platform, and the issue of direct elections, by the rank and file, of 50 percent of the leadership organizations in their confederation.

## The Creative Side of the 1977 Movement

The 1977 movement was possessed of a certain unity, about which Toni Negri, seeking artificially to develop the notion of labor resistance, waxed theoretical when he spoke paradoxically of the "social worker."[20] This notion is unacceptable. What lay at the heart of these struggles was a rejection of industrial culture by a historical subject. This was a subject who, alienated from the notion of individual enterprise, was either indifferent or hostile to work, a subject who was defined more by exclusion than inclusion, and by economic subjugation rather than domination in relationships of production, and who was more concerned with the immediate satisfaction of basic human needs and desires than with preparing for a better tomorrow. The actor here was but a minimally social figure, whose only adversary was the state—a state he at once despised and solicited in order that it behave like a welfare state—and who was hard pressed to find institutional channels through which to press his demands.

The movement had two sides to it, two "arenas," as people said at that time. The one, called "creative," was primarily a repository for cultural meanings, while the other, said to be proper to labor autonomia, rather conveyed social, working-class ideals, and tended towards the use of indiscriminate violence. There is no sharp divide between the movement's two sides, both of which claimed to be "autonomist" and neither of which was foreign or indifferent to what the other set in motion. The creative side was constantly stressing the actor's subjectivity as well as his feeling of being a stranger to his own society. It called for the liberation of the individual, for breaking rules, and enjoying oneself. It denounced politics as a source of social repression, and evoked a heterogeneous group of authors including Agnès Heller for her analyses of the notion of needs, as well as Michel Foucault, Félix Guattari, and the Karl Marx of the *Grundrisse*. Its intellectuals placed a high premium on writing, poetry, and language; and spoke, somewhat after the fashion of Mayakovski, of "transforming life into language" and "abolishing the division between art and life"—to which they added, in a threatening tone, "but this time, Mayakovski will not kill himself, because his little Browning has better things to do."[21] It accorded considerable importance to communication, and founded a number of pirate radio stations, of which the renowned Radio Alice out of Bologna, which Félix Guattari portrayed as "moving into the eye of the cultural hurricane, with its subversion of language and its publication of the journal *A traverso;* and plunging directly into political action in order to better 'transversalize' it."[22]

The most surprising manifestation of this creative side are undoubtedly those of the "metropolitan Indians," those fleeting figures of the spring of 1977. The metropolitan Indians were first of all shamans of language with painted faces, whose expressivity took the form of gala spectacles, street theater, happenings, but most especially iconoclastic slogans whose biting invective exploded the hyperideologization of the student milieu by carrying it to absurd extremes. At the same time, it gave voice, in a way that transcended all other forms of discourse, to student feelings regarding the PCI, the unions, etc. Theirs was also, however, little more than an acceptable way to drop out. Values relative to family, authority, and hierarchy were to be rejected out of hand, while the party and other organizations were to be consigned to a moldering museum of antiquated political systems. This would also explain the metropolitan Indians' cohabitation with the Autonomia Operaia autonomists who, even though they were highly vanguardist, were violently opposed to all more traditional political organizations such as the PCI or the radical extraparliamentary Left. Having broken away from all constructive forms of ideology, the Indians were complacent in their "marginality" and, maintaining that the individual was political, met in small groups to talk about themselves ("in big meetings, one cannot liberate oneself") and, after the fashion of certain feminist groups, to practice *autoscienza*.

The metropolitan Indians were the most spectacular expression of the "creative side" of the 1977 movement. This side has, in the main, been greatly criticized,[23] and it is true that its discourse was indeed quite obscure and confused. Yet, it suffices to read its literary output to see that this was but a weak movement which, while it stressed a rejection of industrial culture, was powerless to play an active role—even when it sought, in the words of "Bifo," to move from a "diffuse and protean alienness toward the reconstruction of offensive forms of action."[24] What is sociologically important here is that this group exhausted itself in its search for an identity, that it had reduced to its own subjectivity; and that, in the absence of any real social adversary, could only exist in a state of dissent from and war against the state. For many, this failure led to total withdrawal, whereas for others, it led to the violence which constituted the other—victorious—side of an action which corresponds perfectly to the concept of antimovement that we defined in the first part of this book. *The 1977 movement was a social antimovement*, and the crisis within it very rapidly spawned *terrorist patterns of behavior*. This antimovement was strongly permeated by themes that were, in the same period, giving rise in other parts of the Western world to new social movements. Here, these new social actors were mapping out the conflicts that would come to be experienced by all societies entering into a postindustrial phase. In this sense, the 1977 movement was not only a manifestation of the end of the left and an especially critical phase in the inversion of the labor movement, but also a moment of inversion within the new social movements.

Here one might draw a comparision with the new social movements that emerged in the same period in France. Like the French movements, the 1977 movement was an indication that Italy was moving towards a new social reality whose conflicts were no longer so tied up in industrial progress and development as with the actor's capacity to set his cultural bearings, to define consumer norms and necessities, and to adduce the meaning of his own existence. Like the Frenchman, the Italian had great difficulty in extricating himself from models bequeathed to him by the labor movement; in breaking with the intellectual traditions inherited from communism and Marxism; and in asserting his own meanings instead of merely yielding, as if to a foreign power, to ideologies in which the main point of reference—however distorted it may have become—was still one of labor action. But the wave of new social movements that swept across France between 1974 and 1978 were able, most particularly in the antinuclear struggle, to link a call to creativity with the search for a social adversary. It had furthermore been able, in certain cases, to generate the notion of a conflict between various peoples, consumers, and regions on the one hand, and a technocratic power, epitomized for the most part by the EDF, the state-run electrical utility, on the other. In Italy, it was impossible to generate such a notion of social conflict. In the midst of a state-level crisis and the intransigence of its institutions, any call to creativity and any construction of a social actor was out of the question. The reaction of some groups was to turn in on themselves, while others, the feminists in particular, responded with a mixture of sectarian obstinacy and cultural innovation. On a more massive scale were those other groups who turned to absolutist and often self-destructive violence, which they claimed to be revolutionary and proletarian. These were kept in line by organizations which, no longer capable of designating a (social) adversary, were still able to point to a common enemy: the state.

It is tempting, as we have already noted, to see in the 1977 movement a vaguely libertarian and situationalist show of feeling by a labor movement that had always been possessed of such sensibilities, as opposed to those proper to Jacobinism or Leninism. However, apart from its appeal to actual experience and to basic human needs—which one finds among all manner of actors, and not merely those proper to the formative phase of the new social movements—the "creative" side of the 1977 movement was too sharply at odds with industrial culture to have constituted itself as a member of the family of new social movements.

It is with this that we come to glimpse the great originality of the Italian experience. Here, terrorism did not proceed from the decline of a social movement (the labor movement) alone, but was also associated with the difficult birth—more properly speaking, the abortion—of the first protest actor whose coming prefigured the future of Italy's social struggles. This was, in other words, a case of *classic inversion*, unidimensional in principle even if its evolution was a long and tortuous one,

coupled with an *inversion before the fact,* linked to the emergence of a
new social actor.

## Autonomia Violence

The random armed violence of 1977 was embodied, at the very heart of
the movement, by a number of groups of which Autonomia Operaia
(Labor Autonomy), heir to Potere Operaio, held the limelight.[25] Yet can
this properly be called an organization? The image of a dense and *quite
informal* network is surely closer to the mark than that of a party. At
most, one might speak of a number of their centers as magnets for the
political and ideological processing of those ideas and theorizations that
were moving along a thousand and one channels at that time. So it was,
for example, that their "penitents" later could speak of *Rosso,* a journal
edited out of Milan, as the "autonomists' subjective secretariat." The
main target of autonomia violence, at least according to its most fundamental statements,[26] was constituted by the PCI and the unions, which
it accused of furthering capitalistic relations, of failing to represent the
interests of the working class, and of being "the right's left." Theirs was
a feeling of exclusion as much as one of betrayal: the PCI and the unions
were the embodiments of an order and a system that rejects you; their
only preoccupation is with the powerful and organized working class.
Therefore, their action was corporatist.

Often, however, autonomia violence could not be reduced to its labor
references, and appeared as little more than blind rage, bereft of any
theoretical or political base. What they wanted was to bear arms, or to
gain access to weapons; and they intended to use those weapons, which
is what they did, especially in demonstrations which at times took on
the look of armed insurrections, as was the case in Bologna in March
1977. Their violence was not especially proper to the proletariat or the
underclass, given that a number of young men from good families were
taking part in it. In the universities in particular, it was tied into ideologies in which all manner of ideas became mingled with one another: the
"spontaneist" nature of their actions for "political rehabilitation" were
justified by the legitimate character of a "reappropriation by the producers" of that which had been extorted from them by capital in the form
of monetary appreciation. A "hypereconomist" critique was deployed in
order to explain a wide array of attitudes, via a Marxist problematic.
An unwieldy ideological discourse, often Stalinist in its overtones, was
set in place. At the same time, all that was derived from the inversion

of the labor movement came to be associated with the 1977 movement's cultural focus, and also proceeded, as a consequence, from a protest which reversed the categories of the new social movements.

The overriding image that emerges from the language and practices of the grassroots violence, the acts of delinquence, and the use of weapons in street operations, is one of confusion. The two sides of the antimovement were intertwined. The "creative" side, when it did not simply disappear entirely, deteriorated into a desire to come to blows and to handle "comrade P 38." In the words of Sabino Acquaviva—who was well-placed to observe it, teaching as he was at the University of Padua, a major autonomia center—violence was made fusion.[27]

The autonomia violence that went hand in hand with street demonstrations was of such an order as to transform Rome, on March 12, 1977, into a city under seige. It also made itself felt in the operations carried out by a smattering of tiny groups which appeared in the same period, under a wide array of acronyms: no less than 24 organizations claimed responsibility for armed operations carried out in 1976, 77 in 1977, and 179 in 1978.[28] "Kneecappings," firebombings of buildings and vehicles, holdups, "proletarian rounds" against small-business owners guilty of black-market hiring, and other acts of violence multiplied, as did the variety of targets—business leaders, security forces, judges, journalists, offices of professional associations, etc.

It was with a mixture of interest and circumspection that the Red Brigades and Prima Linea followed the 1977 movement—a social antimovement whose creative side fell apart to the greater profit of its violent side. Following this, as we have seen, they absorbed—at first cautiously, and later in a less and less controlled fashion—a youth for whom autonomia per se offered no perspective whatsoever.[29] The age of pure terrorism had begun, due in no small part to the surprising convergence of such armed resistance organizations as the BR and PL, and the lost children of the 1977 movement.

# 9

# A Sociological Intervention with Terrorists

Our analyses have, to this point, been based upon a traditional procedure in which historical documents are complemented by available books and articles, as well as by individual or collective observations and interviews. As such, they have so far failed to deal conclusively with the issues raised at least by our two principal hypotheses.

The first of these contrasts two families of interpretation. An analysis based on a crisis occuring on a state, political or cultural level is profoundly different—even if complementary to it—from one based on the notion of the inversion of social movements. The problem that remains is to establish, once and for all, the central place and value of this latter analytical mode.

There is a second hypothesis as well, which cannot truly be tested until the centrality of the principle of inversion has been established. This consists of explaining the 1978–80 intensification of violence into a pure rationale of terrorist action in terms of a telescoping of these two processes. Throughout the 1970s, there had been an ongoing inversion within the labor movement which had become hyperactivated and thrown out of control by a second inversion—that of the 1977 movement. This is more or less our hypothesis: to wit, that terrorism becomes all the more deadly when there is a clash, rather than a combination, of these two courses of action.

The research we will now present is not a mere reiteration of our earlier arguments, because its precise aim is to test two hypotheses. It

engages the actors themselves, former terrorists who agreed to ponder
these matters together with us. We did not solicit their comments merely
as a means to supporting our hypotheses, as is generally the case when
a researcher or a journalist gets together with terrorists. They actually
took part in our analytical endeavor.

## Two Terrorist Groups

The method for sociological intervention used in prior research by Alain
Touraine and myself made it possible for us, in our work on trade unionism as well as Solidarność and other new social movements, to go beyond
mere ideology and to analytically take apart that which historical practice had tended to put together and synthesize.[1] Whence the idea to apply
it to the phenomenon of terrorism, while adapting it to the specific nature
of the subject at hand.

So it is that we very concretely took up a course of fieldwork which
we carried out together with two groups of former terrorists who had
decided to reflect on their prior actions, and who had accepted the idea
of taking part in a series of meetings. Each of these groups successively
met with various co-discussants, all of whom had been located in some
way on the field of terrorist action, as political militants, trade unionists,
etc. Our choice of two groups, and of these two groups in particular,
should be obvious. Our goal was to seriously examine the hypothesis of
a two-tiered process of inversion. Our first group thus brought together
militants whose transition to terrorism had basically been caught up in
the inversion of the labor movement; the second, very different, was
especially made up of active participants in the 1977 movement.

The first group, which we contacted through Alain Geismar, was a
real group, six members strong, composed of former terrorists who had
either fled to or been exiled to Paris. The members of this group had
been bonded together by a leader who was at once their intellectual and
political guide and the person responsible for their material survival,
helping each of them to find housing and odd jobs.

As ex-terrorists, the six members of this group, whose numbers were
soon reduced to five, were first and foremost "dissociates." They had
participated, until 1979, in the Italian experience, where they had all
been based in the same region, in the vicinity of a major city located in
the northeastern part of the peninsula. They had not belonged to the
Red Brigades, but rather to Prima Linea, and their leader was a pioneer
in the theory and practice of "dissociation," which principally involves

acknowledging and accepting responsibility for one's acts without falling into informing and the other ignominious acts implicit in "repenting."

Because this first sociological intervention group was made up of former activists whose guiding model and ideologies were quite distant from the sensibilities of the 1977 movement, it was useful to complement their input with that of a second group, one that was representative of those very sensibilities that had been so visibly manifested in the years following 1977.

Most of the members of the second group came from the great northern urban areas: Turin, Milan, or the region around Venice. Only Carlo was from the south, where he had been a teacher prior to going underground and later into exile. Nearly all had worked in factories, although Maria Pia and Fabrizio were the sole members to have had a long labor experience. All had also known the university system that fell apart in the late 1970s, either as students or, more often, as political activists. The most senior among them, most particularly Luciano, had lived through the whole of the historical process of the 1960s and 1970s, the hopes and student movement of the hot autumn, the extraparliamentary Left, the struggle against fascism, the breakup of Potere Operaio, and autonomia.

We should add that this turned out to be an unstable group, which fell apart after its first meetings, whereas the first group met fifteen times between June and October 1982, in meetings of three hours' average duration (see table 1).

## The Inversion of the Labor Movement

The leftist extremist Italian terrorists constantly declared their solidarity with the working class. All indications lead one to believe, however, that their intensification of violence owes much to the increasingly artificial character of the relationship that obtained between these political militants and the labor struggles as they really existed, no matter how much subliminal violence these may have incorporated.

Here, our sociological intervention confirmed our hypothesis. It produced a great number of accounts, which tended to indicate that there existed a discontinuity, and not a continuity, between labor violence and terrorism; and even led to the notion that terrorism was the opposite of labor action. Each of the two groups' debates with a union leader laid bare the breakdown of Italian trade unionism, and even more so the breakup of the labor movement, both of which had spawned social forms

TABLE 1
CALENDAR OF GROUP MEETINGS

| GROUP ONE | |
| --- | --- |
| June 3, 1982 | Meeting without co-discussant |
| June 9, 1982 | Meeting without co-discussant |
| June 18, 1982 | Meeting with Alain Geismar |
| June 19, 1982 | Meeting with Mr. Sergio, director of an Italian daily newspaper |
| June 30, 1982 | Meeting with Maria (feminist, Manifesto ex-militant) |
| July 2, 1982 | Second meeting with Alain Geismar |
| July 3, 1982 | Meeting without co-discussant |
| | Meeting with Just, a steelworker, and his wife |
| July 7, 1982 | Meeting with Gianfranco, FML union leader |
| July 9, 1982 | Meeting with Mr. Alfa, a corporate executive |
| July 10, 1982 | Second meeting with Mr. Alfa |
| | Meeting without co-discussant |
| July 12, 1982 | Meeting with Mr. Stefano, priest and editorialist for a major daily newspaper |
| July 19, 1982 | Meeting without co-discussant |
| October 23, 1982 | Meeting without co-discussant |

| GROUP TWO | |
| --- | --- |
| November 30, 1982 | Meeting without co-discussant |
| December 6, 1982 | Meeting with a Solidarność advisor |
| December 13, 1982 | Meeting with Maria |
| December 22, 1982 | Meeting without co-discussant |
| January 7, 1983 | Meeting with Giuseppe, FML union leader |
| January 23, 1983 | Meeting without co-discussant |

Note: The Appendix gives an account of the principles, results, and methodological limits of these mediated discussions. Apart from Alain Geismar, the co-discussants' names are pseudonymous.

of violence, and general rage. It was furthermore confirmed that this rage did not issue directly into political violence, and even less into terrorism, but that it was capable of fostering a climate amenable to the expansion of it.

## Labor Violence and Terrorism

In the first group, Paulo and Giancarlo are boundless sources of information. Paulo feels he never had any choice in the matter: he had, in the name of his fellow workers, committed scattered acts of violence—sabotage, intimidation, and nonlethal attacks on owners and management. But was it not immoral, even disgraceful, to kill a man? His answer is immediate: "In my workplace, where four or five workers died over five years, it was almost automatic to throw the boss into the furnace." Paulo, often seconding Giancarlo, has much to say about the brutality of the captains of industry in the region. It was the owners who fired the first shot: having armed themselves back in the 1940s they had, on several occasions, "tried to run down the picketing strikers with their cars." They also sought to eliminate the forms of representation the labor movement had won for itself, and did not hesitate, for example, to lay off elected councillors, or refuse to deal with the union.

Resorting to violence also owed much to union "betrayal," and it was a very natural transition for Paulo when he set himself up on the armed wing of a movement whose institutions were no longer serving their purpose. "We were a small group, and even though lots of people who belonged to it didn't know exactly who you were or what you did, there always was some way for them to let you know that this or that thing had to be done. Relationships with our comrades were personal, I mean, they had worked in those factories, or were still working in them, and we discussed various problems between ourselves, between the members of our group. Requests for our services came to us from the factory, and we discussed whether or not we should take action, and how. To give the place where I worked as an example, they didn't know what I did, but the request would come to me one way or another. They never came to me and said, 'Could you do something for me?' They asked me, 'You don't know anybody, do you, who could shoot the boss in the kneecaps or beat him up while he's on his way home?' Sometimes we even had to step in when they asked for things, and explain that just shooting somebody in the kneecaps wasn't going to solve their problems."

This labor violence could give voice to highly volatile emotions. The workers asked Paulo, as well as a few other persons, "for some specific things . . . one day, for example, that we kneecap two of the bosses," but they had their own problems with wages, families to feed, and would often quickly give wide berth to outright acts of violence.

Finally, for Paulo, the injustice and violence of the social system did not stop at the factory gates, and this was a subject about which he spoke on several occasions. When he had been laid off, the courts had ruled in favor of the owners. More than this, he had not been able to enjoy the benefits of economic growth and democratization. He had neither been able to attend school—"the closest one was fifteen kilometers from my village"—nor enjoy the health-care system, and in the final analysis, he considers the state to only be good for helping owners and covering for fascists.

Owner violence, union powerlessness, and general social injustice brought about a grassroots protest whose protagonists bemoaned the lack of any mechanism for institutionalized arbitration. In Paulo's "white" region, we find ourselves in the presence of recent and rapid industrial growth coupled with weak institutional mechanisms, a situation created more than anything else by the omnipotence of the Christian Democrats there.

Prevailing conditions were apparently of such an order as to encourage the emergence of potentially terrorist forms of violence. Yet the workers, even those who were radicalized, hesitated to take up this course of action. Paulo entered into Prima Linea because without a weapon or an organization, "you couldn't do anything, because you didn't have the technical know-how." After he had drifted for a time towards terrorism, however, he had the feeling that he was "becoming cut off from the workers" and decided to give it up. "I got out of the armed resistance because I was a worker, and that was that."

While Paulo is hostile to the very idea of homicide, Giancarlo is not. Both of them, however, learned the same lesson from their experience with violence: this violence was linked to the weakness of the labor movement. At times, it appeared to take the place of the movement, but as soon as it became politicized and began organizing outside of the workplace, it cut itself off from labor hopes and aspirations.

Paulo's and Giancarlo's reminiscences end with 1977. A number of members from our second group, however, continued to take part in labor resistance until as late as 1980 or 1981.

No sooner did Maria Pia leave school in the little provincial village of her birth than she found herself working in a textile mill. She had participated in actions that often issued into a variety of forms of social violence. Faced with owners who refused to negotiate in the face of increasing demands for higher wages and skill differentials, resistance often hardened, and there were spontaneous outbursts of violence. "When the boss tries to run down a picket line with his car . . . what do you think happens next? His car is destroyed!"

It was not a revolutionary vision or a Marxist-Leninist ideology that led Maria Pia to take up the course of violence. Her participation was rooted in a climate of blue-collar rage that was constantly influenced by the cultural foci of the 1977 movement, its championing of basic human needs, and its desire to create, *hic et nunc,* a new order of interpersonal and social relationships. Her action was carried out within the context of an archaic small-business firm that had no interest in modern approaches to restructuring its machinery of production.

Fabrizio's notion of labor autonomia emerged out of a very different and highly symbolic context—the Fiat plant in Turin. It was in 1969 that Fabrizio, at the age of sixteen, discovered politics and began taking part in actions which, though ostensibly to transform his school, "nearly did it in." Like tens of thousands of others, he had lived the more-or-less bohemian youth of overpoliticized students, taking the odd job here and there. He ended up at Fiat where he became an active militant in labor autonomia, before being fired along with sixty of his comrades, as the result of an executive decision to put an end to "terrorism" and to see through to its conclusion a restructuring program begun several years earlier.

His statement is the occasion for presenting what was, very concretely, the autonomia of the late 1970s. Fabrizio is insistent that there was, in the factory, a form of blue-collar violence that attacked the prevailing relations of production, while remaining distinct from the highly politicized terrorism practiced by the Red Brigades, a terrorism that was nearly always far removed from the workers' consciousness and conflicts. This scattered, subversive violence, mainly consisting of acts of sabotage, was but one facet of a broader action organized by autonomia. This action was, as Fabrizio insists, as far removed from political terrorism as it was from the institutionalized labor actions.

These statements, taken as a group, generally speak to the gulf between labor action, even when it becomes violent, and political terrorism. It even suggests that the two are incompatible. It is easy to understand Paulo and Maria Pia's rebellion and anger. We have also seen that such did not translate directly into a political action organized after the model of armed resistance. In those cases in which such a movement claimed to have taken control of a workers' revolt, and in which a number of workers yield to the temptation to follow their lead, a split occurred. And, when the dust had settled, the workers came to see that their decision had been catastrophic. This had been the experience of Paulo, as well as of Maria Pia, who cries, "In the beginning, violence was brought in as a category you could use, but not one that would end up using you. But from the moment we reached a level where we were theorizing about violence as a possible alternative, I found myself being used. Armed struggle became the basic phenomenon. Everything was confused. It's no longer possible to justify what was justifiable before, because before, it was the struggle that justified everything."

This basic statement, of a veritable hiatus—between labor violence rooted in relations of production and terrorism against the state—will now be greatly reinforced by a description of a blue-collar fundamentalism, as was forcefully voiced by members of the first group in the course of several meetings.

### Blue-Collar Fundamentalism

If we are to believe the first group, the workers could not comprehend purely political assassination or the killing of judges, and were even averse to the use of armed violence. Although they rejected factory violence, they considered it a mistake to try to raise the stakes, and take on the state. Instead, they preferred to lay down their arms. Mario, the group leader, has never been a worker, but has always wanted to live symbiotically with the workers' struggles. "I made a break with terrorism," he explains, "when the four factory workers who were part of our organizaton, workers from a major plant in the region, themselves decided to quit. For me, it was as if an alarm had gone off, which rang louder than any of our intellectual arguments." Besides, Giancarlo adds, the BR's Walter Alasia column, entirely blue-collar in its inception, broke up because it could no longer get along with the workers in the factories. The terrorist course it began following in 1977, epitomized by the kidnapping of Aldo Moro, was a phenomenon that no longer had anything to do with the labor struggle. It was nevertheless part of a process from which the members of the group took some time to disengage themselves.

Mario, who had been a Prima Linea leader at that time, remembers with particular clarity the anger he felt when he heard that the Red Brigades had kidnapped Aldo Moro. "My first reaction was one of rage. I wanted to get even with the BR. It "shot to blazes our campaign on the structures of factory production." Speaking in the presence of a daily newspaper editor who had introduced himself to them as a friend of the late politician, all asserted that for them the affair had been a matter between the Red Brigades and the state. "What happened had nothing to do with us," says Paulo, and the group, agreeing with the newspaperman on a point he has made, stresses that this was the turning point at which terrorism, of a different ideological and political order than the violence of the previous period, truly began.

The model for action adopted by these former terrorists was the radical product of an operaism that had become impracticable. Until 1978, their armed struggle had continued to have the appearance, at least, of an extension of labor action. Down to that time, there had been real solidarity with the workers, who came to them asking for help and advice, and who were even ready to provide them with hideouts and housing. To that point, their violence had been instrumental—but this lost all its meaning in 1978. With the decline of workers' resistance movements, in the general winding down of a cycle begun with the hot autumn of 1969, they had at one time thought it possible to "make a strategic retreat, to regroup," while holding onto their research structures. They were forced, however, to make a hasty choice between a militarization in which "the model was more important than the content, and the form more important than the substance," and the abandonment of armed insurgency. The rapid growth of the Red Brigades, followed by the massive phenomenon of the "repenters," quickly pushed them out of the picture. More than anything else, it was their special attachment to an actual blue-collar community that cut them off from those who had taken up the path of uncontrolled violence. When this blue-collar fundamentalism is absent and there is no concern for maintaining a link with labor resistance, it is much easier to slide into terrorism than when there is a real and concrete relationship with labor actors.

### Trade Unionism and Terrorism

It is a truism to maintain that there were but two actors—the trade unionists on the one hand, and the terrorists led by the Red Brigades on the other—speaking, in the 1970s, in the name of the Italian factory-based labor movement. That this notion is all too schematic was made clear in meetings held between each of our two groups and a union leader, meetings which indicated the consequences of the crisis in trade unionism. This crisis gave rise, on the one hand, to a scattered social violence that did not feed directly into terrorism and, on the other, to the opening of a political arena for activities that were in fact terrorist. In other words, what these meetings primarily showed us was that it had been the breakup of the labor movement that had opened the way to a two-tiered phenomenon of scattered violence and terrorism.

#### Meeting of the First Group with a Trade Unionist

Gianfranco is a highly placed leader in the FML in Turin.[2] He feels that trade unionism was slow to comprehend the impact of terrorism, whose support in the labor environment was significant.

What is tragic for him was the triangular relationship within which the union had to face the onslaughts of terrorism from one side and management from the other. How could it defeat terrorism without becoming a "union that was subordinated to, a junior partner in, or sold out to management?" His question is greeted by veritable howls on the part of Giancarlo, who suddenly rages at him. "You had a lot more to say against the terrorists than you did against management," he cries. "It was you who created the climate!" Until 1978, Giancarlo contends, until the Moro kidnapping, armed resistance was, for the workers, "much more than just the union. It was all the workers had." But is this enough to justify armed insurgency, from the standpoint of labor?

The list of the ills suffered by the unions at the hands of terrorism is a long one. It had made it easier for management to fire people: "All a worker needed to do was to raise his voice when complaining about his hours, and Fiat would fire him for intimidation of a terrorist nature." It introduced fear, doubt, and suspicion between workers, and strengthened the law's arsenal of repression. Terrorism actually presented itself as an alternative to the unions, and it was at this juncture that the latter entered into a strategy of rapprochement with the state. Here, Giancarlo forcefully jogs his co-discussant's memory. "My God, you people were saying, 'If you're not with the state, you're with the BRs'!"

Whereas Paulo saw the armed struggle as a tool that an illegal workers' action could use, Giancarlo found it to be more of a revolutionary mode of action, grounded in the factory and the relations of production. Both felt that the use of violence was a means to compensate for a failure in union leadership. Their plans were torpedoed in 1978, with the transition to violence at a truly political level, a transition spectacularly marked by the kidnapping of Aldo Moro. After this, there would perhaps remain a handful of workers committed to the armed struggle. However, as the first group states insistently, this would no longer have anything whatsoever in common with workers' demands—demands which the unions were nonetheless incapable of helping to answer.

### Meeting of the Second Group with a Trade Unionist

The discussion held between the reduced numbers of the second group and Giuseppe, another FML union leader from Turin, typifies the rift that widened, throughout the 1970s, between a bargaining union that was most concerned with participating in the country's modernization, and a workers' revolt which, left by the unions to its own devices, reverted to the old practices of direct action. In a single act of incomprehension and denial, Giuseppe rejects everything from the Red Brigades and Prima Linea to sabotage, absenteeism, and alcoholism. For him, whatever does not partake of a union-organized strike or arbitration—including direct action, racketeering, and smuggling—are but so many individualized forms of pathological behavior. Fabrizio begins by reminding him of the massive scale of autonomia-inspired subversive practices, the size of autonomia demonstrations, and the success of its workers' collectives. In 1978 for example, it was able to block, for over a month's time, an attempt by the management of the Rivalta factory to enforce mandatory overtime work on Saturdays. Fabrizio underscores the continuity of the low-level conflict that endured for several years, and is insistent that it was often one and the same worker who both fought in the union ranks and who, outside of his union ties, fought in the ranks of autonomia, which was not to be confused with the Red Brigades.

Once again, we are reminded of the existence of a blue-collar violence that was at once external to the unions and distinct from the armed struggle as it was carried out in theory and practice by the Red Brigades. The union co-discussant refuses to acknowledge any positive effects it may have had, but acknowledges the fact that such violence did exist in the 1970s. The debate also points to the arena in which this social violence took shape. This was not only in those innumerable situations, with which we are already familiar, in which the Communist party and the unions proved powerless in their attempts to act constructively on behalf of labor. It also arose in those cases in which changes in the labor market and in the organization of the workplace resulted in hiring from new sectors of society. Fabrizio, like thousands of others, has nothing whatever in common with the uneducated [sans éducation] mass-workers of the 1960s who were transplanted, at times brutally, from the countryside to the urban assembly lines of Taylorized factories. He is a cultivated and highly politicized young man whom the labor market—exemplified by Fiat's massive hiring program in 1978—had steered in the direction of an unskilled position, in factories in the process of post-Taylorized restructuring. He is neither attached to manual labor nor to industrial values, but is quite sensitive to the 1977 movement's innovations of cultural categories. His periods of employment, with a number of companies, have been interspersed with long periods of unemployment.

A large number of workers may, like Fabrizio, be identified with that aspect of working-class consciousness which the union co-discussant judged to be pathological. They speak in terms of the here and now, and are more moved by anger than by a desire to negotiate or to formulate some alternative social order. In the classic model of working-class consciousness,[3] rebellion and negotiation, defensiveness and counterproposals, come together and complement one another to produce a social movement. The debate we have just summarized confirms that this classic model became outdated in 1977 or 1978. Labor autonomia, in Fiat-type factories,[4] was the externalization of a structural modification within a labor movement that would never be able to pull itself back together. Fabrizio and Giuseppe represent the two irreconcilable sides of this social movement, and their exchange shows how little they have left in common.

## The Inversion of the Labor Movement

It now becomes possible for us to offer a general description of violence and terrorism, as concerns their various links with the labor movement.

At the properly social level, labor violence has two sources. The first derives from the labor movement's conditions of existence. When a labor movement cannot do what it was created to do, when it is banned or simply not backed by institutionalized forms of political action, a classical working-class consciousness finds no other outlet than that offered by violence. In such cases, social, indeed revolutionary, violence is clearly experienced as being wholly distinct from terrorism. Here, the act of moving from the former to the latter constitutes a leap from a legitimate action to practices which are perceived, after the fact, as illegitimate or counterproductive.

The second source of labor violence derives not only from the labor movement's opportunities for self-expression, but also from its very nature. Here, violence can arise when the working-class consciousness breaks down, or when a new proletariat goes so far as to question the historicity of the industrial society. In this latter case, when the new proletariat defines itself more by the precarious nature of its employment and its economic demands than by the conflicts inherent to the relations of production, violence can proceed from the social movement itself, or more exactly from its decline and collapse. It becomes an expression of the rage felt by persons who have fallen between the cracks in the institutionalization of labor conflicts, and is much more prone to elevating itself to a political level than in the previous case.

Terrorism proper, as distinct from social violence, derives, in the factory context, from three different models.

The first of these was delineated in 1970 and 1971 by the Red Brigades. This was the model, classic during the time in which left-wing politics was at its height, of a leftist vanguard with a primarily ideological approach. While this group was able to recruit from the labor milieu, it did so out of a sense of mission that had very little to do with actual day-to-day labor struggles. The second pattern, the outlines of which began to emerge after 1973–74, was fully embodied by Prima Linea, which was founded in 1976. In the beginning, the group intended itself to be an armed tool of labor insurgency, its instrumental extension as it were. Its militants were there to afford labor technical and logistic assistance and support, and to develop basic structures within the factories. When this quickly proved utopian, it gave rise to pure terrorism. The third pattern, in line with the basic concepts of autonomia, diverges on theoretical grounds from the notion of forming any type of party whatsoever, and rejects all vertical structures. This was a movement, and not an organization.

Neither of the first two patterns stems directly from social violence. They are primarily political in nature, with their development being a function of weaknesses in the labor movement and of crisis situations (in the state, the political system, etc.). The third, which appears later, affords a continuity of sorts between a destructured social action and a political action that has tailed off into terrorism.

In other words, the inversion present in the first two patterns arises from actors or modes of analysis which are external to the social movement proper. Such would hold to a lesser extent for the third pattern.

These three models, relatively distinct in their basic principles, tend to merge with one another in the chain reactions proper to a flareup of violence. Fusion—in spite of the initial positions taken by autonomia, antithetical to vanguardism and the notion of an organization—occurs within a Leninist framework, which provided a basic mold for armed insurgency in its many divergent forms.

In the final analysis and regardless of ideological and political origins, what resulted was the undeniable inversion of the labor movement.

For all this, is it possible to say that the terrorist upsurge of the late 1970s was the product of this inversion and this inversion alone? Or might we not also ascribe it to a second phenomenon, linked not only to the historical decline of the labor movement, but also to the first abortive manifestations of a number of new social movements?

## The Inversion of the 1977 Movement

The inversion of the labor movement was an intermittent process that extended through the decade of the 1970s, a process that involved the first brigatistes as well as the labor autonomists who were themselves closely linked to the 1977 movement. The inversion of the 1977 movement proper was, on the contrary, swift and violent. Our second sociological intervention group represents one of its sides and is, in a certain sense, its best analyst.

From the moment in which its protagonists became engulfed in armed struggle, the cultural ideals of the 1977 movement melted away into violence. As a social antimovement, closely related in its aspirations to the new social movements, it then became swallowed up by ideologies and practices whose motor was the war against the state. Our research shows us just how this occurred.

Invited in order that the second group might compare its own experience with that of a nonviolent movement, a symbolic figure in Solidarność was invited as a co-discussant. This individual, one of the most influential spokespersons in the Western world, was sufficiently acquainted with Italy to appreciate the innumerable factors differentiating the Polish experience from the Italian movement. Solidarność had represented the whole of Polish society rather than just a few of its sectors; it was a stranger to Marxism which, for it, symbolized the communist powers; it restrained itself and rejected violence in its fight for democracy and against totalitarianism. The group has trouble coming to terms with the image of a progressive actor working not in order to wrest power away from the state, but rather to extricate society from the state's grasp. When all was said and done, they explain to the Solidarność representative, you fell back into the classic pattern, if not into a Leninist model. You were unable to go on resisting the irresistible question of state power. Not only this, but you lost as well. The most they are ready to allow is that Solidarność postponed for as long as possible its confrontation with the state, whereas Italian autonomia quickly brought matters to a head by moving to take power through the force of arms. Why was it that autonomia became so quickly radicalized? The group maintains, long and loud, that theirs was a social and cultural movement, an expression of blue-collar demands and cultural renewal. Why, then, did everything gel into armed insurgency? A primary explanation, recalling the specificity of Italian history and culture and evoking its longstanding tradition of radical movements, has barely been broached before a second one is vigorously advanced: in the face of the all-powerful Italian state, armed resistance was the sole possible and effective form of action to take. Here, the Solidarność spokesperson can hardly believe his ears. The group explains to him that the Polish totalitarian state is, in the final analysis, perhaps not such a powerful one, whereas the Italian state tramples every political institution, closing off "all room for questions, all room for hope" . . . "it controls everything." A state can be "as powerful as the Italian state without having to be strong or centralized," and the Italian state, with its nonfunctional bureaucracy and its many deficiencies, presents a fantastic "capacity for being so contradictory as to end up being unable to change anything, ever." The modern capitalist state, they conclude, "has found the way to be as powerful as a totalitarian state without being a totalitarian state."

What these former terrorists are describing is, perhaps, not so much the state per se as a rigidified institutional system which, more or less corrupted, has been reduced to a mere instrument for maintaining the status quo. Whatever the case, these images show that autonomia, even if it started from a critique of culture and a proletarian condemnation of society, was itself unable to avoid being cowed into taking the state as point of reference. One finds no mediating structures between real experience, the championing of consumer and basic human needs, and demands for immediate changes in social and interpersonal relations on the one hand, and the desire for action and armed confrontation with the state on the other. Nor can one discern any effort to discover or invent modalities for the political treatment of such demands. Terrorism, as well as violence as both a means and an end in itself, were the final manifestations of a process that had been initiated by actors who had believed it possible to overthrow the existing order by creating the necessary conditions for the existence of an action. Yet all the while, these actors knew that they were, through their own initiative, suppressing those very same conditions. The failure of autonomia lies here, in its transition to a war against the state, and in its resignation in the face of those who would actually wage that war.

This failure is closely related to an inversion process. Fabrizio is the first to suggest that the group ought to distinguish between the "movement" prior to 1978 or 1979, and the mass terrorism that followed. As we already have seen, he denies any association between random social violence rooted in labor relations, and political terrorism. Now he details his ideas. When Prima Linea assassinated the engineer in charge of restructuring the automated workshops at Fiat, it acted "outside of any connection with what was really going on at the plant or with the lives of the workers—and expressed a tension that didn't even exist." Again, when the same organization "kneecapped" several students and instructors from a business-teacher's college, "it was foreign to every point of reference and every cause the workers were fighting for." Lucia agrees with him: terrorism appeared when a number of groups decided they were the vanguard of their neighborhood, of a "portion of their class," and presumed to become its representative without their claims having the slightest correspondence to reality.

These analyses correspond to the thesis of simple inversion, according to which action is reduced to the mere reflection of a reversal of categories proper to the labor movement. But these categories were constantly being supplemented by other propositions, which introduced the dual foci of real life experience and basic human needs. These are themes more closely associated with the language of actors from the new social movements, such as were found, in the same period, among militants from the antinuclear, feminist, ecological, etc. movements. So it is that Lucia can relate the intense psychological turmoil she felt when she became aware that violence "represented something completely foreign to concrete experience, to your entire being, to day-to-day life." Flavia remarks that at that time "there were categories, values, and personality traits that you had to bury, to hide, because they weren't a part of the collective experience."

In this group, whose every member fully recognizes himself in the hopes of the 1977 movement, two levels of discourse are constantly being intertwined. The first is the classic discourse of an intelligentsia which identifies itself with the basic demands of society and acknowledges a posteriori that terrorism results from an artifical identification with largely mythical labor demands. The second quite dissimilarly invokes the subjectivity of the actor who speaks in his own name and who emphasizes his own needs. The former is a statement bearing on the inversion of the labor movement, while the latter not only carries this through to its conclusion, but further saddles it with a second inversion, that of the new social movements which emerged out of the wake of the "creative" side of the 1977 movement. The tragedy of autonomia lies first in the fact that it failed as a new sociocultural actor; and second that it became involved, at the time of its fall, with new combatant ideologies and organizations, which engulfed it. In Luciano's words, autonomia was a movement, something in the air; after 1977, however, "ideologies began blowing in the wind, which swept it into a corner.

The armed groups injected their methods into the movement and took it over."

Three major points are hereby confirmed. First of all, the Italian experience of terrorism was brought on by more than an ideological reshuffling triggered by the decline of the labor movement. It was revitalized, in a spectacular way, by the 1977 movement, the powerless public face put on by the new social movements. This movement, like others that were emerging throughout the Western world at the time, was at once a social antimovement that had yet to completely disengage itself from the old battles of industrial society, and a precursor to the conflicts that would be spawned in postindustrial society. Second, we find ourselves obliged to dismiss as false the widely held notion that the 1977 movement funneled directly into the combatant organizations. There was indeed a transition of the former into a number of the latter groups. However, this tilt was, more than anything else, the result of the movement's *failure,* of its leaders' inability to translate into actions its highly subjective positions and aspirations for cultural renewal, coupled with the proletarian demands it claimed to represent.

Thirdly, the 1977 movement's specific themes, themes which allowed it to call itself a new social movement, were never presented in isolation, even when they were inverted. They were constantly linked to a labor-based, anticapitalist focus, even if they lacked the impact of those themes which led to the inversion of the labor movement.

At this stage of our analysis, terrorism appears as the result of two basic processes of inversion: that of the labor movement and that of the 1977 movement. We now must examine the ways in which these two processes, both favored as they were by the state's institutional intransigence and structural weaknesses, became telescoped so as to produce a veritable stampede into armed insurgency.

## The Clash

Is it possible to see the upsurge of autonomia, followed by its activists' embracing of armed struggle, as a mere extension of prior actions, with the only change being one of scale? Or do these events rather introduce a total break with and even a reversal of all that preceded? Here as well, the work of our two intervention groups is highly illuminating, and illustrative of just what it was that lay behind the rise of terrorism. This was the repeated subjection to crisis of the classic Leninist model, a model that favored keeping a tight rein on violence, which was only to be released in revolutionary situations.

## Hatred for the 1977 Movement

If there is a leitmotiv to the first group's discussions, it is surely the repeated expression of its hatred for the 1977 movement. 1977, as Giancarlo explains, was "lower-middle-class terrorism carried out by students." Mario goes even further. "Without the student environment, the armed struggle would not have been a mass phenomenon, it would have been nothing more than a political platform." Paulo is more specific. "The arrival of those people pushed us too far. It cut us off from the workers."

The first group's description of the 1977 movement and, in a broader sense, of autonomia, is reflective of the notion of sets of crisis-related patterns of behavior. Marked by a weakening of the middle levels of society, then in social decline, the violence to which these gave rise "hegemonized" the entire armed struggle to the detriment of the working class. Mario maintains that in 1977, the lower middle class was carrying inside itself an "instinctive and irrational violence," a veritable gangrene that completely destroyed the workers' action. The Roman column of the Red Brigades who held Aldo Moro "were nearly all people who had come out of the 1977 movement." When our researchers bring up the major themes of the movement, and most especially those of its creative side—its chosen causes of real life experience, basic human needs, desire, feminism, or the new social movements—the group's reaction is frank and direct. "I don't care about that stuff," says Mario and all are unanimous in maintaining that nothing really matters but working-class problems and the working-class vision.

In the early days, in the early 1970s, there had been a great cluster of groups who split not so much over basic ideas, as over strategic matters. Following the fall of the student movement, and most particularly the collapse of its base at Trent, the Italian Left rallied around a common vision, which served to catalyze both the armed struggle and the extraparliamentary Left. "It was," as Mario describes, "to work for oneself, to gain wealth for oneself, to live better on a collective level, to do away with capitalism. What separated us was tactics. For the extraparliamentary Left, it was the long road into the institutions; for us, it was armed resistance." The most lofty expression of the model to which Mario refers is to be situated, without a doubt, in 1971–72, before armed struggle had become an issue. This was the time in which Potere Operaio and Manifesto attempted to form a unified party, which would have been capable of bringing together militants from the PCI as well as, according to Mario, from the Fourth International. But, says Paulo, "It was Prima Linea that brought us all together!" When the attempt to form a political organization had failed, many drifted into politicomilitary formations. After 1976, as the members of the group relate, the "original rank and file of Prima Linea began flirting in a big way with the youth movement." Then, with the breakup of the extraparliamentary Left and the emergence of armed groups, a new focus, which had nothing to do with labor, was brought to the fore. This quickly became violent, upsetting the older model. Invited to a meeting with the first group, Maria personifies this very standpoint. Ten years earlier, she had been a militant in Manifesto, and later in feminist groups. She had actively participated in the sociocultural protests of the 1970s, without ever having been attracted to violence. Her confrontation with the group is, on the contrary, a violent one.

The meeting begins on a rather pedestrian note, with the evocation of Margarethe von Trotta's film on the "years of lead." Then, a rift quickly appears, in which the group shows itself to be against all that Maria stands for. Paulo bluntly states that he doesn't care about feminism. As for the right to free speech, to being different if such means being true to one's own self, Mario expresses his opposition by outlining a vision of society in which "there is as little difference as possible." Maria firmly defends her antitotalitarian positions, and the group stands behind its leader and isolates itself in a surprising exchange. As if to bait Maria, Mario states that he believes in totalitarian society and makes a series of abstract and incomprehensible (at least for the researchers) statements on the subjects of the Hegelian dialectic, the division of labor and social homogeneity. "That's doctrinarian diatribe," Maria comments, to which he answers that he does "have a dogmatic and ideological vision of communism that is ultimate and quite nearly religious." Backing him up, Paulo who has always, until now, concentrated his discussion on concrete themes linked to working-class experience, indicates that his is "also a religion of communism." Giancarlo says that he takes Stalin to be his model, while Mario adds that "the difference between Stalin and Lenin is that Stalin was a democrat and Lenin a totalitarian; therefore I am Leninist. Stalin was a Bonapartist father of democracy, and Lenin a democrat of totalitarianism."

■

*This is a critical turning point in our research.* Suddenly, we researchers find ourselves confronted with a sectarian frenzy, which erupts out of the heat of a debate in which feminism, individual subjectivity, and the right to be different, all personified by Maria, run up against the group's working-class ideology.

But rather than dismissing the group, and especially its leader, as non-sensical and irrational, let us rather examine what they are laying on the line in their somewhat troubling extremist discourse. To this point, the Marxist-Leninist positions of Mario and his friends have been powerful, coherent, and calm—and calm would indeed return following the clash with Maria. Beyond purely academic interests, the group has been effecting an intellectual return to Marxism-Leninism. It has read the classics, developed a critique of terrorism that Lenin would perhaps have not disavowed, and established itself in what we have called a communist fundamentalism. However, the debate with Maria has unleashed a radical line of discourse in which the group puts on—for the only time in the course of our investigations—a show of terrorist frenzy. This phenomenon confirms for us the incompatible nature of these two foci, which together brought about the rise of terrorism. The first was inherited from the left, and the second, coming later and linked to the 1977 movement, was associated with the cultural sensibilities personified by Maria. It especially shows us that the meeting of the two had a number of effects on the ideological matrix of the former which, as we know, ended up swallowing the latter. The Red Brigades' or Prima Linea's Marxist-Leninist ideology did not simply engulf the contributions it received from a relatively different ideological horizon. It was rather shaken, modified, and pushed to extremes which, in our group, took the form of the outburst we have just described, and which translated, in the real world, into a terrorist intensification and total collapse. The armed resistance organizations found themselves forced to deal with powerful internal tensions and conflicts for the sake of an ideological model which had itself been shaken and forced, as it were, to justify acts of aggravated violence. It may reasonably be supposed that after 1977–78 the runaway stampede into pure, unmitigated terrorism was very much the result of just this sort of encounter between these two distinct levels. One might also defend a hypothesis according to which the proliferation of murderous acts, the diversification of victims, and the growing membership in combatant organizations was not so much the result of an increase in strength as an uncontrolled tailspin of a mechanism that has run amok.

These remarks, based on our fieldwork, place in a bad light those arguments which see terrorism as an expression of predispositions linked to a given psychological structure. The outburst of frenzy and tailspin into violence stem from a particular situation—i.e. of a necessary yet unrealizable ideological processing of reality—and not by personality traits.[5]

### Autonomia and Armed Struggle: One Rationale or Two?

Ought we to follow Judge Calogero and many others and maintain that there existed a single organization in which terrorism as practiced by the BRs and autonomia added up to one? Ought we to adopt the position taken by Maria, for whom violence is intrinsically linked to the very existence of the nonlaboring social strata, a position which would, at bottom, lead one to see little or no difference between the post-1977 BR and autonomia? All that we have seen heretofore inclines us to reject this viewpoint. Yet, at this final juncture, it behooves us to recognize that as soon as it is rationales of action and trajectories of militancy— rather than mere organizations—that are at issue, the answer cannot be so simple.

Whereas autonomia at first spoke in terms of actual experience, human needs, and existential necessities, the Red Brigades spoke in terms of power, the state, and civil war. Isolated, the first group might have ended up committing acts of random violence and delinquency, or perhaps it would have dropped out, sought to exemplify some ideal, or shown greater cultural inventiveness. Left to their own devices, the second group would have been just another organization of limited scope, comparable to the German Red Army Faction.

But these two phenomena never ceased to jostle one another, to inter-mingle, to find one another mutually attractive—to the ruination of both. Several times, with the second intervention group, which has never-theless taken such great pains to distance itself from the BR, the idea of a certain historical and political unity is put forward. Maria Pia is the first to put it into words, and not without courage. "Autonomia began to draw close to the BR, and the movement began to go downhill. Auto-nomia could and should have been able to provide a real alternative to the BR's political strategy, that is to the strategy of elimination. But they didn't, and so it was the BR who gave the Italian movement its distinctive look. That's why we have to admit that the BR was part of our move-ment, that it was part of our history." Other members of the group fell into step with her. "An entire series of autonomia experiments had noth-ing to do with terrorism. But if someone were to ask me whether or not there exists a continuity between the BR and ourselves, if we share a

common history, I would have to say that they're like us. Even if I never
shared their opinions, I could never say that there is a true difference
between the BR and ourselves. To do so would be to lose sight of the
movement's true essence."

We would perhaps do well to go further back in time, to the end of
the student movement and the appearance of the leftist movements, and
acknowledge that all of the political struggles of the 1970s, including
the armed struggle, had two complementary sides to them, the one sociocultural and the other turned in the direction of the state. This is what
Luciano suggests when he seeks to remind us that quite often, from the
early 1970s on, the same militants could maintain both foci simultaneously. "We cannot separate either the Italian movement in the years
following 1968 or autonomia from a discourse on power. We cannot
say that power never interested us, that the only problem was to change
our lives. The focus of our movements in the 1970s alternated between
needs and power." So it happened that, after the mid-1970s, the parties
of the extraparliamentary Left, and most particularly Lotta Continua and
Potere Operaio, underwent a division in which the military organization,
at first given the task of maintaining order in demonstrations, split off
from the broader organization. "But at that point the division no longer
held," Lucia tells us, "because there had been a kind of cultural revolution where carrying weapons wasn't supposed to be limited to a small
body of militants, but open to everyone who was on that political course.
Everyone was supposed to take responsibility for a weapon—the military
wing had taken over. It was a syndrome."

In the end, the group maintains that it is impossible to distinguish
"terrorists from nonterrorists, the armed struggle from autonomia."
Moreover, "those who didn't bear arms often belonged to the same
family of ideas, and offered shelter to those who had."

At the very outside, it is possible to say that Judge Calogero, the bête
noire of these former supporters of autonomia, would agree with certain
of the group's positions—even if the group has taken such great care to
distance itself from armed insurgency as was theorized and practiced by
the Red Brigades.

These remarks force us to qualify, in conclusion, our hypothesis of a
process of dual inversion. To be sure, the 1977 movement and, in a
broader sense, autonomia did—in order to adopt a focus which was
often close to that of the new social movements—split off, politically,
socially, and culturally, from earlier causes and theoretical models. But
as we have just seen, it is artificial, on the one hand, to separate the

armed struggle, the direct result of the inversion of the labor movement, from an autonomia that was as much an heir to the conflicts of the 1970s as it was an unworkable expression of a new form of action. On the other hand, when the 1977 movement and autonomia failed, it was through various Leninist ideologies—which they themselves also helped to "run amok"—that they, in the final analysis, annihilated themselves. The "creative" side of the 1977 antimovement is much closer to the ecologists, feminists, and antinuclear protests, than to workers' demands, however diluted these might have become. The preoccupations they high-lighted were much more those of a postindustrial society than those of an industrial one, even if only to the extent that it greatly emphasized the theme of communication. In this sense, the fact that it failed in its armed struggle allows us to speak of a second inversion. The way in which it funneled itself, however, into the Marxist-Leninist models within which it was later broken down, points to its theoretical subordi-nation to the principles that powered the first inversion, i.e. the inversion of the labor movement. It raised this first inversion to a higher power, carrying it to its limits in the murderous and nihilist frenzies of the early 1980s. In a certain sense, the 1977 movement constituted a detour, a transition, following which a process begun in the early 1970s became greatly intensified. Leftist extremist Italian terrorism was the product of the long and tortuous inversion of the labor movement. Exacerbated and driven to its heights by the 1977 movement, it briefly attempted to follow the path of the new social movements before drowning in a hyper-Leninist orgy of violence.

# 10

## Conclusion to Part Two

In the Italian case, the inversion process was long and chaotic, involving thousands of activists. Elsewhere, leftist extremist terrorism has developed more quickly, with the terrorist flareup being more immediate and spectacular even if they have mobilized a relatively limited number of militants. In Germany and Japan, the armed struggle never went through that important preterrorist phase in which political violence was combined with authentic labor rage. Nor was it reinvigorated in these places by the rise and the later fall of a movement comparable to that of 1977. In these two countries, terrorism, apparently well aware that it would never be able to draw into its fold a working class that was already highly institutionalized, skirted the factories entirely. At the same time, its immediate rise and expansion, in which it was looking for direction as it engaged in anti-imperialist and anti-Zionist conflicts—which led it, most particularly, into the service of the radicalized sectors of the Palestinian movement—were of a greater magnitude than in Italy.

A second generation of actors belonging to the same family promoted itself in the early 1980s, most especially in France (Action Directe) and Belgium (Communist Combatant Cells). The trajectories of these groups were even shorter. They emerged out of the final convulsions of the leftist movement, rather than its ascendant phase; and they were only slightly influenced by autonomia, whose foci, borrowed from the Italian scene, corresponded but little to reality. The only social base that Action Directe ever had were the Parisian "squatters" of 1978–79,[1] whom these militants were quickly forced to leave behind, before plunging into an underground existence and a tailspin into terrorism.

The Communist Combatant Cells made themselves known through a series of attacks carried out in October 1984, but their experiment apparently came to an end in December 1985, with the arrest of four persons. This group had sought to awaken a subjugated and alienated working class without ever having militated in the workplace. The group had also wished to appropriate for itself the issue of the peace movement, and had presented itself as an actor capable of taking on NATO, by sabotaging a network of pipelines, for example, in December 1984.[2]

Lastly, in a number of Western countries—Greece, Portugal, and Spain—there exist groups that may be compared with those we have just mentioned.

Each of these cases, in order that it be properly analyzed, would have to be made the subject of a specific program of research. Nonetheless, our examination of leftist extremist terrorism in Italy has provided us with data that may be applied more broadly.

First of all, it shows us the uselessness of interpretations which confuse favorable factors or conditions with the sociopolitical sources of a given phenomenon. A state in crisis, a rigidified political system, or an important cultural change, although they may facilitate its emergence, do not create terrorism. The closing off of the public sphere, restrictions in the freedom of speech and communications are but so many contributing factors to the rise of terrorism. So it was that terrorism in Italy diminished when the extraparliamentary Left was flourishing and enlivening public discussion than when such debates were being cut off, restricted, or closed to the public—and the extraparliamentary Left was falling apart.

Radical leftist terrorist actors cannot comprehend themselves without referring to some social constituency. In the Italian case, the plunge into terrorism was indivisible from the growth of the labor struggles. Armed resistance appeared as a program within the context of councilist agitations, at a juncture in which a resurgence of class warfare was imaginable, but in which the union and political organizations had already fallen out of sync with a number of workers' demands. It grew in direct proportion as a very young group of relatively well-educated new proletarians—who had more or less been cast adrift by the classic labor organizations—split off from the skilled or mass-workers, who had a more traditional profile. The more the image of a unified class consciousness, taken in hand by the unions or the PCI, became an artificial one, the more violent the scene became. This violence could be scattered and limited to the factories, or it could become politicized, and issue into terrorism when it disengaged itself from the concrete reality of the labor struggles. After the hopes that had been pinned on it in the late 1960s, the decline of the Italian labor movement resulted in the isolation of the political actors who claimed to be its spokespersons. The course of violence that some of these persons embraced was made all the more deadly for the fact that, rather than seeking to respond to real labor concerns, it sought instead to explode the system's internal contradictions.

This serves to remind us of the central role played by intellectuals in the terrorist phenomenon. There cannot be leftist extremist terrorism without a weakening, decline, or overinstitutionalization of the social movement that serves as its focus. Nor can it exist without that specific group of agents who elevate violence to a political level and who insure its ideological processing, in this case in a Marxist-Leninist mode.

What was peculiar to the Italian and a number of other phenomena was that they downgraded classic Marxism-Leninism to the point of dissociating the very thing that ideology associates; to wit, an actual reference to a social figure, and the identification of its vanguard with the consciousness of that figure.

When Marxism-Leninism becomes transformed into a terrorist ideology, it loses its capacity to serve as a steward of violence. It is no longer able to make a tool of violence, nor can it guide the hand (through the party) of the person who holds that tool, to effect a historical reversal in which the masses must also play a pivotal role. It deserts every one of its social reference groups, believes itself capable of acting without or even over and against the workers (or, in other contexts, the peasants), and catapults itself into activities in which all that really matters is a head-on military confrontation with state power. This transformation of Marxism-Leninism into a pure and aggravated form of Leninism, this abandonment of or disinterest in the social movement with which one had previously claimed kinship, can only be possible if that movement has itself been weakened, institutionalized, or dismantled. It has for its counterpart an overwhelming subjectivism which transforms the militant into the central revolutionary actor, the world historical individual par excellence. This gives rise to yet another paradox since there arises, out of this subjectivism, a kind of anarchism—present in Germany in the Second of June movement, in France in Action Directe, and in Italy in the libertarian facets of autonomia—which connects back up with the destructured Leninism which had provided radical leftist terrorism with its theoretical base.

# Part Three

## NATION, CLASS, AND REVOLUTION:
## THE BASQUE PHENOMENON OF ETA

On a planetary scale, the southern Basque country (Euskadi) is a tiny region of little interest to anyone who thinks in geopolitical terms.[1] Furthermore, the collective violence that has been deployed there is proportionately small if we compare it with other contemporary examples. ETA (Euskadi Ta Askatasuna—Basque Fatherland and Liberty) activism is nonetheless worthy of careful examination. If for no other reason, this is so because it answers a great and venerable question that has plagued thinkers, particularly Marxist ones, for a great many years.[2] Since the nineteenth century, a great number of actors and intellectuals have sought to formulate and promote resistance struggles capable of freeing, in a single movement, a dependent nation and an oppressed social class. ETA tells us that there exists a concrete path for revolutionary nationalism to follow: this is the path of armed struggle.

The question posed by armed resistance groups who claim to be fighting in the name of revolutionary nationalism is easier to formulate than it is to answer. For does revolutionary nationalism not find its necessary—due to a given historical situation—conditions in the most extreme forms of violence imaginable, a violence that therefore extends into terrorism? Or is it more accurate to say, on the contrary, that the most profound meanings of revolutionary nationalism are subverted, perverted, and inverted as soon as groups who claim to be fighting in its name sink into terrorism? This is the essential problem to be resolved by an analysis of the kind of action ETA practices. This case is all the more interesting for the fact that the answer is not an obvious one. In many respects, ETA appears to be caught up in an inversion process and a cycle of indiscriminate violence, as witnessed for example by the attack on a Barcelona supermarket in June 1987. But in other respects, ETA enjoys broad-based grassroots support, and a following and legitimacy of such an order as to prohibit us from speaking of it in terms of a purely terrorist rationale. Should we qualify ETA as a manifestation of revolutionary nationalism, or rather as a terrorist group? Is it possible to link, in a single action, a social focus, a revolutionary vision, and a fight for national liberation, without sliding into acts of violence destined to issue, sooner or later, into terrorism? Such will be our basic question.

# 11

# A History of Armed Struggle in Southern Euskadi

## The Birth of ETA

The armed struggle in Euskadi is a recent phenomenon which began with a crisis in traditional Basque nationalism following the Second World War.

Nationalism appeared in the Basque country at the close of the nineteenth century, and continues to stand in the long shadow cast by its founding father, Sabino Arana. In the beginning, it was the corruption and decadence of Spain that he denounced, contrasting it with the purity of the Basque people. Arana was Catholic, antisocialist, and greatly preferred the past to the present, hearkening back to a mythic golden age in which Euskadi lived in perpetual peace and happiness, and developing an unshakable affection for the *fueros,* the original laws of the former Basque States. He was greatly worried by the advance of modern heavy industry, which was undermining traditional Basque society with its capitalist indifference to the national cause, and its immigrant workers—the *maketos* who, having come from Spain, were incapable of absorption into Basque culture, and who were inclined to subscribe to socialist doctrines.

At the end of the Second World War, the political voice of Basque nationalism, the Basque Nationalist party (PNV), was justified in considering that its time had come. The moving force behind the Basque government in exile, the PNV, which had remained faithful to Sabino Arana's doctrines even as it had sufficiently diversified itself to become an important popular party—of the order that would be called Christian Democrat today—was merely biding its time until the fall of the generalissimo, that friend to Nazi Germany and Fascist Italy. But in 1947, the

Cold War dashed all of its hopes. The United States, in building a network of alliances in which Franco's Spain was a key participant, quickly
placed great reliance on the dictator. It was out of this crisis that ETA
emerged.[1]

ETA began in 1952, in Bilbao, with the creation, by a group of nationalist students, of a bulletin entitled *Ekin* (Act), which denounced the
PNV's confessionalism and which, most importantly, called for action.
For these youth, the PNV's powerlessness was unacceptable in a time in
which unyielding repressive measures were stripping the party of nearly
all of its ranks within the Basque territory. They also found the same
PNV to be too accommodating to a regime that was prohibiting strikes
as it backed an economic order that favored an industrialist middle class
which was losing its Basque patriotism.[2] They had the feeling that the
PNV had become antiquated, and that it was limiting itself to forms of
action that ignored the contemporary situation in Euskadi. Lastly, they
were finding it more and more difficult to accept a policy by which party
directives were being dictated from outside Basque territory, and thereby
rendering all domestic action heteronomous.

Several *Ekin* groups appeared in Vizcaya and Guipuzcoa, and fused
with other youth groups that had themselves left the PNV. In 1959, their
differences with the PNV and its youth organization were so pronounced
that they decided to form ETA.[3]

In its early years, ETA remained close in its ideology to traditional
nationalism, to the point of borrowing its doctrine. It was only when it
sought to put a halt to all racism, by rejecting confessionalism, that it
began to distance itself from the party. At the same time, it maintained
that the time had come to set about the practical building of the nation,
which had ceased to be an entity or an essence and which had become,
for them, a will, a becoming. This they effected, above all else, by teaching the greatly endangered Basque language to children and adults alike.

Beyond these changes, the ETA split was also bound up in the group's
discovery of the labor movement. Traditional nationalism, actuated by
a lower middle and middle middle class concerned with maintaining
social order without conflict, was opposed to socialism and indifferent
or hostile to labor action. In the early 1960s, ETA's early pioneers realized that the only resistance and the only agitation going on within
Euskadi itself was coming out of the world of labor. This was because
the Basque country was a highly developed industrial society that was
presently going through a great industrial boom, the second in its history.
The great strikes of 1962, which first broke out in Asturias, were fol-

lowed on a massive scale in Vizcaya and Guipuzcoa. These strikes, which underscored the amorphous nature of the PNV and its inability to act spontaneously, gave rise to thought. ETA began to take up positions that pointed it in the direction of an estrangement from two of the pillars of traditional Basque nationalism. These were the "Españolist" oligarchy that made up the upper middle class, as well as the patriotic (abertzale) middle and lower middle classes whose patriotism went hand-in-hand with practices that were exploitive of the proletariat. Thenceforth, ETA developed a course of action that was open towards a working class that was itself made up, to a great extent, of immigrants. These would no longer be excluded or ignored, but would rather be brought into the Basque struggle. In the eyes of ETA, the proletariat became the undisputed protagonist in its combat.

Simultaneously, ETA was tending towards a Marxist line that was greatly influenced by nationalist and revolutionary incidents that had shaken the entire world. Fidel Castro, the Algerian FLN, followed by Ho Chi Minh and Mao Tse-tung and still later Che Guevara, came to be figures of reference about whom a great number of young Basques had the greatest awareness, especially when their studies took them to French or Belgian universities. The *ETA Notebooks* and the news sheet *Zutik,* distributed clandestinely, secured the spread of Marxist, Leninist, and revolutionary ideas, which completed ETA's spectacular overturning of traditional nationalism. Its followers discovered Marx, historical materialism, and the critique of political economy. They analyzed the works of Lenin, and the thoughts of Chairman Mao, and appropriated for themselves an anti-imperialist and revolutionary terminology, bandying about the notions of the popular class and the worker's nation. Before long, they had embraced the principle of armed struggle. In less than three years, ETA had become an organization capable of maintaining a simultaneous discourse on the nation, the working class, and the revolution.

## Early Action, Early Schisms

In 1959 and 1960, ETA's activities were basically limited to a few pieces of graffiti that proclaimed "Gora Euskadi" (Long Live Euskadi). By 1962, however, this armed resistance organization, at odds once again with the policies of traditional Basque nationalism, had become a power to be reckoned with, and an indispensable weapon to be wielded against the violence of the dictatorship.

For several years, however, perhaps simply due to a lack of supplies,

ETA activities were only minimally violent, the group's main task being the clandestine framing of an ideology, in the course of which dissension over divergent viewpoints, concerning both political and tactical matters, was not rare.[4] The concept of revolutionary war introduced by Krutwig in 1962, which embraced guerrilla tactics of the order of those practiced by the Algerian FLN, was replaced, in the ETA's Fourth Assembly, by the theory of the activism-repression-activism syndrome. This doctrine suggested that a cycle could be set in motion in which every action would generate a repressive reaction, which would in turn give rise to an even more revolutionary course of action, itself followed by even greater repression, and so on. Already at this time, there came the first clash, within the ETA, between the two poles the organization had sought to unify. In the one camp were adherents to a leftist and Marxist line, more or less labor-oriented, who stressed a sociopolitical focus. On the other side were the Third-Worlders, who placed a greater emphasis on the nationalist character of their action. The latter group accused the former of españolism, while the latter were themselves sometimes treated as "culturalists" by the former.

The Fifth Assembly, convened in December 1966 on Basque territory, constituted a fundamental turning point in ETA history. First of all, it was at this meeting that the organization threw out its "Felipe" (another pejorative term for "españolist") contingent. These Marxists, hostile to armed insurgency, would go through Trotskyist and Maoist phases before forming the Spanish Communist movement. It was also in the course of this assembly's second session, in March 1967, that the organizational model of "four fronts"—military, cultural, political, and economic (which would later become a labor front)—was consolidated. This model was itself subordinated to a more ambitious plan for a Basque national front, that would unite the Basque proletariat, peasantry, and middle classes, in a common struggle for freedom. The middle class would later be deleted from this plan. A strategy was put together, according to which acts of violence would be directed against highly symbolic targets, and would be used to secure the organization basic material needs. This plan was quickly implemented in the form of bomb attacks on various premises closely linked to the regime, holdups, and nails thrown onto the streets during the Vuelta (the annual Spanish touring cycle race). Most important was the assassination, on August 2, 1968, of Meliton Manzanas—the police chief of Irún, notorious for his acts of torture—for which ETA claimed responsibility. This was the first killing planned and carried out by ETA. Shortly thereafter, Txabi Echebarrieta, an important leader in the organization, was killed, reportedly by the Civil Guards during a police check, and another militant, Iñaki Sarasketa, arrested and given a very heavy sentence. Firsthand statements by persons who took part in the decision to kill Manzanas confirmed for us that the decision was only taken after a debate over the ethics of such an action. It was a mature decision taken after much thought, and in no way signaled an entry into a broader campaign of killing.

The years 1968 and 1969 were marked by another incident, concerning ETA's military wing, which is most often referred to by the cover name of its instigator, "El Cabra." This individual (whose real name was Zumalda), a military leader in the organization, had resigned together with thirty or so other militants to mark his disagreement with the "españoliste" line that had dominated prior to the Fifth Assembly. The *cabras*, whose odyssey has been traced in an anonymous work,[5] were in fact hard-and-fast nationalists who, cut off from ETA, survived for over two years before disappearing under the onslaughts of a repression that had hardened after the elimination of Manzanas.

From a military standpoint, the cabras spent much more time drilling than they ever did fighting. What is essential here is that we see their grounds for splitting off from ETA. Their decision, based on a purely military rationale, was grounded in a patriotic nationalism which was entirely divorced from the sociopolitical dimensions of the Basque movement.

Here, we may already glimpse what would become a constant feature of the many schisms that have punctuated ETA's existence. When a faction—like the "Felipes" who were thrown out of the Fifth Assembly—isolates itself on the grounds of class, they do so on the basis of a rejection of the recourse to armed resistance. When, as was the case with the cabras, a rift cuts off a nationalist faction, it becomes the occasion for this group to take up a policy of rapid militarization, even if that faction cannot last.

## Armed Insurgency, Nation, and Revolution

Manzanas's assassination brought about an immediate reinforcement of the machinery of repression, facilitated by new legislative measures. Not only would ETA activism be thenceforward identified with banditry, but anyone who demonstrated, assembled, took part in strike actions or work stoppages, or who upset the "public order," could be indicted for "military insurgency." Arrests were carried out by the hundreds, with broad segments of the Basque population subjected to torture, summary trial procedures, and imprisonment. This considerably weakened the entire ETA structure, with many of its ranks being arrested, and most of the rest being driven into exile.

This was nevertheless a period during which the rapprochement between ETA and the labor movement became concretized, most especially on the occasion of the Vizcaya strikes, in February and March of 1969. This was also the time in which powerful tensions arose within the organization, wherein the practice of armed insurgency was a major cause of contention.

On one side were the Marxists who, especially when they were in exile, were worried by the great emphasis placed on nationalism in the group's armed struggle. On the other were nationalist patriots for whom Euskadi was a colony, and who subscribed to a platform that gave priority to military action. Straddling these two viewpoints was a group of militants who attempted to hold the middle ground.

Throughout 1968 and 1969, the ETA leadership continued to hesitate and vacillate between these two ideological extremes. In August 1970, its Sixth Assembly was convened.

The inner turmoil was of such an order that the organization became split into two blocs.[6] The first of these, which constituted the great majority, was composed of those militants who had called for the meeting in the first place: these would be called ETA-6. The second, in the minority, were those whose intention it was to remain loyal to the principles of the previous assembly: these were ETA-5. The former favored a revolutionary course of action, and therefore the theme of class warfare, while the latter supported the priority given to the independence struggle. It has been this rift, which appears to divide the two components of its action, that ETA has constantly striven to close up. One has the impression that there have been two forms of collective action in Euskadi, each of which has tried to carry out its agenda independent of the other. The first, nationalist, is spearheaded by ETA-5, while the second, revolutionary and intent on maintaining solidarity with related resistance movements throughout the rest of Spain, is backed by ETA-6.

In the minority at the time of the split, ETA-5 maintained its links with the past history of the movement, and in the long run emerged victorious over ETA-6. The latter, having taken up a revolutionary stance, exhausted itself in ideological conflicts with other leftist groups. In 1972, it fell apart entirely. While there had been far more revolutionary ETA-6 militants than there had been adherents to ETA-5, it was this latter group which, although greatly diminished, managed to rehabilitate itself.

It must be said that, however fragmented and marginal ETA may have remained until the end of the 1960s, it had nonetheless become the symbolic core of the various and sundry Basque protest movements in their common struggle against Franco's oppression. In the words of Letamendia, the Basque prisoners claiming adherence to ETA were beginning "to lend a political character to trials which invariably ended in guilty verdicts: the accused became the accusers,"[7] with popular support for them being voiced on a massive scale. The Burgos trial,[8] in which six of the accused were sentenced to death, and ten others given very heavy prison terms, brought ETA to international attention. Moreover, the strikes and demonstrations carried out in its support proved that there existed an impressive popular opposition, which identified itself with the armed resistance organization. The central powers, which eventually caved in to the combined pressure of Basques and Spaniards at a popular level and public outcry on an international level, reduced the death sentences to prison terms. This clemency was, moreover, an indication that the regime was weakening.

ETA-5—which we will henceforth return to calling ETA—swiftly asserted itself as a socialist and revolutionary organization engaged in more than a mere struggle for national liberation. Its strategy was based upon a Leninist model, with the qualification that the people who rallied around the working class under the guidance of a revolutionary vanguard would here be defined in national terms: they were Basques.

Following 1971, ETA was able to translate into action its capacity to simultaneously express the two sets of ideals which the ETA-5/ETA-6 split had pried apart. On January 17 of that year, a commando kidnapped Zabala, an industrialist whose factory had been striking over wages. In this case, the protest movement had taken a spectacular turn: thirteen employee representatives had taken up a hunger strike. The ETA commando holding Zabala immediately made known the conditions for his release: the rehiring, without sanctions, of all workers, wage increases, etc. A few days later, the firm's executives gave into nearly all of their conditions, and Zabala was set free. In the words of Letamendia, "the target had been carefully chosen. Zabala was a Basque owner, who spoke the Euskadi language. Therefore, there was no way that ETA could be accused of collaborating with the Basque middle class."[9] By 1971–72, ETA was being perceived by Basque public opinion as an organizing base for its growing social, national, and political struggle.

## The Labor Front and the Military Front

Prior to this time, the opposition between the revolutionary struggle and the fight for national liberation had provoked discussion and internal tensions on what had essentially been an ideological level. By now, however, ETA's following in Euskadi had grown very large. This being the case, the group sought to actively enter the field of social agitation while broadening its military action, thereby widely expanding the arena of both forms of activism. At this point, the problem of unifying into a meaningful whole the various meanings of their actions was now being shunted to another level and formulated in new terms. The question of the ideological and political opposition between, or the complementarity of, national resistance and sociopolitical action had become one of the organizational and practical relationship obtaining between the grassroots struggle and the armed struggle.

A "preparatory meeting" held in October 1972 was primarily devoted to problems posed by the organization's structure. There had been powerful tensions between its two major "fronts," each of which considered its role to have greater priority than the other. ETA's successes had attracted many young people into its fold, with their numbers generally swelling the ranks of the "militarists." At the same time, the labor-front militants were troubled by an increase in armed actions, which were undermining their industrial actions in the factories, and running counter to the development of a grassroots movement in the field.

In theory, the labor front, following October 1972, was strongly represented in the high-level ETA decision-making process. It was, however, the militarists who in fact controlled the organization. In spite of the significant tensions that remained, one has the image of 1972–73 as a period of relative stability rooted in a balance of power between its militarist and grassroots actions. ETA was able to function on a wide variety of levels, and its record for this period was both impressive and indicative of its mastery in placing its shots in directions which corresponded to the organization's varied agendas. These ranged from support for workers to bombings of headquarters of corporatist unions working in the service of the regime, and attacks on offices (tourist bureaus, for example) whose existence symbolized the political presence of the dictatorship, the Basque country's dependent status, etc. A number of major events pushed the organization's internal tensions into the background. The first of these was the kidnapping of Felipe Huarte, an industrialist member of the oligarchy, who was later released in exchange for

a high ransom and the fulfillment of demands imposed by workers striking at one of his firms. Next, and of even greater consequence, was the
execution, on November 20, 1973, of Admiral and Prime Minister Luis
Carrero Blanco, by the Ogro commando.[10]

Democrats and revolutionaries, freedom-fighters and autonomists, adherents of all manner of social and political causes—who was there that
did not applaud the brilliant coup in which Franco's heir apparent was
liquidated? Activist violence, efficiently directed against a variety of targets, could serve to unify people in a wide array of situations.

But this newfound unity would prove unstable. In 1974, a new split,
reminiscent of the departure of the "españolistes" in 1967 and the
ETA-5/ETA-6 schism of 1970, was provoked by the departure of the
labor front which, while it did not abandon the principle of armed struggle, at least halted its support of practices liable to stand in the way of
their social actions.

## The Military Wing and the Political-Military Front

Those who remained within ETA were faced with a choice between
two opposing views. This time, their opposition was not over the basic
principles of their action, nor did it result—at least in direct fashion—in
a rift between the nationalist and sociopolitical dimensions of the movement. Nor did these divergent views set up an opposition between an
armed insurgency that was most closely allied with nationalism, and a
grassroots struggle more concerned with a social and revolutionary
agenda. Here, the problem was posed on a practical level, and within a
common theoretical framework. In spite of this, the two blocs began to
move apart. The problem was one of discovering a way, in the new
political landscape, to coordinate grassroots agitation with armed insurgency.

One bloc was a minority composed of persons who maintained that
it was out of the question for a single organization to coordinate both
military and grassroots forms of activism. In their eyes, the two had to
be separated. The immediate consequence of this approach was the takeover of this group by its militants. Concentrating their efforts on establishing a strictly military structure, they would become the military ETA,
the Military Wing or ETA-M.

The other bloc was a much larger group which felt that the new
political situation justified an apportioning of its action, on the condition
that both of its components be administered by a single leadership group.
The crisis in the ruling regime was opening up possibilities for a more

active grassroots campaign. Therefore, there was no reason for the organization to abandon its social agitation. This group, which would constitute the political faction within the Political-Military Front of ETA (ETA-PM) considered it indispensable that the organization continue the armed struggle, in the face of the general climate of violence that oppressed the Basque people.

Both sides of this split, between the Military Wing and the Political-Military Front, were acutely aware of the new social and political situation. The labor movement, which was becoming increasingly broad-based and powerful, stood out clearly as the pivotal social actor, and provided the Basque movement with a great mobilization potential. Spain, including Euskadi, was no longer the isolated citadel it had been throughout the 1940s and 1950s. It had opened up, and was now within earshot and in touch with the cultural and social changes that were rippling across the whole of the Western world. The regime, like El Caudillo—whose succession had been more than compromised by the death of Carrero Blanco—had grown old. No one could seriously foresee the changes that would come, but all were caught up in the feeling that they were at a historical turning point, of which a key feature would be the opening of political institutions which had theretofore been kept under lock and key by the government.

The ETA's Military Wing chose to place its emphasis on the necessary separation between social agitation and military action. In other words, it expected less out of the former than it did from the latter, whose policies were, as we know, basically dictated by an independentist agenda. The Political-Military Front of ETA wished to exploit the prevailing sociopolitical climate, and make the most of new opportunities without having to give up the armed struggle. History would quickly show that the Military Wing's agenda was the sole agenda to maintain an unshakable opposition to the Spanish state, and to bar all forms of intermediate compromise—that of limited autonomy, for example. This allowed it, in the best of times, to define its strategy according to its own rhythm, as opposed to that of those other political and social entities that were also leaning towards a break with Spain.

In contrast, the Political-Military Front's agenda theoretically allowed it to juggle the two constituent parts of its insurgency in response to changes in the prevailing situation. As such, it could toughen and step up its military operations when there appeared to be less room for political maneuvering or, on the contrary, announce a truce and even the cessation of armed resistance when the situation favored democracy and the opening of the institutional system. The Political-Military Front, even if it had no intention whatsoever of laying down its arms, had nonetheless provided itself with the theoretical means to do so.

## Problems within the Political-Military Front

In seeking to link together political struggle and armed struggle, was the Political-Military Front not in the process of becoming a party? This was an idea that began to take shape in 1975, most especially in the form of positions taken by one of its principal leaders and ideologues, Pertur, who foresaw the formation of a party that could at once be communist and "abertzale."

At the same time, the Political-Military Front was building up its military wing, the *bereziak* commandos (special commandos), who would take charge of broad-based operations whenever they extended beyond the responsibilities of the leader of a given zone. In the final months of the Franco regime, the Political-Military Front's strategy had become one of exerting military pressure as a means to toppling the regime once and for all and of encouraging and developing social and political resistance groups.[11] Its militants took part in the formation of organizations whose role it was to mobilize these groups, of which the most important was that of the revolutionary Basque Labor Association (LAB) trade union.

Paradoxically, 1975 would be a terrible year for the Political-Military Front of ETA. In spite of the fact that the Franco regime—continued repression notwithstanding—was collapsing, those who had committed themselves to a strategy that was fine-tuned to changes in the political scene were paying dearly for their line of action. First of all, the police—especially following the nomination of Minister Arias who "ran the government as if it were a gigantic police station"—had never before been so active and efficient as they were now.[12] Secondly, the Political-Military Front's internal liason between its political and military operations made the police repression a much simpler task, enabling the police to easily work their way up its chain of command. This was combined with field-based militantism that often blew the cover on the organization, up to its highest echelons.[13] The Political-Military Front was nearly entirely dismantled in the space of a few months, with many of its leaders falling into the hands of the police when they were not killed outright in armed confrontations. Most of Pertur's friends were taken and the organization weakened, with those who came to replace those who had been lost being less and less trained politically, increasingly frustrated, and more and more interested in military activism than in political militancy.

At the time of the dictator's death in November 1975, ETA's Political-Military Front was in the grip of massive internal problems. Five hundred of its militants had been jailed and an even higher number had taken refuge "on the other side," in the northern Basque country, under extremely difficult living conditions. Only one of their military commandos was still operational. The upcoming generation had not been able to absorb the political and ideological experience of the preceding generation, and the leadership was itself in crisis because nearly all of its members had either been arrested or killed.

## The Death of Pertur

For a brief moment in its history, ETA had appeared to be the voice of an all-Basque movement. The first indication that it was impracticable emerged out of an inner conflict. For the first time in the history of this organization—whose image was as of yet largely untarnished—tensions within ETA itself resulted not merely in exclusion or schism, but in the physical liquidation of one of its leaders.

In the spring of 1976, the first spring of the post-Franco era, the Political-Military Front ETA found itself unable to control the insuperable tensions that its own orientations, in that period of opportunity, were generating. While the program to link political activism with armed struggle was an ideological one, it nevertheless turned against the organization. This it first did by rendering it vulnerable to police repression, and later by quickening opposition between the political faction, which was increasingly intent on being in the vanguard of all Basque resistance movements, and the military faction, which was becoming increasingly adamant in refusing all attempts to supervise its activities. The politico-military strategy of this front had reversed the poles of its action, and the dream of an organization that could combine these two approaches was fast becoming a nightmare. Thenceforward, the two factions of the Political-Military Front would be locked in conflict. Beyond their talk of independence and revolution, the first of these groups, dominated by the "berezis," were proving by their acts that only those who toted weapons could call the shots. The other group, within which Pertur would play a dramatic role, held to the principle of a necessary separation between the two approaches, and favored seeking a political way out of the organizational crisis. Pertur, after having taken part in the work of the preparatory meeting, was given the green light to reflect on the theme around which the coming assembly would be convened, and thereby to think through the relationship between armed action and grassroots agitation in the new context that had emerged out of the fall of the dictatorship. Together with a couple of close friends, he went into isolation, devoting the weeks following the preparatory meeting to the construction of a platform that would in fact constitute his political will and testament.

Pertur's overriding desire was to find a way by which political action could continue without having to sacrifice the use of weapons to which, as he never tired of saying, the Basque movement was so indebted. It pained him to see the appearance of machinations, within ETA itself, that were causing the split between its political and military factions to be accompanied by the escalation of a terrorist syndrome. He quite rightly felt himself threatened by this escalation, in which a weapons-based approach was beginning to rage out of control. Every day, he saw how the militants of a just cause, the mighty arm of a popular rage long suppressed by the dictatorship, were becoming more and more a collection of cynical individuals, increasingly superficial in their political considerations, and more and more psychopathic—his very term.

Surely the most poignant of the propositions he drew up just before his passing was that in which he addresses the specific necessity, on the part of the militants, of maintaining their mental equilibrium. In guarded words, he described the very life of the militant-turned-soldier and the pathological transformations, both physical and psychological, that come to affect him. His statements are nearly premonitory in their nature: "We cannot allow the functioning of the organization to be affected by personal crises in the lives of its militants . . . History shows that numerous deviations, especially those linked to the quest for and abuses of power, are directly linked to psychological imbalances, if not to what are more clearly neuroses, paranoid states, or other mental illnesses." With this, he suggests that they arise not only out of individual psychological traits, but also out of increased levels of militarization.[14]

Pertur therefore did not desert his organization. To the very last, he strove to bring together and unify all that had been torn apart by the inner turmoil, and all that was polarizing ETA around two approaches which had become so wildly antagonistic. His efforts blew up in his face. On July 23, 1976, even before his platform had been discussed within ETA, Pertur was ambushed and disappeared—for good—most probably eliminated by his own people.

So ended Pertur's trajectory of militancy. Heretofore, ETA had given the impression of being an organization capable of controlling itself. The turning point, brought on by the post-Franco climate of openness, unleashed a process which placed at loggerheads a majority who wished to return to the institutionalized political scene, and a highly militarized minority. The murder of one of the Basque movement's most visible leaders constituted the apogee of this process. Following this incident, the "berezis" would take to the field, cutting themselves off entirely from the Political-Military Front before joining ranks once more with ETA's Military Wing. The others, the great majority of the Political-Military Front, followed the trail blazed by Pertur. They created a party, the Euskal Iraultzale Alderdia (EIA, the Basque Revolutionary party), out of which would later emerge the Euskadiko Eskera (EE), which remained linked to ETA-PM until 1981. This latter group, at EE's request, declared a truce of indefinite duration; and a press conference at which the *septimos* appeared with their faces unmasked marked the end of the ETA-PM of the Seventh Assembly. There next appeared the *octavos* (PM 8) who decided to continue the armed struggle. Most of these joined ETA-M, with a few remaining isolated.

## The Political Explosion of the Post-Franco Era

With the death of El Caudillo—who was as late as September 1975 still signing death sentences that would result in the execution, among others, of the ETA militants Txiki and Otaegi—came the disappearance of a regime which alone defined, by limiting them, the conditions of expression of Spain's social movements. As a result, the action network in Euskadi, starting with the institutionalized political system, became considerably transformed after November 1975. The constitutional monarchy that had been set up consolidated itself with the voting of a constitution by the Parliament on December 29, 1978. In Euskadi, the period often called the years of transition (1976–77) were the occasion for a veritable political explosion. In 1977, the "abertzale" left was torn apart over the question of whether or not it should participate in the upcoming elections, and whether ETA should run its own candidates while many of its number were still being held in prison.

The elections of June 15, 1977, followed by those of March 1, 1979, permitted a wide array of political parties to express themselves freely. The PNV won 26.9 percent of the vote in the 1979 elections, with 14.8 percent going to the Herri Batasuna (HB), which represented the "separatist" electorate. Euskadiko Eskera, an electoral coalition dominated by persons who had given up the armed struggle even as they maintained their "abertzale" or leftist leanings, mustered 7.8 percent of the vote. Thus the specifically Basque political forces represented nearly 50 percent of the vote, with the remainder going to Spanish parties.[15] The 1978 constitution was supported by a great majority of the Euskadi voters, albeit with a high rate of abstention attributable to the positions taken by EE and HB, as well as the PNV.[16]

Prior to the transition to democracy, the PNV, whose leaders often felt themselves to be fathers of sorts to the activists, had given broad if discreet support to ETA, which they greatly esteemed even if they disagreed with its methods. Following 1977, this partnership came to an end, painfully and often in an ambivalent manner. It is impossible for a father to denounce his children; moreover, armed insurgency may have served as a trump card for the PNV in its political dealings with Madrid. Even in the hands of others, the armed struggle was a tool of some considerable efficaciousness; and it is for this reason that the PNV continues to be accused, even down to the present day, of using this tool to its own ends, and of supporting ETA.

Conversely, the PNV was just as often branded as being autonomist in its leanings. The independentists saw it as a "decaffeinated" actor, and saw its growing hostility towards the armed struggle as but a sign of its disaffection with the sole objective a nationalist organization ought rightly to have—the attainment of statehood. In fact, the more the armed struggle tailed off into what many considered to be terrorism, the more the PNV, well ensconced in the political system yet perceived as controlling an autonomous political power of some significance, had to work to break its ties with ETA, if not to oppose the group.

Euskadiko Eskera (EE) was born out of a desire both to maintain a revolutionary and nationalist activism and to move away (in 1980 and 1981 at least) from armed insurgency, which its founders judged to be incompatible with Spain's democratic future. Numbered among the members of EE were some of the most prestigious of the former ETA militants and leaders; people like Mario Onaindia, one of the persons who had been sentenced to death in the Burgos trial. A medium-sized group, EE would be closely aligned with the PNV in its nationalist agenda, considering the granting, in 1979, of limited autonomy to be a step towards independence. It was, however, at odds with the party on social matters, considering itself as it did to be a labor vanguard opposed to the middle class, for which the PNV constituted, in its eyes, the political voice in Euskadi. Ideologically fragile, it brought together a rather heterogeneous radical left, a blend of partisans of Eurocommunism and persons in favor of self-determination, as well as a number of variant forms of leftist politics that had been on the decline since 1977.

HB was lastly an aggregate of several lesser revolutionary and independentist parties. But above all else, it constituted a political forum for all persons who, for either social or political reasons, maintained a desire for radical disengagement from the much-hated political institutions, which they considered to be undemocratic. HB, even though it fielded candidates in the elections, refused to seat them, even when they had won seats there, in either the Spanish or the Basque parliaments. With the exception of Navarra, it never attended a single one of the Basque *disputaciones* (general councils). On the other hand, it was highly active on a local level and could count in its ranks a number of elected officials who participated, in this case, in the municipal government of cities and villages.

A number of other political entities, whose sphere of action was Spanish, may also be added to these Basque groups. By far, the most influential of these in Euskadi was the Spanish Socialist Labor party (PSOE), however ill at ease it may have been in the Basque context. While this party's electoral constituency was generally leftist, it also supported, to a certain extent, a Spanish centralism to which many Basques were hostile.

There now existed in Euskadi an open political system, in which violence could no longer unite political aspirations which—while they had, under the dictatorship, been united by oppression and repression—were now vying with one another for power. Revolutionaries, democrats, independentists, and autonomists were now at odds with one another, and if armed struggle would thenceforth become a necessity and a positive cause for some, it would be a bane for others.

## The New Face of Nationalism

Basque nationalism was also becoming factionalized. The 1979 statute, by affording the Basque country a significant level of autonomy, split what had previously been a unified group into two camps.[17] In the one camp were those who accepted the statute and who were willing to play along and attempt to administer the new powers, including the right to a Basque government, parliament, media (television and radio in Basque), police force (of limited jurisdiction), etc. that had been granted to Euskadi. In the other were those persons who would accept nothing short of total independence, and who saw autonomy as a dangerous Trojan horse. There were also those who felt that autonomy was a strategic tool that could be integrated into the Basque strategy, and serve as a means rather than an end. Everyone claimed to be nationalist, and everyone wanted a sovereign Basque state. Some, however, placed this requirement before all others, feeling it to be most urgent, whereas others rejected the use of nondemocratic methods towards the realization of their goal, and refused to remain a part of the armed struggle.

Under the dictatorship, cultural nationalism and independentism could appear to constitute one and the same cause; but now they would split apart, as they did in the case of the major issue of the Basque language, Euskera.

Thanks mainly to the *ikastoles*—schools in which teaching was conducted in Euskera—the Basque language had been able to hold out against forty years of a dictatorship hostile to its use. The original ETA leaders and ideologues, people like Txillardegi, Madarriaga, and Krutwig, had placed a primary emphasis upon the speaking of Basque; promoting and defending Euskera was for them part of the same struggle as acting towards national independence.

After 1979, however, it became possible in Euskadi to implement a program of cultural activism and interpret it in independentist terms; or, on the contrary, to see such as falling within an institutional framework. As such, there began a process of dissociation. The campaign for the promotion of the Basque language, now wholly legal, became primarily a forum in which the major political organizations faced off with one another, in the form of associations possessed of their own platforms and aspirations. Great amounts of resources—even if such were judged insufficient by the "separatists"—were available to all who wished to educate their children in the Basque medium. Euskera was neither the sole nor compulsory language, and it was becoming increasingly clear that language—which should have been at the heart of Basque activism, and which defined the Basque identity in the eyes of many—was not being perceived by all concerned as a requirement; and that it could even become a hindrance to progress, or an element of injustice. Children sent by their parents to be schooled in the ikastoles complained that they could see no good reason for the extra work involved in learning a second language. Many were those who learned Basque as adults in order to gain access to public-sector jobs that were closed to non-Euskera speakers. Language was becoming a condition for finding work, if not an occasional means to upward social mobility.

Even though democrats and autonomists alike committed significant resources to the protection of the Basque language, those who noted a relative disinterest in the language (which no longer had to resist repression but which could simply grow of its own accord) linked the popular lack of will in this sphere with the autonomist cause, which for them epitomized all that ran contrary to independence. In the eyes of the separatists, language could only live and take hold if there existed a strong and independent state, which could even go so far as to make monolingualism compulsory. In the meantime, it was appropriate that it be used as a symbolic cause in the independence struggle and mobilization, at the same time as an instrument for liberation, a means by which to denounce Spain's linguistic imperialism and to legitimate nationalist action. In the mid-1980s, there was a divergence of views on the question of Euskera, which centered around two major poles. In the one camp were the autonomists, for whom cultural progress was linked to the transfer of power projected by the 1979 statute and the establishment of institutionalized changes. In the other were the independentists, for whom language was, through the struggles it inspired, both an end and a means.

## The Decline of the Labor Movement and the New Social Movements

After the mid-1970s, social resistance movements were possessed of two major features. The first of these was a strong labor influx, followed by a collapse of the labor movement; the second was the rise of such new social movements as the antinuclear cause, which would also collapse in the space of a few years.

Down to the late 1960s, the most active sectors of trade unionism in Euskadi were monopolized by labor commissions closely linked to the Communist party. Even before the death of Franco, labor protests were becoming increasingly frequent and exacting in their demands. Counteroffensive in nature, they resulted in a veritable wave of councilism, which often approached that of the Italian movement of the early 1970s. This "assemblyist" movement went much further than had the underground labor organizations out of which it issued. A grassroots activist movement, it gave the impression of great strength, and of a capacity to raise its insurgency to the level of a revolutionary process. The high point of the labor struggle, the assemblyists began to fall apart in 1976–77, with labor meetings becoming more like theaters for political manipulation than forums for the voicing of the working-class consciousness.

At the same time, there appeared a trade unionism which epitomized the two increasingly divided factions within the labor movement. The first of these, eschewing all revolutionary models, instead sought to par-

ticipate in the development of a political economics and to strike a balance between the labor and management viewpoints. The latter, more
defensive in nature than the expression of any constructive platform,
was more separatist than conciliatory in its tendencies. These two faces
of labor consciousness—the former organized by the Basque Socialist
Movement (ELA) and the General Union of Workers (UGT), and the
latter by the LAB—were greatly affected by the crisis that rocked
the labor movement in Euskadi and the entire Western world. With the
former institutions, we find a protest torn between its own increasing
corporatist tendencies, and its negotiations with a management waving
the specter of factory shutdowns and job losses. In the latter, we see a
separatist current which, revolutionary and seething with blue-collar
anger, was nevertheless incapable of mobilizing worried and defensive
workers, winning as it did only a small percentage (5–10 percent) of the
votes in union elections. Here too, we find ourselves in the presence of
the dislocation of all that Franco-era political conditions had brought
together.

The antinuclear protest in Euskadi took on the look of a powerful
movement, constituting as it did the sole case in world history of a
movement which succeeded in blocking an electronuclear project, and of
halting the construction of a nuclear power plant. Francis Jaureguiberry's
excellent analysis of this struggle clearly points to both its similarity with
its French homologue (studied by this author in 1978) and its specificity.[18] In 1972–73, with the announcement of four groundbreaking projects, later reduced to two (the Ea and Lemoniz nuclear complexes), resistance was at first localized and provoked by doubt and fear. Beginning
in 1976, this widened into a broad-based movement, attacking the cold-
blooded nature of the central government's decision, the absence of democratic procedures, and the technocratic omnipotence of Iberduero SA,
the Spanish equivalent of the French EDF. As in France, this was complemented by a culture critique, spearheaded in the main by its most "ecological" components. Above all else, however, the antinuclear struggle
was a complex action, the proper implications of which were constantly
being absorbed—even if at the risk of being completely denatured—by
a nationalism that had itself been stimulated by the armed struggle.

In December 1977, after announcing its intent to respond to the "terrorism" of Iberduero SA, ETA carried out its first armed raid against the
Lemoniz power station. Many others would follow, of which the most
spectacular were the kidnapping and killing (as announced by ETA,
which had accorded Iberduero and the central government a week to

decide to give up the project) of Ryan, the head engineer of the Lemoniz plant in January 1981, and the assassination of Pascual, the Lemoniz project leader, in April 1982.

The impact of the antinuclear movement, especially in the development of a number of antinuclear committees, remained strong until 1981. In a number of other contexts—in France, Germany, and the United States, for example—such would have marked the birth of a new kind of actor, unique to a programmed society and fundamentally different from that of the labor movement. Weighted down by revolutionary and especially nationalist themes in Euskadi, resistance here became a job for ETA which, as Jaureguiberry clearly shows, left the social actor unhappily relegated to the sidelines. The movement, in its properly social and cultural dimensions, became undermined by a violence that stole away its own action and linked its ideals to practices that it itself had found questionable.

The feminist movement, even if it was not subjected to such trials, underwent a similar evolution. It also emerged in the mid-1970s, showed significant vitality into the early 1980s, and then fell apart, exhausted, not unlike its French and Italian counterparts. Outside of widely accepted currents of opinion, it only survived in scattered groups which, closed in on themselves, gave more the impression of an antimovement than of a social movement. Its trajectory was not, however, thrown off course or inverted by ETA intervention, as the antinuclear movement had been.

## Towards an Inversion Process?

Beginning in 1976, a two-pronged aggregate of conditions, which held the potential for triggering an inversion process, were present.

On the one hand, each of the activist movements' three major ideals was capable, in isolation, of facilitating the transition into a rationale of terrorist action. The political system had opened up and become diversified, making it impossible to target a single symbolic enemy in its resistance. Nationalism was being interpreted on two levels, rather than in a single unified way. The social struggles had become greatly weakened, if not destroyed—a primary condition, as we have seen, for an inversion process.

On the other hand, the pursuit of maintaining a single level of discourse and a unity of action with regard to these three causes was becoming an increasingly artificial one, if only because each of them referred to relatively different spheres, goals, and adversaries.

During the decade that followed, ETA would project a twofold image of itself: one of a geometrical increase in lethal, sometimes highly terrorist, actions; and one of an organization which, having recovered its balance, had managed to avoid the tailspin into which it might well have fallen. Following Pertur's death, it would not be until 1984—with the liquidation of Miquel Solaun, and again in 1986 with that of "Yoyès"—that this armed resistance organization would physically eliminate one of its active or former members.[19] On a broader level, the years of transition as well as those of an established Spanish democracy saw ETA functioning along the lines of a model that would undergo but few major modifications. As for the former Political-Military Front—the septimos (born out of the Seventh Assembly) and the octavos (born out of the Eighth Assembly)—most of its members returned to normal social and political lives. Only a few of their number—like the seventeen "milikis" who had rejected the social reinsertion accepted by the majority of the "octavos" in 1983—rejoined the Military Wing to provide ETA with technical know-how, especially in electronics.

Between 1976 and 1987, ETA was practically the sole group to occupy the field of armed struggle in Euskadi, and its relations with the autonomous commandos, of anticapitalist inspiration, were nonexistent or even conflictual—as was the case after the latter assassinated a business leader who had been paying the revolutionary tax levied by ETA.

The ideology of the ETA leadership, clearly presented in its KAS (Koordinadora Abertzale Sozialista) platform, consists of the following five points, which are accepted by several organizations: the amnesty and liberation of all Basque political prisoners; the legalization of independentist parties; the expulsion of Spanish state police and military forces from Euskadi territory; the improvement of living and working conditions for the lower classes; and an upgrading of the autonomous status of Euskadi, which was tantamount to independence in the very near future. The list of ETA armed actions, enumerated quite regularly in *Zuzen,* the ETA news bulletin, was impressive in these years: the killings of Spanish military personnel and "collaborators"; wide-scale sabotage, thefts, and holdups (designated in organization vocabulary as actions against the financial oligarchy); kidnappings; and the levying of the revolutionary tax. In each of these years, more than a hundred military operations were carried out, resulting in several dozen deaths. The armed struggle was never so deadly as in the years following the transition and the changeover to democracy in Spain. At the same time, ETA was being weakened by attacks from the Antiterrorist Liberation Group

(GAL),[20] by the effectiveness of the Spanish governmental repression and inflexibility, and by the spectacular reversal of French governmental policy between 1984 and 1986.

ETA now appears to have distanced itself from a pure rationale of terrorist action, and seems capable of controlling its members and of seeking an end to armed insurgency. At the same time, it does at times fall into an indiscriminate and truly terrorist violence.

# 12

## An Analysis of ETA Violence

In the historical reconstruction we presented in the last chapter, we were constantly brought back to two essential themes. The first of these is that it is ETA's apparent intention to speak in the name of three types of ideals: nationalist, political, and social. The second is that it is a difficult if not impossible task to unify these three orientations within a single movement.

### A Hypothesis on the Subject of ETA Violence

To say that ETA intended to embody the most elevated principles of protest action in Euskadi by no means implies the group succeeded in doing so. ETA has always seen itself as the symbolic and concrete steering organization for an ensemble of struggles which together make up an *all-Basque movement,* that is at once national, revolutionary, and social. This pivotal role is not one that can simply be taken for granted, and one may even say that it is mythic in nature. When reality does appear to correspond to the mythic image of an all-Basque movement, violence can be held in check and the self-regulating armed struggle can continue. When, however, the myth unravels and diverges from reality, it can only be maintained at the cost of an inversion process and an upsurge in terrorism.

We will begin by describing the three constituent parts of the myth of an all-Basque movement.

## The Struggle for Statehood

To borrow a term from Clifford Geertz,[1] it is through a *complex associa-tion* of powerful feelings, of both political and territorial scope, that there have emerged two distinct facets to nationalist struggle, the comple-mentarity of which can never be assumed.

On the one hand, it is a cultural affirmation, an expression of self-identity by a people who intend to preserve and promote their culture. Such an affirmation need not be conflictual and may even tend towards an interest in folklore, described and replenished in the form of schol-arly—and especially ethnographic—works on the subject of associa-tions, gourmet societies, *cuadrillas*, and other forms of communal life which the Franco dictatorship had been unable to uproot.[2] Traditional-ism, "machismo," industrial and often preindustrial values were the main features of a culture which served as a base for a solid framework of communal solidarity. Of essential importance here was the Basque language, Euskera. Through its ikastoles, schools in the Euskera medium, previously clandestine and greatly repressed but now legal and often aided by the autonomous institutions of the Basque government and mu-nicipalities, the Basque movement was able to educate broad segments of Basque youth in a language the Franco regime had sought to eradicate. This positive side of a nation—which now defined itself in terms of its culture—is inseparable from largely mythic references to a historical, or indeed a transhistorical or ethnic unity of the Basque people.

On the other hand, the primary demand of Basque nationalism is independence, and therefore a Basque state possessed of the attributes proper to every modern state (a law-and-order apparatus, an army, cur-rency, diplomatic corps, etc.). Since its goal is to extricate the country from the foreign rule that enslaves it, Basque nationalism has a belliger-ent relationship with Spain, which it considers to be an occupation force, in which nothing is negotiable, short of total independence. Just as Basque *cultural affirmation* seeks to defend a threatened national identity and to secure its continuity, so *independentist nationalism* champions radical disengagement and the formation of a state.

Historically, these two facets of nationalism did not emerge simulta-neously, and a complex dialectic relationship continues to obtain be-tween the two. The birth of ETA proceeded from a crisis in traditional nationalism, in which an agenda of cultural affirmation and an upsurge of independentist themes had been prevalent. The bonding together of these two nationalist components was not, moreover, immediate or self-evident. When the Franco dictatorship attacked the Basque nation on all fronts, the two facets could easily be combined, with the call for independence defining the political conditions necessary for the defense of Basque language and culture. All it took, however, was a change in the political situation for there to appear, under a democratic Spain, an ever-widening rift within autonomous Basque institutions between cultural practices—which were not merely tolerated, but were actually encouraged—and the independentist rhetoric of radical disengagement (even when the independentists themselves were promoting, albeit in a different spirit, actions of a cultural order).

## Social Protest Movements

Both in the Franco years and after Franco, social agitation was primarily the work of a labor movement whose demands were leveled against the social actor constituted by management, which had dominated society through its organization of labor in the factories. While the labor struggles were at their height from the late 1960s into the mid-1970s, their golden age covered but a short period of time, which extended from the fall of the Franco regime to the beginning of the economic crisis and recession, which began to make itself felt in 1977.

As a social action, the labor movement cannot be dissociated, in Euskadi, from the wide array of struggles that were shaping Spanish industrial society. From this standpoint, differences between the Basque country and other regions mainly concern the relative impact of the various constituent parts of this struggle. Between 1910 and 1940, the anarchist presence was hardly felt in Euskadi, whereas the UGT[3]—together with a Christian trade unionism that was itself sensitive to the paternalism of a portion of the Basque middle class—was highly influential. Starting in the 1950s, the UGT was on the decline, with the labor commissions linked to the Spanish Communist party predominating. These latter began to weaken considerably in the late 1960s, in tandem with an upsurge, on the part of rank-and-file workers, which took on a councilist form. The UGT would not reappear on the scene in any significant way until after Franco's death. The labor movement in Euskadi was, however, possessed of a number of unique features. These mainly took the form of its specifically Basque organizational structures, the Basque Socialist Movement (ELA) and the LAB. The ELA was originally a very moderate Basque labor union, composed of workers who, concerned with gaining access to consumer cooperatives, generally accepted the brand of paternalism backed by the PNV. It was not until the late 1960s that it underwent significant changes and became an organization comparable in its ideology to the French CFDT. The LAB, born in the 1970s, was more of a hard-line union, of a revolutionary stamp.

We thus find that while the organization of the labor struggle in southern Euskadi was tied into Spanish structures, mainly through the UGT and the labor commissions, it remained specifically Basque through the ELA and the LAB.

As we have seen, the field of social insurgency opened itself, in 1972, to the new social movements, of which the most important in Euskadi was, without a doubt, the antinuclear movement. The antinuclear and feminist movements in Euskadi exhibited exactly the same dual nature as did the labor movement. These were social movements whose sphere of operations was pan-Spanish, if not pan-European. At the same time, they were uniquely Basque, if only because their organizations emphasized their "Euskaldu" character to the point of making it their predominant theme.

### Political Action

In the case of the Basque movement—if we exclude from our analysis those currents which, although significant, were external or marginal to it—political action was organized along two axes, which the collapse of the dictatorship and the transition to democracy in Spain pried apart, to such an extent that they have remained antagonistic down to the present day.

On the one hand, we find the championing of the revolution and the establishment, through separatist actions, of a socialist state. This was a current that predominated through the 1960s and down to 1976 or 1977. Here, the references were Marxist-Leninist, within a broad spectrum of leftist ideologies, with the majority also resorting to a Third-Worldist rhetoric that described the Basque country in terms of domestic colonialism and imperialistic dependence. Also present, however, were a number of communistic and self-deterministic tendencies. On the other hand, there was the championing—which grew stronger with the political opening of Spain in 1975–77—of participation in the democratic system. For many, this had indeed been the goal of the entire struggle against the Franco regime.

To this distinction, between "revolutionaries" and "reformers" or "separatists" and "democrats," a second must be added, a distinction also defined in terms of the relationship to the Spanish state. The more strictly political positions, whether revolutionary or not, were drawn along class lines, the more they tended towards the properly Spanish arena of political conflict—whence the accusation of "españolism" wielded against those who had such an orientation. In contrast to these were those political platforms whose aim it was to build a Basque state or to administer the autonomous Basque institutions provided for in the 1979 autonomy statute—institutions that have been progressively set in place. Consequently, here too, we also run up against the dualism inherent to the Basque action which, while it has become involved in Spanish causes, both social and institutional, has also continued to operate on a specifically Basque level.

### The Myth of the Basque Movement

We have now set up an analytic model for the three facets of the Basque action. We have, however, sketched out this image without giving any detail on the formation or the composition of each of its facets, and without attempting to apply it to any particular moment in Basque history. The struggles that correspond to each of these facets arise out of different social and political situations. They designate adversaries who can only artificially be reduced to a single principle of opposition; they correspond to goals that have nothing in common with one another; and they mobilize their actors in the name of a self-image that varies from one facet to the next. One cannot take a practical synthesis between these facets for granted. Any composite image into which all might be decanted so as to form a single all-Basque movement thus runs the risk of being a mythic one. We may state, nonetheless, that there was a period in which these struggles appeared—more than at any other time—to converge, and that there was thus a historical juncture at which a unified action appeared capable of taking charge, of processing, and of unifying their divergent ideals with a minimum of contradictions. This juncture was that of the final breakdown of the Franco regime, at a moment in which the dictatorship still served as a common focus for the various protests that were inspiring Euskadi resistance. At the same time, the regime had been sufficiently weakened for each of these groups to realize a potential for true self-expression. The foundation of the all-Basque movement is a myth that was never so close to coming true as in 1974–75. A model of this all-Basque movement is given here (see figure 1).

In this model, it appears that political nationalism and cultural nationalism can easily be made to complement one another: the former impels the latter to the extent that it appears as its necessary precondition for

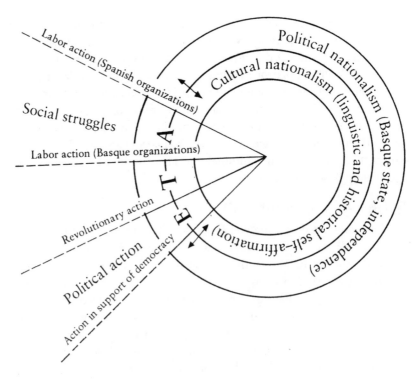

Figure 1. The myth of an all-Basque movement.

development and growth. Communication is established here, to a wide extent, through intellectuals who provide a two-tiered discourse of national liberation and the promotion of Basque culture. The social and political struggles are indicated by solid lines embedded within the area circumscribed by the nationalist struggle—the meaning being that this latter had the capacity to take the former under its wing. They are indicated by a dotted line for all that relates to their insertion into the Spanish field of action, both social and institutional. In 1973–74, social activism was mainly labor-based. The new social movements did not appear in force until 1976, for which reason they do not figure here. But there is a place for them (within "Social Struggles"), which they would come to fill in later years. Political activism managed to intertwine, in a still rather vague fashion, both the revolutionary orientations and the championing of democratic institutions. Social activism and political activism overlap one another to a certain extent. In the Basque country, as in every industrial society, working-class consciousness raises itself from the relations of production to an overall vision of society. Mediating between the two is a political consciousness which defines, through a wide array of variant forms, the kind of state that is to be created in order that management and capitalist domination might be brought to an end.

In conclusion we can say that down to 1975 the various mythic elements appeared to interact with relative ease, due to the fact that all were fighting the same adversary. Management, even if it considered itself to be nationalistic, was directly controlled in its activities by the Franco government, and the corporatist operating procedures that characterized the regime. The dictatorship constituted a rival to which a wide array of political currents could manifest their opposition and which, to conclude, epitomized a centralist Spain which overshadowed and denied the very existence of a Basque nation.

It is simple to draw a theoretical link between the myth we have just presented and the armed struggle. The latter could not have been conceived were the issue not one of bringing together the disparate elements of the Basque movement, and thereby of refusing to allow their dissociation. It remains inseparable from the vision of an all-Basque movement, and therefore from the myth behind it. At nearly no time whatsoever did nationalism proper, long embodied in the Basque Nationalist party, preach armed struggle on its own. It was only in the early 1960s, with the crisis in traditional nationalism and with the construction of complex ideologies in which the nationalist element was strongly complemented by a sociopolitical agenda, that this theme first appeared, even in theoretical form. As in Spain, the labor movement in the Basque country could become greatly charged with a social rage that bordered on riot and rebellion. Yet at no time, not even in the darkest hours of the dictatorship, did it as such ever extol or encourage a transition to organized violence. More than this, participation in labor or even covert action was always viewed as a choice which required that a certain distance be maintained vis-à-vis the armed struggle, even if the latter could at times be perceived as complementary or useful to it. Finally, in Spain—with the exception of a few tiny groups that were not even on the same scale as ETA—the political forces hostile to the Franco regime hardly ever carried their armed struggle outside the Basque borders. This would indicate that ETA was only capable of implementing its political strategy to the extent that it went hand in hand with the struggle for statehood. It is for this reason that the birth and growth of ETA can only be comprehended in terms of the image it gave itself of a revolutionary nationalist movement whose aim it was to speak *simultaneously* in the name of the nation, the social insurgents, and a certain concept of the state and its institutions. Whence the unique position occupied by ETA in our portrayal of the myth of a Basque movement: this organization was both the changing house for the various principles that undergirded the Basque action; and the embodiment of the will, perceived as a necessity, to champion those same principles. It was the arena in which the myth played itself out, first on a symbolic and later on an increasingly violent level.

■

Violence is one of a number of ways by which to both control a complex action and to hold it together. When symbolic integration is a relatively simple matter, violence can be held in check to the point of only being employed in exceptional situations. The more difficult such becomes, and the less the constituent parts of the myth are reconcilable, the more compelling the alternative of armed struggle (another alternative being the abandonment of an action). At the same time, when internal splits begin to manifest themselves with increasing frequency, a group can—as was the case with ETA—give up its quest for a unified action. Finally, when each of the many principles behind a group's action becomes so degenerated, destructured, or antagonistic towards other such ideals that total unification becomes entirely meaningless, armed insurgency, having become the last desperate manifestation of a factionalized movement, carries its participants over the brink of an inversion process.

Such is our hypothesis. What now remains, beyond the analyses we have already put forward concerning the history of ETA, is to validate it.

## A Sociological Intervention

We have advanced the hypothesis that violence gathers or fuses together the various principles that found an action. We should therefore be able to offer a diversified presentation of it in which we can analytically disassemble that which practice appears to assemble. We have also expressed the notion that armed insurgency can be the *sole* means of synthesis left to a group, and we should therefore be capable of demonstrating that those who reject violence, even as they endeavor to maintain control over the meanings it brings together, must fail in their attempt. It is our feeling that, since the death of Franco, the armed struggle has had an increasingly difficult time of staving off a terrorist groundswell and appears to be falling into an inversion process which may or may not be well advanced already. We must therefore find the means by which to pinpoint ETA and its supporters along the path that leads from limited and controlled violence to a rationale of terrorist action, from revolutionary nationalism to its negation in indiscriminate violence.

These varied requirements may be filled through the use of the method of sociological intervention. Applied to the problem of violence in Euskadi, this method had to be adapted in ways that will be presented in the Appendix. Here, let us simply delineate the concrete modalities of our research.

In our study of violence in relation to national, political, and social ideals, we have brought together two groups of militants, each of which has been committed at one time to an action that corresponded, at least in part, to these ideals. The first of these, whom we will call the veterans, is made up of a group of former ETA militants or leaders who are unanimously opposed today to the use of weapons. All are still seeking, to varying degrees, to link together the struggles for statehood, the social struggle, and political action. Most of the members of this group previously belonged to Euskadiko Eskera (EE), an organization which, through the mediation of its present general secretary, was of considerable assistance to us.[4] It put us in touch with a great number of militants agreeable to participating in our inquiry, and more particularly provided us with valuable suggestions which led to the definitive formation of the group. It was in this way that we were able to bring together former ETA members from a variety of age groups and social milieus: four blue-collar workers, of which one was unemployed, a teacher from an ikastola, a student, the feminist militant friend of an exiled ex-member who had recently broken with ETA, an older woman who had always emphasized the democratic nature of her action, and an office worker. These militants had entered and left ETA at different periods in the organization's existence, and their participation in the armed struggle covers, overall, a period extending from the birth of ETA for the first to enter, to 1983 for the last to leave.

The veterans met on sixteen occasions, for meetings of an average of four hours in duration. After a "closed" session (without co-discussant), it was visited by two Navarran priests; Basque nationalists with close links to Herri Batasuna (HB) whose "separatist" stance epitomized that of their organization as a whole; two PSOE leaders; a separatist nationalist who stressed the centrality of the language question; two Basque Nationalist party (PNV) leaders; two Basque business leaders; a teacher from the Goyerri region which has historically provided ETA with many of its militants and leaders; a *pasota,* a term meaning one who "passes over" political matters and is disinterested in everything save perhaps music, the beach, and drugs; and an antinuclear activist. The final meetings were devoted to a presentation by the researchers (Michel Wieviorka, Jacques Garat, and Francis Jaureguiberry) of our general hypotheses on the Basque movement and Basque violence. This was followed by long discussions of our hypotheses, which were at once accepted, modified, and utilized by the militants in their own evaluations of their action, both past and present and, more broadly, of the history of armed insurgency in Euskadi.

The separatist group brought together militants from a number of different resistance groups, with all being closely linked to or members of HB. This organization, through the contacts we were able to have with certain of its directors, did not choose to encourage or aid us in our research. Those members of the group who remained the most faithful to our investigation were blue-collar workers from the LAB labor union, an antinuclear activist, a teacher, an HB city councilman, and an artist. Its meetings (nine in all) were fewer in number but of longer duration than those of the veterans. It received visits from two PSOE directors, a PNV leader, two Basque business leaders, an antinuclear activist and HB sympathizer opposed to armed struggle, a woman director of a small white-collar firm, a feminist militant who had cut her ties with HB, a pasota, and the mothers of two jailed ETA members. It devoted fifteen hours to discussing our hypotheses and to carrying out, together with us researchers, an autocritique of its action. The separatist group—which sees ETA as the cutting edge of the Basque movement—is as strongly convinced of the inevitability of armed resistance as the veterans are opposed to it. In our investigation, researchers and militants came together to develop a common analysis, and not to reconstitute past events. It is not necessary to know the extent of the commitment that any given member of the separatist group may or may not have had in ETA. What is clear is that this group was close, both ideologically and politically, to the organization's policy of armed resistance.

Our work with these two groups was carried out serially, and not simultaneously. It was therefore impossible for us to arrange a meeting between the two, as we had once envisaged. It was complemented, in the case of the veterans, by a series of long personal interviews. Each session was tape-recorded, with the proceedings nearly exhaustively typed out in both French and Spanish. Our inquiry was carried out, discreetly but legally, on the premises of the University of San Sebastián, with the authorization of the university administration.

In June 1986, each of the two groups received a first draft of this text, and each had the occasion, in the course of a final meeting, to discuss its contents. The final draft takes into account the various remarks made at that time.[5]

With this, we have assembled the raw materials that will serve to ground the content of the pages that follow. It is now possible for us to enter directly into our inquiry, carried out with various scattered fragments of the Basque movement. In the one camp are separatists who favor armed insurgency; in the other, veterans who reject it. Both, however, claim to be speaking in the name of the same social (labor, antinuclear, feminist) and national ideals, and both also consider *contemporary* repression to be a clear and present danger.[6]

# 13

## The Work of the Veteran Group

It has been tempting, since the late 1970s, to reduce ETA to the image of a broken-down antimovement that has, since that time, fallen into a barbaric killing frenzy. Our primary diagnosis must, however, be a more guarded one. The language of inversion, when applied to ETA, not only serves to take the place of analysis, but also allows those who employ it to avoid or put off any true analysis indefinitely.

It is for this reason that we will present the work carried out with the veterans as a series of initiatives (interspersed with moments of crisis) which was characterized, at its inception, by an overwhelming rejection of violence, which the group closely identified with a total loss of meaning. It was by distancing itself from this initial standpoint (often under the unyielding pressure of the researchers), by ceasing to content itself with a mere denunciation of ETA terrorism, and by truly examining itself that this group helped us to better comprehend ETA action.

Let there be no mistake about the import of this work. The veteran group was composed of militants who, although they had left the armed struggle, had nonetheless remained politically active, this time legally, in ways that allowed them to continue to speak in the name of the nation, the Basque social movements, and for some at least, the revolution. In other words, this group saw itself, at the outset, as a nonviolent version of an action which corresponded to the myth of an all-Basque movement.

It will be recalled that all of our arguments concerning armed insurgency associated this myth with the violence that was the sole practical means for its concrete realization. If our arguments were correct, then we should be able to contend that the veterans are simply exhausting themselves in their attempts to move from myth to action, and that it is impossible to maintain the vision of an all-Basque movement while rejecting the principle of bearing arms.

The work we did with the veterans was therefore not a series of collective interviews, but a sociological demonstration. If this group had proven itself capable of making an actor of itself and of showing a real ability to bring together the diverse components of an all-Basque movement, then our hypothesis would have been proven false. If the opposite had occurred, it would have been greatly strengthened, if not validated. We will now follow the consultations we held with our veterans, consultations which unfolded in four stages. At first, they would only talk about people other than themselves, about perpetrators of actions that were insane, irrational, and terroristic in their eyes. Then they pulled themselves together to become an actor, passed through a highly charged moment of crisis, and finally engaged in an analysis of armed insurgency.

## The Veteran Group's Working Hypothesis

From its very first session onwards, and in its meetings with the majority of its co-discussants, the veterans posited a theory of armed struggle which turned on the explicit notions of inversion and the loss of meaning.

These former ETA militants, many of whom had held positions of great responsibility in the organization, were at first inclined to believe that it was an irrational universe they had left behind.

> MARIA: I got out thinking anyone who stayed in was crazy.
> IDOIA: But they are crazy! They're all paranoid!
> JUAN: The ones who stayed in get more paranoid, less normal, by the day. It's like an addiction for them, a kind of drug.

For these people, the armed struggle has become a profession for its activists, the sole profession that they, having entered the organization at a very early age, are capable of practicing. The only thing they know how to do is to handle a revolver or a charge of dynamite: "It was inertia that got ETA started. It simply made violence its stock in trade, an end in itself," says José, who goes on to compare the present-day ETA militants with the American Vietnam veterans who, lost and in psychological turmoil, committed suicide, took drugs, or took up a life of crime at the close of the war. A primary theory begins to emerge, one of a subjective

rationale according to which violence obeys no one and nothing, save
the immediate demands of warfare. "Instead of saying, 'we use weapons
for this or that reason,' they say, 'what reasons can we find to go on
using weapons?'" The group pursues this notion—of soldiers driven by
a subjective rationale—with a set of highly unflattering appraisals of
present ETA leaders, who are so many "mafiosi" who live comfortably
on the money they have extorted in the name of the "revolutionary tax."
Contrary to what took place from the 1960s down to 1977, there no
longer is an impressive replenishing of the ranks, but, rather, as José
puts it, "a system where the leaders never wear out. They're at the top,
where they have a kind of job security. A lot of militants come in and
burn themselves out in the intelligence commandos, or at best in the
support commandos, and they never rise any higher because the rest of
the hierarchical ladder is so overloaded and top-heavy." The group mus-
ters a few figures in support of its arguments: in 1984, there were about
six hundred activists hiding in France. "Forty are leaders, the rest are
marginals." "Why does there continue to be violence? Because there are
a few guys up there who've made violence their job, and they don't want
to be taken off the list. They don't want to learn new skills." ETA has
long since stopped being a democratic organization, if indeed it ever was
one: "There's no dialogue." The group's critique is sometimes pushed
to extremes, and the notion of a vicious circle—typical of an organization in which uncontrolled violence has become the sole agenda—is
applied to the ETA of the Franco years. The 1974 attack on the Correos
Street café in Madrid was but one particularly deadly example of a
generalized "barbarism of imprudent actions" that was always screened
by a real policy of "impunity" within the organization itself.

Was this but a syndrome typical to armed insurgency? Not necessarily.
A second, complementary, theory even more directly applies to the notion of inversion. Here it is argued that ETA violence is no longer dictated or informed by any meaningful principles. Rather, it has become
disconnected. This being the case, the organization's targets have become
increasingly random, with bombs going off, for example, in bank buildings, "killing innocent people." A baker, a plumber, and a marble carver
were liquidated on quite nonexistent grounds, or simply because ETA
suspected them of having "ratted." ETA blunders have multiplied, but
"when they knock people off by mistake they explain themselves in the
same way as the dictatorship used to do: 'it was an accident'!" People
join ETA for less-than-glorious reasons: "I know," says Juan, "a lot of
young people who joined ETA not to fight repression or the economic

crisis, but because the police were after them for some petty crime."
Recruitment is totally unselective: today one finds "young people under
twenty in ETA who have ten murders on their conscience. That would
have been unthinkable in 1970." Nor is there the intellectual rigor that
characterized the earlier period: "We tried to think things through," says
Luis. "We read, we learned things, and we tried to communicate what
we knew to the people in the villages, to persuade them to join our fight.
All that has been forgotten, and the problem has became 'Gora ETA
Militarra' (Long Live the Military ETA) versus 'Contra ETA Militarra'
(Down with the Military ETA)." In order to maintain its popular support, ETA no longer emphasizes the underlying principles of its resistance
in Euskadi, but rather highlights its own victimization, especially its
martyrs and victims of torture. It commemorates its dead, whom it "uses
as a political weapon," and has developed "a taste for necrophilia, a
veritable cult of the dead." More exactly, the group accuses ETA of
pushing to its limits the workings of the action-repression-action cycle.
It "purposely lets its militants rot away in jail" and "is [so] uninterested
in prisoners" that when a general amnesty was declared in 1978, and all
prisoners were being released from prison and the amnesty committees
preparing to dissolve themselves, a number of ETA sympathizers successfully opposed their dissolution. In the prisons as well, ETA has been
responsible for a certain reign of terror.

On a wider scale, ETA strives to scuttle anything that smacks of peace
or negotiation. During the transition period, as Juan (who was at that
time the leader of the "jailed Political-Military Front's negotiating
team") tells it, "the Military Wing did all that it could to stall negotiations—physical threats against prisoners who were ready to negotiate;
and the assassination, on the outside, of Ibarra [one of the great industrial oligarchs of Vizcaya], to show the government just how wrong it
was to free the 'etarras' detainees." The refusal of anything that might
open the way to negotiation goes hand in hand, according to the group,
with ETA's guiding principle. In its blood frenzy, ETA maintains that
the dictatorship, in spite of its facelift, is just as alive, and as oppressive
and repressive, as it has ever been—which ETA strives to demonstrate
by maintaining the action-repression-action spiral.

Today, more than ever, ETA is cut off from reality, living in its own
little world, feeding on the only comforting news it knows—the news
that it itself propagates. This mechanism too is an old one. Juan explains
that already in his time "when we went to France to see the people living
in exile there, it wasn't to give them news from home, but to flatter

them. When we went to see a prisoner, it was to tell him that whatever he knew was true." José adds, "people were pulling strings everywhere. People only said what they wanted to say, only heard what they wanted to hear." Even though there was no correspondence between it and popular aspirations, the isolated little world of ETA couldn't understand that the time had come to give up the armed struggle. When people returned from exile or came out of prison, they were no longer honored as village or neighborhood heroes. In the end, the veterans' unanimous conclusion is that a catastrophic separation has taken place between ETA and the Basque people.

All agree that ETA actions have been responsible for a chaos that is threatening to ruin their country. It is a blot on the democratic struggle, that has "impeded the processes of social change," cut off debate, and embroiled the political process. "Alliances between Fraga and Carrillo, and Onaindia and Vizcaíno. That's what ETA succeeded in doing, bringing people like that together!"[1] Armed insurgency is the opposite of social action. "When the labor movement goes down, militarism goes up," observes Joxeba; ETA is destroying the Basque nation, and fighting—even if still indirectly—the PNV, and is "targeting not only people on the outside, but also certain segments of the Basque population itself." In a word, it has become the inverted image of the Basque movement it embodied but ten years before.

This analysis draws together and greatly unifies the members of the veteran group. Each has contributed to the discussion, and each has considered his contribution to be based in solid fact. This analysis was advanced in many of the meetings in which the group's co-discussant was not from the separatist camp. This was the case with its co-discussants from the PNV (from which the group diverges mainly on the grounds of its own leftist—sometimes Marxist and occasionally revolutionary—political references); the PSOE (which it reproaches, for its part, for having systematically abandoned its positions of openness towards Basque statehood); and the young pasota, whose disinterest in politics and refusal of all militant commitment it attempted to fathom. It is not shaken when a separatist co-discussant attempts to unnerve the group by speaking Basque, only to discover that he has ten perfect Euskera-speakers sitting before him.

Finally, this analysis was shared with other actors, most particularly with two of the business leaders and members of the Basque employers' organization, Confebask, who met the group. According to these managers—whom none in the group challenged—small-, medium- (and sometimes large-) scale business owners had often supported ETA in the Franco years, giving money to exiles, refusing to fire persons for political reasons, and voluntarily rehiring persons upon their return from exile or release from prison. They are not hard on their employees, but are rather paternalistic in their policies, anxious to contribute to improving relations with their workers through negotiation. For these company directors, the effects of violence are always catastrophic. Terrorized by ETA and its "revolutionary tax," business people hardly invest at all in Euskadi, for fear that they will give the impression of having large financial resources. They buy less, using for example vehicles with small engines. Those who are less patriotic leave altogether, or at least think about doing so: why risk one's life and that of one's family, why force one's family to live a life of terror when elsewhere, in Spain, it is possible to invest and do business? Many leave their villages for the city, where relationships are more anonymous, and where their wives are not insulted at the grocery store and their children not threatened at school or the local bar. Hindering them in their entrepreneurial endeavors, the armed struggle's primary consequence is thus the impoverishment of the country. Modernization is halted and all efforts to overcome the crisis situation are paralyzed.

More than this, it lays the foundations for a random violence which replaces the social relationship between labor and management with a climate of terror. "Anything that has anything to do with decision making, discipline, or the chain of command in the firms is completely undermined." Not only is the desire to invest critically reduced, but so too is the capacity for coordination and direction. Floor managers and white-collar employees are constantly being physically threatened: "For a yes or a no, a foreman starts getting threatening letters signed ETA." In this climate of fear and dread, social relationships become strained and hardened, with the result being that floor bosses and personnel managers begin shirking their responsibilities. "Everything gets sent upstairs," and it becomes impossible to deal with the business's internal tensions. For management, then, terrorist violence and the random violence that accompanies it involve much more than the dangers of kidnapping or extortion. It is the negation of all entrepreneurial activity, the destruction of—or the creation of a crisis situation in—social relationships. It is behavior that has, in the final analysis, nothing whatever to do with the class warfare for which the terrorists claim responsibility—even when they themselves are not interested in it. "The revolutionary tax is not a class-based social action. It is levied for the money and for the survival of the organization." These business leaders would like to foster a genuine social relationship, but violence destroys that relationship. In this difficult time of economic crisis, these Basque patriots too want to "put the [Basque] house in order," but violence keeps tearing it down. From their standpoint as well, ETA action derives from an inversion process that negates both the system of social action and the nationalism it so loudly champions.

It is an immense gulf that presently divides the interpretation presented by both the veteran group and the management co-discussants just mentioned on the one hand, and the notion that ETA is the manifestation of a Basque movement, and is thereby justified in speaking in the name of the nation and the revolution, on the other. The veterans' theory on the spontaneous eruption of the armed struggle is so strong as to appear unassailable. Ought we therefore to abandon our investigations, and simply second the group's radical image of inversion, an image in which they have been supported, as we have seen, by their co-discussants from management? The answer is no.

### The Veteran Group as Actor

The veterans have just become aware of the notion of a foundation for an all-Basque movement. The researchers remind the group of the essential elements of the course they have embarked upon together, and now ask that they stop talking about others, about people still belonging to ETA. We challenge them with the following question: now as before, is the problem not one of following a course of action capable of unifying both national and sociopolitical agendas?

The group's first remarks confirm that this is indeed what is at stake, if one is to remain on the field of action. Within the group, however, a diversity of positions begins to emerge. Some consider that its first priority should be to chart a new nationalist course and agenda. Others insist that it is sociopolitical issues that ought to occupy center stage.

But it is 1984, and much has changed since the 1970s. The notions of both nationalist activism and sociopolitical activism have greatly evolved. Great gains were made in the winning of autonomous status in 1979, and the matter at hand is now one of intelligently administering that autonomy. Indeed, most of the members of the group appear to be content with—or prepared to reconcile themselves with—the regional autonomy accorded to the Basque country. The labor and social protest movements are on the decline. This being the case, the issue is not to champion socialism or a dictatorship of the proletariat, but rather to find an equitable and speedy way out of the present economic crisis. The veterans thus begin to develop a model for action in which a regionalist approach (the new face of nationalist action) and a policy for economic modernization (the new face of social agitation) can be adapted to one another. With this, the tension begins to mount, for the first time, between the group and the researchers.

The latter underscore the fact that such positions are quite distant from the aspirations these same militants had held some ten years earlier. They note that the dream of an independent Basque state and of a society led by its workers and producers is over; and that the dream of a Basque version of the taking of the Winter Palace has been abandoned. The group reacts strongly. Its members explain that national and social oppression have gone down and are still on the decline. The problem is not one of linking national action with social agitation, but rather of distinguishing between an anachronistic form of political activity—the armed struggle provoked by the Franco dictatorship—and political activities that fall within the institutional structures of a democracy. The researchers are adamant, saying they find it unacceptable that an altered situation, no matter how great the change has been, could transform actors inspired by such a visionary platform into mere agents of cultural and economic modernization. They insist that there had to have been some link between their abandonment of the armed struggle and the radical narrowing of their vision; and that ETA, for its part, had been forced to step up its level of violence precisely in order that it might be able to go on speaking in the name of independence, the revolution, and the labor movement.

This argument is provisionally rejected by the group, and most especially by José, who applies the theory of inversion towards a definition of the armed struggle. It is a critical moment for the group. José is the first to recognize that "we're pretty much pasotas ourselves . . . we're not the militants we once were." Francisco admits that today he doesn't feel "altogether good about myself . . . I expect it's universal, that everybody feels that way." Juan considers that "the frustration and even the anger we feel could come from the fact that there have been two camps since 1977. One group placed its bets on a total break and for them, obviously, everything's been totally frustrating because we're further than ever from breaking away. The other group is frustrated as well because, to the extent that all the political talk has had no effect on society, one has the impression that everything has gotten blurred." José and Idoia emphasize the institutionalization of the various conflicts:

playing the institutions' game means "going soft." The session ends on a general note of irritation. The militants have the feeling that they have been challenged, criticized, and even accused of being "reformist."

## The Crisis in the Veteran Group

The next session began with the question of nationalism. Francisco is the first in the group to suggest the need of drafting a new national platform, one of a democratic nationalism without "any vanguard, outmoded aspirations, or platforms for national salvation." Rafael insists on the need to reject piecemeal the vanguard's entire mythic discourse on labor.

Now the group begins to fluctuate between its analysis of actors other than itself—HB and the PNV—and a consideration of its own action. It is the latter which the researchers propose to systematize, along the lines of two models. The first, which qualified as the horizontal approach, and had dominated the previous session, turns around two poles: (1) a campaign aimed, within the context of Euskadi's autonomous status, at taking over the institutions, and exerting pressure towards modernization—for example through education and the media—as a means to securing the nation's cultural development; and (2) a sociopolitical campaign which, grounded in propositions concerning the restructuring and retooling of industry as well as in a defense of the principles of democratic partnership between labor and management, would seek to generate economically responsible and socially equitable solutions to the crisis.

The second approach which, qualified as vertical, had to this point only been touched upon by a few members of the group, is grounded in another concept of action. Rather than working from a necessarily violent independentist line of a radical disengagement from existing structures, this approach would, through grassroots actions whose national import would be felt in every sphere, gradually build up a nationalist base. A nation so constructed would be the issue not only of cultural usages but also of programs carried out at a village or neighborhood level, as well as within factories, feminist and ecologist groups, etc. In each of these grassroots actions, a heavy dose of nationalism or a clear *ezkualdun* reference would be the essential element. The two approaches are not necessarily mutually exclusive. In a sense the action of EE, the party to which most of the group members claim allegiance, incorporates elements of both.

These two models of action, which emerged out of group discussions, are the only alternatives available to it as an actor. The group has already examined the former, albeit not in any depth, since it was over this issue that it experienced its first tensions. The latter constitutes the first tentative efforts to devise, in the wake of traditional nationalism and revolutionary nationalism, a third form of nationalism.

At this point, the reader may have the impression that these investigations have carried us far away from the problem of violence. This is, in fact, not the case. The veteran group is more than a mere heir to earlier struggles; its members, nearly all of whom had at some time to live underground, and in many cases in exile or prison, left the armed struggle without ever giving up their commitment to militant action. Should they succeed in drafting a stable, broad-based, and visionary activist platform, this will constitute a proof for them that violence is in fact foreign to the causes in the name of which they have been fighting, and that it is neither the necessary condition for nor the ineluctable result of said causes. Should they fail, such would prove or at least suggest that it is impossible to abandon the armed struggle without also surrendering the lofty principles in the name of which the struggle is being fought. The group is well aware that much is at stake here.

It is not without hesitation that the group begins by examining the first, the horizontal, approach. A radical version of this orientation is allowed by Idoia. This energetic and courageous woman had, since the early 1950s, taken part in a great number of battles against the dictatorship. Today she points to the need for overall modernization on both cultural and economic levels. Others share her perspective, but place a greater emphasis on the necessity for sociopolitical agitation, not only to help the country to weather the economic crisis, but also to take its place in the ranks of modern societies, and to avoid falling into a Third-World situation. The researchers do not underestimate the importance of a modernization campaign, so long as it can remain focused on the popular forces in society. They wish, however, to divorce the question of impact from that of the risks involved. By opening the country up to the outside, cultural modernization might very well result in a diluting of that same traditional Basque culture that still very much fires the nationalist rhetoric. "Developmentalist" economic pressure appears to be far removed from the image of a labor struggle whose aim it is to provide society with radically new guidelines. Voices are raised as the group realizes that this approach, as realistic as it may appear, is greatly limited in its scope, at least in comparison with the visionary platforms of the 1970s. The recognition of this cold hard fact plunges the group into turmoil. José becomes unnerved and launches into an endless discussion intended to explain that there is no one in Euskadi who separates social and national issues. But it is Idoia who becomes especially incensed, as she denounces what is for her the greatest of all evils. This is Basque patriotism which she considers to be a Basque version of nazism. For a moment, José and Idoia lose all control. The "N" on the researchers' chart, doesn't it stand for nazi rather than nation? Francisco himself, who a few days earlier had claimed that he could not "water down his nationalism," now says that it had always been the social issues that had motivated him. "I never played the nationalist game," he asserts. At the same time, he shares his concerns with us: "If the Basque majority is socialist, it will end up by foisting its own Españolist culture on us." To hear him tell it, Juan is only a nationalist in order that he might "smash the capitalist system here." The nation, José explains, is never anything more than a set of social problems, problems which people would rather work out locally than from a distance, through a centralized system. Luis is the only member who refuses to be swept over by the wave that is carrying the group so far away from its nationalist self-identity. He remains an abertzale nationalist, and continues "to define [himself] as an independentist. But for the time being . . . I refuse to abandon our nation's flag, the building of our nation, so long as the question of our own sovereign institutions remains unsettled, so long as our Basque cultural heritage has not been recovered and raised up, so long as the problem of language, the language of every one of us, is not resolved, and so long as our country does not take the slow but democratic road towards 'eskualization.'" Maria supports Luis, and the pair explicitly advance the second approach, which we referred to as vertical. Both feel that it is a grassroots movement that must form and take charge if the nation is to move towards independence.

But is this activist strategy as feasible and realist as Luis and Maria claim? Luis develops his argument: activism is necessary in the neighborhoods, in the towns, and "everywhere that concrete programs are being organized," to rouse the interests of young people and promote cultural activities. Maria explains that the sum of concrete activities carried out by each person in his proper sphere "implies, when all is said and done, that what we are doing is building a nation, that everything is part of a unified whole." But implicit in her position—and she would confirm this later in an individual interview—is a certain critique of all-embracing theories and broad-based discourse. She would rather participate in grassroots politics and act practically than subscribe to all-purpose ideologies for the construction of an all-Basque movement. This vertical approach is a fragile one, and is in fact a soft version of a model we will encounter later, with the second, separatist group. It says more about Luis's difficulties in divorcing himself from violence than it does about his commitment to a new form of action. The researchers recognize the desire to build a fairer, livelier, and better-educated society in his statements, but still are at a loss to know how a number of scattered actions might be combined concretely into a unified national whole. Luis's and Maria's attempts to explain are drowned out by a veritable storm of rage that erupts when José and Idoia mention Hitler and then go on to compare Basque patriotic nationalism to the activities of Khomeini who sent "all who were capable of sullying the fatherland before the firing squad."

## The Veteran Group's Autocritique

The departure of Idoia and José, who leave the meeting before it is over, defuses the tension. For the moment, the verdict is clear. The horizontal approach that predominates in the group had given rise to a rejection of all independentist ideas, and to a veritable crisis in which José and Idoia had been the main protagonists. Rather than clarifying matters and helping them to settle on a realistic activist strategy, it had destabilized its potential spokespersons, inciting them to make statements that were either extreme (e.g. there is hardly any difference between the nazis and HB) or incoherent. The vertical approach was not so much defended as intoned as a kind of prayer.

In the end, neither of the two strategies was definitively affirmed or firmly established. More than this, the discussion that had followed had brought on the breakup of the group—which renders the likelihood of the two ever interacting at a party level (that of EE in this case) rather implausible. Those who today denounce armed struggle after having abandoned it are incapable of formulating their own model of action.

The meeting continues with the group, now reduced in number, pacified. Both Jon and Juan offer scenarios which illustrate their desire to participate in an institutionalized system that turns on one's will to exert pressure, from within, upon a political system. While both thoroughly defend the 1979 autonomy statute, Juan phrases his arguments in terms of a strictly political opposition between the PNV and the PSOE. The session concludes on a highly analytical note with a long exposé by Luis. He emphasizes the issues over which he is in disagreement with HB and the Military Wing of ETA. There already exists in Euskadi a certain degree of self-determination in the educational system, as well as in health care, language, and certain economic spheres. Within the limits of this self-determination, the Basque people enjoy democratic expression. HB and the Military Wing deny this reality, asserting that the Basque people remain totally dependent. For them, violence serves in fact to diminish this self-determination, which in turn allows them to better advance the argument that the situation is one of total dependence. This is why, as Luis explains, they will one day launch an attack on the Ertzaïna (the autonomous Basque police force). Luis then presses for the complementary notion that violence is fueled by problems internal to a Basque community in which culture is principally "being brought to a boil" by the economic crisis.

Luis's analysis is valuable inasmuch as it frees the group from the crisis situation in which it had found itself. Its theoretical import is also appreciable. Luis's approach has in fact shown that there is a certain discontinuity between the theses of syndrome and inversion. According to him, HB and the Military Wing of ETA base their actions on demands which either stem from the economic situation, or which point to the fact that there remain wide areas in which Basque self-determination is still being denied. Theirs is not an entirely irrational approach. The session ends on a note of satisfaction, with all feeling that "very useful work" has been accomplished.

The following day, the entire group gathers for a final meeting. The atmosphere is now perfectly calm. Everyone is conscious of having weathered a crisis the day before, a crisis which had not begun to abate until José's and Idoia's departure and the clear analytical presentations of Juan and Luis. Very relaxed, the group reviews its entire history of the previous twenty years. Much of what the group members say concerning the splits within ETA has been used in the historical introduction with which Part Three of this book opened. One last time, however, the group returns to its theory of spontaneous violence. José calmly reiterates that the armed struggle is the sum total of both a subjective rationale embraced by militarist elements who only know how to wage war, and of a process which brought about the dissociation of ETA from the thoughts and hopes of the "real people." Under the dictatorship, there had hardly been any forum for public opinion. Under the changed conditions of the democratic regime, it was possible to see just how wide the gulf was that existed between popular aspirations and the language of armed insurgency. This former ETA leader (who took part, from the side of the Political-Military Front, in the ETA-M/ETA-PM schism) thus refuses to budge from his earlier positions. He explains with great clarity that the further the "people" turn away from ETA and HB, the more this aggregate would find itself forced to step up its violence in order to impress upon the same people's minds its own version of what must be. As for a subjective rationale, he states that it can stem from a number of processes, including the dominance of pure militarists over politicists, a lack of reserve, and the loss of political control over the use of weapons. The same notion of subjective rationale can be used just as easily to explain the suspension of armed operations. There was a year and a half, as José notes, when the Military Wing had stopped using its weapons for reasons linked to its weak infrastructure as well as to the effectiveness of government repression.

This return of the group to its original arguments is, however, short-lived. It is abandoned as soon as the researchers advance a hypothetical scenario of politicization, in which repression has ceased and in which all the militarists have gone far away, to distant foreign lands for example. If the theories of syndrome and inversion are well-founded, then violence ought to entirely disappear. The group rejects this hypothesis outright, returning to the myth of the Basque movement. Violence would rear its ugly head yet again, it explains, because the myth would still be operative. As long as the myth exists, the armed struggle will continue to manifest itself. Thus echoing (although not explicitly) analyses worthy of Georges Sorel, the group links violence to the unrealizable image of an all-Basque movement, and draws the logical conclusion. For the armed struggle to stop, the myth must be stopped, exploded.

Here concludes the work we carried out with the veterans. This group had first presented a long analysis of the armed struggle which held to such notions as inversion and the syndrome of violence, dismissing ETA as meaningless, barbaric, and irrational. Called upon to define itself as an actor, it was rocked by a powerful crisis, finding itself powerless to develop a broad-based visionary model of action, and incapable of settling on a model of more modest proportions, a "watered-down project" in the words of Francisco. Returning to its analysis of armed insurgency, the group defended its earlier positions, recognizing however that violence is at least partially grounded in matters of true significance—all of those spheres in which the Basques did not yet enjoy self-determination, in the words of Luis—and most especially in the mythic notion of an all-Basque movement.

With this, we may draw two definitive conclusions. The first has to do with the failure of the veteran group. This was a collection of ten or so militants who endeavored—both in terms of their personal quests and their political life—to speak in the name of a multiplicity of abert-zale, social, and leftist ideals. From this standpoint, the group's efforts had not succeeded. It had been unable, in the role of self-critical actor, to advance any all-embracing model of action. It had only been comfortable when contemplating its historical past or, especially, criticizing contemporary perpetrators of violence. The question arises as to whether another group of militants, of similar tendencies, would have arrived at the same results. It is likely that they would not.

The group had explored, at great length, a wide array of potential courses of action, and had found itself stymied by the unfeasibility or the contradictory nature of all the possibilities it had taken very seriously. The crisis it had weathered, and out of which it could not emerge until it had distanced itself from its prior analysis of its own practices, carries the weight of proof for us: *today, it is impossible to develop a visonary program of action or to support, by linking them together, the principal ideals of an all-Basque movement, without resorting to armed struggle.*

A second conclusion may be drawn from the group's realization—especially at the conclusion of its series of meetings—that violence had a certain sense to it. The idea of a pure inversion was in fact attacked by the very same persons who had first defended it with the greatest ardor. This they did as soon as they allowed that Spanish democracy was incapable of responding constructively to the sum total of demands coming out of Basque society. Within the Spain of the PSOE, there are things that are not unifiable and there are things that have not been unified, and it is precisely on these matters—which the democracy cannot or will not secure—that the armed struggle concentrates its efforts. It is hard for someone who has renounced violence and become a vehement critic of ETA to defend such an idea. The fact that it was presented as such by veterans—who had little or no stake in political ideologies that consider democracy to be capable of solving the world's every problem—gives it an even greater impact.

# 14

## The Work of the Separatist Group

On the one hand, then, we find a violence that has become aggravated since the late 1970s, while on the other, a Basque movement whose main components have become divorced, disjointed, and often weakened at the same time.

Does there remain a link between the organized practice of violence and the nationalist, social, and revolutionary principles that fostered Basque activism during the days of the dictatorship, some ten to fifteen years earlier? If so, what is the nature of this link?

For the veterans, this link had long since been broken and the armed struggle had become purely terroristic. We know, however, that this judgment is not wholly acceptable. A good number of militants and their sympathizers in Euskadi identify themselves with a separatist vision of national and social emancipation, and consider ETA to be the legitimate vanguard of that vision.

Will the separatists be capable of analyzing their own activism in such a way as to overturn, completely or partially, the thesis of inversion and the terrorist syndrome? Will they be able to relate—in sociological and not ideological terms—their often highly selective participation in social struggles to their national consciousness, their political commitment, and the principle of armed struggle as such is put into practice by ETA? These are the issues that are at stake in the discussions of the separatist group, a group composed of approximately ten highly active militants. Some belong to several organizations, specializing in labor, neighborhood, ecological, prisoner-support, and strictly political causes. This group, even as it acknowledges the legitimacy of the armed struggle, refuses any direct identification between HB and ETA, as well as between itself and HB. This is not only because the separatist cause has a broader base than this political entity, but also because these militants identify themselves with a *movement* rather than with an *organization*.

### Separatist Strength

The group's first three sessions are devoted to meetings with adversaries: representatives of the PSOE, the PNV, and the business community. Adversaries? Perhaps the better term here would be "enemies," especially in the case of the PSOE. Separatism in fact implies that a state of war exists. Their confrontational stance is inalterable, nonnegotiable, and ultimately nondiscussable. When it meets its socialist co-discussants, two important leaders of the PSOE in Euskadi, the group's separatism is immediately carried to extremes. The socialists, as the group explains in a single voice, are the representatives of Spanish centralist policies whose aim it is to annihilate the Basque people. Through such policies, the dictatorship "disguised as reforms" lives on, perhaps more insidiously than it did under Franco. This it does in the form of a total disrespect for human rights, ongoing repression and oppression, the covering up of acts of torture if not the "covert war" being waged by the GAL, emergency laws, the ZEN plan, a refusal to legalize either HB or HASI, the prohibition of the expression of ideological support for ETA, and so on.[1] The widely hailed democracy is not democratic, and terrorism—because terrorism does indeed exist—is a creation of the state and of the socialists who support it. These so-called socialists dare to speak in the name of the working class? The group maintains that they destroy social movements wherever they find them, and not only in Euskadi. Their policy is to funnel off, absorb, and finally dissolve popular movements, and to promote a hyperinstitutionalization which paralyzes all grassroots action—for example, by founding a Women's Institute which was against all that the women's movement stood for. Antidemocratic, anti-social, the PSOE is first and foremost anti-Basque. It suppresses the Basque language and stands in the way of the people when they attempt to give a proper burial to their *gudarris*—the heroic patriotic victims of the Civil Guards that have become even more murderous than they had been under the Franco dictatorship. It encourages informers, and allows drugs to corrupt the Basque people.

The group will hardly listen to the responses offered by its co-discussants, who explain that the socialist party has long been established in Euskadi, that it respects human rights more than does ETA, that the Basque country's autonomy statute is the most comprehensive of its kind in Europe, that the Basque language is widely supported and promulgated, etc. This is not so much a dialogue as two very strained parallel monologues, punctuated by outbursts of anger. On one side are those for whom the socialists are *txakurak,* dogs; on the other, those for whom HB, ETA, and the separatist movement are assassins, madmen, and enemies of democracy who torpedo all social and political progress.

When it meets the PNV representative, the group is less inclined to reject him and his cause out of hand. This it does not only on fundamental grounds but also because this particular co-discussant happens to be a historical figure in the anti-Franco struggle and, although a senator, someone who is relatively marginal within his own party.

The discussion with him opens along two distinct lines. The first of these is nationalist. Are we not, suggests the co-discussant, committed to the same activist cause, even if along different paths, of which the one is slow but reasonable and the other, while more rapid in appearance, is unrealistic and lethal? A wide gulf emerges between him and the group. The path of reform, which presupposes an acceptance of the Constitution and the autonomy statute, has nothing to offer to the group. It is a path for selling out, for compromise and collaboration with the Spanish government, a path that leads to a form of regionalism whose objectives have nothing in common with abertzale, a path of complicity with a dictatorship that is still very much alive. Here, the co-discussant is unable to follow the group's arguments, and emphasizes the fact that the statute preserves the Basque people's historic rights. More importantly, he opens up a second line of discussion, on the subject of the revolution and totalitarianism. It is not so much the group's independentist nationalism that separates him from them as it is the collectivist and totalitarian political system into which a revolutionary process cannot but lead. He is against all dictatorship, including that of the proletariat. It is true that the kinds of revolutionary sentiments and Marxist-Leninist ideologies the group flaunts cannot but shock a man for whom negotiation and discussion within an institutional framework, even with his most bitter adversaries, are in no way tantamount to treason or self-compromise.

The group states that there is no common ground for understanding. Rather than there being a common objective (independence) with two possible modes of access, there are rather two distinct conflicts, the one national and the other sociopolitical, concerning which they are in total disagreement with their co-discussant. The "umbilical cord," although it was still intact in the 1960s, between a PNV perceived as a regionalist administrator working in the service of the middle class and the independentist separatists who speak in the name of the proletariat as they champion the revolution, has now been cut.

The business leaders' critique of the armed struggle has already been presented. Here too, they come as a pair to meet the separatist group, which presses them to avow their allegiance to the PNV. When the two claim to be nationalists themselves, the group responds with a class-based discourse. The business community is part and parcel of the privileged class, and as such is the exploiting agent of international capitalism, which totally exploits the people of the Third World. It is powerless in the face of the economic crisis, which it nevertheless turns to its own profit and encourages through automation and the introduction of new technologies. It seeks to domesticate the workers, no longer invests in its community, manipulates the justice system in its own favor, all the while demanding that the government give it more room to maneuver through the enactment of new laws and statutes. It also destroys the environment, only respecting the ecological balance when forced to do so, etc. Even as the group attacks these co-discussants by arguing from a standpoint of class warfare, and attempts (in vain) to challenge their abertzale credentials, they nevertheless let them have their say. Their arguments are solid, especially on the subjects of the economic crisis and the labor market, concerning which they point out that wages are higher and the salary scale more equitable in Euskadi than in Spain, and that in the courts "it's always the owner who takes it on the chin and the worker who wins." In particular, they stress the fact that while Basque trade unionism is quite powerful overall, the separatist positions defended by the group correspond to those of the LAB, a minority union with a very small following.

Somewhat charmed by these co-discussants whose jokes concerning the pettiness of their Catalan homologues provoke laughter and introduce a certain complicity, the separatist stance of the group is also weakened, very slightly, by the declarations of one of its number. Pedro, an LAB union member, states in no uncertain terms that he has no desire to discuss the revolution, but would rather seek to "improve what we have here and now." The group rallies itself however by championing a certain universality. Because the struggle is a universal one, one has no right to go into the details of this or that action for fear that such may constitute a pact with the devil. As Antonio puts it, "By compartmentalizing our problems, we may well be able to find a solution to some of the differences existing between ourselves . . . but if our analysis loses its universality, it loses its meaning."

This first series of meetings is clearly indicative of the nature of the relationship obtaining between separatism and its social and political adversaries. It is a combative relationship in which discussion either leads to confrontation—as in the session with the PSOE representatives—or an attempt to reduce to absurdity or treason the adversary's positions by playing on a tightly argued two-tiered register.

It reproaches the PNV for its degenerate nationalism and, most particularly, for its middle-class stance. It responds to the business leaders' powerful nationalist discourse with the language of class warfare and the revolution. And should the group find itself even momentarily placed in a position of potential agreement with its co-discussant on some point pertaining to either of these registers—the national or the sociopolitical—it falls back on the universality and the necessarily synthetic nature of its cause. Separatism refuses the "compartmentalization," the internal diversification of the import of its action. It reinforces its positions through a marked ability to combine every element into an all-embracing discourse which, in the final analysis, allows it to maintain a veritable breach between itself and co-discussants with whom it might otherwise agree on certain limited points. This is a confirmation of one of our hypotheses, i.e. that violence is inseparable from a universalizing definition of the categories of action, the highest expression of which is to be found in the myth of an all-Basque movement.

Does this mean that the separatist group is motivated by the power of separatism and nothing else? Here we must introduce a second minor but real dimension to our analysis, one that is related, moreover, to Charles Tilly's theories on violence. The critique with which the group faces off against its adversaries is not merely revolutionary and independentist. It is also that of an actor who is both aware of and perhaps even desirous of entering onto the institutional scene. It is for this reason that the group demands certain rights and militates for improvements in the justice system and free speech at the same time as it maintains the necessity of a total overthrow of the powers in place. And, while it does not reject the principle of negotiation out of hand, the terms it sets just to come to the bargaining table are so categorical—e.g. the demands of the KAS platform for amnesty, the legalization of independentist parties, removal of the police force, etc.—as to be unacceptable to Madrid. In the same way that HB is an active participant on the municipal scene, the "separatist" group also occasionally manifests a desire to take part

in the political game, from which it finds itself excluded and marginalized.[2] At no time, however, does this component of its discourse ever
gain the upper hand. One may, in response to a given situation, fight for
specific demands, reforms, or improvements. But, as Antonio explains,
separatism is the way of the future, the only way.

## Three Registers

From the outset, the separatist group has viewed itself as symbolizing a
multifaceted assembly of popular actors led by an ETA vanguard, which
alone is capable of taking an all-embracing view of a wide array of
Basque protest movements. For it, violence is unavoidable, if only because of the oppression and repression that reign in Euskadi. We would,
in fact, devote an entire day of research to an exploration of this double-
faceted movement, which fuses into a single principle a wide variety of
meanings, and which claims its legitimacy to be that of a people who
have been bullied by power. In the course of this day, the group would
be visited by a militant pacifist who sympathizes with the Basque cause
but who is against the armed struggle; a manager in a white-collar business who is a nationalist torn between her abhorrence of violence and
her separatist sentiments; a pasota; a militant feminist; and two mothers
of imprisoned ETA militants jailed in the Herrera de la Mancha peniten-
tiary, some four hundred miles from San Sebastián. These co-discussants
arrive in succession but, with the exception of the pasota, remain with
the group until the end of the day.

In order to present itself as the unifying link between the various
Basque insurgencies, the rationale of separatism operates on three registers. By isolating each of these registers, our inquiry will aid us to comprehend this rationale.

The first register is that of a championing of *convictions*. It is grounded
in the notion that there exists a direct link between the meaning of the
lesser conflicts and the rationale of separatism; and that the actors in the
lesser conflicts are capable of recognizing that link. The second register
is that of *intimidation*, which plays itself out in tests of strength and
thereby oppositions between the separatist militants and the actors
whom they intend to unite under the separatist aegis. Separatism refuses
to see itself as the extension of this or that lesser conflict. It therefore
must force them to follow in its wake—which constitutes a telltale sign
of inversion. Finally, the third register is that of the *denunciation of the
enemy*. Here, separatism counts on the excessive acts of those whom it
opposes to aid it in expanding its following and strengthening its action.

This too indicates that it has entered into an inversion process, since what matters is not that one speak in the name of some social or national cause, but rather that one win over a more-or-less amorphous group by denouncing repression—quite often even as one is contributing to its intensification.

We will now give an account of the day's proceedings, which not only brought to light these three functional modes, but also showed how they fit together with one another.

### Convincing

With the militant pacifist, the task at hand is a relatively simple one. This person defends the principle of exemplary, nonviolent behavior, referring on several occasions to the Greens of West Germany. He sees himself as a radical, even as he maintains that a certain level of institutionalization can be highly beneficial. He asserts that the armed struggle ceased to be a liberation movement in 1977. Here, the group is too strong to be shaken by such arguments. The practice of nonviolence is tantamount to giving free rein to the armed forces, to yielding ground to central state repression. At Lemoniz, on the one hand, the armed struggle forced the state into retreat; in West Germany, on the other, the Greens were unable to halt the installation of American missiles. The only reason there are no American bases in Euskadi is that American imperialism is afraid of ETA. The group also develops, on the spur of the moment, an argument which Georges Sorel would not have disowned. Violence, they assert, is the necessary condition for the continuation of the movement: "If the Military Wing was to lay down its arms, a very high percentage of the abertzale movement would take up a life of sheepherding and pot smoking." If there is no violence in Germany, this is precisely a sign that its social movements are falling apart, and most especially that its labor movement has been institutionalized to death. Finally the group explains that armed insurgency is a means by which to break through the wall of silence and the disinformation campaigns that surround national liberation movements all over the world. The co-discussant, faced with a group that is not hostile in the least, retreats from his original position, stating that the only place for a peace movement in Euskadi is within a popular front of which the armed struggle must constitute a vital component.

The business manager is full of good intentions, but she irritates the group when she voices the torments and doubts that assail her. She is in favor of peace and the pursuit of negotiated solutions. At the same time, she is viscerally opposed to the notion of the "political branch-office," and is therefore independentist. She votes for HB and understands its refusal to take part in institutional politics, but when a law she strongly supports, such as that concerning abortion, is debated in the Spanish Parliament, she feels cheated by the abstention of the legislators she helped to elect. The group argues but little with her, rather reasserting its role as popular spokesman and denouncing yet again the institutionalization process which, it claims, transforms popular mobilization and grassroots activism into a politicized life whereby one delegates to others, through one's vote, any commitment one may have had to charting the course of one's community.

## Intimidating

Everything changes with the arrival of the pasota. This young man believes neither in socialism nor in the independentist cause—"Their values don't interest me." He says he feels "assailed by politics," and attacks so-called militant generosity, which tries "to force its truth on others." He has no desire whatsoever to learn Euskera and, in a broader sense, pleads for a private, individual experience. At first, the group tries to convince him, saying that the oppression and difficulties he experiences as a person are experienced by other people than himself. Because they are collective, they demand collective action. Antonio goes a long way in this vein. He acknowledges the importance of personal problems and experiences, which are all too often lost in the shuffle of militancy; and admits that he attempts, not without difficulty, to retain the personal element in his dealings as a social actor. Not only does the pasota cling to his positions, but also criticizes, via the group itself, both HB and ETA: "You are just as capable of repressing me as is the cop next door," he says as he denounces the violence to which the separatists force him to submit. Tempers rise, and when the pasota accuses the members of ETA of being killers, and the group of "being on the same level," the group's anger takes two forms. The first is one of indignation, and Angel, one of whose close relatives is an ETA member who has recently been tortured in prison, prefers to leave the room rather than "bash [the co-discussant's] head in." The group will brook no criticism of those who altruistically give their blood and lives for the cause. This pasota, Antonio adds, talks just like Fraga. Following on the heels of Angel's indignation and exit, an even more shocking incident occurs. Pedro, extremely agitated, puts the young pasota through a veritable interrogation. After having declared, "I hate you, there isn't a single clear idea in that fuckin' head of yours," he assaults him with a rapid-fire series of police- or terrorist-style questions: "What do you talk about from the moment you get up in the morning until you go to bed at night? Do you greet people in the street? Do you know how to say hello? Do you critically evaluate your own opinions? Does someone else prepare your lunch or do you fix it yourself? Do you enjoy it when you get an erection?" and so on. The pasota, unnerved, nevertheless answers every question, albeit briefly. The group then begins to howl with laughter as they make vague threats about his job. Calm is then restored, and the discussion is taken up anew in a polite tone, with the matter at hand being the causes of this communications breakdown between the group and its co-discussant.

The separatist group had swallowed the pacifist militant whole. It had at first attempted to win over the pasota, but when he had resisted, it resorted to intimidation and—the word is appropriate here—verbal terrorism. The pasota's sin was not that he took an individualist position, but rather that he had placed himself at odds with the group, and especially with ETA and the armed struggle. Once he had done so, the question was no longer one of convincing him, but rather of silencing him.

### Convincing Revisited

When it meets Magda, an Aizan militant (a feminist organization closely linked to HB), the group, led by Antonio, at first tries to use its powers of persuasion on her. This woman has backed every separatist movement of the past fifteen years, continues to support HB, and takes part in demonstrations. She is, however, disenchanted or, in her words, "burnt out." This is because the feminist cause, or her understanding of it, has absolutely never been integrated into the broader movement. In everyday life, male militants or sympathizers often behave like macho men or, at worst, women-beaters. At best, they understand feminism as an egalitarian movement, whereas for Magda it constitutes a redefining of culture, human relationships, and the way one lives one's life. The group is divided over the issue. Ricardo, who is an antinuclear activist, shows himself to be truly understanding, and attempts to draw the group closer to Magda's standpoint. For his part, Pedro, an LAB trade unionist, shows himself to be totally indifferent to feminism. In another context—in France for example—the distance between Pedro, a revolutionary syndicalist, and Ricardo, an antinuclear ecologist, would be infinitely greater, given that feminism and the antinuclear movement both belong to the sphere of postindustrial struggles, whereas trade unionism, especially that of the LAB type, is deeply rooted in values endemic to industrial society. Here, however, everything tends to become merged together into a single action, in which the matter of independence is predominant. Magda vigorously attacks Pedro, denouncing his "pasotism." In order to satisfy him, she would have to join in workers' protests and take part in demonstrations for wage demands in which she has no stake. At the same time, there is no reciprocity on the part of people like Pedro. Women have been isolated by the specific themes of their action. As the meeting goes on, Magda increasingly emphasizes her differences with the group and, in spite of the efforts of Antonio, who pleads for a greater openness towards feminism by the Basque movement, Magda declares that the meeting has further alienated her from the HB umbrella.

The group is aware that its session with Magda has brought a troubling fact to light: that one of the protest movements, one of the meanings of its action, is seceding; and that it is impossible to meaningfully integrate it into the movement. Antonio's statements carry but little weight in comparison to the indifference towards feminism and "macho" practices which characterize the majority of HB militants and their affiliates. Antonio is saddened by this, and asks that there be created "channels and a climate in which a complementarity between these movements [feminists, homosexuals, etc.] can exist."

### Denouncing Repression

The day is not yet over, however, and it is now the turn of the mothers of imprisoned ETA activists to take center stage. These two women describe the sufferings they have endured, sufferings that are but small in comparison to those of their sons. They tell of how the prison administration humiliates them, and of the difficult conditions of visitation; and the discussion turns around the themes of oppression and repression. Here, more than ever, the group is both unified and possessed of arguments that help it to score points with its co-discussants. Magda, whom as we just saw had distanced herself from the group, declares, "It's things like that that make it impossible to ever give up entirely, and become a pasota. That's the reason I'm still here." The business manager herself denounces the emergency measures taken by the state. The antinuclear militant and the pacifist declare themselves ready to show the world, through the intermediary of the peace movement, the ways in which the state exerts its repression. The presence and testimonies of these prisoners' mothers bond the group together with its co-discussants, even if the latter have no illusions—"we are supporting something," concludes Magda, "that is in fact nothing more than the consequence of something else that we are refuting."

The impact of the discussions we have just summarized goes well beyond the life of the group itself. They *epitomize* the present-day practice of the separatist camp of the Basque movement. Here, the group attempted to rally, unify, and convince militants and sympathizers who had distanced themselves to some extent from the armed struggle. When faced with open hostility, it attempted to intimidate its interlocutor. Most importantly, it was able, through the spectacular highlighting of the plight of real victims of repression, to gain back some of its support, some of the commitment it had lost. The group, which has to this point been used to symbolize the struggle, will now analyze it.

## The Separatist Group's Autocritique

The analyses of the veteran group served to prove the point that one cannot expect an activist movement to unify nationalism, social movements, and the revolutionary cause without engaging in violence. With the separatist group, the stakes are similar, and the questions with which it is faced, even if posed from a different perspective, are exactly the same.

If our arguments are tenable, this group ought to find in violence the means by which to direct a number of movements and protest groups through a single coordinated strategy. It ought also to recognize the fact that such is the prime function of violence, i.e. to unify a number of more-or-less contradictory causes.

This is the most favorable argument that can possibly be advanced on the subject of ETA, which considers armed resistance to be the medium of expression for a variety of demands. Such an argument renders it impossible, however, for us to fully answer the basic questions underlying our research. While it does not demonstrate the existence of a *real* relationship between violence and actual protest in Euskadi, its treatment will nevertheless constitute a first analytical step for us.

The group's original statements were, in fact, quite distant from such a notion. Its spur-of-the-moment theory on the armed struggle was a militant discourse which blended together two minor and one major interpretation. Violence can be presented at times as a simple response to the violence perpetrated by another, to central state terrorism. One may also consider it to be a means by which to intensify the crisis in or

the decay of the prevailing system. Primarily, however, the armed struggle is a global response to a problem which itself cannot be correctly
perceived except in its globality. It is for this reason that when the researchers proffer the notion of the unification, through violence, of a
multiplicity of causes, the group rejects it out of hand. Here as in every
situation that would follow the group strongly resists any suggestion
that theirs might be a diversified movement. Thus, there is for it but one
form of nationalism. Purely cultural nationalism does not exist, save
when it is sublimated into folklore studies or PNV regionalism. It also
explains that if the nationalist cause has become strengthened since 1977,
this is because it has been purged. Yesterday's allies have become today's
adversaries, with the PSOE and PNV clearly taking the side of the ruling
powers. The communists have also distanced themselves from ETA. At
first, this reinforcement isolated the nationalists. As they have taken on
new life, however, these have shown themselves to be the sole persons
capable of taking care, through their struggle, of the various and sundry
needs of the people. The national liberation movement offers the social
activists, whom the reformists had briefly hoodwinked, their sole work-
able perspective. It alone has a platform, a promise for a fairer and
more rational society. The researchers, who maintain their analytical
distinction between social causes and national causes, are vigorously
challenged. The group reproaches them for a lack of comprehension and
for their insistence in compartmentalizing a unified whole. If it was theory they had wished to discuss, the researchers would have done better
to have convened the *burus,* the heads of the movement. National and
social, the group explains, are inseparable; and in the arena of social
struggles it is artificial to presume to draw distinctions or point out
contradictions, between the labor movement and feminism or the antinuclear struggle, for example. Theirs is a global platform, in which a
clean break with the past, through the founding of a new society and
national liberation, is the solution to every problem. More than mere
unification, separatism implies the *fusion* of the diverse components of
the Basque action. It simultaneously entails a Leninist agenda, according
to which the armed struggle serves as a rudder to guide political action.
None but ETA, the vanguard of this struggle, is capable of viewing the
situation from a sufficiently elevated perspective. The rank-and-file
actors, with their special causes, could never presume to have such an
overview.

Defending their arguments, the researchers ask that the group examine
a theory of armed resistance according to which the armed struggle

would have stemmed from a multitude of actions begun by special-interest groups, each with its own principles—nationalist, ecologist, labor, etc.—to defend. These would then have been unified through a separatist political discourse, and translated into action via ETA-inspired armed insurgency. Once more, the group widely rejects such an analytical procedure, and critiques its practical consequences. If one allows that there are a plurality of causes worth fighting for, then one must also allow that each separate struggle has its own specificity. This opens the way to separate treatments of each struggle, which in the end can only lead to an institutionalization judged by the group as the kiss of death. This refusal to negotiate and to institutionalize conflict is inseparable from a concept of action in which the agitation of the special-interest groups and the armed insurgency must rely on one another for their very survival. The armed struggle complements the grassroots protests by providing them with the necessary conditions for continued growth; but the converse is also true, for as Manuel explains, "without popular mobilization, the armed struggle would die."

The separatist group tends to become close-mouthed whenever the researchers attempt to introduce analytical approaches by which to deconstruct their action into its constituent parts. Its great strength, which is also an obstacle to communication, is its rejection of anything and everything that goes against its universalist reading of its action.

Yet, as this long discussion between the researchers and the group progresses, a pattern—according to which the group accepts a compartmentalized image of the different components that violence fuses together—begins to develop and take hold.

Hereafter, ETA is viewed as an instrument by which constituent actions can be brought to their conclusion. ETA shows workers that they can use force to make their bosses yield to their demands; and antinuclear activists that they can paralyze the Lemoniz power station by physically eliminating its directors, etc. It is also, and above all else, a vanguard and a synthesizing force. "It brings together the forerunners and the heel-draggers, and synthesizes, rationalizes, them," often taking a long lead on the special-interest activists whose field of vision is limited to this or that particular issue.

There is no concrete proof, however, that such a harmonious relation between the special-interest groups and ETA exists, even if ETA postulates such a model. Contrariwise, there is nothing to stop us from thinking that ETA destroys social movements much more often than it furthers them, or that it is more of a bane than a boon to the Basque nation.

## The Paradoxical Convergence of the Two Groups

For the veteran group, the armed struggle—even if it does at times betray the inability of the Spanish democracy to address a certain number of demands and protests—is the fruit of an inversion and the result of a loss of meaning. For the separatist group, the armed struggle is meaningful, constituting as it does a national and social liberation movement's most elevated expression.

On the face of things, the two groups are in total disagreement, in their militant practice as well as in their theoretical analysis. In truth, however, the two converge and complement one another.

The veteran group rejects violence but is incapable of developing a broad-based visionary model of action. The separatist group has elaborated such a strategy and states that it must necessarily entail armed insurgency. In both cases, violence is, in the final analysis, defined in the same way: it constitutes the only possible answer to the problem of unifying a wide array of social struggles with the political and national struggles. Organized violence fuses together a multitude of action principles and raises them to a higher power. These principles, while real for the separatists, are mythic for the veterans, and it is here and here alone that they truly part ways.

Our research has thus brought us to a definite conclusion concerning the relationship that obtains between activist principles and violence. The armed struggle is, as we have demonstrated for both of the groups, inseparable from a revolutionary nationalist platform.

The abandonment of this platform by the veteran group enabled it to engage in a lively critique of the armed struggle. This platform continues to be embraced by the separatists, i.e. by militants who bear witness, by their simple existence, to the concrete reality of the grassroots struggles.

Once again, we must acknowledge the unstructured nature of these various struggles. LAB trade unionism, as we have seen, has but a small minority following, has little use for negotiation, and is quite estranged from ELA or UGT activism. The antinuclear movement was considerably weakened by deadly ETA interference. Feminism is hardly taken seriously within HB. Yet, in working-class neighborhoods, one finds a constant presence of this organization or of groups or associations closely connected with it. This is especially the case where community demands have become radicalized and anger is rampant, but where there is also some organization by which to exert sustained pressure on municipal and other authorities. HB's electoral support, often close to 20 percent of the total vote, moreover corresponds primarily to an intransigent nationalism which is of a different order from the PNV's more moderate policy of negotiating its nationalist platform.

For all of these reasons, it behooves us to recognize that the militants of the separatist group do represent popular sentiments which have their roots in neighborhoods or factories and are possessed of a high sense of purpose. At the same time, we must acknowledge the fact that the movements which have served as mouthpieces for such sentiments have lost much of their strength and cohesion.

ETA violence is primarily the result of the increasingly difficult task of simultanesously speaking in the name of the suppressed nation, social movements, and the revolution. It is aggravated by the fact that the meanings of each of these three components have themselves become diminished or deconstructed.

# 15

## Conclusion to Part Three

In the Basque country as much as anywhere else in the world, it is impossible for a movement's universalist platform—at once national, social, and revolutionary—to translate directly into an enduring and well-organized action capable of limiting and controlling its own use of violence. From this perspective, our research has brought a number of points to light.

The armed struggle can only truly exist when the three central ideals of the Basque movement are evoked conjointly. Pure nationalism, however independentist it may be, a one-issue social agenda grounded in the labor movement, or a strictly political activism of Marxist-Leninist inspiration can never give rise, in isolation, to the long-term practice of organized violence.

At the same time—as the intense debate within the veteran group demonstrated—it is impossible to simultaneously maintain a broad-based, visionary platform and attempt to pull together the major components of Basque action without engaging in armed resistance. For anyone who would presume to maintain such a unifying perspective, the rejection of violence must necessarily entail a tempering of national aspirations, an acceptance of an institutional or negotiated handling of social conflicts, and a certain distance from the Marxist-Leninist models amended by the left in the 1970s.

These observations should aid us in understanding ETA's historical trajectory. With the end of the Franco era and the beginnings of the Spanish transition to democracy, the task of holding the basic components of the Basque movement together became more difficult than ever. The common enemy, at once Spanish, authoritarian, corporatist, and dictatorial, was gone. The more artificial the unification of the Basque movement became, the greater the tendency to rush into violence as a means to affording it a unity that no longer corresponded to the multiplicity of Basque struggles, causes, adversaries, and actors.

The unique evolution of each of the component parts of ETA action further tended to broaden the armed struggle. As soon as it became possible for institutions to satisfy, at least partially, nationalist demands, as soon as the economic crisis began to erode and weaken the social protest movements, as soon as the Basque and Spanish political systems diversified and began to function in a democratic fashion, Basque separatism had to break its ties with Basque negotiation. It in fact turned against the latter, giving voice to and radicalizing a nation's anger on the one hand, and distancing itself from the actual experience of those greatly weakened persons whom it claimed to be representing on the other.

Today, it is impossible for us to identify the armed struggle with a rationale of terrorist action. ETA's power base extends well beyond the quite considerable 15 or 20 percent of the electorate that votes for HB. The independentist and separatist tendencies for which it is the mouthpiece themselves generate tensions that are felt in the internal workings of the PNV itself. ETA enjoys popular support that can only be qualified as social, in spite of the situationalist rhetoric of HB's political adversaries. The armed struggle is linked to the radical faction of popular protest movements as well as to demands which, under the prevailing cultural and economic crisis, have flared into social rage. It does, moreover, retain certain contacts with the loci of meaning it claims to represent. In a certain sense, it reinjects the political scene with all that had been voided from it, providing a society in crisis with a forum of expression it would not find elsewhere. It is thus impossible to speak of inversion here.

*Although we may shock, we must therefore conclude that, sociologically speaking, ETA violence is, on the whole, not terrorist.* It has clearly been tending in that direction, pushed there in part by international factors—not the least of which was the 1984 French policy reversal—which have played against it. It is not, however, possessed of terrorism's character of blind frenzy, nor is it marked by the total disjunction from every support base that defines terrorism.

The acceleration of an inversion process in which ends become confused with means, and in which the armed insurgent functions in a strictly ideological mode disconnected from the practices of those he claims to represent, constitutes a dangerous risk for ETA. It may, in the end, be the price ETA will have to pay before such trends—which, while they continue to be generated out of political violence, can at times veer off into terrorism—disappear.

This is truly a paradoxical situation. The more Euskadi benefits from the transfer of power, the more the declining labor movement falls apart or becomes institutionalized, the more the political system in both the Basque country and Spain functions in a democratic fashion, the more the armed struggle—perhaps relieved of a large number of its present activists and still in pursuit of its primal and unalterable myth—will tend to engage in deadly forms of action. In the present situation, in which it is appropriate to speak, in overall terms, of political violence rather than of a rationale of terrorist action, military or police intervention cannot hope, through independent action, to wipe out the armed struggle, whose popular support base remains massive. At the same time, one should not hope for some hypothetical negotiating process to put an end to the violence. This remark, which is based for the most part on the work carried out with our research groups, in no way implies that political or repressive action would be totally ineffective. It simply serves to remind us of the impossibility of reducing the armed struggle to nothing more than so many outbursts of violence; and of the difficulty if not the impossibility of arbitrating nonnegotiable positions. Here too, we see the limits of those analyses which are too quick to diametrically oppose violence and democracy to one another. The Basque experience shows us on the one hand that a social entity which has been expelled or reprocessed by a democracy can readily reemerge, in some new and radical form, in such unexpected forms as armed resistance. On the other, a nationalist phenomenon, when it takes the form of a call to separatism and independence, is difficult to introduce into the same arena as those demands with which a democracy is capable of dealing.

# Part Four

## INTERNATIONAL TERRORISM

Terrorist actors have always been capable of moving in circuits not necessarily circumscribed by national borders. So it is that specialist literature has often hearkened to the foundational and paradigmatic phenomenon of the Assassins, whose "well-tempered terror" spread itself, at the beginning of the millennium, across the farthest reaches of the Muslim world.[1]

Yet, the very notion of international or transnational terrorism has only come into its own in recent years, in the context of the airline hijackings carried out in the name of the Palestinian cause. This group neither holds the monopoly nor the patent on actions of this kind. At no time, however, has a national liberation front ever carried out a terrorist-type action on such a planetary scale.

Faced with such a phenomenon, one may be tempted to choose for one's standpoint that level at which the armed struggle operates, and see it as a tool put to calculated use for the wielding of influence over geopolitical relations, both on a regional (Middle East) and a global (East-West) scale. Our viewpoint will, however, be of an entirely different order as we attempt to deal with these two sets of problems which have catapulted international terrorism into the important place it occupies today. The first of these, of central importance throughout the 1970s down to 1982 (when Israeli troops entered Lebanon), is the Palestinian question. The second is the Lebanese question.

A strategic or geopolitical analysis, while it can make it possible to reconstruct and even anticipate terrorist strategy, cannot explain how this or that actor came to take up the course of terrorist violence, and tells us nothing about the sociopolitical or ideological process out of which the very idea of resorting to extreme forms of armed resistance

215

emerges and becomes practically applied. It isolates a particular level—here, that of international relations—which it views in a relatively autonomous fashion, while taking a relatively limited interest in the trajectory that brought the actor to this particular level. It further leaves out of its analysis the actual experience of that people, class, nation, or community in whose name the terrorist action is carried out, and the ways in which this experience fuels or dampens its action.

The bounds within which a sociological analysis of international terrorism (a problematic term, as we will show) may be carried out become all the more restricted when one goes beyond the threshold of the most deeply cherished ideals of a given activist movement, and rises to that of the interplay of political and military forces. At this level, violence is apparently reduced to a stupefying blend of barbarism and tactical rationality, of meaninglessness and strategy. This does not mean that such analyses should ignore these political and military levels, and entrench itelf within a sociologically more classical treatment of those levels at which social relationships and community consciousness first take shape. Its particular contribution will consist in describing the relationship that obtains between these two levels, and in bringing to light the ways in which they are mutually informing.

The two phenomena we will be studying here shade into one another, and present a certain unity. Given that both proceed from the same world region, the Middle East, this is, from the outset, a geographical unity. Theirs is also a unity of form, since the two founded by themselves the very notion of international terrorism, at least on a popular level. Lastly, there is the historical unity. The violent developments that have occurred in Lebanon, and terrorist violence in particular, are intimately connected to the presence and departure (in 1983) of the most central organizations of the Palestinian movement.

Nonetheless, this is but a partial unity. In a certain sense, the Lebanese question is a reverse image of that presented by the Palestinian movement. The former does not stem from the constitution of a historical subject whose aim it was to build a nation-state. Its origins rather lie in a fragile state whose disintegration opened the way to patterns of behavior that have spanned much of the spectrum of human violence, from petty crime to international terrorism. In both cases, our basic objective will be to analytically disentangle the various currents of thought that have combined to form what Western opinion has rather confusedly grouped under the single oversimplified all-purpose heading of international terrorism.

# 16

# The Palestinian Movement

Viewed from Israel, the Palestinian movement is essentially a terrorist movement. This is a hard-and-fast definition which, widely accepted even beyond the borders of Israel, proceeds from the discourse of the actor himself.[1] Conversely, the Palestinian resistance generally takes exception to such a definition of itself. It explains that terrorism is in the main foreign to its action, and argues that it is in fact more proper to the forces of Zionism, who are experts in such matters; to wit, in the activities of the Irgun and the Stern group, particularly in the critical postwar years from 1945 to 1948. This too is an example of an actor's discourse. Here, let us rather approach the matter on the topical and limited basis of the hypothetical link that may be established between the various truly terrorist episodes that have marked the history of Palestinian struggle and the Palestinian movement itself.

The events we will treat here are peripheral to any full-scale war or guerrilla war being waged against Israel. They also differ from domestic terrorism, from those actions of blind fury which, carried out by Palestinians within Israeli-controlled regions, are generally directed against civilian targets. These are rather actions that fall under the heading of terrorism targeting or carried out against non-Israeli populations, i.e. international or state-sponsored terrorism. These include airline hijackings, assassinations, bombings, kidnappings, and other criminal activities which, carried out outside the strictly geographical zone of conflict, and in accordance with a terrorist rationale, purportedly bear an

217

indirect if not convoluted relationship to both the Palestinian movement and the actual experience of the Palestinian masses in whose name such acts are perpetrated.

As soon as one takes the position that every Palestinian action is, by definition, terrorist in nature, one abandons all claim to ascertaining the specificity of the kinds of incidents we have just enumerated. Furthermore, such a position forces one to postulate a continuity that manifests itself on two levels, i.e. the continuity between the Palestinian movement and every act of terrorism committed in its name, or simply by Palestinians; and the historical continuity between the first airline hijackings (1968) and those that followed, as well as the Munich massacre (1972), the Entebbe affair (1976), the assassinations organized by Abu Nidal in the years following 1975, and so on.

Refusing to treat these, even hypothetically, as terrorist acts makes it impossible to understand these episodes, generally considered as external to the Palestinian movement. As for their perpetrators, these become reduced, out of hand, to so many madmen, traitors, and irrational actors.

Neither of these two perspectives are acceptable. The terrorist patterns of behavior we will be studying can only be understood in the context of the Palestinian movement as a collective action; this does not imply, however, that they ought necessarily to be viewed as direct expressions or agents of either the movement or the national consciousness that founds it. It is more appropriate in fact to note the discontinuities and breaks between practices which, although they may be identical in form, are nonetheless embedded in particular historical situations and thereby disclose different meanings. In some cases, terrorism is an outward manifestation of internal conflicts, while in others it is a movement's most exalted and meaningful self-expression. In still others, it can also betray a deep-rooted crisis, or simply be the fruit of a situation of heteronomy which, in the unraveling process whereby a movement loses its independence and any sense of meaning it may have previously had, triggers a group's self-destruction and the destruction of the struggle out of which it originally emerged.

For all of these reasons we will, instead of working from the rhetoric of Israeli or Palestinian actors, give a sociological account of the movement. Such an approach will help to explain patterns of behavior which, while they have nothing in common with the guiding principles of the movement, nevertheless remain incomprehensible outside of the Palestinian cause.

## Ways of Approaching Palestinian Terrorism

It is important that we locate our methodology in relation to the major approaches that have been put forward on the subject of Palestinian terrorism. We have already mentioned the first two of these.

The first is based on acts, both accomplished and projected, which are seen as so many instrumental responses to a situation that itself stems from a network of constraints upon the capacity of the concerned organizations to act. In this case, analysis consists of an examination of the international system into which an actor, whose calculations have led him to draw upon that most unusual resource known as terrorism, flings himself. This methodological approach relegates to darkness or shadow any phenomenon that cannot be reduced to an interplay between terrorism and counterterrorism. It is an approach that is most amenable to more-or-less superficial analyses of the fanaticism or insanity of activist insurgents[2]—or of their obliviousness to reality, which in turn renders them vulnerable to outside manipulation, most often from Moscow.[3] At times, terrorism can even become hypostasized. No longer a phenomenon to be understood, it becomes an explanatory category.

The second aforementioned approach proceeds from a refusal to acknowledge any notion of differentiation between the Palestinian movement and its organizations on the one hand, and the practice of terrorism on the other. In this perspective, the Palestinian movement is consubstantially and essentially terrorist in nature, an umbrella organization that combines the most extremist of groups into a system in which every actor, including the "moderates," profit from a terrorist policy. "It has in no way been proven," writes Annie Kriegel, "that these apparently dissident operations (the Rue Copernic attack, for example) fall outside of PLO control: it is standard procedure for the leaders of the Palestinian high command to lay the blame, for terrorist attacks it has in fact programmed but which for a variety of reasons it does not wish to claim responsibility, at the feet of groups of unverified PLO affiliation."[4] It is true that one often finds, even at the heart of Fatah, the most central and often the most moderate or negotiation-oriented Palestinian organization, an ambivalent mixture of declarations that are overtly hostile, in both precept and practice, to international terrorism, and manifestations of joy or support for these same precepts and practices. It is not difficult to delineate a multitude of levels of discourse, often highly contradictory in appearance, in the statements made by Palestinian leaders.[5] Similarly,

we may fail to note that a single speech may be pitched to several different publics—Western, Arab, or socialist-bloc governments; Western
public opinion, the movement's own social base, etc.—who will at times
hear it in a wide variety of ways. This or that denial, for example, will
be taken literally or rejected as false by the Western public, and viewed
by the Palestinian masses as a disclaimer carrying the weight of an affirmation.

The more one is committed to or identifies oneself with the state of
Israel, the more difficulty one will have in treating the Palestinian movement as anything other than a relatively tightly integrated whole whose
many-faceted threat is grounded in its great unity. Differentiating features are therefore minimized, denied, or presented as so many proofs
of a manipulative subtlety whose aim it is to cloud the picture, thus
making an apparently dissident operation yet another manifestation of
Palestinian perversion. In broader terms, anything that does not directly
fit into the framework of such a monolithic rationale is reinterpreted or
inverted in such a way as to make it fit.

While this standpoint is too extremist to be accepted out of hand, it
may be that it deserves more credit than we will give it here. In the
absence of solid data, one ought perhaps not to exclude the existence of
secret or well-concealed links in places in which we might otherwise tend
to see an absence of continuity. There nonetheless comes a point where
the image of a relatively well-integrated terrorist movement can no
longer hold up, especially when we note that the terrorist acts here are
the work of groups who will not stop until they have blocked every
possible avenue of negotiated solution to the conflict with Israel and
have, furthermore, physically eliminated any Palestinian who has attempted to back such a solution.

A third approach, belonging to the field of political science, concentrates on those internal decision-making processes of the Palestinian organizations which may trigger a transition to terrorism. It is in this vein
that Alain Gresh,[6] in his excellent book, analyzes the functioning of the
PLO, its decision-making processes, its internal debate, the evolution of
the organizations which take part in its meetings, etc. This approach is
already more sensitive to the meanings of group actions, and to the social
and nationalist values it espouses or attacks. Its limits are the same as
those of any sociology of organizations. Here, action is analyzed on the
basis of its most visible and structured manifestations. The actor—who
is not reduced to his terrorist activities alone—is nonetheless defined, as
in the previous approach, by his calculations, strategies, or his capacity

to realize his objectives; that is, by the changes he can implement or by which he can be influenced more than by that which he sees as providing meaning to his resistance. The emphasis placed on the political character of the organizations can also lead scholars like Gresh to minimize and give short shrift to the practical magnitude of the terrorist phenomenon per se. Bard E. O'Neil, in his analysis of the armed struggle in Palestine, treats terrorism in terms of instrumental violence, taking up an approach in which the matter at hand is to identify "a number of factors having a major bearing on some outcome or dependent variable (in our case the success or failure of a strategy of protracted revolutionary insurgency) . . . to suggest those conditions under which specific factors are more critical than they might otherwise be."[7] More precisely, O'Neil studies from his particular standpoint a variety of strategies which lead him to treat "popular support" as an element of strategy: in order to gain their support, the actor must greatly impress his constituency, using such means as material assistance, terror, etc. to both call for their support and win them over.[8] In this perspective, terrorism proper is a tactical instrument used either by the movement as a whole or by a given organization whose aim it is to make its voice heard either within the movement or on the international scene. It is, according to O'Neil, a form of warfare, on a par with conventional and guerrilla warfare. This means however that any terrorist action which cannot be related to some form of instrumentality must fall outside of the scope of his analysis. It is for this reason that this third approach is at odds with the second one, which takes all terrorist acts, regardless of their political origins, to be its starting point, and which tends, in a rather heavy-handed way, to link them with the Palestinian movement as a whole, without inquiring about that movement's internal debates or political jockeying.

The argument we will defend takes the *Palestinian movement*, a movement that is not defined as a political actor, but rather as a poorly unified combination of national and sociopolitical ideals, the immediate manifestations and permutations of which can at times be carried to the point of terrorism—as its starting point. Rather than considering "popular support" to be a mobilizable resource, it rather stands O'Neil's argument on its head and takes this base or "support," which generates the meaning of such actions, as its starting point. The Palestinians are not a great heteronomous mass which an array of techniques would serve to align with this or that political organization. They are rather the heart of a movement capable of providing itself with organizations, and influencing their political and strategic workings. This brings us to the central issue of whether terrorism is an expression of these very workings, or whether it rather stems from processes which serve to alienate the Palestinian movement from the actions of those who claim themselves to be the spokespersons or vanguard.

There is no sense in treating the preceding approaches as hopelessly incompatible. They essentially correspond, each in its own area of strength, to three relatively independent and hierarchized problematics. These three registers feed on, fuel, and interact with one another, even as each retains its uniqueness, whence the analytical development we have chosen to put forward. *Starting with the Palestinian movement, we will look at the political organizations and processes it implements and by which it is influenced, and conclude with a treatment of terrorism proper.*[9]

## Palestinian Nationalism

The Palestinian movement, gradually gaining in momentum, was not immediately perceived as the formation of a national consciousness that had been abused, flouted, and denied by another national consciousness which had succeeded in realizing its aims, i.e. that of the Zionist Jews living in what became an independent state in 1948. More important than the Palestinian uprisings of 1921, 1924, 1933, and 1935, the great strike of 1936 was a combination of social demands and opposition to Jewish immigration into Palestine which, taking the form of political pressure, was at times accompanied by violence directed against the British, the then dominant colonial power in that part of the Middle East. After the Second World War, at the same time as the Zionists were preparing to found the state of Israel and the British were more and more clearly headed towards the withdrawal the Americans had been encouraging, the Palestinians were having a difficult time in holding their own against an adversary that was driving peasants off their lands and out of their villages, and resorting to the use of force to enforce its own agenda. The Palestinian resistance was poorly organized, clumsy in its relations with the British authorities, and backed but little by neighboring Arab governments. Most important of all, there was no Palestinian national consciousness to carry it forward, and even less to unify it. Elie Sanbar has shown that something that has been liquidated is not so much a state (and even less a nation-state) as it is a community defined by traditional social relations: a certain relationship with the land, and forms of political organization in which clans and local powers backed by small groups tend to predominate.[10] Like a number of others, includ-

ing Nadia Ben Jelloun-Ollivier,[11] he stresses the uniqueness of the relationship, or rather the nonrelationship, that was inaugurated in the course
of founding the Jewish state in Palestine. The Jews did more than simply
assert their domination. They drove a people off its land with the seeming
intention of wiping out an entire society. The Palestinians were transformed into emigrants and exiles instead of being colonized, and the
relationship of exclusion or of alienation that arose between themselves
and the Israelis carried with it consequences which have been described
at length by Ben Jelloun-Ollivier. No attempt was made to assimilate or
integrate them, or to generate intermediate strata of Palestinians capable
of participating in the economic, political, and cultural life of the Israeli
state. The Palestinians who stayed behind would be restricted to jobs
within nonstrategic sectors, often with great distances between their
workplace and their homes.

One can hardly qualify their defensive action of 1948 as a nationalist
insurgency. This date was the beginning of a long period characterized
by the incapacity of the Palestinians—many of whom had moved into
refugee camps in countries bordering on Israel—to go beyond their feelings of emptiness, of loss, of the death of a society, or to translate their
ever-present dream of returning into some constructive form of activity.
To be sure, influential Palestinians were active on the Arab scene, but to
little effect, and the notion of a Palestinian cause was barely perceptible.
The Palestinian government established in Gaza in 1948 under the aegis
of the Arab High Commission was stillborn. Later, when the Palestinians
came to be represented at the Arab League Council, it was the council
itself which designated their delegate—which tells us something about
the inability of the Palestinians to devise their own forms of representation. "At the end of the 1950s," says Ahmed Hamzé, "people had
stopped using the name of Palestine. It was as if the Palestinian question
had been forgotten for good."[12]

In 1952, a group of young officers overthrew the king of Egypt and
Nasser came to power. Hereafter there developed, throughout the Arab
world, a revolutionary nationalism which would, down to 1967, domi-
nate the political thought of a number of popular movements as well as
a few governments. The first traces of the construction of a Palestinian
action bore the stamp of the Nasser ideology, while the first attempts to
politically organize the Palestinians were inspired by Arab nationalism
and directed by regimes which, taking the Egyptian lead, clamored after
the nationalist cause. We will return shortly to this orientation and the
many forms it took. Although Arab nationalism may have been the

cradle of the earliest attempts to organize a Palestinian action, it never-theless remains the case that the veritable forging of this action took place *not in the development of nationalism, but in its overturning, and in the assertion of the primacy of the Palestinian cause.* This overthrow was the work of the founders of Fatah, who have remained the backbone of the movement ever since.

Until the early 1960s, the very idea of a Palestinian nation was practically absent from Palestinian discourse. None of the criteria which would allow one to speak of a nation could truly apply to the Palestinians whose political elite, rather than delineating its own unique constituency, located itself within the much wider cause of the Arab homeland. The notion of a properly Palestinian history or culture was but rarely advanced. There had been no Palestinian state in the past. All the Palestinians had known was administrative and territorial dislocation, first under the Ottomans and later under the British. Now it was a total dislocation which they were experiencing, with a portion of their population being spread across a number of Arab countries and the remainder remaining in Israel and the so-called occupied territories (the Gaza Strip and the West Bank, which the Israelis prefer to call Judea and Samaria). *The Palestinian nation is an invention devised for the most part by the core founders of Fatah.*

Since their student days in Cairo in the early 1950s, Yasser Arafat, Salah Khalaf, and a few others have cherished one central idea, an idea that was as simple as it was healthy: the Palestinians could not and should not have to rely on themselves. Arafat himself has often explained the genesis of this idea. Even as late as 1984, he was still speaking indignantly of the postwar period, of the careless and indolent Arab League, and of the humiliation he felt when the order was given to disarm the "irregulars" of which he had been a part.[13] This idea took shape throughout the 1950s, during which time the nucleus of Fatah founders had established itself in the Gulf states, and most especially in Kuwait, where the governments in power allowed them the greatest freedom of movement, and where they saw the greatest potential for setting up an organization. Fatah was created in 1959 (according to Salah Khalaf; according to Khaled al-Hassan, the group was founded in 1962). The Palestinian nationalist platform, as it was drawn up at that time, was based on five principles: (1) the goal was the liberation of Palestine; (2) armed insurgency was necessary for the realization of this objective; it would thus be necessary to (3) rely on the Palestinians' ability to organize themselves, (4) to cooperate with allied Arab powers, and (5) with sympathetic international powers.[14] Viewed from our present-day perspective, it is easy to see how these principles, which have remained unchanged, have dominated the history of the Palestinian movement. But in the early 1960s, these principles stood out in marked opposition to the then-predominant ideologies. This not only marginalized the group, but even made it difficult for it to maintain a real organizational base in countries like Egypt. This was, in fact, the height of Arab nationalism and of the political ideology of Arab unity. Applied to the specific question of Palestine, the theme of Arab unity implied the subordination of the struggle to a cause of much greater magnitude which, were it to succeed, would insure the liberation of Palestine. In practical terms, this theme made the Palestinians powerless and pale actors, whose specificity was of but secondary concern within the context of the pan-Arab action.

Until 1967, the Palestinian nationalist cause was limited to a cluster of tiny groups which, at odds with and crowded out by more widely accepted ideologies, enjoyed but limited support. When in 1964 the Arab nations founded the Palestine Liberation Organization (PLO)—and provided it soon after with a military wing, the Palestine Liberation Army (PLA)[15]—they turned over its leadership to Ahmad ash-Shuqayri, an influential figure who had a long background in inter-Arab diplomacy, with the idea of creating a locus for Palestine representation within the broader context of the Arab nation, and thereby under strict Egyptian control. Prior to the Arab defeat in 1967, the PLO, riddled with internal tensions and dissension, was totally ineffectual. Most particularly, it was marked by the ascendancy of an Arab nationalism which was, by definition, hostile to the reversal of priorities inherent in the kind of Palestinian nationalism championed by Fatah. The charter drawn up by the PLO in 1964 made no mention of Palestinian self-determination in a liberated homeland. "The very idea of a specifically Palestinian struggle or of a particular role for the Palestinian people [was] treated as regionalism (iqlimiya) and [was], as such, suspect."[16]

Fatah carried out, to the best of its still quite modest abilities, commando operations against Israel which were generally considered to have contributed secondarily to the outbreak of the 1967 war. A catastrophe for the Arab nations, the Six-Day War constituted a historic opportunity for Fatah. In effect, what had been a stinging failure for Arab nationalism was, for Fatah, an opportunity to embark on a course of action in which it has yet to be either defeated or humiliated. Hereafter, it was the meteoric rise of Fatah which, after briefly seeking to chart a course across the occupied territories with the hope, quickly dashed, of organizing a Palestinian uprising there, quickly took up other strategies.

From here on in, Fatah's (successful) line of action would consist of maintaining optimum relations with the Arab countries as a group—which placed it squarely within the sphere of Arab unity—while maintaining an autonomy and independent existence that could only be sustained through broad-based support by the Palestinian people.[17] Fatah won this support, particularly in the refugee camps that were forming or growing as the result of the Six-Day War, in a way that was nothing less than spectacular. The spread of Fatah ideas and thus the development of a Palestinian national consciousness were inseparable from the practice of armed insurgency. In March 1968, the Battle of Karameh was the first occasion for Fatah to display its military prowess. Fatah resistance to an Israeli army that had converged on this village on the east bank of the Jordan to wipe out the Palestinian guerrilla movement was, in the eyes of the Arab world, a symbol of Arab honor, courage, and efficiency that cut across the images left behind by the debacle of the Six-Day War. Nasser became an active supporter of Fatah, introducing Arafat to Moscow, while King Hussein of Jordan, who had declared "Now we are all fedayeens" after the defeat, was impressed. In the following months, the Palestinians would mobilize on a massive scale,[18] providing Fatah with sufficient stature to take control of the PLO in 1969, with Nasser's blessing. Even following Shuqayri's resignation, however, the organization remained a kind of Palestinian parliament rather than an offshoot of Fatah. The Palestinian national charter, which founded PLO doctrine, was modified in July 1968 with the important introduction of articles underscoring the direct link between the armed struggle and the national consciousness: "The armed struggle is the sole means to liberating Palestine. It is also a basic strategy, and not merely a tactical phase. The Arab population of Palestine affirms its absolute determination and its firm resolution to continue in its armed struggle and to work for a popular armed revolution for the liberation of its homeland . . . Commando operations constitute the core of the Palestinian people's war of liberation."

Over a period of some ten years, a national consciousness arose which, as the repository of the basic ideals of the Palestinian movement, asserted itself as a power to be reckoned with. This consciousness was, first and foremost, concerned with contributing to Arab unity, effecting with regard to Arab nationalism what we have termed a reversal, rather than a break. "It was not the Palestinian revolution," said Arafat in the afore-mentioned interview, "as should have been the case, which found itself at the top of the pyramid, supported by a healthy Arab world. It was rather that which bore the weight of the entire Arab world during one of the darkest periods of its history."[19]

Fatah did not break with the theme of Arab unity, but rather reordered its mythic structure, which the 1967 defeat had greatly shaken. In so doing, it put forward a new strategy by which to reconcile ends and means, the desire for Arab victory, and the definition of realistic objectives. As is often the case, it was during an ideological crisis—in this case, the crisis of Arab nationalism—that a new self-image (here, that of Palestinian nationalism) sprang to life, at the same time as armed resistance came to be viewed as indispensable.

This reversal took the form of a number of political actions, out of which certain constants emerge. The more the Arab world appeared to be divided and torn apart, the more Fatah insisted upon a policy of non- (or strictly limited) intervention in the internal affairs of the individual states, and the more its strategy consequently became a difficult and at times highly sophisticated game of diplomacy.

Fatah made it a principle to neither support any regime against its opposition, nor to support any opposition to a given regime. This position became untenable at times, especially within host countries harboring a large number of Palestinians, in which Fatah's operational needs required a degree of freedom which could at times compromise governmental authority or state sovereignty. In the course of Fatah's short history, there were two long episodes during which the organization was unable to maintain this prudent policy of refusing to meddle in an Arab nation's internal affairs, and most especially those of a host country. These occurred in Jordan, where the Palestinian organizations were driven out on the heels of the terrible hostilities of September 1970; and in Lebanon, following that country's second civil war (1975). Even in these cases, however, this policy left its mark. As a number of observers have noted, Fatah bucked, for as long as possible, the strong pressure exerted by the PFLP (Popular Front for the Liberation of Palestine) to heighten the conflict with King Hussein of Jordan in 1970. In Lebanon, in 1975–76, it worked harder than any other group to avoid a split with Syria, and to avoid entering into too close an alliance with Junblatt's Progressive Socialist party. It has been its refusal to rely upon any single country or to take Arab unity for granted that has permitted Fatah to portray itself as the author of that unity. This was explained by Arafat to the journalist Eric Rouleau in the course of a long monologue: "The Palestinians will not commit the errors of the past; never again will they be the tools of the Arab governments who used them to further their own interests; it is the Palestinian revolution that will catalyze Arab nationalism, and not the opposite" (as had been maintained by every manner of pan-Arabist, the Nasserites, the Ba'athists, etc.).[20] Fatah's problem is not only one of placing itself squarely within a real cultural unity, or of attempting to transform that into a political unity. It is also, in more concrete terms, one of benefiting from the assistance and support of the widest and most diversified sources possible, without letting itself be drawn into conflicts that might someday arise between those who answer its call, and without itself appearing to constitute a threat to any given Arab country. As Khalil al-Wazir (Abu Jihad) once stated in an interview, "The PLO (dominated by Fatah) does not enter one axis in the Arab world against another; quite the contrary. The Palestinian cause demands the greatest possible Arab support from all sides."[21]

A second constant, closely linked to the first, devolves from the realistic and pragmatic nature of Fatah's discourse and activities (as opposed to the "ideological" nature of the PFLP and the PDFLP [Popular Democratic Front for the Liberation of Palestine]). Its guiding principles are clear and vigorous, not only because its leadership core has remained unchanged since its founding,[22] but also because its internal debate (and even its changes of direction) have been dictated much more by tactical and strategic imperatives and evaluations of relative strength in given situations than by abstract or ideological considerations.

Throughout its transition from subordination to the Arab League to a pivotal and autonomous status—as well as in its felicitous contention that it did not constitute one of the expected effects of the triumph of the Arab state but was rather its primary condition—Palestinian nationalism has become a guiding light for a number of other causes, and a major point of reference for resistance movements whose highest ideals it supplies from without. This has primarily been the case with political activism inside a good number of Arab nations, as well as political actions carried out by the Arab states themselves. It has also held throughout the world, for a wide array of anticapitalist and anti-imperialist protest movements, some of whose militants have worked for the Palestinian cause itself. Having become relatively independent, the Palestinian consciousness has sanctioned an activist diplomacy which has at times bordered on the arrogant. Relations with Moscow in particular have never been reducible to one of vassalage, as the proceedings of a meeting held between Gromyko and Ponomarev and a delegation led by Yasser Arafat indicate. Each side apprised the other of its situation, differences were noted, and at no time did the Palestinian delegation appear to be subordinate to or even overshadowed by its Soviet interlocutors.[23] An appreciable consequence of the pivotal role gained by Arafat has been of a financial order. The considerable sums siphoned into the PLO are admininistered in a wholly independent fashion. This not only ensures that the organization functions smoothly, but also allows it to supervise, through its distribution network and in clientelist fashion, an extremely broad political spectrum.

## Revolution and Class Warfare

The Palestinian movement does not hesitate to call itself a revolution, with the term mainly belonging to Fatah discourse. We can, however, provide a more exact meaning for this word, and define it as an action directed toward the overthrow of a regime and the takeover of state power. As soon as we do so, we find ourselves forced to recognize that it is indeed an implication of the insurgency which, distinct from Palestinian nationalism per se, has been spread and championed by a number of groups other than Fatah.

The revolutionary subgroups existing within the Palestinian movement also emerged out of a spinoff from—but more especially from the great crisis in—Arab nationalism. Their earliest spokespersons were, first and foremost, resolute opponents of Zionism and imperialism, who had also taken part in the rise of Arab nationalism. George Habash and Hani al-Hindi, who would later found the PFLP, dreamed in the late 1940s of an Arab state extending from the Persian Gulf to the Atlantic Ocean. They were indifferent, if not hostile, to socialist and communist ideologies, and the activist group of which Habash would become the great leader was, until 1967, essentially pan-Arab and anti-imperialist. The Palestinian militants who joined to form the Arab Nationalist Movement (ANM) refused, until 1964, any "regionalist" temptations, and were more concerned with the question of their organization's place within the Nasserist fold.

Living in a number of countries in the region, these were often intellectuals, professionals, and students.[24] Nonetheless, the ANM created a Palestinian branch in 1964, mainly as a reaction to the creation of the PLO and the formation of Fatah. The Marxist-Leninist and revolutionary ideologies had already made visible advances among these militants, but it was the Six-Day War, and the collapse of Nasserism and the pan-Arab dream it implied, that was immediately responsible for the group's development.

Here, rather than there being a reversal of polarities between the liberation of Palestine and Arab activism, *there was rather the addition—to a perspective which, while still Arab, had been placed in jeopardy and thereby in crisis—of a new necessary condition for a real and effective engagement on the part of the concerned countries: the establishment of revolutionary regimes.* As George Habash put it in an interview,[25] the process of liberating Palestine would be "the climax of unification and the radical change that will overtake the whole Arab region and especially the area bordering Israel." In the context of the crisis in Arab nationalism, Fatah advanced the cause of the Palestinian national consciousness, whereas the PFLP grafted onto its preexisting ideology a platform which consisted of rallying the people and calling for the overthrow of conservative or pro-Western Arab governments, all in the name of Palestinian liberation. This shift toward ideologies preaching direct revolution in a number of Arab nations did not follow a straight line. On the contrary, it resulted in a veritable cleavage which formed along two major fault lines.[26]

In the one camp were those who, wishing to link pan-Arabism with the revolution, held out against overly socialist, Marxist, or communist-inspired doctrines and remained attached to the old ANM slogan of "unity, liberty, revenge." In the other were those who, placing increased emphasis on social causes and the class struggle, sought to construct a political movement along Marxist-Leninist lines. While it was over the issue of promoting a revolution against those regimes which, starting with that of Jordan, qualified as traitorous or reactionary, that the two camps collided, it was over the matter of the makeup of their social constituency that they parted ways. Whereas the latter group took its social base to be a strictly grassroots one, the former defined its base in somewhat broader terms with their differences taking the shape of what William Quandt has so beautifully termed the "esoteric issue of the role of the middle classes and intellectuals."[27]

So it was that the PFLP, created out of the ANM and a number of smaller groups in 1967, began in 1968 to experience considerable internal tensions which erupted into a fundamental split. Out of this there emerged the PDFLP whose leader, Nayif Hawatmah, went so far as to envisage the creation of "soviets" in northern Jordan.[28]

The revolutionary model that the two organizations continued to share led them to take issue with a number of Fatah positions. Whereas the latter group spoke in terms of independent action and the Palestinian consciousness, the PLFP and the PDFLP were banking on changes and splits within the Arab world. Whereas Fatah spoke in terms of a Palestinian nation, the PLFP and the PDFLP spoke in terms of the Arab people.

It is for this reason that the PLFP's and PDFLP's strategic orientations were so different from those of Fatah. These two organizations could in no way presume to be external either to interstate friction or to internal conflicts in any one of the Arab states. They defended and received aid from regimes they considered to be progressive, and took sides against those they felt to be reactionary. In absolute terms, they were much more fragile and vulnerable than Fatah, more liable both to falling under the control of friendly governments and power groups and, conversely, to being viewed as a direct threat to Arab regimes who, while ready to support the Palestinian cause, remained reluctant to enter into the kinds of conflicts toward which these groups gravitated.

The question of the revolution, which gave rise to the 1969 split between the Habash and Hawatmah camps, was undergirded by not one, but two activist principles.

The principle which George Habash has continued to personify down to the present day is essentially anti-Zionist, anti-imperialist, with a tendency towards attacking reactionary Arab regimes. The war against Israel and revolutionary violence against this or that regime have dictated his acts much more than has any vision of building a Palestinian society or state. It is for this reason that the PFLP has often pioneered extremist strategies, pioneering as it did the Refusal Front in 1974; and that it has appeared to be the most intransigent among the Palestinian organizations in the positions it has assumed, refusing any and all negotiated or intermediate solutions to the Palestinian question.

The current embodied by Hawatmah has diverged from the former first through its pro-Soviet, and later its pro-Chinese stance. Both of these positions, beyond their ideological proximity, are very much bound up in strategic concerns internal to the PLO. Gaining Moscow's recognition allowed the PDFLP to better hold its own against Fatah and Arafat, who took some time to become Moscow's most favored interlocutor. What mainly distinguished the PDFLP from the PFLP, however, were the former's attempts to imagine a Palestine of the future and to chart the democratic system of the future Palestinian state. In its desire to be overtly proletarian, it called for the fusion of the popular Jordanian and Palestinian movements, and promoted the notion that the Jordan-Palestine division was an artifact imposed by the British at the time of

their colonial presence. Most importantly, however, the PDFLP was explicit in its acceptance of Jewish culture, to the point of taking such
initiatives—as in Hawatmah's resounding interview printed in the
March 22, 1974, edition of the Israeli *Yedioth Aharnot* newspaper—to
attempt to reach out to the Israeli left.[29]

In a certain sense, its relatively classic Marxist-Leninist line and its
reference to class warfare have led the PDFLP into much more nuanced
positions than those of the PFLP. It was, for example, the first group to
seriously envisage such limited solutions as that of a Palestinian "mini-
state." Its class orientations have made it into an actor capable of thinking in terms of popular action while openly transcending the national
question of a Palestinian or (especially) an Arab homeland. It has also
been more amenable than the PFLP to a rapprochement with Fatah as
it has attempted, through practices verging on negotiated compromise,
to reconcile if not combine national consciousness with revolutionary
aspirations. If it has taken issue with the notion of prioritizing Palestinian
nationalism, it has done so not so much in the name of Arab unity as in
that of a leftist revolutionary perspective. It has also done so because it
generally identifies the Palestinian national consciousness with the interests of a middle class that would have the most to gain by the creation
of a state, in its own image. As Abu Jihad explained it in a July 3, 1970,
interview, "the Palestinian revolution is an inalienable part of the Arab
revolution, and any attempt to 'Palestinize' the Palestinian question is,
in the final analysis, rightist and questionable from a nationalist perspective."[30]

## Social Base and Political Ideology

In the eyes of its most critical observers, political discourse, whether of
a Palestinian or revolutionary nationalist order, is always quite distant
from popular aspirations, and ultimately corresponds to the specific preoccupations of intellectual elites. "The burning issue," writes Bernard
Lewis, "is not so much of a people without a country as one of an elite
without a state."[31]

According to those actors most sympathetic to the Palestinian national
consciousness, this reproach is only valid for revolutionary factions in
the movement, whose positions they dismiss as resulting from their distance from zones of conflict and direct popular mobilization. In the
words of Abu Jihad, "taking no physical risk . . . and lacking for nothing,
[the revolutionary intellectuals] can offer themselves the luxury of inflex-

ibility without ever having to fear eternal exile."[32] Can this question be reduced then to a gulf between a matter of a revolutionary radicalism cut off from the masses versus a national pragmatism that corresponds to real popular experience? Many have often gone overboard in making this contrast, thinking to explain it in terms of the social, geographical, religious, etc. situation or origins of the principal leaders. Thus there is, for example, a relative homogeneity in the religious (Sunni), geographical (Gaza Strip), and political backgrounds of the Fatah heads, whereas the PFLP and PDFLP leaders are more often non-Muslims with a more wide-ranging political experience.

Apart from the fact that this kind of argument can only ever be but partially validated through a concrete examination of the militant population, it teaches us very little about the gulf that can separate the world of the activist from his popular base. On the other hand, studies such as those carried out by Rosemary Sayigh and Pamela Ann Smith are better indicators of the direct communication that opens up as soon as it is the Palestinian national consciousness rather than Arab revolution, and resistance rather than class warfare, that are championed.[33]

Palestinian society, such as it has constituted or reconstituted itself in exile, is a fragmented society composed of peasants stripped of their land and vocation, and middle and business classes living in Lebanon, and in even greater numbers in the Gulf states, etc. To be sure, the masses of rural origins now living in refugee camps, uprooted, impoverished, often exploited by local authorities, and deprived of many of their rights, have a number of social axes to grind.

Yet, it is the theme of Palestinian national resistance that unites them, and which they reciprocally reinforce. Thus, in the eyes of Rosemary Sayigh, the peasants "contributed more than other classes to the national resistance movement . . . A peasant who has been dispossessed, his moral universe overturned, and then given access to knowledge through modern education, does not easily give up his struggle. His deeply rooted sense of possession, his obstinacy and patience, his long time horizon, combine to make him an enemy more formidable because his weakness is obvious, his strength concealed."[34] The theme of a struggle that is at once social and revolutionary is by and large an artificial one, not only because it is arbitrary to identify a people who are for the most part poverty-stricken with a social movement, but also because the networks through which political mobilization takes place correspond more closely to communal forms of organization than they do to some shared social identity. Militant participation in revolutionary organizations owes much more to traditional affinities maintained in spite of exile, to membership in a given clan or extended family, than it does to ideological choices motivated by social demands. Similarly, within the major Palestinian organizations, the distribution of power is based on the ability of their leaders to attract followers whose attachment to them, defined on the basis of affinities, increases in proportion to the number of financial favors they are able to rain down upon them.

This is why we should not be surprised at Fatah's ability to recruit from among the unwashed masses, even if classic Marxist thinking would maintain that its strongest base ought to be the middle strata of society. This is also why the Palestinian movement is, taken as a whole, so nonsocial. To be sure, its leaders have, especially since Lebanon in 1970, been anxious to ensure that the community run smoothly. But whether they be mainly Palestinian nationalists or Arab revolutionaries, they are not the least bit concerned with creating the conditions for such dialogue and conflicts as may produce a Palestinian society. The political organizations, though they may strive to control the community's inner environment and to protect it against the world outside, refuse to tolerate—sometimes to the point of force—the existence of any element liable to lead to internal protest.

Compared to the theme of revolution, which moreover draws the Palestinian cause into various relationships of subordination to foreign powers, the theme of national resistance is more pragmatic and less ideological. It is therefore not astonishing that it should occupy a central place in a movement that functions more on the basis of communal (family, clan, native village) ties—ties that incite inter- and intraorganizational opposition—than from a set of guidelines for demands and protests of a social order. The movement tends more towards a utopian dream of a return to the homeland and to unity than towards a desire to deal with its internal differences on a political level.

Marxism-Leninism has always enjoyed a certain ascendancy among the Palestinians. The principal form it has taken, however, especially in the PFLP, has been one of a discourse or jargon which, maintained together with a program of action whose aim it is to change the course of history through strategy alone, has a greater stake in popular despair, the desire for revenge, rage, and impatience, than on plans to overhaul society. It is a strategy more concerned with maintaining recruitment levels than with ideologically and politically organizing a mass action.

## Dependence and the Loss of Meaning

With no territory of its own, the Palestinian national consciousness is limited in its ability to transform itself into autonomous action. As such it finds itself constantly forced to improvise, compromise, negotiate, and find its niche within a fluid and protean political and diplomatic context. The forms this political interplay takes are determined by international factors—in particular the system constituted by the Arab states—all of which greatly limit Fatah's freedom of movement.

The revolutionary spirit, which tends, for its part, towards plans of action that attack certain governments, finds itself obliged to make certain strategic choices that tie it to various power blocs or governments, and tend to isolate or marginalize it by limiting its freedom of movement. To speak in terms of dependence or vassalage would however be to overstate the point, as each of the tendencies we have just mentioned is capable of generating its own political, military, and diplomatic strategies. This statement does not hold, however, for a number of groups that have become so many malleable instruments in the hands of the Arab governments that directly control them.

Here we must differentiate between two distinct processes. In the first of these Palestinians—living in a host country that has succeeded in gaining military control over its Palestinian population and most especially over the refugee camps—find themselves, *nolens volens,* absorbed into the prevailing power's policies and international strategy, with a very slim margin of autonomy.

The second is one in which actors who have, for one reason or another, split off or become alienated from the Palestinian movement opt for a strategy by which they exchange subordination for financial, military, or other kinds of support.

Sa'iqa falls under the first heading. In the beginning, this was the Palestinian wing of the pro-Syrian Ba'ath party, the formation of which was decided in Damascus in September 1966. From the viewpoint of Salah Jedid, who ruled Syria until 1970, the Palestinians constituted a heteronomous mass to be manipulated. The Sa'iqa, whose headquarters were quite naturally located in the Syrian refugee camps, was conspicuous in its active support for the Jedid regime. In the years 1969–70, this was a support that was most amenable to an alliance with Fatah, with which it aligned its positions as early as 1968, when the latter was taking over the PLO. Sa'iqa's conundrum was that it was thereafter torn between its insertion in the PLO and thus a Palestinian self-identity, and its subordination to its masters in Damascus. When Hafiz al-Assad took power in Syria in November 1970, he threw out the Sa'iqa leaders, because of their links with his predecessor, and put the organization under his direct control. What little margin of autonomy Sa'iqa may have previously enjoyed became further reduced, and it was all its men could do to avoid being drawn into the Syrian military hostilities in Lebanon in 1976. When President Assad turned to the Christians to attack the "Palestinian progressives," desertions occurred on a massive scale, emptying the Sa'iqa ranks.

Iraq also attempted to avail itself of a tool comparable to Sa'iqa. This country was, however, too far removed from the immediate field of conflict, and refugees too few in number, for there to be a recruitment pool of any size there. The Arab Liberation Front, formed in Baghdad in 1969, was furthermore a minor organization, never capable of doing anything more than to carry out Iraqi orders. Within this family of actors, the experience of the small group headed by Ahmad Jibril was a relatively unique one. At first, Jibril, himself a former officer in the Syrian army, and a number of persons close to him, moved by the desire to "carry out a war of nerves against Israel," considered joining Fatah. Too closely linked to Syria to do so, however, they instead joined the PFLP, which they left in 1969 to form the PFLP-General Command. Jibril then returned to a dependent relationship with Syria which he maintained until 1970, before turning to Iraq for assistance. All the while, Jibril sought to maintain his autonomy, for which the price was a group of very limited dimensions and very radical and extremist positions.

This second general tendency brings us into the fields of state-sponsored terrorism, that is of the use by Arab states of Palestinians—or Palestinian sympathizers—who have come to offer or sell themselves into the service of a given regime, secret service, or even a given cause.

Certain of these are Palestinians who have split off from the PLO, the most notorious among these being Abu Nidal, one of Arafat's former lieutenants. Given the task of representing the PLO at Baghdad, he became friends with Iraq's Ba'ath leadership, following which he openly disputed PLO executive council decisions, fomented incidents in Palestinian camps in Lebanon, and in the end entered into battle against the very organization to which he had belonged. By now a full-fledged terrorist, a semimercenary working—out of a manifest hatred for the PLO—in the service of Iraq and later Syria, he was condemned, in absentia, to death by the latter group.

Colonel Qaddafi's Libya has also made a specialty of recruiting Palestinian Fatah or PFLP dissidents. Starting in 1973, it began offering them both financial support and training camps, and has since used them as mercenaries directly recruited, trained, and used to Libya's own ends.[35]

Here we have reached the outermost fringe of the Palestinian movement, a fringe often cut off from the movement itself, a grey area whose actors move from a relationship of dependence into one of heteronomy. Here, losing touch with the original meaning of their struggle, they often fall, at times with the frenzy of those consumed by self-hatred, into the abyss of actions carried out in obedience to positions that are foreign, indeed hostile, to the movement whose cause they presume to be defending.

# 17

# Palestinian Terrorism

To each of the constituent parts of the Palestinian movement, it has been possible for us to attach the names of groups or organizations. An organization (or a group) is, however, always a complex historical entity which, more-or-less stable and coherent, can never be reduced to the sociological meaning it embodies. Furthermore, internal and interorganizational dialogue so affects the circulation and transformation of ideas and meanings as to make it impossible for us to freeze the movement into a static image composed of its juxtaposed or combined parts. Let us illustrate this observation with an a example: interviewed by the *Revue d'études palestiniennes* for its special issue "The PLO: Twenty Years On," George Habash, whom as we have seen is anything but a personification of the Palestinian national consciousness, affirmed that "the revolution's most important contribution has been the consolidation of the national identity and the establishment of a political and moral entity. In the early 1960s, and even down to the end of that decade," he went on, "the Palestinian national character had not yet fully emerged . . ."[1] In the same vein, one finds Third-World, Maoist, and other currents of thought within Fatah. While the Palestinian organizations have themselves theorized to excess over their ideological differences, it suffices to scratch the surface to see the extent to which these groupings correspond to clan, family, or clientelist structures.[2]

The movement is basically structured along the lines of two sets of meanings, both of which appeared or were strengthened in the vacuum left by the decline of Nasserite Arab nationalism. There were, however, other meanings that were introduced into the Palestinian struggle, the most important of these being Islamic ones. In the late 1940s, while they were still receiving their political schooling, Yasser Arafat and a number of people close to him belonged for a time to the Muslim Brotherhood. It would appear that their ties with this group have never been fully broken. Abu Ammar, Arafat's nom de guerre, as well as the name Fatah, the names of the PLA brigades and, on a wider scale, a great number of the movement's symbolic images refer directly to the vocabulary of Islam.[3] At no time, however, has the Palestinian movement ever taken up the path of Islamic activism, which it has, on the contrary, always viewed as a threat or a sign of weakness. Likewise, there have at times been hints of former nazi or neonazi elements in the Palestinian camps, and indications that the Palestinians have had ties or affinities with the Syrian Popular party (PPS), a pan-Syrian group, of fascist inspiration, based in Lebanon. This violently anti-Semitic group is alleged to have supplied some of the personnel responsible for the slaughter that took place in Munich in 1972. Here too, we would do well to see this as a marginal cause and an instrumental relationship in which the PPS was likely taking its orders from outside (before tilting into the Syrian camp in 1982).

Now that we know the movement's guiding principles, it should be possible for us to describe the relationships that obtain between their violent activities and the ideals upon which they claim such activities to be based.

## A Minority Organization's Tool

The Palestinian movement's first phase of expansion occurred in the years between 1967 and 1970. At a time when Syria constituted a safe base for fedayeen activities, and Jordan was becoming increasingly worried over the massive presence of the Palestinians whose self-organization was beginning to threaten the sovereignty of King Hussein, Lebanon was already finding it impossible to control the Palestinians, and agreed in Cairo in 1969 to sign accords giving them great latitude. Nasser was helping Fatah to take over the PLO, financial aid was pouring in (mainly from Saudi Arabia and Libya), and the PLO and other Palestinian organizations were growing, with training camps springing up everywhere. At the same time, there was relative agreement that no compromises could be made with Israel and Zionism, that Palestine had to be liberated, and that the armed struggle was the sole viable means to this end—a thesis that the founders of the future PFLP had not wholly embraced prior to 1967. Possessed of a number of good reasons for aligning their positions (the PFLP having agreed to fully participate in the PLO in 1970), the movement's three principal organizations stood together in rejecting the Rogers Plan which, proposed by the United States, was on its way to being accepted by Egypt, Jordan, and Israel.[4] Nonetheless, important differences divided them, and the first of these was ideological. This was a period that saw the rise of Marxism-Leninism which, because it was more-or-less linked to the Arab nationalist agenda, was rejected by Palestinian nationalism. In spite of their shared opposition, the PDFLP and the PFLP were also at loggerheads with one another, with the latter presenting a platform for Arab unity over and against the former's nascent doctrine of a democratic state. The three organizations were also in disagreement over the strategy to be adopted in Jordan. The PFLP felt the time had come to do away with the Hashemite monarchy, and was pushing for a confrontation with Hussein's army, which became concretized in 1970;[5] the PDFLP, even as it shared this objective, was unsure about the ripeness of the moment, while Fatah refused to be drawn into a policy not its own.

It was in this period that the first significant manifestations of international terrorism, carried out by PFLP militants, occurred. The strategy employed by George Habash and his partisans first consisted of transferring the war against Israel to a level at which the Zionist state appeared more vulnerable than elsewhere, i.e. that of international communications. Jacques M. Vergès, who was a barrister in Algiers and defense attorney for a number of the first Palestinian terrorists at the time, has reconstituted, in a book that appeared in 1969,[6] these actors' rationales and explanations for their actions. For them, the hijackings or attacks on El Al airplanes, the most elevated expressions of the Palestinian resistance, were acts of war that respected the "neutrality [or] the nonbelligerence of the concerned states" (in this case, Greece and Switzerland) while attacking Israeli military targets.[7] The civilian nature of El Al's activities was contested, with counsel stressing the care the terrorists took to avoid taking civilian lives, even those of Israelis.

In these acts of aviational terrorism, the policy adopted by the PFLP and from time to time by much more autonomous militia groups has fundamentally been one of a minority organization seeking to assert itself at a juncture in which the Palestinian movement was on the rise. Fatah, which was dominant in this movement, declared itself hostile to terrorism, with Yasser Arafat branding as "contrary to the general interests of authentic fedayeen action" (*Al Hayat,* Beirut, June 13, 1969) the sabotage of a pipeline carrying oil from Saudi Arabia to Saida, in Lebanon, for which the PFLP had claimed responsibility. Yet Fatah itself was carrying out commando operations that were themselves direct attacks, often at the borders of its territory, against the state of Israel. Following its first Arab "victory" at Karameh, its popularity increased spectacularly, and volunteers began flooding in. In the beginning, international and more specifically aviational terrorism serve as a means for Habash and his cohorts to bring the Palestinian insurgency to world attention. By doing so in a spectacular way, he also put his own group in the world limelight. Terrorism had both the foreign (the war against Israel) and domestic functions of projecting his organization as efficient and active and of thereby enlarging its following and pool of potential recruits. Whence the paradox, appropriately stressed by Ann Lesch in her review of a significant collective work on the Arab-Israeli conflict:[8] those who reenlisted in the PFLP at this time were more motivated by feelings of humiliation and a desire for action than by a newfound attraction to the organization's rhetoric or ideology.

There is always a self-perpetuating autonomy to terrorism, which feeds off its own practice, and the skyjackings initiated by the PFLP were no exception. Not every attempted hijacking or attack on planes on the ground was crowned with total success. Militants were being arrested and jailed, so that the game now became one of winning, through identical terrorist means, the freedom of detainees. Starting in 1969, there began a spiral in which aviational terrorism became further saddled with this strategic requirement, thus giving an international dimension to the conflict with Israel, and obliging a number of countries to not only take greater precautions, but also to take part in negotiations they could well have lived without.

In 1970 however, the thrust of these activities became altered. The PDFLP and especially the PFLP were eager to take on King Hussein and to set up a popular regime which would afford the Palestinian resistance greater freedom of movement. Here, aviational terrorism became a critical element in a strategy which further sought to bar the implementation of the Rogers Plan, which Egypt and Jordan were on the verge of accepting. An attempted hijacking failed in London, with one terrorist being killed and another, Leïla Khaled, jailed by the British.[9] However, every other operation carried out in early September was successful. An American flight was forced to land on an abandoned Jordanian airport, baptized the "airport of the revolution" for the occasion, and its passengers evacuated from the planes which were then dynamited. Negotiations led to the freeing of the passengers, but this was quickly followed by the liberation of PFLP militants held by a number of European nations. The PFLP, although its activities had been suspended at a meeting of the PLO's central committee, was leading the parade. Incidents between fedayeen groups and the Jordanian army were on the increase, and calls for a general strike and civil disobedience were being sounded. On September 15, King Hussein announced the formation of a military cabinet, an indication that he had decided to take a hard-line approach to the Palestinian question on Jordanian territory. From September 17 to 27, 1970, the Jordanian army launched a number of offensives which shattered the organized Palestinian presence there. This it did in spite of a brief Syrian intervention, which was withdrawn as the result of diplomatic exchanges in which Henry Kissinger proved to be especially active and efficacious.[10]

Here, terrorism did more than to seek to block a peace plan which the Palestinians as a whole had found undesirable, and to force a show of strength with the Hashemite government. It had also played the internal role of committing Fatah, the predominant PLO organization, to take up confrontational positions it disfavored on both strategic and philosophical grounds. This was therefore once again a case of a minority organization raising the stakes, in ways perfectly coherent with their own overall positions, as a means to drawing an entire movement in a direction opposite from that preferred by its predominant organization. The consequences of this extremist swing are obvious. The Palestinian movement, removed from the political and military scene in Jordan, was thrown into turmoil. The PFLP strategy had borne its bitter fruits, with the group's own powers considerably curtailed as the result of having carried out an offensive that had weakened the movement as a whole.

### Black September: The Terrorist Movement

Brutally expelled from Jordan, militarily weakened, and incapable of initiating attacks on Israeli soil in the wake of that country's reinforcement of its defenses (and the loss of the east bank of the Jordan as a base from which to launch operations), the Palestinian movement as a whole was, in the fall of 1970, plunged into a deep state of crisis. Even Fatah was considering equipping itself with structures that were sturdier and less permeable to outside influences or foreign penetration, as well as better training for its recruits who had been too numerous to benefit from a proper political and military education. But the biggest question by far was whether or not to take up undercover operations. The temptation to terrorism, always linked to the temptation to secrecy, actualized itself all the more quickly under the prevailing situation, in which the fondest dream of all was to take revenge against King Hussein and show the world that the Palestinian resistance was still alive and well. "At that time," explains Salameh, one of the principal founders of Black September, "we had been driven into obscurity, a terrible obscurity. We *had* to get out, and that is what we did . . . We came out of the shadows to tell the world: Even though you temporarily chased us out of Jordan, we still exist."[11] To these remarks may be added Fatah's concern with not disappointing Palestinian youth, who were capable of throwing their lots in with a PFLP camp that was more radical in its words and deeds. Paradoxically, the weapon of terrorism, which had sped up the catastrophe of September 1970, would this time be used not by a minority organization, but rather by Fatah and, by extension, the PLO.

There are two accounts of the founding of the Black September terrorist organization, which was so named in reference to the events we have just described.[12] The first of these underscores the spontaneous or marginal character of the group which subsequently placed itself under the wing of Fatah; the second presents it as an initiative taken by that organization's leadership, and principally by its "leftist" faction. But this is of little importance. What matters is that Fatah itself recognized and administered a relatively controlled terrorist group whose designation as Black September insulated Fatah from the appearance of immediate involvement.

The goal of the group's first successful operations was revenge against the Hashemite regime. On November 28, 1971, the Jordanian prime minister was assassinated in Cairo; then, in December, the Jordanian ambassador in London was attacked, but survived his wounds. These two attacks would be followed by a variety of operations. Beyond vengeance, however, Black September's activities were geared to respond to the feeling—and to the accusations raised by the rank and file—of impotence and passivity, to remobilize Palestinian opinion, and to compensate for the movement's military and organizational weakness.

The massacre carried out on May 30, 1972, at Israel's Lod airport, although it had all the marks of a Black September operation, was not one. It was rather the PFLP which claimed responsibility for an action in which three Japanese men opened fire, killing twenty-six—but the same PLFP was working, at the time, in close collaboration with Black September. The Munich attack was a Black September operation through and through and was, in all likelihood, one of the last far-reaching terrorist actions in which Fatah played an instrumental role. On September 5,

1972, a Black September commando unit entered the Olympic Village
and kidnapped eleven members of the Israeli Olympic team. The operation ended in massacre. The PLO officially dissociated itself from Black
September, even though it also stated that the killing had served the
Palestinian cause. Other less spectacular operations would follow. Taken
as a whole, these terrorist acts gave rise to three types of processes.

The first of these constituted a new dimension—analyzable in isolation—to the war between Israel and the Palestinians. Apart from more
classical responses (reinforced precautionary measures, reprisals, diplomatic action), Palestinian terrorism gave rise to an Israeli counterterrorist
campaign which used methods comparable to its own. In response to
the assassinations, letter bombs, and other forms of a terrorism which
most often targeted persons accused throughout the world of working
in the service of Zionism, the Israelis adopted identical practices, giving
rise to a relatively two-sided engagement between terrorist specialists
from both sides. Michel Bar-Zohar and Eitan Haber's engrossing book
gives a particularly well-documented account of this phenomenon, from
the Israeli perspective.[13]

A second process led the PLO (and Fatah in particular) to distance
itself even further from Black September terrorism. This latter was running up against international opinion, where the name of the game was
convincing people, through spectacular actions, of the justice of the Palestinian cause. More than this, it was an embarrassment to Arab governments. Later, when the movement raged out of control, it was a source
of reprobation not only for them but also for Fatah, which could no
longer simply ignore it. After Munich, Fatah distanced itself from terrorism even as it, in the words of Helena Cobban, gave it its basic orders.
The Khartoum operation would oblige it to harden its opposition to
such methods, since it was becoming impossible to go on organizing
(discretely) and backing (more openly) actions which—by resulting in
the deaths of diplomats, including the American ambassador in Khartoum—was undermining the authority of the president of Sudan. Fatah's
abandonment of these terrorist orientations was not dictated by its strategic and diplomatic alternatives alone. It also owed much to the
strengthening of the movement as a whole, which had found a way to
reorganize itself on Lebanese soil and which had by now weathered the
crisis that had followed its expulsion from Jordan. Bard E. O'Neil, who
offers an analysis of this process in a stimulating article in which he
bases his arguments on a typology put forward by Richard Schultz,
concludes on the subject of Palestinian terrorism: "when bad strategy, a

poor environment, organizational defects, low active popular support in the target area, and limited means for conducting guerrilla warfare are combined with the effectiveness of the counterinsurgent side, we are able to arrive at a more comprehensive explanation of capability reductions and, in turn, terrorism."[14] But we must go beyond such conclusions, which imply that a stengthening of the movement ought to correspond to a decline in terrorism.

The third process, linked to the second, accompanies the evolution of Fatah. As is often the case when a movement reorients itself strategically and gives up certain armed resistance activities, internal tensions develop in which partisans of such activities become pitted against those who have decided to cease and desist. These tensions may lead to splits or factionalizations, which may themselves issue in deadly confrontations between two camps that have arisen out of a single original group. The departure of the Abu Nidal faction, as well as the formation of a number of pro-Libyan groups, generally correspond to the exact moment in which Black September's brand of terrorism was abandoned by the PLO. In a certain sense, the price that had to be paid here was—as in a number of other movements that choose to give up a given form of armed struggle—the departure of a number of elements which seceded in order to carry on with their terrorist efforts. Once these elements have become nearly wholly unaccountable to any base whatsoever, they come to identify themselves with the cause for which they are fighting, adopt extremist and radical positions, and dismiss the essence of the movement as treason while seeking aid from political powers or governments which waste no time in using them to their own ends. In 1973, at a time when Fatah was disengaging itself from the practice of international terrorism and taking up a policy of negotiation and diplomacy even as it continued its guerrilla insurgency against Israel, a number of individuals (more often than groups) who had broken away from it or who were simply not integrated into its action were willing and able to take charge of operations which others were hastening to organize. Although it had not distanced itself so greatly from terrorism, a comparable phenomenon occurred within the PFLP, albeit on a much more modest scale. In 1972, George Habash announced that his organization had decided to suspend the practice of airline hijacking, explaining that "foreign operations" were not "Marxist-Leninist tactics." This decision gave rise to powerful tensions within the group, which culminated in the departure, in February 1976, of Wadi Hadad, who had been one of the PFLP founders and, most especially, the organization's "foreign operations" chief. Thereafter, Wadi Hadad found himself in Baghdad and later Aden, out of which he directed, until his death in 1978, a far-flung terrorist network, which was responsible in particular for the hijacking of an Air France flight over Entebbe in 1976.[15]

## The Inversion

Following 1973, it becomes increasingly difficult to analyze, in terms of the internal workings of the Palestinian movement, the rationale behind the terrorism carried out in the name of the Palestinian cause. To be sure, the PFLP continued to wield the arm of terrorism, and remained a pivotal organization in the planning of terrorist operations. Starting in the mid-1970s, however, terrorism became factionalized into the work of a number of dislocated groups, whose planning was done by a number of Arab regimes. One might even contend, on grounds treated at length by Nadia Ben Jelloun-Ollivier, that terrorism was the continuing manifestation of an armed insurgency which was unable to take on the more classical form of a guerrilla insurgency. The Israelis had entirely sealed off their own national territory, there were no large cities within which an urban guerrilla war could be developed, etc. From our perspective however, what is essential must be sought in another direction, in those activities in which the meaning of one's acts no longer bear anything more than a distant and distorted relationship to the movement as we have defined it.

Whether the matter be one of an internal split and the departure of a group—however small, of the order of those led by Abu Nidal or Wadi Hadad—or of isolated individuals in search of a radical form of action, but also at times simply moved by a martial activism, we find ourselves faced with a veritable inversion of the major categories of action.

Palestinian nationalism gave way to pan-Arab causes which, already present, were simultaneously strengthened and rendered increasingly artificial as a torn Arab world became glaringly less capable of fostering any sort of unity. There sometimes also appeared a pro-Islamic agenda, which was tantamount to a submission to the strategic interests of the state sponsor that was arming, financing, and directing the activities of the actor. Now, even though Islam often constituted a common reference for the movement, it was never a central factor in its unification or its self-identity. This was not only because about 10 percent of the Palestinians were Christians: in the words of Yasser Arafat, "denominationalism is a mortal danger that we must root out."[16] As the PLO's guiding principle, the armed struggle was no longer a direct guerrilla-based confrontation with Israel, but had rather become an international terrorism directed against targets which at times had very little to do with the Israeli-Palestinian conflict. The notion of the adversary and of a conflict that the movement might at some time have settled through negotiation, had become transformed into a dualistic opposition between the forces of good and evil, with anti-Zionism often taking on the appearance of overt anti-Semitism. This is a point of major importance: whether it is limited to verbal outrages of Shuqayri, who vowed to push the Jews into the sea, or of George Habash, who explained from the very beginning of his career that the enemy was the Jew and international Judaism, and that his terrorism targeted Jews as Jews and not as Zionists,[17] the identification "Jew = Zionist" has always been a sign of weakness or of the inversion of the movement. The revolutionary vision of imposing a popular regime upon the Arab countries, no longer expecting much from the concerned masses, was becoming transformed on the one hand into a revolution of global proportions—embodied by an international terrorist network—and, on the other, by a participation in a state-sponsored terrorism that was an extension of state diplomacy, a diplomacy that took the form of physically eliminating all opposition. For the PLO and Fatah, hatred had so replaced any adherence to or sharing of a given ideology as to become the major catalyst for their action. It was as if there was nothing of greater urgency than to destroy those organizations which had joined the camps of traitors to the cause, or of collaborators with the Zionist or imperialist enemy. Carried to its limits, this inversion reduced action to the elementary principle of the elimination of evil, and facilitated a blind submission, sometimes to the point of self-sacrifice, to orders to attack targets identified with the polymorphous forces of evil.

It is nonetheless difficult to apply the oft-used expression *manipulation* to qualify the heteronomy of those who placed themselves, at the end of an inversion process, in the service of a regime or a political power whose objectives were foreign to a Palestinian cause that had itself become an empty point of reference having little to do with the actual movement. This was much more a case of adaptation and accommodation between the extremely radicalized options of certain Palestinians and the interests of those who would make use of their services, than it was one of an ideological working over and brainwashing of an order that would have resulted in manipulation.

Here, it is possible to delineate a number of more-or-less advanced stages of inversion.

Inversion is still relatively limited when the protagonist retains a certain level of autonomy, a capacity for an action of his own, which stands out to the extent that it no longer directly conforms to the basic work of the movement. A group that no longer has to maintain a dialogue with other organizations, that no longer seeks to remain in touch with a popular base or with a given public opinion, becomes accountable to itself alone. It has no obligation to make any sort of political effort, and is therefore capable of operating by the force of arms alone. The rationales of its leadership become reduced to strategic and military calculations, which issue into operations which may be carried out quite totally unhampered. If the group has managed to build up or enter into international networks, it may very well be able to avoid slipping into total dependence, supply itself with weapons and other tools of the trade, and manage to endure for a time. However, the most common tendency, here as in other insurgencies, is still to move in the direction of subordination to a given state, a subordination which can become more-or-less absolute. Yet the mark of the Palestinian cause, although inverted, nonetheless remains, even when it takes the form of an obstinate hatred for the PLO or Fatah, or of a murderous anti-Semitism.

### Interactions with Other Breakaway Factions

In the Arab countries of the region as well as in Europe, Asia, and Africa, a wide variety of support has been offered to the various Palestinian organizations. Elsewhere, more long-standing networks have at times worked in favor of this or that group. This is especially the case with such former militants of the Algerian FLN as Mohammad Boudia (a one-time close friend of Ahmad Ben Bella, director of the Parisian Théâtre de l'Ouest) whose aid to the Palestinians was quite significant in the early 1970s. In June 1973, this openly pro-Soviet individual was assassinated by the Israeli Mossad, which considered him to be Black September's number-one man in Europe.[18] The most important relationships were, however, those which developed with movements that appeared on the scene after the Algerian FLN.

One is tempted to present the massive influx, beginning in the late 1960s, of militants from the world over into the Palestinian resistance as the result of a symbiotic support policy in which the Palestinians welcomed, schooled, and trained militants from Japan, Germany, Italy, etc. In a number of cases they supplied technical and financial aid as well as weapons, in exchange for which they were able to rely, in a certain number of operations, on the support and participation of those

foreign organizations with which links had been established. This working procedure was a source of encouragement for a great number of
internationalist militants from the Third World—as well as from Europe—in conformity with (especially) PLFP expectations. Here we must
differentiate between those actors who, in their own world regions, manifestly drew their support from social or national movements capable of
practically maintaining their autonomy, and those who came into the
Palestinian struggle to recover the meaning they had lost back at home.
When the relationship of the former with the Palestinians went beyond
one of mere ideological proximity, it took on an overtly instrumental
character in which each group retained its specificity. For the latter, the
same relationship derived from a search for meaning which ultimately
transformed them into low-level mercenaries in the service of those who
had offered them a cause with which to identify themselves. It would be
simplistic to draw an overly sharp opposition between these two typologies of the encounter between foreign militants and the Palestinian cause.
Yet, it clearly appears to be the case that the greater the loss of—and
thereby the search for—meaning among the foreign militants, the more
they were attracted to or taken under the wing of groups which had
themselves split off from the PLO, or at least from its predominant Fatah
organization. In its relations with foreign terrorists, it was the PFLP that
most often fused together the two relational typologies we have just
described. This is solidly supported by the compelling testimony of Hans
Joachim Klein, a militant from the Revolutionary Cells (RZ) who went
through the many phases of this loss of meaning in Germany: "I had
taken to the streets because of Vietnam and was beat up for it. I had
taken to the streets because of racism against the blacks in the United
States and the plight of the migrant workers in West Germany and was
beat up for it. I was living in the streets because of the demolition of a
residential neighborhood, and was beat up for it."[19] He ended up working together with the notorious Carlos, organizing and carrying out, on
behalf of the PFLP, the December 20, 1975, kidnapping of eleven minis-
ters representing their countries at the OPEC meeting in Vienna, minis-
ters who were only freed after a high ransom had been paid. He also
relates how his organization had been able to plan the assassinations of
Jewish community leaders, people who "were of absolutely no interest
to us but . . . that's how it goes, the head of the PFLP doesn't give
anything unless he gets something in return."[20] The most spectacular
terrorist escapades have often resulted from such a collaboration, between actors from movements that had lost all contact with the social

realities of their own countries—most especially Germans from the Revolutionary Cells or the Second of June movement—and dissident Palestinians like Wadi Hadad, who was linked to the Entebbe and Mogadishu
operations.[21]

It is for this reason that we must draw a distinction—even if, in practical terms, the correspondences and interactions are constantly present—
between the activities of the PFLP, which organized an international
network which a variety of movements turned to their own profit but
which nevertheless had the PFLP as its core; and those of increasingly
heteronomous groups which followed the same trajectory, but mainly in
the service of terrorist states. When the PFLP set up the Badawi meeting
(near Tripoli, in Libya) in 1972, the order of the day was the creation
of a revolutionary—and in reality terrorist—International, in which the
PLO was to be a participant. As a consequence, what had been presented,
in sensationalist terms, as a "pact" and a veritable terrorist "conclave"
disbanded: Fatah abandoned Black September terrorism, the PFLP
ceased to play a confederating role, and the various groups began to
deploy their own strategies.[22]

## The Terrorist States

Three states—Iraq, Libya, and Syria—specialize in the use of Palestinian-
mediated international terrorism. *Our analysis took the Palestinian
movement for its starting point. These states are its endpoint.*

### Iraq

With Iraq, we find two relatively distinct mindsets behind a single
Palestinian-actuated terrorist phenomenon. This does not preclude, as we
have seen, the existence of organizations like the Arab Liberation Front,
which has no terrorist contacts and which operates as a government-
controlled Palestinian army.

First, there is Abu Nidal, who left the PLO in 1973, and whose activities have followed two guidelines. The first of these has been to do the
Iraqi regime's dirty work in its battle against its Syrian homologue. When
war cannot be countenanced, diplomacy is out of the question, and
terrorist violence becomes the rule, Abu Nidal has been the agent of such
violence—in places like Damascus, where a team of killers gunned down
four guests at the Hotel Sémiramis in September 1976; and in Amman,
where the Syrian foreign minister barely escaped a machine-gun attack
that killed ten persons at the Hotel Intercontinental. Abu Nidal's second
task has been to wage a deadly war against Fatah and the PLO, accused

of betraying the cause and of attempting to reach a negotiated solution with Israel. Rome, London, Kuwait, etc. have been so many venues for assassinations of PLO representatives. Through a process we have already had the occasion to observe, this in turn has provoked a counterterrorist effort on the part of Fatah, which has employed comparable methods. Rather than directly attacking cohorts of Abu Nidal, himself comfortably sequestered in his Iraqi sanctuary, Fatah agents terrorized Iraqi representatives and diplomats. The journalist Dominique Baudis has retraced one of these episodes in the deadly war between Fatah and Iraq, through a reconstitution of the hostage-taking incidents carried out by Palestinian agents in the Iraqi embassy in Paris, on July 31, 1978.[23]

There has always been some weak link between these two policies. On the one hand, the Abu Nidal organization has, as a tool of state-sponsored terrorism, taken the place of diplomacy. On the other, it pushes to its very limits a rationale which has itself constituted the most deviant form of an extremist strategy initiated ten years earlier by George Habash's PFLP. More than merely an inversion or a split, the deadly hatred the group has felt for Fatah has also constituted an attempt to force the movement, by working from outside the PLO, into taking up a more radical line, to block all "moderation," and to thereby destabilize Yasser Arafat. After a rift with Baghdad in 1980, Abu Nidal left Iraq for Syria, where we will again meet him shortly.

Even before he left Iraq for southern Yemen (even if he did not, it appears, split with Baghdad, where he retained his bases of operations) Wadi Hadad's activities derived from a relatively different model of action. His basic concern was to promote revolution throughout the world, and he therefore had no interest in physically attacking Fatah or the PLO, or in directly serving Iraqi interests. Wadi Hadad's terrorism was more an institutional distancing from the PFLP than it was a break with its ideology. His most illustrious acts—Mogadishu and Entebbe—highlighted both the special relationship he maintained with German terrorism and his constant concern for securing independent financing through the use of ransom demands. Wadi Hadad's installation in southern Yemen may also be interpreted in terms of his desire for autonomy vis-à-vis Iraq. The welcome given him in a host country controlled by the Soviets placed him in a relationship of logistic and political dependence, which allowed him, paradoxically, to avoid becoming the tool of any one state in the region. Much more than Abu Nidal, he was his own boss. He died in 1978, and his funeral oration was pronounced at Baghdad, before a great crowd, by George Habash.

## Libya

In Libya, it is clearly Colonel Qaddafi's perspective that one must take if one is to understand the terrorist activities, of which but a small portion are the work of Palestinians. The Libyan head of state has often helped or encouraged a variety of organizations engaged in armed struggle, financing, in the Palestinian case, all manner of operations, placing his embassies or diplomatic pouch in Black September's service (especially in the 1972 Munich affair), and welcoming as conquering heroes the authors of the Vienna operation (December 20, 1975) organized by Carlos on behalf of the PFLP (see above). But Qaddafi has not been interested in merely giving aid to revolutionary or terrorist organizations. He has also worked to further his own designs, both international and domestic, by using terrorism as a tool. Through a process not unlike that of the formation of the Abu Nidal organization, a Palestinian organization began to take shape in Libya in 1973. Abu Mahmoud (Ahmad Abdul Ghaffour), originally a PLO representative in Tripoli, broke away and placed himself under the direct orders of the Libyan regime (he would be killed in Beirut late in 1974). His organization was given responsibility for a number of highly diversified operations which had much less to do with the Palestinian cause than with Libyan diplomacy or Colonel Qaddafi's will to physically eliminate all of his opponents who had taken refuge abroad. The Palestinians who placed themselves in his service were, more than Abu Nidal or Wadi Hadad, the pure and simple tools of a terrorist political policy. The body of often sensationalist literature on this subject has generally contented itself with the simplistic explanation of Qaddafi's megalomaniacal personality, instead of concerning itself with the important sociopolitical processes involved.[24] The use of terrorism and therefore the recruiting of Palestinian terrorists (among others) cannot be understood without looking at Libya's own internal revolutionary processes (the revolutionary committees of 1973, the hunting down of opponents, popular militias, etc.). These are further extended or complemented, in the context of Libya's relative diplomatic isolation, by an Arabo-Islamic revolutionary program intended to embrace the entire Arab world, and which claims to be the sole program capable of ending Israel's existence.

It is not our goal here to go into a regime-by-regime analysis, even when the regimes in question are terrorist. We can, however, offer a hypothesis on the subject of the Libyan regime which relates to our arguments concerning terrorist actors. We ought to see, in Colonel Qaddafi, a manifestation of the crisis in Arab nationalism which—not unlike the PFLP splinter groups—is weighted down with a religious baggage that places it in holy alliance with the most radical of the pro-Islamic movements. As with a number of terrorist groups, we seem to be in the presence, once more, of a dual process in which a specific, strategic, and calculating reason is placed in the service of a limitless and irrational expansionist policy, and in which the actor defines himself in a hypersubjective fashion while hyperobjectivizing his enemies.

## Syria

In Syria as well, Palestinian terrorism is but a minor element in a much broader agenda, which is that of strengthening a still weakly constituted state. Gérard Michaud's analyses clearly show the ways in which violence is as much the rule of domestic political struggles as it is its regime's pursuit of a foreign policy.[25] It is a violence that is just as capable of massacring thousands of the regime's detractors—the hard core of whom are members of the Muslim Brotherhood—as it is of spreading terror on the international scene. Here too, hypotheses of the same order as those we advanced above on the Libyan regime seem to be more adequate than the more common fare on the subject of Hafiz al-Assad, who is often portrayed as the Bismarck of the region, in spite of the weakness of his regime. We need, however, to be careful here. While an analysis of state-sponsored terrorism may well carry us beyond the Palestinian question, and lead us to ponder the instrumental role of violence in the foundation of the nation-states in this part of the world, we will nevertheless limit ourselves here to describing the modest role played by the Palestinians in a situation which appears to be largely dictated by President Assad's strategy.

Theirs is not an exclusively terrorist role, far from it. The Syrian army controls Sa'iqa, playing a role in the Palestinian movement's internal conflicts and championing military and political opposition to Yasser Arafat. As far as the 1970s are concerned, it is only possible to speak of a single punctual event in terrorist terms. Prior to the October 1973 war, Sa'iqa had organized an operation in which hostages were taken in Vienna in order to block Austria from facilitating the transit of Jews from the USSR toward Israel. This episode has been widely interpreted as a diversionary tactic aimed at diverting attention from Israel and from the preparations for the war that would be started, one week later, by Syria and Egypt. As far as we are concerned, Syria did not truly emerge as a terrorist state until 1980, at which time Abu Nidal left Iraq to become the ringleader of a number of operations launched out of that country. Later, other groups and individuals, closer to Islam than to any Palestinian cause, would also come into play.

The object was to eliminate opponents of the regime who had taken refuge in foreign countries—people like Salah al-din Bitar, who was assassinated in Paris in July 1980—and to resume, after a relative lull of two years, the deadly war against the PLO and Yasser Arafat. Another goal was to use terror to gain a position of relative strength on the international scene, in order that Syria might implement its Lebanese agenda. The spectacular series of attacks carried out against Jews in Europe—the October 1980 Rue Copernic attack, as well as the August 1982 killings in the Vienna synagogue and the Rue des Rosiers (like the operations which, carried out in Lebanon, ended in the death of Louis Delamarre, the French ambassador, as well as the embassy cryptologist and his wife)—often carried the signature of Abu Nidal.[26] Here, the Syrian regime's geopolitical interests had become fused if not amalgamated with its blind visceral anti-Semitism and its redoubled efforts to weaken the PLO and to block all mediation between it and Israel. This was an amalgam which, here as in other cases, clouded the national and international political picture, introducing dissimulation, allowing for ambivalent strategies and double-talk, reinforcing attitudes of fear and uncertainty among its targets, and bewildering public opinion. Such was, for example, the case with the Jewish community in France which, after the Rue Copernic attack, was convinced that this was the harbinger of a rising anti-Semitism within its own society. This was also an amalgam in which, moreover, all of the specificity of and every reference to the Palestinian cause, even inverted, tended to break down. Well into the mid-1980s, Syria employed or encouraged an international terrorism whose actual actors were often individuals or groups who had nothing to do with the Palestinian cause.

## Extensions and Spinoff Groups: ASALA and LARF

Pure Palestinian terrorism has had its imitators, which have on many accounts worked from comparable worldviews. Out of the decaying Lebanon of the 1970s, we have seen the appearance of an Armenian brand of terrorism on the one hand, and of a revolutionary and nationalist Arab terrorism on the other, with both being relatively independent and greatly inspired by the Palestinian reference group.

Armenian terrorism derives in part from a rationale that has little to do with the dismemberment of Lebanon. In the early 1920s, Armenian militants, in the wake of a veritable worldwide manhunt, assassinated the Turkish leaders who had been responsible for the genocide of their people.[27] Armenian terrorism is not, however, an extension of this act of vengeance, but has rather emerged out of splits that occurred, within the Armenian diaspora, in the years following 1970. In 1973, a survivor of the genocide gunned down two Turkish diplomats in Los Angeles and thereby inaugurated, fifty years after Operation Nemesis, a series of attacks orchestrated or backed by the Dachnak party (Armenian Revolutionary Federation). It was at this time that Armenian youth banded into underground organizations whose "targeted" actions were well-funded by various Armenian communities.

While this evolution towards armed struggle was not unique to the Lebanon-based Armenian community, Lebanon was clearly its epicenter. This was first of all the case because this community is relatively large and, more importantly, relatively concentrated here, especially in the Sinn El Fil and Borj Hammud neighborhoods of Beirut. This is secondly the case because, like every religious faith—even if it has been less active than other faiths—it has not been able to avoid the winds of civil war that are tearing the country apart. It therefore has, here more than anywhere else in the world, been steeped in a culture of violence and death. Lastly, the Palestinian organizations have afforded it a model and object lesson for its own activism, as well as a real potential for mobilization.

The Armenian Secret Army for the Liberation of Armenia (ASALA) first appeared in Beirut in 1975 out of a combination of three factors: the disenchantment of the Armenian community in its realization of the lack of impact its political activism had had on international awareness of its genocide at the beginning of the century and its claims to its homeland; the boom in terrorism as a political tool; and Palestinian inspiration.[28] Born out of a crisis within the traditional Armenian political parties, it began to receive active support from the PLO, most especially from the PFLP. Until 1980, "[terrorist] strikes were considered pure, useful, and agreeable to the community. Pure because they were aimed at representatives of the Turkish state that had authored, profited from, and been an apologist for genocide. Useful because they had, in the space of a few years, advanced a cause that had been stagnating for over half a century. Agreeable because the Armenians savored the cunning of history which, at the four corners of the world, had come to subject their tormenters' descendants to the constant threat of the grandsons of their survivors, who had themselves been scattered over the entire planet."[29] There followed a series of indiscriminate attacks, most notably that carried out at Orly Airport in July 1983, and a gradual clarification of ASALA's ideological base. This was nothing less than a wholesale renovation of the Armenian position: a priority given to the use of weapons; subjectivity on the part of the actor who proclaimed himself to be both the voice and strength of the Armenian people; references to the Third World, and a pro-Soviet stance.

Nationalist with no qualms about attacking its own community, Marxist-Leninist without a social base, ASALA was, in a word, a classic terrorist group, the product of an inversion. This inversion gave rise to both an unbridled violence and an ideology that championed specifically Armenian causes, in spite of the fact that the diaspora was sickened by its violence and its dreamlike calls for revolution. Its trajectory was in no way special. We have just noted its two opening phases (Turkish targets until 1979, followed by a diversification of violence, if only as a means to freeing activists being held in Western prisons).

In the years between 1980 and 1982, ideology hardened as the organization reached the peak of its power. Ties were established or strengthened with a variety of Armenian movements throughout the world, as well as with all manner of revolutionary and nationalist groups. In this period, ASALA was also distributing its own journal and regularly broadcasting its views over an Armenian radio station based in Lebanon.

There then began a third period, a period of decay and a tailspin into terrorism hastened by the entrance of Israeli troops into Lebanon. ASALA, at first torn apart, consolidated itself into two factions: in one camp were Hagop Hagopian's hard-liners, who for the most part found themselves in refugee camps under Syrian control and who aligned themselves more or less with the Abu Nidal organization. In the other were those elements who wished to avoid inversion and heteronomy, and whose desire it was to return to a mainly anti-Turkish resistance. In both cases, the number of activists was greatly limited, and the two camps of the old ASALA greatly weakened. This did not, however, prevent its most hard-line elements from maintaining an extremely violent and anti-Semitic level of discourse, in which they demanded, for example, that Jean-Paul Kaufmann's kidnappers kill him for the simple reason that he was an alleged Jew.

ASALA terrorism, while it clearly thrived under the Lebanese crisis, was not one of its byproducts. Its inversion paralleled that of the Palestinian movement, and its factionalization, which often appeared to imitate that of the Palestinians, belonged to the same family of processes. Such was also the case with the Lebanese Armed Revolutionary Faction (LARF).

Since the wave of attacks that occurred in September 1986, the press has provided us with a great wealth of information on LARF. In the beginning, George Ibrahim Abdallah, the future leader of the organization, was a militant in the Syrian Social Nationalist party. This party, more often referred to as the Syrian Popular party—the PPS—was a Lebanese party favoring a plan for a greater Syria, of clearly fascistic inspiration and most strongly implanted in a number of Maronite Christian and Greek Orthodox villages in northern Lebanon. Sensitive to Lebanese Communist party doctrine, Abdallah militated for the Palestinian cause and, more importantly, placed himself under the PFLP umbrella group which controlled the region's two Palestinian refugee camps. In this, he followed Wadi Hadad who was—prior to creating his own organization, which is best remembered for its hijacking of an Air France Boeing jet over Entebbe in 1976—one of the PFLP's main organizers of international operations. Throughout the 1970s, Abdallah was on the move in Europe as well as in the Middle East, where he maintained open links with Syria and perhaps Libya. He later drifted away from the PFLP to found LARF, together with a number of friends and relatives from his native village of Kobayat.

His trajectory, hereafter a matter of common knowledge,[30] culminated in a number of attacks, assassinations, and assassination attempts against American and Israeli targets in France and Italy, and in the kidnapping, in Tripoli, of the director of the French Cultural Center. The series of ruthless terrorist attacks carried out in Paris in September 1986, for which the CSPPA claimed responsibility and which the police and press at first attributed to LARF,[31] appear to have been the work of other, pro-Iranian actors, even if these attacks were explicitly presented as means for pressuring the French authorities into quickly freeing Abdallah.

In the light of this analysis, it is impossible to view LARF's trajectory as a gradual process in which a series of crises and a growing alienation from the popular masses' actual experiences finally led to international terrorism. Here the action is, from the outset, strictly politicomilitary. *The divergent path taken by men like Abdallah was built upon the foundations of other divergent paths,* most especially that of the PFLP but also, at some deeper level, that of an Arab nationalism that history had constantly denied, as well as those of European armed resistance movements with which he had maintained a variety of relations.

This process, in which a tilt towards international terrorism and its corollary—subordination to terrorist states—is grounded in a network of organizations which are themselves already heavily committed in this direction, indicates the immense gulf which existed, from the outset, between the group and any and all social or communal movements it may have claimed to have been fighting for. It is for this reason that whenever the police or journalists attempted, in their investigations, to discover the locus of meaning from which the group's action proceeded, they found themselves plunging downwards through the thick tangle of denominational and social relations that make up the Lebanese scene until they hit rock bottom on the sole social base from which the organization operated—a family clan in a straggling village in the north of the country. In its war on imperialism and Zionism, carried out in the name of an Arabo-Marxism itself threatened by an upsurge of radical Islam, the sole identifying principle that LARF had to show was one of an overpoliticized village group. The group's impressive ideological apparatus, which one finds in a thesis written by a family member,[32] was built upon a social void. Contrary to other terrorist phenomena, this was not the upshot of a gradual process of disengagement from reality, since this disengagement was more-or-less given from the outset. LARF terrorism was even less an extreme manifestation of communal violence of the Hizbollah type, or a modality of the crisis within the Christian denominations of Lebanon. It was rather a direct extension of the heteronomous experience of all political actors who placed themselves in the service of the most extremist factions of the Palestinian movement. By closing itself in upon a radicalism which claimed to maintain this identification in a Marxist-Leninist, Arab and pan-Syrian mode, it constituted a unique variant form of Lebanese political and military action.

This variant which—like ASALA—could not have come into being outside the climate of deterioration and the culture of violence proper to the Lebanese civil war, was nevertheless not its direct by-product. It was, in its own way, an extension of the Palestinian experience, and more specifically of its terrorist spinoff, which first took the form of the PFLP. It constituted a special kind of permutation on the many spinoff groups that arose out of a locus of meaning which remained, in a confused manner, that of the Arab nation and the Palestinian cause.

While ASALA and LARF did not issue out of the Palestinian movement, they did grow in part out of processes comparable to those by which the latter became inverted. They also owe much to it, on both an ideological and a practical level. It is for these reasons that the international terrorism one may attribute to them ought, in the final analysis, to be sociologically assimilated to that associated with the Palestinian movement.

## Conclusion

It is difficult to distill the Palestinian practice of terrorism down to a single essence or to qualify the Palestinan movement, once and for all, as a terrorist movement.

We may isolate the crisis in Arab nationalism as the primary source of the international terrorism that began to appear in the late 1960s. The two main ideological elements that were advanced in the course of this crisis—Palestinian nationalism and Marxism-Leninism—were more often on opposite sides of the fence from one another than on the same side. Each of the two built up its own brand of terrorism, with even an Armenian variant emerging out of the throng of Palestinian nationalist groups. In the one camp, the early spinoffs of Palestinian nationalism (Black September, etc.) were of limited duration, a sign of great weakness and of a temporary inability to organize a military insurgent operation out of a territorial base. In the other, revolutionary anti-imperialism, which was more Arab than Palestinian, spawned a number of spinoff groups whose earliest manifestations betrayed their minority character. On the national front, international terrorism remains a substitute for an unwageable war; on the revolutionary front, it remains linked to an Arab agenda which, in the light of the powerful conflicts that have erupted between Arab nations and the recent pro-Islamic upsurge, is unrealistic. It is also associated with Marxist-Leninist ideologies whose social bases and links to actual social causes are highly questionable.

Palestinian nationalism becomes more radical—most notably in the case of Abu Nidal—when its activists cut themselves off from the actual experiences of the masses, and turn against the movement's more moderate elements. It no longer has to concern itself with the concrete problems of those in whose names it claims to be fighting, and its intransigence, which one can no longer measure in terms of the expectations of their popular constituency, goes hand in hand with a sometimes total dependence upon terrorist states. The same holds for ASALA's Armenian nationalism. The Marxism-Leninism and pan-Arab anti-imperialism of organizations like those of George Habash and Wadi Hadad have also had an affinity for radicalized activities. These, rather than being the actualization of popular demands, have constituted an attempt, of negative impact, to recruit militants in search of a fight—yet another expression of a growing heteronomy of which a particular variant, from outside the Palestinian movement but within a very similar ideological purview, has been LARF.

Finally, international terrorism is, in this case, not merely the upshot of the spinoff groups that mainly stemmed from one of the two major elements of the Palestinian movement. It also owes much to their contradictory nature, which is brought to the fore whenever a possibility for openness or negotiated settlement is in the wind. Terrorism is also a tool that directly or indirectly provides the movement's revolutionary component—especially when it is in the midst of a process of inversion—with a means for blocking all negotiation (which is in any case unjustifiable when relations are poor) which the nationalist component might wish to undertake.

Our study of the Palestinian movement ends in 1982, the year in which Israeli troops drove the PLO out of Lebanon. Since that date, it has only considered the particular spinoffs constituted by ASALA and LARF, whose terrorist rationale expanded or reproduced those we had already encountered in a number of Palestinian groups.

Our research greatly damages any theory that would view the Palestinian movement as being terrorist through and through, and rather shows how the terrorist alternative can derive from a multitude of causes. Terrorism can at times constitute a *method* to be used at a particular juncture (Fatah, Munich 1972), or to be combined, with varying degrees of control, with a broader array of strategies for action (PFLP). It may constitute its own *rationale of action,* in which case it becomes the expression of a veritable inversion. Such either arises out of an ideal of nationalist resistance (Abu Nidal), or out of revolutionary ideals (Wadi Hadad and his successors). It is also well disposed to promulgating an ideological synthesis: the Abu Nidal organization, for example, has also called itself Fatah-Revolutionary Council, by which it considers itself to embody a dual affiliation.

At times, terrorism can become so estranged from the central meanings of a movement as to invert them; in others it can, on the contrary, come to constitute a desperate expression of those same meanings. Moreover, the very existence of a competing rationale of terrorist action can, on occasion, force a movement's moderate elements to resort to terrorism. Alternatively, it can force them to admit its usefulness, if only as a means to showing that they are neither passive, impoverished, nor powerless in a given situation. It is for this reason that, even as we underscore the significant differences that exist within what appear to be international terrorist activities, it behooves us to acknowledge that they share a certain problematic unity. It is absolutely essential to understand, however, that this problematic cannot be understood if one takes the terrorist phenomenon to be one's starting point. Only when one starts from the movement itself—from its political and ideological foundations, its internal tensions, and the tendencies of certain of its elements to split off and invert the meaning of its action so as to ultimately find themselves in a situation of partial or nearly total heteronomy—can this problematic take on its greatest fullness of meaning.

# 18

## Lebanese Actors: A General Analytical Model

Throughout the 1970s, the Palestinian cause, whose imposing legitimacy overshadowed even that of the Lebanese state, was the center of gravity for every facet of Lebanese political life.

The departure of the PLO in 1983 did nothing to reverse the general downward trend of the Lebanese state and political system. On the contrary, it had a catalyzing effect, as if the structured presence of the Palestinians had constituted a valve which had held back a pressurized liquid explosive. The explosion of violence that followed, on both the domestic and international levels, was manifestly linked to the principles which the Palestinian question had at once masked, obscured, or subordinated to itself, but which it had also helped to generate.

Not all was terrorism within this climate of violence, and even less was international terrorism, especially if we put aside the cases of LARF and ASALA, which have already been mentioned in terms of their proximity to Palestinian terrorism.

It nonetheless remains that the Lebanon of the 1980s, both before and after the 1982 Operation Peace for Galilee, was viewed by the world as a headquarters for an international terrorism that had simply shed its nationalist and Marxist-Leninist ideologies to become pro-Islamic. The question nevertheless remains as to whether the attacks carried out against the West, the kidnappings of European and American citizens, truly deserved the qualification of "terrorist." Another question concerns the applicability of the notion of inversion to these phenomena. Such an approach implies that we ought to concentrate on actors, much more than the system within which they move.

The violence—and especially the international terrorism—that origi-
nates out of Lebanon appears to stem primarily from exogenous processes and external interference, which affect a country whose government and political system are fragile and artificially integrated. By
applying a sociology of systems we should be able to account for the
violent activities that have been erupting throughout the history of this
structural and ever-deepening institutional crisis. The grounds for such
an approach become all the more apparent as soon as we consider one
of the major consequences of the deterioration to which we alluded a
moment ago: this has been the universalization of a veritable culture of
violence which no one in Lebanon has been able to avoid.[1]

It is nonetheless impossible for us to reduce the properly Lebanese
actors to their heteronomy or, at best, to their limited and short-term
interests; or their violence to a combination of tactical instrumentality
and patterns of crisis behavior shaped by a breakdown of governmental
structures and the proliferation of a culture of violence.

Whether they be political or social powers, whether or not we define
them in denominational terms, and whether or not they be pawns in a
greater strategy, the Lebanese actors nevertheless do have aspirations,
goals, and historical interests of their own, which influence their short-
term military and political calculations.[2]

## The Proliferation of Violence

In Lebanon, it is difficult to define the actors, at least in a primary
overview, without speaking of the Christian and Muslim communities
or, more specifically, of the two major faiths themselves.[3]

The matter at hand is not to describe these denominations as a means
to distilling from each some essence that could then be singled out as
inclining it towards violence. It is rather to make sense of a series of
shifts which have, over some thirty years, resulted in the outbreaks of
violence we are so familiar with today and which, as we will see, but
rarely derive from a terrorist rationale.

It is possible to view these shifts from the perspective of each of the
separate denominations.[4] Catalyzed by the deterioration of the state and,
until 1983, by the Palestinian presence, they in fact derive from the
same movement. Behind the specific features of each of these confessions
however, there has been a real unity to Shiite, Sunnite, and Druze actions.
It is for this reason that it may be useful—even before we look at the
cases of particular actors who have chosen a course of aggravated violence, or consider the potentially terrorist nature of such violence—to

set out a general model for the activities of the Lebanese insurgency as a whole.

The model we will present here applies to a common arena of tension, conflict, and incompatible goals and interests, which are becoming increasingly resolved through communal isolation and the proliferation of violence. It is constructed along three axes, with each axis oriented toward three poles: an offensive pole, a defensive pole, and a pole of radical dislocation. Is this last pole terrorist? When an actor begins his trajectory as a popular protest figure, as may be observed in the cases of the Shiite movement of the disinherited and the Sunnites of the Bâb Tebbâné neighborhood,[5] this dislocation results in a social antimovement. What we mean here is that its activities continue, *without there being any dissociation* between perpetrators of violence, clergy, or their communal constituency. Here we find a powerful bond of unity between both religious and secular leaders, violent insurgent groups, and a given popular base. Here, when a split mobilizes a community that is centered on itself rather than on some isolated vanguard, *the actor is not, sociologically speaking, a terrorist, and one cannot speak in terms of a rationale of terrorist action.*

When the actor does not, from the outset, have a strong social identity, as is particularly the case with the Christians in Lebanon, his dislocation comes to look more like a breakdown than a social antimovement. It nonetheless overlaps the latter inasmuch as it too takes the form of separatist behavior or self-isolation. For this reason, we will continually employ the term of antimovement to designate the third pole of our general model. We may now turn to the three axes of this model.

The first of these is social. It indicates the ability of actors to speak as social movements and as popular figures of protest. We will call this ability offensive when the actor is able to promulgate alternative programs for economic development, to stimulate programs of modernization, or to protest those offered or administered by his social adversaries. We will call it defensive when the actor seeks to protect turf he has already won or to highlight popular demands proper to the poor and downtrodden classes, classes possessed of a social rage and a marginal consciousness which eventually lead to separatism and mob violence. We will use the term *antimovement* when the actor has ceased to define himself socially in order that he may rather champion a communal identity grounded in a refusal to interact and a tendency towards self-isolation. Such is the case, for example, when a neighborhood becomes transformed into an armed citadel or sanctuary.

The second axis is that of integration into the state and the political system. This centers around an offensive pole, of which the primary feature is the desire to enter into and remain within this system, and even to widen its powers and enhance its impact on political decision making. Its defensive pole is constituted by the championing of revolutionary separatism and the goal of taking over state power. Its transformation into an antimovement may be heralded by a desire to create homogeneous territories—each having the key attributes of a state—for each separate denomination, or at least for one's own. Its image becomes sharper when its activities, whether deliberately or not, serve no other purpose than to accelerate the collapse of the state and the Lebanese political system. Along this second axis, and most particularly at its offensive pole, violence becomes instrumental in nature. At its defensive pole, it has less to do with a certain capacity for control or a political will, than with a state or political crisis, to which it contributes when it becomes transformed into an antimovement. Here it is constantly aligning itself with more specifically social themes, as well as with the defensive side of popular movements, and the rage of the poor and downtrodden.

The third axis is that of the assertion of a national identity. Its positive pole is one that calls for a Lebanese nation, itself a subunit within the Arab nation. It is only through such a definition that the actor can continue to act within the bounds of his own society, and assert himself in the face of increasing interference on the part of foreign powers. Its defensive pole may lend a certain priority to Arab nationalism—to the detriment of Lebanese nationalism—which may result in the championing of some common trans- or infranational principle. In this case, the principle will generally be religious, based on Islam, one of its denominations, or Christianity. The tilt towards an antimovement leads to an orientation towards either the Western or the Soviet bloc, or to strictly communal or ethnic constituencies. Here, the pole of radical dislocation is characterized by heteronomy—actors placing themselves in the service of foreign powers—or else by a sectarian anti-Western stance which may lead to fanaticism and, in extreme cases (but less often than has been intimated on the subject of suicide missions), self-destruction.

## A General Model

Table 2 summarizes this general analytical framework. Rather than ideal types, what it delineates are axes and poles. Each actor can, at any given moment, be pinpointed on this table in terms of the position he occupies

TABLE 2

| | OFFENSIVE POLE | DEFENSIVE POLE | POLE OF RADICAL DISLOCATION: ANTIMOVEMENT |
|---|---|---|---|
| Social axis | Counterproposals; calls for development and modernization | Defensive action to protect turf already won or to speak in the name of the poor; popular rage | Communal self-isolation |
| Axis of integration within a territorial collective | Institutional pressure | Revolutionary separatism | Catalyzation of state crisis |
| Axis of self-identity | Assertion of Lebanese nationalism | Arab or religious self-identity | Anti-Western stance, fundamentalism, pan-Islamicism, heteronomy |

on each of the three axes. It is in fact this tridimensionality—i.e. the tendency to simultaneously speak out on social matters (the social axis), vis-à-vis the state (the axis of integration), and in terms of a national or religious entity (axis of self-identification)—that distinguishes Lebanese activism.

This table may first be read along historical lines. The more deteriorated the state and the political system have become, the more the behavior of these actors as a group moves from the offensive activist pole to the defensive pole, and finally towards antimovement. This inversion process is not one of simple transposition, but is rather much more characterized by an increasing tension between the three poles. As long as these remain unseparated, each actor remains torn between a radical activism and an attempt to maintain himself within—and thereby to defend his own political, economic, and cultural interests therein—the traditional Lebanese context. When they become disconnected, adherence to the same faith does not necessarily preclude internal splits or intracommunal violence.

On a broader level, table 2 should allow us to better grasp what this violence signifies in the Lebanese context. First of all, this violence varies from one square of the table to another. At the offensive pole, it hardly enters into play at all as concerns the social axis; it is instrumental and greatly limited when the goal is one of exerting institutional pressure; and it translates into a potential insertion into foreign struggles—mainly with Israel—when it is expressive of Lebanese national identity. On the social level, the closer one moves toward antimovement, the more violence tends to take the form of the mob violence that stems from crowd behavior and popular insurrection. Whenever the dangerous classes become involved, such violence will tend to degenerate into classical forms of delinquence, which have grown considerably in Lebanon. The refusal to take part in a nation-state takes on the form of a revolutionary violence, for which the ideology, originally pan-Arab in the 1960s and 1970s, has become increasingly religious, taking the Iranian revolution to be its overall (but not exclusive) model. Among Christians, it has also taken the form of purely military attempts—of the coup d'état variety— to found a strong central power over homogeneous territories, which function as if they were independent states. Finally, the reference to a trans- or infranational identity generates a violence which, while many have taken it to be fundamentalist in nature, may derive more from a policy of simple communal defense, or else from some separatist (anti-imperialist, anti-Western, anti-Muslim) inspiration. Such violence is more often directed against domestic Lebanese targets (denominations other than one's own) than foreign ones.

These various and sundry forms of violence may become combined, through either constructive or destructive interference with one another, both of which can give rise to even higher levels of violence. When it is fueled by a social rage or religious extremist calls to separatism, the action may quickly veer from the defensive pole toward the point of radical dislocation. Pure sources of violence can easily lead into practices which amalgamate a number of such sources. The further one moves down the defensive slope, or continues in the direction of antimovement, the more reasons one finds to seek military, political, financial, and ideological support from outside of Lebanon, support which a number of Arab powers are still quite happy to provide. In such cases, violence tends to take on new meanings, because the actor has placed himself in a position of dependence, which quickly transforms him into the hit man of the groups that provide him with financial or ideological backing. He becomes an aggregate of internal meanings and external leanings, which are reconciled all the more easily when the actor himself has broken with his own society or state.

Inside each of the religious groups, violence is moreover a preferred means for solving the tensions which link and oppose the poles we have identified here. How can one possibly maintain, for example, a working relationship between a form of action which prioritizes institutional pressure and an action carried out in the name of a single community which refuses any insertion into the existing political system, save by force? The sharper the swing towards antimovement becomes, the more it forces those actors located on the offensive pole—who prefer to convince others of their positions through the negotiation and other processes—to yield to power politics and armed insurgency.

We should, however, avoid overly simplistic arguments. The transition from an offensive pole towards the radical dislocation of antimovement need not exclusively or necessarily lead to an increase in violence, whose pure forms may combine into increasingly terrifying amalgams. The collapse of a historical system of action may also culminate in activities of a nonviolent nature. In Lebanon, one also finds cases of more-or-less sectarian communal isolation, the inclination to flee the country and emigrate (what Hirshman calls the "way out"), or to assume a transnational identity which need not necessarily lead to war.

The general model we have just presented will now help us in providing a more detailed analysis of the Shiite community. This community is associated, in the Western imagination, with an image of a fanatical and international terrorism that knows no bounds. This is why it is appropriate that we analyze the conditions and processes specific to the proliferation of violence within this community. It is only through such an endeavor that we shall be able to differentiate between communal violence on the one hand, and a possible rationale of terrorist action on the other.

# 19

# The Disinherited, Communal Violence, and Terrorism

Attacks in Beirut, outside the French embassy (May 1982) and against the United States embassy (April 1983), raids on the American marine headquarters as well as on the French paratroopers' Drakkar base (October 1983) and the Frégate base of the French contingent (December 1983), airline hijackings, kidnappings of French, British, American, German, etc. nationals (journalists in particular), as well as responsibility claimed—albeit with little grounds for proof—for raids in Kuwait, Turkey, Spain, France, etc.—is it not fair to say that we have entered into a new age, in which international terrorism has become dominated by pro-Islamic actors, of which a majority are Lebanese Shiites aligned with Iran?

We know that the breakup of the Lebanese state has favored the expansion of a hydra-headed violence. The moment has now come to show how this violence, in the Shiite case, can be carried to the point of taking on the guise of terrorism. As in our previous analyses, we will take the movement out of which this violence first emerged as our starting point.

## The Formation of the Movement of the Disinherited

Shiism, the earliest politicoreligious schism within Islam, considers the infallible interpretation of the law to derive from the Prophet's family alone, and awaits the coming of the twelfth Imam, the hidden Imam. In Lebanon, the Shiites constitute a community that has long been concentrated into two zones, one in the south of the country (but not in the city of Sa'ida, in which the Sunnites are predominant), and the northwestern portion of the Bekaa Valley, around the city of Baalbek. A rural community, the Shiites hardly had any part in the country's development, which began in the middle of the last century. Both economically and culturally, the Lebanese Shiites have long been left out of the important changes that have swept over Lebanon, and it is not surprising that they remained relatively marginalized throughout the period of French administration as well as under the national pact and independence. They were a traditional society, represented by local potentates who, linked to the great landowning families, had decided to take part in the political system.

Within thirty short years, however, this society was considerably transformed, at the culmination of a process admirably described by Salim Nasr.[1] Migration into the cities and urbanization, entrance into the modern Lebanese economy, the formation of a merchant middle class—even the most traditional social relationships were becoming shaken and beginning to break down, as the agrarian structure became modified and an impressive exodus was funneling a poverty-stricken proletariat towards Beirut. These mainly settled in the suburbs to the south of the capital. General Chehab's presidency, from 1958 to 1964, was undoubtedly a decisive period in this process. More than any other Lebanese president, this individual personified the will to build a powerful state, especially on a military and adminstrative level, which only hastened the collapse of the traditional system of local potentates. He built up the educational system, which lent itself to a politicization of the people and the emergence of an intelligentsia open to such political ideas as Nasserism, revolutionary Marxism, etc.—which gave rise to protest. It was in the same period that there occurred a powerful wave of Shiite emigration into the oil-producing Gulf states and, on an even greater scale, into Africa. This in turn gave rise to the funneling of money back into the native Lebanese communities, where social relations were being further upset by the emergence of a new middle class.

In order to grasp the full impact of the changes that were rocking the Shiite community, it is appropriate that we emphasize the impressive demographic explosion that raised its numbers from 225,000 (or 18.2 percent of the total Lebanese population) in 1948 to 750,000 (or nearly 30 percent) in 1975.[2] Like all figures in Lebanon, where census-taking has long since become a political impossibility, these too are open to discussion. Their magnitude nevertheless cannot be denied. It is out of these multiple upheavals that new economic, cultural, and intellectual elites emerged—but there also came into being an urban underclass, which came together in a movement whose structure constituted the original foundation for the Shiite movement.³ This foundation, which corresponded as much if not more to the offensive side of our general analytical schema than it did to the defensive side, may be dated to 1969. It was then that Imam Musa Sadr founded a Supreme Islamic Shii Council which, taking up a focus of social protest which had been introduced by the Marxist left into certain sectors of the Shiite community, shook the very foundations of Shiite feudalism and its local potentates.

## The Movement of the Disinherited

Pioneered by the charismatic figure of Imam Musa Sadr, this movement was possessed of the following key features:

It was present, on a limited level, at the positive or offensive pole of the social axis, in the form of a call for increased development and modernization in regions with high Shiite concentrations. Its presence was stronger, however, at the negative or defensive pole, where it championed the cause of the downtrodden masses. Demanding greater justice and civil rights, it went so far as to call for a fairer distribution of wealth and for a holy religious state.

Along the political axis of integration into the Lebanese state, it unambiguously called for admission into the state and participation in its political system. From this standpoint, it was highly offensive, and although it did at times brandish a threat of separatism, such was always done in the name of citizens who, having been excluded from the political system, wished to enter into it. This dimension of its action championed an insertion into the political scene, which presupposed the fact that more traditional modes of participation had been outmoded. This necessarily implied an opposition to the old system of representation by figures from the landowning class—which brings us back to the movement's popular and social axis. What is important here is that this movement located itself squarely within the Lebanese context, that it thought in terms of the Lebanese nation-state and—as a number of observers have noted—that it never criticized the Lebanese army, but rather those who held state power.

On the national axis, this movement was defined by an antiimperialism which placed it at odds, because it was Lebanese, with the state of Israel. This also drew it, albeit not without creating powerful

TABLE 3

|                     | OFFENSIVE POLE | DEFENSIVE POLE | POLE OF DISLOCATION |
|---------------------|:--------------:|:--------------:|:-------------------:|
| Social axis         |                |       X        |                     |
| Axis of integration |       X        |                |                     |
| Axis of self-identity |     X        |       X        |                     |

tensions, toward both the Palestinian movement, whose cause it at times espoused, and a Marxist-oriented and strongly anti-imperialist left. In no way did this movement herald an upsurge of Shiite Muslim fundamentalism. Here, religion was essentially a vehicle for self-identity, holding the community together as it defined its principles of justice and an exemplary way of living.

In the mid-1970s, the "movement of the disinherited," as it called itself, had the configuration shown in table 3.

Violence was not wholly absent from this configuration. On the social as well as the political axis, it constituted a threat rather than a reality: "If our demands are not met, we will set about taking them by force," exclaimed Imam Musa Sadr in a speech quoted by Itamar Rabinovich.[4] Its presence was more manifest on the national axis, on which the movement wished to take part in the war with Israel, establish a Lebanese national resistance, train itself militarily, and arm itself in order to avoid becoming future Palestinians.

Beginning in the years 1976–77, this original configuration fell into turmoil, in which all that the movement had managed to bring together began to fall apart. Civil war, an increasingly overt Syrian presence, tensions with the Palestinians aggravated by Israeli reprisals carried out on Lebanese territory, as well as the *active influence of the Iranian revolution* after 1980, brought about a split in the movement which would thereafter incorporate two factions. This dissociation was quickened by the mysterious end of Imam Musa Sadr, who disappeared while traveling to Libya in August 1978. Both of these two factions were characterized by a powerful militarization and a political discourse that betrayed a relatively high level of activist training. Prior to opting for one side or the other, the members of the Shiite political rank and file often received their first military and ideological training within the Palestinian organizations. Throughout the 1970s, a good number of militants moved from support for or participation in the Palestinian movement into Shiite activism, with this trend becoming greatly accelerated by the 1982 Israeli invasion.

## The Amal Movement and Hizbollah

Those who followed the former of these two factions continued to concern themselves with ensuring Shiite access into the Lebanese political system. Having distanced itself from the Palestinian resistance, it found itself caught in a bind brought on by two of its principal causes: its anti-imperialist agenda and the hostility to Israel it implied, and the survival of a Lebanese state increasingly threatened by a continuing PLO presence. In the face of Palestinian resistance, a political and military machine whose activities had resulted in Israeli bombings and reprisals against Shiite villages in the south of the country, as well as a Marxist and communist Left, which was actively recruiting from its own popular base, this faction had but one strategy left to it. This was a trend towards accelerated militarization carried out in tandem with a search for alliances which would at times place this actor in a position of great dependence with regard to Syria. This faction, which organized itself politically and militarily under the name of Amal, became in 1974 the political heir to the movement of the disinherited. Its first objective, beyond those we have already mentioned, was to defend the south, even if this meant associating itself with the Palestinians, against the Israelis. The latter, finding Lebanon to be a powerless political entity, was in the process of using a policy of reprisals to expel the Shiites from a region in which they constituted a large majority of the population. Later, the Amal movement would on several occasions show its hatred for the Palestinians. This mainly took the form of an attempt to take over their refugee camps, especially following the 1982 Israeli invasion, in the massacres they carried out in 1985, and in the 1986 "war of the camps." Generally speaking, the group's militarization went hand in hand with the community's decision to look after its own social problems (distribution, health, etc.). Its differences with the local potentates and the great feudal families were decreasing, because these traditional leaders were by now coming around to the Amal viewpoint, and arguing for a negotiated insertion into the Lebanese political, economic, and cultural spheres. The slight increase in power they came to enjoy was mainly the result of a crisis in the original movement, of an increasing tendency towards heteronomy in the hands of Syria, and a weakening of the social themes that had previously placed the movement of the disinherited under its control.

Represented by such figures as Sheik Shamsedine, a religious leader and president of the Supreme Islamic Shii Council, or Hussein el-Husseini, these traditional leaders were not key actors on the Lebanese stage. The great novelty was, on the other hand, the meteoric rise of a second faction, which we may designate by the name of Hizbollah (Party of God), even if this appellation only corresponds to an organization that asserted itself as the political symbol of a nebulous aggregate of still-unstable tendencies. This faction, whose symbolic leader is Sheik Muhammad Husayn Fadlallah, has been separatist in both its social and political positions, and seething with popular rage. It has put but little trust, or very moderate trust, in a political insertion onto the Lebanese scene, and has placed itself at a great distance from all references to the Lebanese nation. It has rather preferred a policy of aggravated anti-imperialism, which has become transformed into an anti-Western stance, with the idea of the nation being replaced by the transhistorical principle of the battle of good against evil. Here, the break with all that has preceded has become greatly advanced if not quite nearly consummated. Their goal has been the formation of an Islamic republic and not a Lebanese state, and their call has been to a total fusion of every category of social, political, and historical action into a single guiding principle for the functioning of both public and private life: Islam. Especially following the Israeli occupation of southern Lebanon, Hizbollah has never abandoned the notion of Israel as the enemy. On the contrary, the Lebanese Christians have never been openly referred to as enemies; and leaders like Fadlallah have repeatedly stressed the absence of differences between the Christian and Muslim peoples. "The difficulties," as he explained in the course of a long interview, "are brought about by the Christian leaders, as well as a certain number of Muslim leaders who lie, who use violent methods, and who defend the interests of the privileged."[5] Hizbollah speaks in the name of the people, and does most of its recruiting, mainly through funding from Khomeini's Iran, among the oppressed of Beirut's Shiite suburbs, as well as among college and high-school students.

This second faction consolidated itself in the years following 1982. It appears to have been created in Baalbek, where mullahs and revolutionary guards were responsible for establishing its ideological and practical guidelines. Next came the task of taking over the Beirut neighborhoods,[6] and of effecting a union between an originally fragmented political mindset and a mindset which, proper to the popular masses, was heir to the most defensive tendencies within the movement of the disinherited. This aggregate has not always been a perfectly homogeneous one. On the one hand, it has fluctuated between exemplarity and violence, with its social-antimovement character, appeals to absolute principles, and general rejection of the Lebanese state leading, at certain times, towards nonviolent, and at times exemplarist, attitudes. On the other hand, whenever the Iranian revolution has been its point of reference, the group has interpreted its own place in history in an irreconcilable mode. While some of its number anticipated an Iranian victory over Iraq, and a subsequent regional and later global expansion of the Islamic revolution, others were of the opinion that the revolution would be born in Lebanon itself.

There has often been a tendency to speak about the Shiites in terms of an awakening of Islam. It is nonetheless quite clear, in the light of the changes that have occurred in the Shiite world and the meteoric rise of Hizbollah, that Islam—Shiite in this case—cannot suffice to explain the formation of a movement founded in its name. Elsewhere, the notion that there occurred an eruption of something that had been stifled or held down for centuries cannot account for all that happened in this context. In the case of Hizbollah, one is in the presence of the proliferation of a social antimovement, of a type of communal isolation that has found its meaning in a particular reference. This reference, as Daryush Sheyegan has demonstrated in his work on the Iranian revolution, has consisted of an ideological blend of elements which, derived from the Islamic revolution as well as from Western philosophy, has been subsequently reinterpreted.[7]

It is now possible for us to summarize these remarks, which describe the fragmentation and subsequent inversion of the original grounds of the Shiite movement. Figure 2 provides us with the overall structure of a Shiite movement that had fallen apart and was heading towards inversion.

The two lines along which these factions took shape are analytical constructs. Both are, in practical terms, more complex and ambivalent, with the dominant features of one being secondary in the other, and vice versa. Sheik Fadlallah, for example, has never maintained that immediate action was necessary for the establishment of the Islamic republic. This man, close to certain circles of the Khomeini regime, has never—in contradistinction to the Iranian line—referred to the states of the region as puppet states, and has never wholly abandoned the cause of a Shiite Lebanese state.

Within each faction, we may also note internal differences which result

*1970–1976*

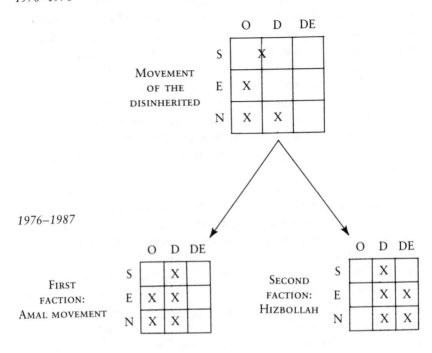

O : OFFENSIVE POLE              S : SOCIAL AXIS
D : DEFENSIVE POLE              E : AXIS OF RELATIONSHIP TO THE STATE
DE: POLE OF RADICAL DISLOCATION   N: AXIS OF SELF-IDENTITY

Figure 2. Factionalization of the movement of the disinherited.

from the geographical—or, more properly speaking, geopolitical—
situation of its actors. In the Bekaa Valley, a region under direct Syrian
domination, one does not adopt the same attitude toward Syria as one
would in faraway southern Lebanon. On a wider level, both factions are
prey to internal tensions, which have given rise to increased levels of
armed violence and heteronomy. This latter phenomenon is reflective of
a complex and unstable interplay of strategies that are internal—but
also increasingly external—to the Lebanese scene.

The opposition between these two factions has become sharper and
sharper over time, with the action of the one often being viewed as
contrary to that of the other. Their denominational unity has in fact
been a very fragile one, behind which there have loomed a number of

conflicts and rivalries. These in turn have given rise to platforms, if not antagonistic visions and perspectives, which need to be defined in political terms. While the former have favored revolution and separatism, the latter have tended more toward a mixture of political pressure and instrumental violence. As for the traditionalists, their effort has remained centered on the common practices of negotiation and political maneuvering.

We cannot but note the correlation between the factionalization of the original movement and the intensification of violence.

The former faction, which has enjoyed a strong popular base of support in urban neighborhoods and villages, and which has been able to develop a wide diversity of social programs (housing, health, etc.), finds its political expression in the Amal movement led by Nabih Berri.[8] This figure has equipped himself with a militia whose role it has been to ensure his control over areas with a high Shiite population—southern Lebanon, Beirut neighborhoods, and the capital's southern suburbs—as well as to pressure the state and the Lebanese political system and actually run entire regions. We should note that here, as everywhere else in Lebanon, a process of disintegration has been at work. So it is that even in the zones under its control, the Amal movement has been at constant odds with all kinds of militia groups, down to the level of neighborhood gangs which, led by low-level za'ims, have enjoyed a relatively independent if marginal status. It has often been the case that organized political violence has shaded into practices which, often under the Amal aegis but in a more-or-less independent fashion, have tended toward the scattered incidents of violence one generally associates with gang activities than with political action. We should also note that Amal's military capabilities have not been as great as its ambitions, as proven by its failure to wipe out the Palestinian camps, as it attempted to do in 1986–87. Its troops are of a decidedly inferior order of mobilization than those of Hizbollah.

The second faction, of which the structured form is Hizbollah, arose from the merging of two perspectives. The first of these was one of grassroots violence, which emerged out of the decomposition of the defensive pole of the movement of the disinherited. The second, consolidated by politicoreligious agents who, acting under Iranian influence, had been especially successful in schools and the university, championed the establishment of a revolutionary order and a religious reign of terror through intimidation, threats, and a variety of other practices. This violence, when channeled and organized, could also take on (however weakly) an instrumental and more immediately political character, without ever appearing to be interested in increased access to state power.

These two perspectives have competed with one another much more often than they have been allied, with this competition commonly resulting in sometimes deadly confrontations. This use of violence was aggravated by Lebanese resistance to Israel throughout that country's occupation of southern Lebanon. Here, resistance was more often marked by one-upmanship and rivalry more than by a desire for reconciliation. In purely strategic terms, one of the goals of this policy of constantly raising the stakes was the political and military control of southern Lebanon, which Amal had no desire to share with anyone else, not even Shiites. This rivalry also took the form of a very different set of relations with the Palestinian movement. The Amal movement, very close at the time to the Syrian regime, was deeply implicated in the deadly operations which, especially after 1980 and its violent altercations with Fatah, sought to eradicate all organized Palestinian presence in Lebanon. Conversely, Hizbollah became increasingly aligned with the PLO. Such are the major thrusts of these two lines of strategy behind which one finds, underlying the Amal and Hizbollah opposition, an indirect confrontation between the geopolitical interests of Syria on the one hand, and those of Iran and the PLO on the other. These two lines are themselves fragile, especially threatened as they are by yet another actor, Iraq, which while an enemy of Iran often retains close relations with the PLO.

## Is Hizbollah an International Terrorist Group?

Western and southern Beirut, the northwestern Bekaa Valley, and southern Lebanon: these three Shiite population centers are also regions out of which there have emerged, above and beyond a general climate of (political) violence, patterns of behavior which, generally characterized as international terrorism, have been directed against both Israel and the great Western powers, most particularly the United States, France, and Great Britain.

This behavior has taken two particularly spectacular forms. The first of these has been one of suicide attacks, which contributed greatly to the American and French withdrawal from Lebanon in 1983.[9] The second of these, so many cases of extortion against Western governments and public opinion, has consisted of taking European and American nationals hostage (which should not lead us to forget the kidnappings, at times to wholly dissolute ends, of hundreds of Lebanese citizens) or the rare airline hijacking (such as that of the TWA Boeing jet, hijacked on a Beirut airport runway in June 1985, which the Western press was invited to report live).

In the former case, we find ourselves at the limit if not the outside of the Shiite movement's most radicalized factions, and in the presence of self-destructive forms of behavior which disclose more a total loss of meaning than religious fanaticism. In the latter, on the contrary, we are more often witness to various manifestations of Hizbollah's communal anti-Western stance, in alignment with Iranian political interests.

We must be highly cautious here, to the point of reading the lines that follow in the conditional, given that the information placed at our disposal—most often generated by intelligence agencies or by the actors themselves, without any possibility for outside verification—has been of questionable value at best.

We will first look at the suicide missions carried out against the United States and France in 1983, as well as those that targeted Israeli troops, especially prior to their total withdrawal from southern Lebanon in 1985.

The first group to practice this type of action emerged out of a split within the Amal movement. In June 1982, Husain Mussawi, at logger-heads with the political positions of Nabih Berri (who was in favor of American mediation and ready to join the Christians in a committee for national salvation), founded his own organization, the Islamic Amal, and established himself at Baalbek. It is he who was, according to American and Israeli intelligence, allegedly behind the operations of 1983. Behind Husain Mussawi himself, some have seen the hand of Syria or even of Moscow, and others that of Tehran. In 1983, Mussawi was still claiming to membership in the Hizbollah: "Hizbollah is the march of the people. It is a people's state . . . any believer who fights Israel in southern Lebanon, who defends the honor of the Muslims of Beirut and the Beka'a Valley, or who has ties with the Islamic revolution belongs to the Hizbollah . . . We are working for Islam and the Islamic revolution. That is why we belong to the Hizbollah."[10]

The hypotheses advanced by the intelligence services are not at variance with Mussawi's contentions. In 1983, his organization was still a tiny one, and its obviously heteronomous terrorist actions may be seen as so many expressions of the relative lack of a Hizbollah presence, which did not take on significant proportions until 1984–85.

The 1985 suicide missions derive more from the implementation of policies directly dictated by Syria than from the actual experience of the

Shiite masses. Irrefutable documents (terrorist interviews intercepted by the Israelis or the Army of Southern Lebanon—the Christian militia created by Israel in southern Lebanon—before they were able to carry out their plans) suggest that these suicide missions were the acts of persons of weak character who, caught up in personal or family crises, were manipulated more by the the Lebanese Communist party—or, more often, by Syrian agents acting through the Syrian Popular party (PPS)—than they were motivated by any politicoreligious fervor.[11] It moreover appears that in a number of cases, the "suicide" in question was not one at all, the driver of a truck loaded with explosives being the victim of a lie, with his explosive charge being blown up from a distance even though he had been told it was on a delayed fuse. Here, in the case of the PPS at least, we are far removed from Hizbollah, and rather find ourselves in the presence of the military policy through which Syria sought to force its will upon the Middle East, while suppressing all reference to any communal movement, however fanatical it might have been. In the case of the PPS, we are also witness to the crisis strategies of a political party, for which suicide missions were a means to gaining attention, recognition, and respect both in Lebanon and in Damascus.

So it is that the first of the two rationales of international terrorism implemented by Shiite radicals appears to correspond to actions carried out by individuals or groups with very limited social bases. The pro-Islamic discourse of these persons and groups corresponded to two phenomena, both of which left them open to manipulation by a state power: the weakness of their popular support, and their own personal or psychological difficulties. These factors are sufficient to integrate this rationale into our classic arguments concerning inversion and alienation from the social or communal context which the actor claims to be representing.

The same does not hold for the second rationale, which emerged out of a broader context of violence and, more importantly, from the much more autonomous nature of its actor's self-justification.

Forcing its way into a number of neighborhoods in west Beirut and its suburbs, Hizbollah never wavered in its practice of a combination of politicoreligious mobilization and domestic terror aimed at ensuring its growing control over a number of areas. This terror, which often had a strong moralist tinge to it—a war on alcohol, depravity, theft, and banditry—took on a new direction after 1984, when it began targeting foreign elements in Beirut. This campaign took the form of hostage-taking, assassination, and terrorist raids, for which responsibility was claimed by the Islamic Jihad, the name used by most of the groups working within this umbrella organization.

Here, terrorism is nearly totally devoid of the self-destructive character we mentioned above with reference to the suicide missions. There is also an appreciable difference between it and the terrorism practiced by a number of Palestinian organizations and, on a broader scale, the terrorism of the 1970s. We may even contrast the two, as Percy Kemp and Asaf Khoury invite us to do when they speak of a transition from a "terrorism of demands" to a "terrorism of destabilization."[12] This new form of terrorism, they maintain, places a premium upon "purely situational structures, which often only exist for the duration of an operation," and gives rise "to a parallel phenomenon of indiscriminate, unpremeditated, random terrorism which, while it is not directly manipulated by it, objectively serves [the terrorist organization]."

The Shiite "terrorists" are anything but actors who have become lost or isolated within an environment that has no place for them, or who are controlled by the powers that arm them and that dictate their activities to them. They are, quite the contrary, like fish in the water, protected by a community that understands and often accepts their action, and based in neighborhoods where, besides being able to organize, they can also count on resident support. They express the ideals of a communal movement, and give voice to its rejection of the West and its religious orientations. They do not take their inspiration from ideologies that have no connection with real life, but rather live like warriors fighting in the defense of a generally common cause, in close contact with the community's political and religious leaders.

Just how autonomous is Hizbollah and the groups which, following in its wake, have used the name of Islamic Jihad or, somewhat later, that of the Revolutionary Justice organization? United behind leaders who—unlike Nabih Berri, the secular and relatively westernized Amal leader—are possessed of both political and religious powers, they have remained greatly loyal to the Iranian revolution. In the Baalbek region, they are also loyal to Syria, which exercises a certain military and thereby political control over them. Their degree of freedom is thus somewhat limited, for while Iran remains at the ideological heart of their movement, the Syrian regime is also capable of exerting a powerful influence over them. Most essential for these groups is the continued existence of their broad social base, which ensures a continuity between a locus for the production of meaning and the implementation of violent forms of behavior. Such behavior, although it is always more-or-less dependent or subordinate, nevertheless manages to remain relatively autonomous.

We have the tendency to fuse together, under the heading of "terrorism," a heterogeneous aggregate of actions whose actual unity only occurs on a formal level. This fusion is facilitated by the innumerable connections that exist between more-or-less identifiable groups who are capable of trading hostages with one another, taking inititatives whose international implications may extend well beyond their reach, and acting on a political register one day and a criminal one the next. It is nonetheless necessary that we draw an analytical distinction between communal forms of violence which, giving rise to a kind of underground war, are nevertheless backed by a strong popular base; and pure terrorism which, capable of reconciling itself with totalitarian entities, is bereft of any social base and much more directly manipulated and motivated by state sponsors of terrorism. While it is the case that these two forms of violence are, in actual practice, in constant interaction, they nevertheless derive from two distinct rationales. Ultimately, Hizbollah violence, as repugnant as it may be on many accounts, is worthy of being qualified as something other than terrorism, at least as far as its anti-Western activities are concerned. It's anti-Western stance is religious, communal, and separatist. Pretotalitarian, the movement is neither blind, nor lost, nor cut off from the lives of those for whom it claims to speak. It is also perhaps much less suicidal than previously thought.

This body of remarks leads us to reconfirm or to detail a number of the points we made in our general arguments. Our first point concerns Shiism itself. In contrast to the oft-held notion (as, for example, by Assemaani Leba), we cannot consider the "present-day Islamic awakening to be mainly due to the combative nature of Shiism [wherein] the traditions of the 'hidden Imam' gives the Shiite collective consciousness a revolutionary power that is lacking among the Sunnites."[13]

In this case, twenty-five or thirty years ago, the Shiites must have been holding their "revolutionary power" cards under the table. Rather than a cultural constant, it is a recent evolution in their movement. Furthermore, various sources (journalistic and intelligence-based) indicate that Hizbollah has also recruited from among the Sunnites who, according to the *Economist*,[14] count for up to 40 percent of its active membership—no doubt an inflated figure. The strength of the Sunnite contingent within Hizbollah is also linked, among other factors, to the fact that a number of Sunnite militants in Fatah, whose early links with the Muslim

Brotherhood have already been pointed out, drifted into the ranks of Hizbollah.

Our second remark concerns the place of the interdenominational conflicts in Lebanon. To ground an analysis of the Lebanese question upon the matter of these conflicts advances but little our understanding of either the origin of the Lebanese drama or the forms it is currently taking, given the fact that what we are witnessing, in the final analysis, is an ongoing fragmentation or factionalization taking place within these faiths.

Our third remark links back up with the first. The notions of Muslim fundamentalism or fanaticism are in no way explanatory notions. The reference to Islam provides a foundation, but it is also a social factor, a construct which, forged out of the ruins of the original movement and its transformation into an antimovement, became the rallying cry for a total fusion of every category of practice. In this sense, the position taken by an Orientalist like Mohammed Arkoun, who attacks the pro-Islamic movements by way of denouncing their conceptualization of Islam, are generally well-founded. Unlike those who relativize the importance of the history of Islam in order to emphasize the timeless nature of Islam, and unlike those who insist on a particular reading of its message, this author points out that the pro-Islamic movements generate their own particular conception of Islam.[15]

A fourth remark has to do with the rejection of the Lebanese state that one may distill out of the sum total of Hizbollah discourse. This rejection is fundamentally religious, with the reference to Islam taking the place of that of the nation-state. Here, we may draw a parallel between the existence, within the Jewish diaspora (especially in New York), but more importantly within Israel itself, of a mystical movement known as the Naturi-Karta (the Guardians of the Citadel), for which the state of Israel is a sacrilege. For Naturi-Karta, only the coming of the Messiah can sanction the reconstruction of Israel. This is the justification it gives for its own militant anti-Zionism which, often highly aggressive, has sought support from the Jordanian authorities, Palestinian leaders, and even from the PLO. The two groups are of an entirely different order however, given that Hizbollah has mass backing, whereas Naturi-Karta is a very minor group. Both show us however that a religious referent can lead to a twofold split of varying degrees of violence, with regard to both nationalism (Arab Lebanese, or Zionist) and to the political form of the state in which one lives.

Our final remark concerns the upsurge in violence, and its insepara-
bility from the championing of both an exemplary lifestyle and community initiatives to take care of their own problems of health, education,
consumer demands, etc., without calling on the state or being drawn
into conflictual relationships. Hizbollah, often with the help of Iran,
buys weapons, but also founds clinics and schools, and gives material
assistance (pumping stations, etc.) to farmers, at the same time as it
attempts to establish moral order and wage war against the West. Communal self-isolation and exemplarity constitute one side of a coin upon
whose obverse violence reigns, a violence which is at times complemented by the use of terrorism as a method. We must however draw a
distinction between this terrorist alternative—as a means to breaking
away from the West and as the manifestation of an antimovement—and
a rationale of terrorist action. The latter, which appears to turn up on
the fringes of Hizbollah, seems at first blush to be more fanatical than
that of an antimovement, capable as it is of contemplating suicide, and
expressive as it is of a loss of meaning and a powerful heteronomy.

The Shiite movement, in its transformation into an antimovement, has
generated a communal and pretotalitarian violence which has at times
borrowed from the store of terrorism without it being possible for us to
speak—for any but its fringe groups—of a total inversion or a pure
rationale of terrorist action.

# 20

## Conclusion to Part Four

Long associated exclusively with the Palestinian cause, so-called international terrorism has since diversified. It continues to originate from a single region, the Middle East, a part of the world that often reminds one of the Balkans of a century ago. It is, more than ever, inseparable from the breakdown of the Lebanese entity, of a nation-state that could never realize a lasting unity for itself. Its essential principle, to wit, the linkage of groups of states, remains unchanged. Lastly, the violence committed in the name of Islam is not as terrorist in nature as has often been claimed.

Can such a statement fundamentally affect our arguments? When violence that calls itself Islamic appears to be terrorist in nature, ought we not to introduce new categories and, for example, speak of and place great importance on the religious "factor"? The answer is no.

Three important lessons may be drawn from the analyses that have taken up Part Four of this study.

The first of these concerns a theoretical choice which consists of explaining terrorism from the bottom up—on the basis of the movements and antimovements, and social and community actions—rather from the top down, from the standpoint of the international system, the state, or even political systems. While disorder at the top, generally referred to as a *crisis,* can create conditions that favor violence in general, and terrorism in particular, it can never stand as an explanation for the latter. The extreme case of Lebanon, verging on anarchy in the exact, Hobbesian sense of the term, does not undermine this perspective: our understanding of LARF and ASALA terrorism, Shiite communal violence, or of fanatical acts (or acts presented as such), is increased as soon as we view them in terms of the real or mythic image of a movement.

The second lesson deals more directly with religion. Contrary to a widely held notion,[1] this does not constitute a direct explanation for violence, not in the Shiite or any other case. The importance of the role played by religion lies in its ability to weld together a community, to provide it with a common matrix, and to unify an originally disunited and differentiated body of discourse into unified language. In short, it stands as a totalizing force which is made all the more spectacular for the fact that it concerns a *popular actor passing from a movement to an antimovement, from conflict to radical disengagement and communal isolation.*

Religious totalization especially leads, however, to separatist violence, an anti-Western violence that falls under the wider patterns of behavior associated with communal violence. Such activities were overshadowed, in the postcolonial period, by nationalist ideologies that provided a number of struggles with the same principle of unity and identity that radical Islam furnishes present-day Lebanon. Therefore, just as an armed struggle carried out in the name of a nation is not truly terrorist until the nation itself changes course or turns a blind eye to violence, so it is difficult to qualify as pure terrorism the Shiite (or Sunnite) violence with which great numbers of people identify themselves today.

This leads us to our third lesson, which is a confirmation of the usefulness of a distinction separating a terrorist *method* from a *rationale* of terrorist action.

We have already seen terrorist method in the actions of Fatah at the time of the Munich Olympics, as well as in Hizbollah's practice of communal violence. As for a rationale of action, we have seen this in the dissident Palestinian groups—whether they arose out of Palestinian nationalism (Abu Nidal) or a blend of Arab nationalism and Marxist-Leninist ideology (Wadi Hadad and his successors)—as well as in ASALA and LARF, and lastly in the limited number of agents of suicide missions. Between these extremes, the PFLP occupies a unique place, inasmuch as it is at once a center of gravity around which a number of terrorist experiments have taken shape, and a political actor capable of resisting the temptations of a purely terrorist rationale.

The more terrorism becomes a method, the more the individual terrorist is capable of asserting his autonomy. The less it is a method, the more dependent he becomes. Given that its relationship with Iran is in no way one of pure and simple subordination, the case of Hizbollah does not contradict this rule. The more terrorism becomes a rationale of action, the more its relationship with a movement—or indeed an antimovement—or a community becomes artificial and strictly ideological. What holds for ASALA, LARF, and the Palestinian dissidents also holds for the perpetrators of "fanatic" acts, about whom we learn after the fact (when such is possible) that they acted on grounds that were hardly politicoreligious, or that they were manipulated in ways that involved deception (in cases where a "suicide" mission was programmed by organizers of the attack without their agents' knowledge).

The term "international terrorism" thus covers processes that, while distinct, do not truly blunt the efficacy of our analytical tools. In practice, these processes never cease to interact with and interpenetrate one another, whether the case be that of the PFLP camps of the mid-1970s in which Carlos, Hagopian (ASALA) or Abdallah (LARF) received their schooling;[2] that of Fatah in which a number of activists entered into the militia or the leadership of Amal or Hizbollah; that of a general culture of violence, or again that of the complex play of Syrian and Iranian and, by association, Libyan and Iraqi "state-sponsored violence." "International terrorism" thus gives an image of real fluidity and of an intense circulation of men and money; yet we should not underestimate the specificity of the distinct processes it encompasses, even if it often also fuses them together.

Since 1982, this specificity has itself been difficult to evaluate, given the omnipresence of violence in Lebanon. In this situation of widespread decay and multifaceted violence, there is no such thing as a sociologically pure act of violence. A single act can at once be highly vicious and highly political, of independent origins and claimed by a political power or even a foreign regime, a case of institutional pressure on this or that party or religious faith of a country, and a radical disengagement with the West. We have endeavored to trace the boundaries between these various registers, and in particular to draw a distinction between communal violence and a rationale of terrorist action. This distinction is rooted in analysis and is, we feel, useful. It should not cause us to forget, however, that we are dealing in Lebanon with an endemic violence whose various forms have never ceased to interact, overlap, and stimulate one another, in a frightful series of chain reactions that have become increasingly unintelligible over time.

# General Conclusion

In the end, what remains of the notion of terrorism? In Italy, scattered incidents of prepolitical or political violence which were, for a long time, verbal rather than lethal, only became submerged by a veritable wave of terrorism following the kidnapping of Aldo Moro in 1978. In the Basque country, ETA is entering into an inversion process, but with the two principal components of its struggle pulling in opposite directions. At the same time as a Marxist-Leninist platform is having increasing difficulty in prolonging the existence of faltering social movements, the independentist cause, grounded as it is in a strong national consciousness, makes it impossible for one to speak of a rationale of terrorist action. Apart from a few episodes of short duration—when, for example, Arab nationalism and Marxism-Leninism have attempted to appropriate the Palestinian national consciousness for themselves; or more significantly when a number of dissident groups which, subordinated to regimes that have provided them with aid while controlling and using them to their own ends, have engaged in radical action that is simultaneously a life-and-death struggle with the most central and moderate elements of the PLO—it is only on its outermost fringes that the Palestinian movement has spawned terrorist factions. The hydra-headed violence one finds in Lebanon has been conditioned by the failure of a nonexistent state and the militarization of the political system. Here, the tendencies towards separatism and communal self-isolation have been so many striking examples of the formation or reinforcement of antimovements. Even in the activities of its underground groups, however, it is difficult to discern the formation of a rationale of terrorist action. The armed confrontations, kidnappings, and raids have been but so many manifestations and intensifications of already existing inter- and intracommunal rifts, and have more closely resembled warfare than they have manifested any sort of divorce of these perpetrators of violence from their social base. There has often been a tendency to associate radical Islam with terrorism. So long as the pro-Islamic movements manage to avoid a state of total heteronomy and absolute dependence upon foreign bases, however, this is an exaggerated notion. Pure, indiscriminate terrorism, as a rationale of action, in its Lebanese variety, has primarily been the work of a few groups whose plunge into terrorism derives from two sorts of processes. They have either been so many manifestations of a nationalism (Arab, Armenian, pan-Syrian) which, in crisis, is nearly always heavily laden with Marxist-Leninist baggage; or else they have been spinoffs of a more personal than collective order which, taken over piecemeal by a party or state, have tended to foster an often false image of fanaticism.

So it is that a rather limited body of research has brought us to reject the systematic use of the notion of terrorism. Firstly, the term is inappropriate in every case in which one would do better to speak in terms of political or communal violence, or of all-out war. Secondly, by fusing them together, it hides a basic distinction between two phenomena. Terrorism is always a method. In a number of cases, this method comes to be placed in the service of a movement, front, or insurgency that enjoys a solid base in a given social group—a class, nation, or community— which views it as furthering its own interests, as a situational means to its own ends. In other cases, means become confused with ends at the same time as the sole legitimizing basis for an actor's violence disappears—to wit, a social base or a reference group. When this base ceases to exist anywhere outside in the ideology of the actor, terrorism becomes more than a mere method. It becomes a rationale of action.

The training of truly terrorist actors is therefore less common than any spur-of-the-moment sociological analysis would at first lead one to believe. Given that at least two sets of conditions are necessary to it—the former deriving from the ideological and organizational formulation of violence, and the latter from the concrete collective symbolic entities to which this formulaton refers—it is the result of a convergence of phenomena.

It is for this reason that we have constantly drawn a distinction between two families of problems, even as we have attempted to relate them to one another. In the absence of a certain conception of ethics and history, of ideological, doctrinal, or religious ideologies; that is, in the absence of specific agents for their theorization, adaptation, and transformation, there can be no rationale of terrorist action. Such is an ideologicopolitical phenomenon in which thoughts and deeds tend to become confused with one another, and in which it is the intelligentsia that lays down the guidelines for both precept and practice.

Such a rationale can, moreover, not exist unless a certain number of preconditions are fulfilled regarding collective figures of reference. The weaker these are, the more mythic the landmarks they represent, and the greater the tendency becomes to perpetuate violence in their name. The championing of a lofty cause becomes totally artificial when the task of processing meaning has become totally divorced from the actual demands of a real social or community group. Terrorism, as the saying goes, is the weapon of the weak. While this statement holds for the terrorist method when such is used situationally by a movement in trouble, it cannot hold when the matter is one of charting the spectrum of rationales of terrorist action. Whether a movement be social, national, or communal, *the organized practice of indiscriminate and irredeemable violence is not a faltering movement's last best hope or final act of desperation but rather a substitute for a movement which has either become imaginary or has fallen out of sync with the hopes pinned on it.*

■

The course taken by a terrorist group is not only traceable through these processes of designification, or of a sudden alienation from its founding principles. It is also an ideological and pragmatic attempt to recover a meaning that has been lost—or at least to afford itself some significance or legitimacy by attaching itself to some given cause—and perhaps, in the end, to reduce its isolation and thereby quicken or reactivate currents of sympathy for it. Such an attempt can at times take the form of returning to one's roots, as for example when leftist extremist organizations, already well on their way to armed insurgency, undertake or envisage an old-fashioned campaign of militancy in the factories or countryside. More often, however, this quest for meaning takes on the appearance of a forward retreat, which can bring it to parasitize other sociopolitical struggles and enter into relationships of relative dependence or heteronomy. This is called parasitism when an already existing group reorders its ideological framework and slants its actions so as to appear to be supporting a cause it has discovered along the way and with which it originally had nothing in common. We have seen this in

Germany, where campaigns of anti-NATO and anti-imperialist violence have attempted to identify themselves with pacifist protests. It becomes a relationship of relative dependence when a group searches for meaning by collaborating with actors who are foreign to the violent insurgents' own society. This can lead—as was often the case with the radicalized sectors of the Palestinian movement—to a subordination of the group to a movement not its own. Alternatively, it can lead to a participation in programs or networks on an international scale, such as those which the dictatorships in Spain, Portugal, and Greece maintained for rightist extremist terrorist groups until well into the mid-1970s. It can finally become heteronomy when an armed insurgent group, at the end of its rope, falls under the control of regimes who use it to further their own ends while according it only a limited degree of freedom.

During an inversion process, the original meanings an action may have had are more than merely inverted, perverted, or subverted. Violence takes on new meanings, which themselves become rapidly inverted. So it is that when a revolutionary struggle carried out in reference to a social entity becomes an anti-imperialistic struggle, it has to redefine the state it is attacking. No longer a set of mechanisms for the reproduction of internal relations of dominance, a given state becomes a tool in the hands of a foreign power base; and the resistance group, by projecting its struggle onto a global arena, abolishes all distinctions between domestic and international violence to become the purveyor of both. So it is that, through a play of mirrors as it were, a communal—for example, nationalist—action can become revolutionary and proletarian (the leftist version); or else it can take the form of an anticapitalism possessed of strong xenophobic or anti-Semitic tendencies (the rightist version).

In its most radical forms, terrorist violence commonly conflates meanings borrowed from both registers of collective action, by effecting the synthesis of an action which claims to be simultaneously communal and social. In its own way, it thus resolves, through the use of arms and a program of all-out and even global warfare, the contradictions inherent in the desire to speak on both of these levels. This syncretic task of combining such signifiers can at times precede the fall into violence, with the violence itself often being triggered by a crisis in an original model that had already brought together signifiers from the two major families of collective action—populism, leftism, and revolutionary nationalism, for example. The syncretic task always results in a totalization which broadens the scope of the struggle by affording it a universal scope. It becomes a civil war fought outside of all civil relationships, a social struggle engaged outside of all social relations, a national liberation struggle that attacks states which are, at best, only indirectly concerned. Hereafter, any number of factions can become aligned, and any number of currents flow together into what may be described as a terrorist nebula or galaxy.[1]

This ideological totalization is, nonetheless, never fully realized or stabilized. Always sensitive to changes in its environment and within the reference group, it never realizes an absolute nondifferentiation between the various signifiers that give meaning to armed insurgency. Whence the internal debates, the splits and alliances, the departures and exiles, and often the fall into a syndrome in which terrorism, now transformed into a rationale of action, has no limits save for those forced upon it by the military or police forces arrayed against it. The ideological totalization that is part and parcel of terrorism implies a close proximity to the phenomenon of totalitarianism, inasmuch as both combine into a single aggregate of precept and practice the categories of state and society, the mission of emancipating a social class and founding a nation, and a simultaneous championing of both specificity and universality. Both reject the notion of a domestic forum for open discussion and, more profoundly, a basic principle that lies at the very heart of democracy. In the words of Claude Lefort, this is the principle of conceiving of power as existing distinct from and inappropriable by any one person or group.[2] Rather than refusing to acknowledge the symbolic or imaginary nature of power, both instead objectivize it, in order to either wield it (totalitarianism) or to attack it (terrorism). But the great totalitarian regimes of the present century were originally rooted in a relatively broad-based mobilization, whereas terrorism conversely proceeds from a demobilization or a nonmobilization, and from a mythic or artificial reference to collective entities.

■

Do domestic and international terrorism partake of the same rationale of action? We know the latter to often be an extension of the former. But there is also a fundamental difference between the two, which derives from the fact that the latter tends more to negotiation while the former, left to its own devices, can only veer out of control into a cycle of indiscriminate violence. International terrorism often takes advantage of the press and public opinion, which are more-or-less unaware of its underlying implications and strategies. Its violence is, however, most often intended to serve as a sign, a warning, or a sanction vis-à-vis a given political entity, in the knowledge that a small number of its representatives will be capable of interpreting it. This does not hold for domestic terrorism, which takes part in no political game whatsoever—not even a secret game known to but a few initiates. This distinction is one that merits further consideration.

Domestic terrorism can in no way be reduced to mere delinquency or criminality. Once it has, however, become cut off from its social or communal base, the sole legitimacy remaining to it is a self-proclaimed and subjective one. As such, its deadly interference is of the same order as what Hannah Arendt termed a dereliction of politics. Whether it be of leftist or rightist extremist orientation, it is fundamentally different from political violence. Quite the contrary, it signals that its perpetrator has left the field of political action. From here on in, the objectives of his violence become unlimited, as they come to transcend both an abscondent social reference and a political system whose principles and processes it defies.

Can a mythic cause for which violence is the sole concrete expression, or an attitude of denial towards politics, be considered political? Working from a critique of representative democracy and the party system, Carl Schmitt contended that "the denial of politics is the very mark of a political mind."[3] It is difficult for us to follow Schmitt here, however, if only because he contrasts the legality of democratic institutions with a popular legitimacy of which the terrorist actor is unable to avail himself. By objectivizing his enemies, and viewing himself as the hero in a resistance movement carried out in the name of values and principles which he alone is capable of justifying (and which he has no desire to discuss), the terrorist actor exits the political arena with no thought of ever returning. On the far left, he is, by himself, Justice, the Good, History, and the Proletariat. On the far right, he is a champion of order, and the immediate embodiment of a rejection of democracy which proceeds, as François Furet has shown, from a predemocratic tradition of which he is a residual expression.[4] Whereas leftist extremist terrorism proceeds from the painful experience of having failed to mobilize a social entity—for which the terrorist then substitutes himself—his right-wing homologue, often maintaining ties with organized crime, secret services, and the police, more often substitutes himself for a state or for its top leaders, whom he considers to be unqualified for their positions. Whereas the former postulates a pandemic division within society or even the entire planet, the latter notes a lack of order or a number of deficiencies, and then reacts against them—when he is not seeking to amplify them, as in the Italian strategy of tension, as a means to better achieve the order to which he aspires. While leftist terrorism projects itself from below, through an unrealizable or imaginary reference to oppressed actors whom it is unable to keep within its fold, the latter works from above, by championing an authoritarian power capable of ensuring social and national cohesion. Whereas the former constitutes an increasingly artificial and desperate rebellion and an exit from the game of politics, the latter is a negation of the rules of the game itself. Although their premises differ, the result is the same, given that both are characterized by their *exteriority* to the political arena.

From this standpoint, so-called international terrorism introduces an important distinction. To be sure, the reversals of direction and processes of inversion out of which it emerges are comparable to those of domestic terrorism. Similarly, what we see of its no-holds-barred, do-or-die, all-out combat, which seemingly goes well beyond the relatively codified interplay of violence or war as we know it between two countries, would apparently prohibit us from granting it any political status. But what is it that we see? Not only does the actor in this case weigh his options and calculate relative means and ends, but all signs further point to the fact that, even in the most extreme cases, he belongs to a system of action that cannot be reduced to the law of the jungle. The ends—forcing a state to free its prisoners, raising funds, blocking or unblocking diplomatic intitiatives according to its own interests—often concern him directly. They can just as well often betray, whether simultaneously or not, his heteronomy, in which cases the ends are defined not by him but rather by the regime who "sponsors" him.

Here, the actor is participating, at least to a certain extent, in a political system. The means he employs—raids, kidnappings, assassinations—even as they defy the negotiation process are at once a response to or even a form of participation in it. As Charles Villeneuve and Jean-Pierre Péret have brilliantly demonstrated,[5] not one single act of international terrorism carried out against France over the past ten years falls outside of this strategy, which consists of coercive diplomacy and secret bargaining as much as it does of pure violence.

It is a separate reality that underlies the opinions of a public which, kept in the dark, only sees the events themselves; or the misreadings of the facts on the part the judges who generally concern themselves with the dark undersides of affairs that nearly always fall into their hands through political bungling or as the result of interagency conflicts. Here, terrorism is clearly codified—a French garden, in the words of Villeneuve and Péret. It is part and parcel of a set of relationships whose rules are well-known to the leaders who have to deal with it; and has a recognized place in the processes of decision making and high-pressure bargaining.

More important, international violence, in spite of its disdain for our conceptions of politics, does not seek to undermine our institutions or destroy our democratic institutions. Rather, it takes advantage of its weaknesses and limits, which allow it to function at optimum efficiency. The distinction here is an important one.

Ought we then to contrast a dead-end domestic terrorism that is foreign to every political arena, with an international terrorism that is embedded in political operations which—although they are kept secret because they are shameful to democratic governments—are nonetheless real? The answer is no.

It is in the nature of the factions that veer into international terrorism to proceed from the same loss of meaning as that which generates domestic terrorism. However, once he arrives at this point, the actor changes levels, finding himself no longer in a void but rather in situations in which his motivating rationale of terrorist action locks into the strategies of already existing political entities.

The political character of his particular form of intervention therefore has less to do with him than it does with the governments and powers with whom he casts his fortunes at propitious moments. In and of itself, the tailspin that plunges a group into international terrorism is of the same order as that which results in domestic terrorism. What changes is not its rationale of action, but rather the possibilities a given regime offers it for entering into the political arena at a higher level than that at which it was founded. In the final analysis, the rationale of terrorist action remains the same.

This unity remains imperceptible for as long as one holds to the perspective of communities that have been victimized by terrorism. Given the fact that the phenomenon involves a large group of countries, both weak and strong, upon which it can exert a debilitating or tonic effect, the type of state which it affects cannot constitute a criterion for explanation. Nor does this unity derive from the homogeneous threat that it allegedly constitutes, from both within and without, for the Western democracies who have been called to present a common front to this common danger.

Domestic terrorism can also be directed against dictatorships, which also know how to use its potential threat to their own ends. It is not so much democracies per se that international terrorism attacks as it is nations, and the spectacular failure of international cooperation to combat terrorism show all too well that the phenomenon cannot be treated merely through a united resistance on the part of the Western democracies.

The unity of terrorism is also not to be found in the constituencies it claims to champion, constituencies which we have found in the course of this work to be highly diversified: working class, peasantry, nation, religious community, etc. It can only be defined by referring to those forms of collective action which constituted its starting point. In its purest—and most extreme—manifestations, terrorism always betrays the disintegration of some collective action. Wherever the social, national, or communal consciousness is strong, and wherever a social or any other kind of movement is capable of being formed, there can be no place for terrorist spinoffs. These appear and take shape—and become rationales of action rather than mere situational combat strategies—through the disintegration of a collective consciousness, or in the collapse, breakdown, or failure of a social, national, or communal movement.

The downward spiral that leads into terrorism can begin as soon as the signs of crisis begin to appear within a collective action, when movement becomes antimovement, and when the priority is given—at times in the heat of a conflict, which can give rise to great illusions—to defensive attitudes, localism, tribalism, corporatism, and references to a specific group rather than to a broad vision of action. But the terrorist inversion and the long-term commitment to terrorism can only by triggered when crisis becomes metamorphosis, and eventually a radical disengagement from and the destruction of a model for resistance and action; or conversely, but more seldom, when it carries with it the unrealistic championing of a movement still in its infancy. In order for there to be a terrorist process, a great number of conditions—related to the international order, the state, a political system, culture, and intellectual leadership—must be present. But beyond these conditions, which render every instance of terrorism unique, this phenomenon finds its sociological unity, on a global level, in that to which it most often gives voice. This is the reshaping, by an intellectual leadership within a given ideological or religious context, of the final convulsions of a now moribund and decaying collective action or, less often, a unilateral transposition of itself into an action in search of itself.

# Appendix

## On Methodology

The original aim of the method of sociological intervention was to bring to light the traces of a social movement that had seemingly been occluded by other meanings inherent to the struggle in which it was embedded. This we did with reference to new and still-fragile social movements,[1] as well as to a labor movement going through what appeared to be an irreversible process of decline.[2] The first applications of this method, carried out in the form of a number of investigations led by Alain Touraine, had already opened the field to more complex problems as it sought to show that there could exist, within a single struggle, a combination of two or three elements of great sociological significance. So, for example, the Occitanist movement had tried in vain to combine a social movement with a nationalist movement; Solidarność was at once a Polish social, labor, and national independence movement, and an antitotalitarian and democratic political action.[3] The methodological gains made through these studies, as well as the practical experience of our fieldwork, have greatly aided us throughout our work on terrorism.

It nonetheless remains that the application of the method of sociological intervention to the study of terrorism is not self-evident. When we were analyzing trade unionism, the student protests, and Solidarność, we were dealing with positive forms of behavior, in which the actor in question, through his engagement in various conflicts, and through his place within a network of social and political relations, had been able to assert his self-identity in quite powerful and immediate ways. With terrorism, the gap widens—between the armed activist and the meanings to which he refers in a more-or-less mythic mode—to the extent that one must in certain extreme cases, speak in terms of inversion.

The sociologist's problem here is not to isolate, out of a group of potential meanings, those which may be the most important to the action in question, and which may otherwise be screened by less important attitudes. It is rather to deconstruct that which violence fuses together, to bring lost meanings to light, and to rediscover the face of a movement, if not that of an antimovement. Here as before, sociological intervention becomes a tool for analytical deconstruction. That which it seeks to isolate, however, is lost more often than hidden, and weakened more often than distorted or inverted.

As a concrete research strategy, sociological intervention, when applied to terrorism, runs up against an untold number of difficulties. These do not, however, prohibit its implementation. We managed to successfully apply it on two occasions, and the pages that follow are intended to elucidate the lessons we have learned, from a methodological standpoint, from these experiences. We should add here that we had also become convinced that sociological intervention could be applied in those borderline situations in which passion, ideologies, and an omnipresent belligerent discourse appeared to render it unworkable.

## THE CREATION OF AN INTEREST AND THE FORMATION OF RESEARCH GROUPS

When it studies a collective action, a sociological intervention seeks to provide its actors with a perspective from which to analyze their own insurgency. Two preconditions are necessary, from the very outset: on the one hand, unless there exists an interest on the part of the concerned actors, it is impossible; on the other, it implies that the researchers must be capable of convening one or several groups composed of militants who are willing to take part in a long process leading to an autocritique of their action.

The more violent a conflict the less a researcher can hope to encounter a high level of interest. This is not because the actors necessarily reject any such self-reflection, but rather because terrorist violence goes hand in hand with highly structured ideologies which are hostile to all dialogue. Short of becoming an all-purpose intellectual or of presenting himself as being of some instrumental value to the actor, the sociologist is therefore rejected, from the outset, as a potential threat or as an enemy. The researcher thus finds himself in the presence, at best, of strategists, who may in certain cases realize some political gain by participating in a sociological inquiry. At worst, he can find himself faced with combatants who, caught up in absolutist do-or-die mentalities, consider the meaning of their action so self-evident as to be suspicious of the very notion of subjecting it to analysis. It is for this reason that sociological intervention cannot work with highly structured organizations which are already heavily committed to armed insurgency or to truly terrorist rationales.

If, however, we are excluded from placing ourselves at the very heart of terrorism, in which the rules of secrecy and the game of war, indeed of terror, prohibit the presence of sociologists as such, it nevertheless remains possible for us to plant our tent on the edge of its crater—at a vantage point from which we may gaze upon the already-cooling lava, the now-calm vapor jets—in zones in which the patterns of behavior in question either refer to the past more than to the present, in which they herald a future course onto which they have not yet truly embarked, or in which they are sufficiently close to those of armed resistance groups to inform us, nearly directly, of the latter's intentions.

Whence our first tack, which we followed on three occasions, and which consisted of working with former terrorists, deserters from the armed struggle, or survivors of some episode from the historical past. Our second tack, which we took up with a fourth group, led us to convene militants whose action, which bordered on the legal, took part in a movement for which weapons and secrecy were a nearly natural extension.

How does one exit a movement of armed insurgency? In certain cases repression, having effected a military defeat, isolated a group's actors in order to efficently hunt them down. At no time, however, in democratic countries, has the failure of such a movement been the exclusive result of police action. It has always been accompanied by a political collapse, the loss of all public support, and a rejection of violence by social or political powers which had previously shown it some measure of understanding. It is for this reason that the end of an armed struggle often takes on the look of a tailspin into extremist practices, internal collapse, and the internalization within an organization itself of the deterioration of a situation that had theretofore been favorable to it.

Can persons who have managed to escape repression and find sanctuary, by fleeing their country for example, become interested in research of this type? The Italian refugees in Paris with whom we formed two intervention groups show that this interest was both weak and ambiguous. It was first of all undermined by the condition of exile itself with all the material difficulties it entails and, in this case, its political uncertainties, given that the extradition of many of these refugees had been demanded with insistence by their own country's justice system, and that the French authorities had not always adopted a coherent policy in their regard. So it is that interest can arise for reasons that are at wide variance with those of the researchers, who come to gain new knowledge. Some saw their participation in the research of a French scholar with obvious institutional support as an exercise that might accrue to their political or administrative advantage. Others hoped to gain some financial profit from it, often taking the same attitude toward the French institutions as they had had vis-à-vis the Italian state. On the one hand, they wanted to wring as much out of it as possible, while on the other, all they talked about was destroying it. In this case, interest in research became a matter of bartering with the researchers, to whom it was suggested that they should be paid, given written statements in recognition of their compliance, allowed to use the telephone, typewriters, etc. All of this was accompanied by an overriding disdain for the institutions to which these same researchers belonged. In the case of such actors, whose lives have been shattered by failure, it is not easy to find any who truly wish to deliberate over their own action.

Even when one manages, as I did, to pull together an intervention group, there can still remain much room for misunderstanding as well as concrete problems in formulating a research procedure. At one end of the spectrum, the group may shield itself from analysis through sectarian attitudes and barricade itself behind its ideology as it places itself under the protective wing of its leader—who closes off discussion when it suits him, or else filibusters, and so blocks any possibility for differentiating between the members of the group, and all progress in its autocritique. At the other extreme, the group may more-or-less rapidly fall apart, finding itself incapable of functioning on a stable or sustained level.

One encounters quite a different situation when the activists in question decided to abandon their armed insurgency on political grounds, especially when their abandonment has been facilitated by the attitudes of the public authorities. Here, the interest is much stronger, especially when leaving the armed struggle does not necessarily imply that one has rejected or forgotten the principles one felt it embodied. Can one maintain one's revolutionary ideals, and go on speaking in the name of the labor movement or agitating for national independence, without engaging in violence? How can one be true to oneself while playing along with the democracy that was founded after the death of Franco? These were the questions our veteran group from the Basque country asked itself. This kind of self-interrogation can feed directly into an interest in the type of research we were proposing, as we quickly came to realize in the course of our first contacts with Euskadiko Eskera, the political party to which nearly all of the members of our Basque veteran group belonged. Can actors who located themselves before, rather than after, the fact of the armed struggle also be interested in such research? An affirmative answer to this question was forthcoming in the convening of our Basque separatist group.

When an armed resistance group has not (yet) fallen by a rationale of terrorist action, when it is recognized as necessary and useful by broad sectors of the population and, more exactly, when rank-and-file militants accord it a high legitimacy, it is possible for interest to arise out of the following basic question: to what extent is violence necessary, indeed indispensable, in the eyes of the movement for which it is an expression? It was in these terms that the Basque militants, all of whom were nationalists and members of a variety of movements (labor, antinuclear, amnesty, etc.), wished to ponder, together with ourselves, the ties between these movements and the use of violence. Here, it was out of the strength of these links that problems arose. The more mythic they were—that is, the weaker and more atrophied these movements became—the more violence ceased to be the self-expression of a real movement and the more it came to speak in its own name alone. In such cases, it became difficult to assemble a study group and even more difficult to make it function. Here we may say—and this is indicative of the nature of ETA itself—that the relationship between the researchers and this side of the movement was often strained, but never broken.

We should perhaps go into greater detail here and indicate how, in practical terms, researchers can generate interest within a group. In the case of our Italian group, which met with us in Paris, we had no difficulty in meeting these Italian exiles because many of them were currently leading active cultural and political lives in France. In the Basque country, contacting the former *etarras* who had converted to legal political activities was as easy as knocking at the door of Euskadiko Eskera, where a comprehensive understanding of our procedure was immediately forthcoming. We could not, on the contrary, have brought our separatist group together so quickly had it not been for the participation in our research group of Francis Jaureguiberry, who was able to turn to advantage the great confidence he had inspired in the course of several years of fieldwork in Euskadi.

THE CO-DISCUSSANTS

A basic principle of sociological intervention is its refusal to place actors in the classic situation of a sociological investigation. Rather than posing questions to resistance leaders, it instead leads them through a process in which they are brought to analyze their own attitudes and behavior. It is for this reason that an intervention group's proper research begins with a series of meetings in which it invites a series of co-discussants, each of whom embodies an adversary of or a partner in the group's action. This phase of the work tends to break down rigid ideologies and to prepare the group for self-reflection. Here, however, we found ourselves in the presence either of highly structured groups, in which ideology went hand in hand with sectarian practice; or of fragile groups on the brink of collapse. When faced with a "hard-line" group, a co-discussant, rather than initiating a dialogue and opening the group up to an evaluation of its relations with the outside, ran the risk of triggering defensive reactions and increased ideological isolation. When faced with a weakened group, he ran the risk of accelerating its dissolution. Prior to this study, sociological intervention had studied actors who were active resisters. But in the case of former activists, who had left the field of violence, were such dialogues with co-discussants not artificial? Yesterday's enemy could at times become today's partner. Conversely, yesterday's friends could today be treating you as an enemy or traitor. The co-discussants, like the groups themselves, shuttled between past and present, and their meetings, even as they threw light on their current relationship, could well have eclipsed the essential matter of their relationship at the time in which the members of the group were perpetrators of violence. In addition to these problems, other much more practical difficulties could and did arise. The law or their own political persuasions at times prevented potential co-discussants from even countenancing the idea of meeting former terrorists. So it was that when certain of our Italian invitees came to Paris to talk with one of our groups, they would only do so on the condition that we guarantee their anonymity; a number of co-discussants (especially communists) whom we contacted simply declined our invitation. In other circumstances, fear and a general climate of violence discouraged co-discussants. In the Basque country, it took real courage for certain of our invitees to come and take part in a meeting with militants who treated them as enemies or traitors.

It was easy enough to circumvent these practical obstacles. The other problems we experienced (the risk that the group withdraw into its shell or fall apart, time lags between the dates of their action and that of our study) led us to introduce certain permutations on the standard procedure of such an intervention. Faced with a group with sectarian tendencies, it was better to resort to whatever means were possible for progressively drawing the group out; whence the particular attention we gave to the order in which we presented our co-discussants. For our first Italian group, these meetings began with the visit of Alain Geismar, who already had been a favorable influence in our primary contacts with these refugees or exiles. This former leader of the Gauche Prolétarienne not only vouched for our research by his mere presence, but he was also able to introduce, with indisputable legitimacy, themes for discussion that would otherwise have been rejected had they been presented by anyone else. Similarly, the visit by an Italian priest, a great writer in his own right, also had a very positive effect on the group. This churchman was able to speak to each and every member of the group, thereby facilitating a differentiation between the members which unfolded in a climate of great trust. Rather than going into further detail, let us summarize our remarks here. When there is the danger of ideological self-isolation by a group, meetings with co-discussants should begin with those invitees who can somehow be made to appear as friends, or at least as sympathetic and attentive ears. Only later does it become possible to program meetings with adversaries, in the hope of avoiding discussions at cross-purposes, or the mutual rejection of the other's arguments as nonsensical.

In addition to this reversal of an order, which in former interventions had started with adversaries and concluded with allies, we also introduced a technical procedure which consisted of staggering the group's very first meetings with its co-discussants with a series of interviews, which we held with each of the militants on an individual basis. These personal discussions, the content of which could, according to prior agreement, be introduced into the collective discussions, afforded each individual the possibility to openly express her or himself. This weakened both ideological pressure and sectarian tendencies, and further allowed us to introduce the element of internal differentiation that is the necessary condition for this type of analysis. Faced with a fragile group threatened with rapid dissolution and with a tendency to turn against the researchers and, most importantly, to abandon the project altogether, it was necessary on the contrary to do everything possible to weld its members together and foster a greater general interest in the research. Our experience with the second Italian group was, as we are well aware, a partial failure. The practical conclusion we drew was that one must, in such a situation, concentrate the intervention—or at least its primary phase—within a single time and space, instead of adopting a program of several weeks' duration. By holding a closed session with a group for a few days and choosing as its first co-discussants persons who by their adversarial relationship with the group would help to solidify the group, researchers might be able to more easily avoid its premature breakup.

The further removed actors were from the heat of battle and armed insurgency, the more their meetings with the co-discussants were artificial, if not surrealistic. It was therefore of primary importance that they be organized in such a way as to place the group members, to the greatest extent possible, in the position of actors. Even if they had given up violence per se, this did not necessarily mean that they had given up on the causes for which this violence was the expression. This being the case, we had to use every means at our disposal to reinfuse, with their original force, the ideals that had first led them to take up armed resistance. In this way the group, rather than carrying out an objective and detached analysis of phenomena with which it no longer had anything in common, instead engaged in an autocritique of actions whose significance was still a powerful presence in its members' lives. Therefore, when faced with a group which only faintly identified itself as an actor, it was necessary to quickly invite co-discussants who, epitomizing national, social, or political ideals, could rekindle their passions or feelings, and remind them of the fact that violence always stems from a meaning worth fighting for. The further a group had distanced itself from violence and the more it was inclined to behave in a detached way, the more we had to work to force it into the position of an actor. So it was that our first Basque group was only capable of analyzing the armed struggle after it had gone through a series of meetings in which a number of co-discussants had reminded them of the importance of the Basque national cause and the need to fight for a society that was fairer or more open to labor aspirations.

## SELF-ANALYSIS AND CONVERSION

After its meetings with various co-discussants, each sociological intervention group is invited to analyze itself, that is, to generate an analysis of the struggle to which it had theretofore been witness. Most importantly, it is invited to effect its own "conversion"—that is, to discuss and adopt hypotheses advanced by the researchers on the nature of its action. This endeavor takes the form of an active intervention on the part of the researchers, who present a general argument and ask not only that the group accept it, but also that it apply it. The more a group is able to grasp the researchers' hypotheses and apply them to interpret its own history and, more importantly, that of the movement to which it belonged, the more possible it is for us to consider our hypotheses to be valid ones.

Here too, we ran into novel difficulties, together with some of the same difficulties we had encountered in prior sociological interventions. With our first Italian group, which was constantly on the verge of closing in on itself, the researchers had to go at it hammer and tongs in order to introduce to it the notion that there were internal differences within the group. This was a constant struggle, in which the group at times accepted the notion only to reject it just as quickly. As for the group's conversion, this was stopped cold by its leader, with the result being that only one member of the group was able to truly accept the researchers' analytical viewpoint. He then put forward a model quite similar to the hypotheses they had just advanced. The second Italian group's breakup precluded any effort on its part towards self-analysis or conversion. This is why our research on Italian terrorism ended up somewhere halfway between group meetings and an authentic sociological intervention. With the first group, a coherent series of meetings with co-discussants was followed by an attempt at conversion, the results of which were not especially convincing. In this case, our research constituted a consultation of sorts, and even if the group did not engage in an authentic analysis, it did take the first steps in an analytical process. The second Italian group did not, as we have seen, get far beyond the stage—difficult in itself to implement—of attending group meetings. Therefore, any methodological gains we may have realized in the central "conversion" phase of our intervention must be looked for in the context of our Basque sessions.

Our first Basque group, made up of former terrorists who had left the armed resistance movement to take up legal forms of political activism, proved slow to militate and quick to analyze. Too quick, it may be said, since its analytical lights were much less often turned on its own actions than on those of other people, in this case persons still practicing armed resistance. In the beginning, its meetings with its various co-discussants reminded it of the demands of its action, of the importance of the homeland question, and of the social dialogue in which it claimed to still be engaged. But when the time came to present an analysis, the researchers intervened forcefully in order that the group situate itself in relationship to its own action. The researchers repeatedly stressed the importance of the Basque resistance, with sometimes violent discussion pitting them against the group, which was all too ready to abandon the focus of its own action in order to better analyze the practices of others. In this case, tensions ran very high and, while the researchers were very hard on the group, the strategy paid off. They forced the group to relive the hopes that had inspired its past action, and pressed it to recall matters that had been pushed back into the depths of its memory, rather than having been truly forgotten or left behind. This long process allowed for a subsequent conversion, which carried the weight of proof for us. Through it, we were able to conclude that a renunciation of the armed struggle was tantamount to an abandonment of the ideals of independence and social revolution. This led us to broader conclusions on the violence in Euskadi: the wider the gulf between armed resistance and the concrete reality of the social and national struggles, and the more the latter tend to break down or falter, the more violence becomes terrorist violence.

The "conversion" of an actor who has, by political choice, deserted the armed struggle requires much effort on the part of the researchers— albeit less in the presentation of their hypotheses than in the period leading up to it. This therefore implies a sometimes long and tortuous phase during which they must attempt to remobilize the group as it were, and force it to play the role of a movement defined by a search for a combat strategy which excludes the alternative of armed resistance.

If they are successful and the group manages to get over this hump without falling apart, its conversion presents no major difficulties. More than this, it can become the occasion for a definitive reassessment of the history of the phenomenon under study. So it was that our first Basque group, when pressed and incited to do so by the researchers, generated and enriched all existing analyses of the history of the armed struggle in Euskadi since the inception of ETA.

Our second group was composed of activists for whom armed action was an extension or the central element of the Basque movement. Confronted by a variety of co-discussants, it was impressive in its solidarity. When put on the defensive, as we have seen, it not only serried its ranks but also manifested a barely contained violence. It was difficult for us to separate self-analysis and conversion within such a group. The researchers' central thesis was that the armed struggle was the necessary consequence of a decision to combine a number of distinct resistance groups, which were themselves on the verge of collapse. Now this idea, placed at the very heart of our discussions, implied a capacity on the part of the group to acknowledge the diversity of meanings underlying its action, which would normally be the stuff of self-analysis. This is why self-analysis (the conscious realization of diversity) and conversion (the acceptance of a general argument on violence) became caught up in a single process. Here, the researchers were at once insistent that the militants stop confusing matters in their analysis (which was a reflection of their fusing of matters in their practice), and that they agree to see violence as a reference to its highest national and social ideals, which they could not maintain except through violence. Here too, the researchers had to defend their arguments tooth and nail, and constantly struggle against the group's tendencies to reject their analyses and to fuse the principles of their action into a single all-embracing, monolithic image. Faced with a highly militant group living in close proximity to violence, the researchers could not hope to carry this long process of self-analysis through to its end before effecting the conversion of this group. They were forced to intervene forcefully, directly, and swiftly, in the knowledge that the group's autocritique would be effected simultaneously with its conversion, or follow in its immediate wake. Here, the acknowledgment of internal differences occurred after, rather than before, conversion, being its product rather than its precondition.

The proof of a sociological intervention lies in its ability to lead an actor back into his action; i.e. in giving the actor the means to apply the arguments developed by the researchers to better read and perhaps even redirect the history of his action. A moment ago we mentioned that our first Basque group had been able to go back deeply into its own history. It was hardly possible to envisage such an endeavor with the second group. Its conversion was a long and tense process in which it became clear that violence was, for the actor, linked to the desire to combine a great number of heterogeneous movements—which were losing their capacity to champion a broad-based visionary platform—within a single line of practice. It was impossible for us to go further. Had we returned to the group's history, it would have distanced us from our analysis of the then-current situation, and would have implied a change of register that would have been incompatible with the prevailing climate within the group. The militants, who left with the feeling that they had gone very deep in their analysis, had only one remaining desire: to become themselves again, and have done with our study. Under the prodding of the researchers, they had suddenly pulled themselves up to a new level—which they just as quickly abandoned.

## THE RESEARCHERS AND THEIR SUBJECT

A sociological intervention can only work if the researchers, having carried out their own "conversion," not only identify themselves with a given argument and defend it relentlessly, but also master the relationship they must maintain with the group they are studying.

The first research team, brought together to study Italian terrorism, was made up, apart from its director, of two researchers, the one Italian, Carla Bertolo, and the other of Italian origin, Suzanne Famery. Both of these researchers already held doctoral degrees and had long since proven themselves in the field. The second team, brought together to study the Basque movement, consisted, in addition to its director, of two researchers of Basque origin: Francis Jaureguiberry, the author of a doctoral dissertation on the Basque question, and Jacques Garat, a historian. All of these researchers had, each in his own way, been directly touched by the action they were studying. In the Italian case, there occurred a great sensitization, a mixture of sympathy and horror, with regard to these activists with whom the researchers had shared many hopes and convictions five or ten years earlier. The same was true in the Basque case. Only the research director was foreign to the past actions of the intervention groups.

Such a situation can have a certain number of advantages. Sociologists with a solid understanding of these struggles, their past discussions, and subsequent development can facilitate a climate of both confidence and rigor, and help the group to pass into the stage of autocritique. But this proximity can also give rise to a number of difficulties. These can take the form of a certain inflexibility on the part of the researcher, who can fluctuate between understanding and repulsion, and even begin to behave either like a member or an enemy of the group—but no longer like an analyst. In the worst of cases, such a researcher can paralyze analysis at the precise moment in which he has asked the group to enter into a process of autocritique or conversion that is also painful to him. There is only one way to deal with such problems. This is through an autocritique, on the part of the intervention team, of its own investigation and of the effects of the research on the researchers. Through such a procedure, it can monitor these effects and avoid falling apart itself. The more a researcher identifies himself, positively or negatively, with the actor, the more he rejects those in the team who do not share his viewpoint, but rather defend that of the research itself. Misunderstanding reigns, and the intervention itself, threatened by an uncohesive or incoherent team of researchers, turns at best into a series of collective discussions, or at worst into an ideological forum.

Let us be perfectly clear in stating that our groups, while they at no time came close to such a breakup, did go through some moments of great tension. Fieldwork carried out in groups of three already was a guarantee against the loss of control of any one member. Discussions held within the research group, in which the behavior of each member was considered in the light of the overall approach of the entire intervention, helped to avoid breakups which may at times have been in the offing in the course of our fieldwork.

# Abbreviations

| | |
|---|---|
| ANM | Arab Nationalist Movement |
| ASALA | Armenian Secret Army for the Liberation of Armenia |
| BR | Brigate Rosse |
| CCC | Cellules Communistes Combattantes |
| CFDT | Confédération Française Démocratique du Travail |
| CGIL | Confederazione Generale Italiana dei Lavori |
| CISL | Confederazione Italiana Sindacati Lavoratori |
| CPM | Collettivo Politico Metropolitano |
| CSPPA | Comité de Solidarité avec les Prisonniers Politiques Arabes et du Proche-Orient |
| EDF | Electricité de France |
| EE | Euskadiko Eskera (Basque Left) |
| EIA | Euskal Iraultzale Alderdia (Basque Revolutionary Party) |
| ELA | Euskal Langileen Alkartasuna (Basque Socialist Movement) |
| ETA | Euskadi Ta Askatasuna (Basque Fatherland and Liberty) |
| Fatah | Harakat Tahrir Falistin |
| FGCI | Federazione di Giovanni Comunisti Italiani |
| FLN | Front de Libération Nationale |
| FLQ | Front de Libération du Québec |
| FML | Federazione Metalmecanici del Lavoro |
| GAL | Groupe Antiterroriste de Libération |
| GAP | Gruppi d'Azione Partigiana |
| HASI | Herriko Alderdi Sozialista Iraultzalea (Popular Revolutionary Socialist Party) |
| HB | Herri Batasuna (Popular Unity) |
| IRA | Irish Republican Army |
| KAS | Koordinadora Abertzale Sozialista (Patriotic Socialist Coordination Group) |

311

| | |
|---|---|
| LAB | Langille Abertzalean Batzardea (Basque Worker's Association) |
| LARF | Lebanese Armed Revolutionary Faction |
| NAP | Nuclei Armati Proletari |
| NATO | North Atlantic Treaty Organization |
| OPEC | Organization of Petroleum Exporting Countries |
| PCI | Partito Comunista Italiana |
| PDFLP | Popular Democratic Front for the Liberation of Palestine |
| PFLP | Popular Front for the Liberation of Palestine |
| PFLP-GC | Popular Front for the Liberation of Palestine—General Command |
| PL | Prima Linea |
| PLA | Palestine Liberation Army |
| PLO | Palestine Liberation Organization |
| PNV | Partido Nacionalista Vasco |
| PO | Potere Operaio |
| PPS | Parti Populaire Syrien (or Parti Syrien Nationaliste Sociale) |
| PSI | Partito Socialista Italiana |
| PSIUP | Partito Socialista Italiana di Unità Proletaria |
| PSOE | Partido Socialista Obrero Español |
| RAF | Rot Armee Fraktion |
| RZ | Revoluzionare Zellen |
| SIM | Stato imperialista delle multinazionali |
| UGT | Union General de Trabajadores de España |
| UIL | Unione Italiana Lavoratori |
| UN | United Nations |

# Movements, Organizations, and Some Proper Names

MOVEMENTS AND ORGANIZATIONS

1977 movement
Action Directe
Action Française
Amal movement
Antiterrorist Liberation Group (GAL)
Arab High Commission
Arab League
Arab Liberation Front
Arab Nationalist Movement
Armed Proletarian Nuclei (NAP)
ASALA
Autonomia Operaia
Avanguardia Operaia
Ba'ath
Bande Noire
Basque Nationalist Party (PNV)
Basque Socialist Movement (ELA)
Basque Worker's Association (LAB)
Black September
CISL
Committee for Public Safety
Communist Combatant Cells
CSPPA
ETA
Euskadiko Eskera (EE)
Euskal Iraultzale Alderdia (EIA)

Fatah
Fatah-Revolutionary Council
FGCI
FLN
FLQ
FML
Gauche Prolétarienne
General Union of Workers (UGT)
Herri Batasuna (HB)
Herriko Alderdi Sozialista Iraultzea
  (HASI)
Hizbollah
IRA
Italian Communist party (PCI)
Japan Committee
Koordinadora Abertzale Socialista
  (KAS)
LARF
Lotta Continua
Magistratura Democratica
Manifesto
Metropolitan Political Collective
  (CPM)
Military Wing (of ETA)
Muslim Brotherhood
NATO
Naturi-Karta
OPEC

313

Organisation de l'Armée Secrète
Palestine Liberation Army
Palestine Liberation Organization
Partisan Action Groups (GAP)
PNV
Political-Military Front (of ETA)
Popular Democratic Front for the Liberation of Palestine (PDFLP)
Popular Front for the Liberation of Palestine (PFLP)
Potere Operaio (PO)
Prima Linea (PL)
Progressive Socialist party
Proletarian Revolution
PSI
PSIUP
Red Army Faction (RAF)
Red Brigades (BR)
Revolutionary Cells (RZ)
Revolutionary Justice organization
Russian Revolutionary Socialist party
Sa'iqa
Second of June movement
Sendero Luminoso
SIM
Sinistra Proletaria
Solidarność
Spanish Communist movement
Spanish Socialist Labor party (PSOE)
Supreme Islamic Shii Council
Syrian Popular party (PPS)
UIL
UN
United Red Army

SOME RUSSIAN AND ARABIC PROPER NAMES

Abdallah, George Ibrahim
Amri, Ibrahim El
Arafat, Yasser (Abu Ammar)
Assad, Hafiz al-
Bakhtiar, Shapour
Ben Bella, Ahmad
Bitar, Salah al-din
Boudia, Mohammed
Chehab, General
Fadlallah, Muhammad Husayn
Ghaffour, Ahmad Abdul
Guerchuni
Habash, George
Hadad, Wadi
Hassan, Khaled al-
Hawatmah, Nayif
Hindi, Hani al-
Hussein (king of Jordan)
Husseini, Hussein el-
Jibril, Ahmad
Jihad, Abu (Kahlil al-Wazir)
Junblatt
Khalaf, Salah
Khaled, Leila
Mussawi, Husain
Nabib, Berri
Nechaev
Nidal, Abu
Qaddafi
Sadr, Musa (Imam)
Saidan, Mahmud
Salameh
Salem, Selim Abu
Shamsedine, Sheik
Shuqayri, Ahmad ash-

# Glossary

*Autonomia Operaia:* Worker Autonomy—extreme left-wing group which grew out of *Potere Operaio* and declared the autonomy of the working class with respect to the party which historically represented them (the PCI); a substantial part of *Autonomia* subsequently transformed into a myriad of groups of the so-called *terrorismo diffuso.*

*Avanguardia Operia:* Worker Vanguard—extreme left-wing group operating in the worker tradition which emerged at the end of the 1960s.

*BR (Brigate Rosse):* Red Brigades—the main left-wing terrorist group in Italy which emerged at the beginning of the 1970s and lasted despite the transformations in its strategy and leadership, and its splitting-up into various groups (cf. CCC, PCC) and wings (fr *militarismo, movimentismo*), until the end of the 1980s.

*CGIL (Confederazione Generale Italiana Lavoratori):* General Confederation of Italian Workers—one of the three most important trade unions in Italy together with the CISL and the UIL; mainly Communist, but with Socialist and extreme left-wing components.

*CISL (Confederazione Italiana Sindacato Lavoratori):* Italian Confederation of Unionized Workers—Catholic trade union, once tightly linked to the DC, now more autonomous.

*CISNAL (Confederazione Italiana Sindacati Nazionali Lavoratori):* Italian Confederation of National Workers—a right-wing trade union linked to the MSI (Italian neo-Fascist party)

*CL (Comunione e liberazione):* Communion and Liberation—political association founded in the 1980s with a strong Catholic integralist nature.

*COLP (Comitati per la Liberazione Proletaria):* Committees for Proletarian Liberation—groups organized by ex-militants from *Prima Linea* with the objective of freeing imprisoned terrorists.

*CPM (Collettivo Politico Metropolitano):* Metropolitan Political Collective—a group formed in Milan in September 1969 by students from the Faculty

315

of Sociology at Trent University together with Milan factory workers; it was this group that took the decision to initiate the strategy of the armed struggle in 1969 and gave birth to one of the historical nuclei of the BR.

*DC (Democrazia Cristiana):* Christian Democratic Party—the political party, with a strong tradition of Catholic political commitment, which has been in power in Italy without interruption from the end of World War II to the present day, either alone or in coalition with other parties to its left and right.

*DP (Democrazia Proletaria):* Proletarian Democracy—political party of the far left of the political spectrum (dissolved Spring 1991).

*FGCI (Federazione Giovanile Comunista Italiana):* Federation of Young Italian Communists—the youth wing of the PCI.

*GAP (Gruppi armati proletari):* Armed Proletarian Groups—political groups founded in the 1970s, particularly in Milan, which championed the armed struggle; the name is reminiscent of the *Gruppi di Azione Partigiana* (Partisan Action Groups), active during the Resistance and the War of Liberation against the Nazis.

*LC (Lotta Continua):* Permanent Struggle—political organization of the extreme Left which published a newspaper of the same name; a part of the *servizi d'ordine* of LC subsequently formed themselves into armed groups which first became *Senza Tregua* and subsequently *Prima Linea*.

*MPRO (Movimento Proletario di Resistenza Offensiva):* Proletarian Movement of Offensive Resistance—term used by the BR to refer to all those who did not share the political strategy of the parties of the official left and who constituted fertile ground for recruitment to the armed struggle.

*MSI (Movimento Sociale-Italiano):* Italian Social Movement—extreme right-wing neo-Fascist party.

*NAP (Nuclei Armati Proletari):* Armed Proletarian Nuclei—terrorist group particularly active in the south of Italy, especially around Naples.

*OCC (Organizzazioni Comuniste Combattanti):* Organizations of Fighting Communists—one of the factions into which the BR split.

*P-2 (Propaganda Due):* the secret Masonic Lodge, which counted almost 1,000 prominent national figures from the world of politics, defense, and law and order among its membership, and was implicated in a range of criminal activities including right-wing terrorism in the late 1960s and early 1970s.

*P-38*—the name of the gun frequently used by terrorists at the time and which became a symbol unto itself; see the book by F. Calvi in the bibliography entitled *Camarade P 38*.

*PCC (Partito Comunista Combattente):* Fighting Communist party—armed party created by the BR and subsequently one of its factions.

*PCI (Partito Comunista Italiano):* Italian Communist party.

*PGPM (Partito della Guerriglia del Proletariato Metropolitano):* Guerrilla Party of the Metropolitan Working Class—the prison-wing of the BR.

*PL (Prima Linea):* Front Line—the other main trend in Italian left-wing terrorism apart from the BR; PL had "movimentist" tendencies and was an instigator of the so-called *terrorismo diffuso*.

*PO (Potere Operaio):* Worker Power—political organization in the "works" tradition: a part of PO, in particular part of its *servizi d'ordine*, gave birth to terroristic groups.

*PSI (Partito Socialista Italiano):* Italian Socialist party.

*SIDA*—"yellow" or "the owner's" trade union.

*SP (Sinistra Proletaria):* Proletarian Left—grassroots collective in Milan which generated one of the historical nuclei of the BR.

*St. (Senza Tregua):* No Truce—organization formed by militants from Lotta Continua's *servizi d'ordine* who then joined *Prima Linea*.

*UIL (Unione Italiana Lavoratori):* Union of Italian Workers—Republican-Socialist oriented trade union.

# Notes

FOREWORD

1. Let us indicate from the outset that classical sociology has shown but little interest in terrorism, which is absent from most dictionaries and treatises whose aim it is to present a general survey of the discipline. A noteworthy and already venerable exception is J. B. S. Hardman's article "Terrorism" in *Encyclopedia of the Social Sciences*, 14:575–79.

ACKNOWLEDGMENTS

1. *Sociologie du terrorisme,* Doctorat d'Etat, EHESS, 1988. Original length: 1,058 pages.

CHAPTER ONE

1. For more details on this incident, see chapter 17.
2. For considerations that are often close to our own, see Bigo and Hermant, "Relation terroriste." See also Foss and Larkin, *Beyond Revolution.*
3. See Touraine, *Self-Production of Society.*
4. "In totalitarianism," writes Claude Lefort, "one seeks to complete the process by which society as an institution is entirely occulted . . . Before all else, totalitarian discourse abolishes the opposition between state and civil society. The party and its militants set themselves up as repositories of knowledge and power; they control the worker, the peasant, the engineer, the teacher, and the writer, establishing norms and concentrating the virtues of activism in themselves. The party then discovers the vocabulary and syntax of activism to be part and parcel with its own discourse, such that it introduces itself into the very workings of its ideology" (*Formes de l'histoire,* pp. 309–11). See, by the same author, *Democracy and Political Theory.*
5. "Any social movement can degenerate and transform itself into a social antimovement, which may at times call itself a sect and which may also, at the

most macro-social level, take the form of a totalitarian regime which moreover functions, for the most part, like a sect." Touraine, *Méthode de l'intervention sociologique,* p. 26.

6. Arendt, *Origins of Totalitarianism,* p. 471.

7. Ibid., p. 471.

8. Baumann, *Tupamaros Berlin-Ouest,* pp. 159–60.

9. Vidal, *Malheur et son prophète,* p. 186.

10. Charnay, "L'homme est un zoon politikon," p. 11.

11. Touraine, Wieviorka, and Dubet, *Workers' Movement.*

12. See especially Hobsbawm, *Primitive Rebels.*

13. See especially Dubois, *Travail et conflit dans l'industrie.*

14. See Durand, *Chômage et violence.*

15. Perrot, *Ouvriers en grève.*

16. Ibid., pp. 344–45.

17. Beaubernard, "*Laboratoire social,*" p. 175.

18. The Molly Maguires appeared in the 1870s, in a coal-mining region of Pennsylvania. The fifteen murders for which they were responsible were more the upshot of ethnic than social conflicts. These were basically attacks by Irish shopowners or saloonkeepers on Protestants of English, Welsh, or Scottish origins. These murders were not linked to labor unrest, but were treated as such by the mine owners, who presented them as being linked to labor strikes. See Broehl, *The Molly Maguires.*

19. Bonnell, *Roots of Rebellion.*

20. On the German experience, see Salomon, *Outlaws* and especially *Fragebogen.* On Poland, see especially Marcus, *Jews in Poland.*

21. Mongin, "Terrorismes," pp. 1–7. See also the *Rapport du Sénat sur le terrorisme* and Severino, *Techne.*

22. See especially Sterling, *Terror Network.*

CHAPTER TWO

1. Cohn, *Pursuit of the Millennium.*

2. A rather similar viewpoint may be found in Sigal and Verón, *Perón o muerte,* in which the authors explain (p. 14), with regard to the language of Peronism and its tilt towards violence (particularly among the Montoneros), that this was "an element which, under a particular set of circumstances, arose out of a set of signifying mechanisms that defined the nature of the conflict and the positions taken by its protagonists . . . [Such discourse] is linked to the same signifying matrix as that which affords it meaning, and which, in the end, gives rise to it as a form of behavior rooted in a symbolic and imagic order."

3. See also Shils, *Intellectuals and the Power* (p. 3), who describes intellectuals as "persons with an unusual sensitivity to the sacred, an uncommon reflectiveness about the nature of their universe and the rules which govern their society . . . [persons who] are inquiring, and desirous of being in frequent communion with symbols which are more general than the immediate concrete situations of everyday life . . . [and who] need to externalize this quest in oral and written discourse, in poetic or plastic expression, in historical reminiscence or writing, in ritual performance and acts of worship."

4. "The knowledge of the intelligentsia is also the expression of its own structural interests to the point that, if it were to organize itself into a class, its knowledge would be subordinated, before all else, to its own class interests." Konrad and Szelenyi, *Marche au pouvoir des intellectuels,* p. 15.

5. Tocqueville, *Old Regime and the French Revolution,* pp. 145–46.

6. Aron, *Opium of the Intellectuals,* p. 218.

7. Coser, *Men of Ideas,* pp. 148–49.

8. Confino, *Violence dans la violence.*

9. Several passages from his *Critique of Dialectical Reason* and his celebrated preface to Fanon's *Wretched of the Earth* moved Raymond Aron to write: "What I hate is not the choice, *hic et nunc,* at a particular conjunction of circumstances, in favor of violence and against negotiation, but a philosophy of violence in and for itself, not as a means that is sometimes necessary for rational politics . . ." (*History and Dialectic of Violence,* p. 192).

10. Gavi, Sartre, and Victor, *On a raison de se revolter,* p. 87.

11. See, for example, Geismar, *Engrenage terroriste* or, for a more guarded analysis, Liniers, "Objections contre une prise d'armes."

12. See Weber, *Action Française,* especially chapter 28, "The World of Print."

13. Negri, *L'Italie rouge et noire.*

14. Aron, *Opium of the Intellectuals,* pp. 35–36.

15. Raynaud, "Origines intellectuelles du terrorisme."

16. Besançon, *Origines intellectuelles du léninisme,* p. 25.

17. Klein, *Mort mercenaire.*

18. Weber, *Action Française,* p. 398.

19. See especially Gramsci, *Benedetto Croce,* as well as his renowned essay on the southern question (*La questione meridionale*), outlined in 1926 and interrupted by Gramsci's arrest.

20. Nizan, *Chiens de garde.*

21. See Naville, *Révolution et les intellectuels.*

22. See, for example, Morel, *Roman insupportable.*

23. RAF document entitled *Uberarbeite und aktualisierte Ausgabe 1983.* Cf. Steiner, *Fraction armée rouge.*

24. Rodinson, *Marxism and the Muslim World.*

25. Laroui, *Crise des intellectuels arabes,* p. 216.

26. Rodinson, *Marxism and the Muslim World,* p. 72.

27. Ibid., p. 262.

28. Coser, *Men of Ideas,* p. 3.

29. Kepel, *Muslim Extremism in Egypt.*

30. Venturi, *Popolismo russo,* 2:31.

31. Cited in ibid., 2:48

32. Kepel, *Muslim Extremism in Egypt,* p. 142.

CHAPTER THREE

This chapter is basically a reworking of matters discussed in the book I published together with Dominique Wolton: *Terrorisme à la une. Media, terrorisme, et démocratie.* This work itself grew out of a series of private meetings which we organized between a group of journalists specializing in terrorism and various invitees (judges, lawyers, a former terrorist, members of government, etc.), each of whom came on a separate occasion.

1. Cf. notably, for their high quality, *Crusaders, Criminals and Crazies* and *Aggression et violence dans le monde moderne*, both by Friedrich Hacker.

2. See for example Dufour, "Ressorts psychologiques."

3. Let us cite, in particular, for West Germany, Gert Ellingham and Günther Rayer, "Arbeitsmaterialen zu einer vergleichender Untersuchung der Presseberichterstattung über die Entführung des Berliner (CDU)—Vorsitzender Peter Lorenz," analyzed in one of the few works devoted to the relationship between terrorism and the media: Schmid and De Graaf, *Insurgent Terrorism*. For Italy, see Losito, "Violenza e politica," Bentivegna, "Violenza politica e quotidiani di partito."

Elsewhere on these problems, see, apart from Wieviorka and Wolton, *Terrorisme*, my article "Terrorisme et media occidentaux."

4. This idea, applied to Islam, lies at the heart of Edward Saïd's work *Covering Islam*.

5. This theme, of the role played by the media in the transition from social movement to increasingly spectacular and violent activism, constitutes one of Jerry Mander's critiques of television in *Four Arguments for the Elimination of Television*. We find this theme developed, on the subject of changes in the American New Left in the 1970s, by Todd Gitlin in *The Whole World Is Watching: Mass Media in the Making and Unmaking of the New Left*.

6. Heinrich Böll, according to several journalists, allegedly received, in response to his marginal positions criticizing the repression and imprisonment of German terrorists, a great number of signed angry letters, and a few letters of support which were anonymous.

7. Villeneuve and Péret, *Histoire secrète du terrorisme*.

8. This idea is developed by Yehezkel Dror in several texts, most notably in "Terrorism as a Challenge to Governments."

CHAPTER FOUR

1. Geismar, *L'engrenage terroriste*.

2. Charnay, "Théorie stratégique," p. 217.

3. Giorgio, *Profession: terroriste*. On Carlos see for example Dobson and Payne, *Carlos Complex*.

4. Dispot, *Machine à Terreur*.

5. Clutterbuck, *Living with Terrorism*.

6. Solzhenitsyn, *August Nineteen Fourteen*.

7. Chaliand, *Guerilla Strategies*, p. 1.

8. Notarnicola, *Révolte à perpétuité*.

9. See Commission international d'enquête, *Mort d'Ulrike Meinhof*.

10. Klein, *Mort mercenaire*, p. 260.

CHAPTER FIVE

1. In 1971, the leaders of the Red Army, the product of a fusion of a dissident Trotskyist group with a Maoist group, first assassinated two, then later twelve of the thirty-one militants wandering with them in the mountains. These murders

were explained at the time as resulting from conflicts generated by the militants' dual origin and by the group's social and political isolation. See Kawahara, "Terrorismo giapponese."

2. Klein, *Mort mercenaire*. This former terrorist of the Revolutionary Cells most notably relates how his group prepared the assassinations—on German territory—of Galenski and Libinski, the presidents of the Jewish communities of West Berlin and Frankfurt.

3. Raynaud, "Origines intellectuelles du terrorisme," p. 128.

4. Pécaut, *L'ordre et la violence*.

5. Crouch and Pizzorno, *Resurgence of Class Conflict*.

6. On the relationship between the revolutionary left and the Japanese labor movement in the late 1960s, see the very partisan work of Beraud, *Gauche révolutionnaire au Japon*.

7. Chaliand, *Guerilla Strategies*, p. 222.

8. "When the method of action—that is, armed struggle, and particularly the rural guerilla war—replaces the program of action, technical means become transformed into ends in themselves. The imperative—that one must fight—now comes to be conjugated in the indicative tense: things being as they are, how does one fight?" Debray, *Critique des armes*, 1:16.

9. See Marian, "Terrorisme arménien." The ASALA question is taken up with greater precision in the final part of this book.

10. Manoukian, *Fruit de la patience*, p. 148.

11. Touraine, Wieviorka, and Dubet, *Workers' Movement*.

12. Maitron, *Mouvement anarchiste en France*. See especially 1:206–50, "L'ère des attentats, 1892–1894."

13. See Julliard, *Fernand Pelloutier*.

14. "The problem is the following: I'm an anarcho, I want to spread my ideas, what ground will they best take root in? I've already talked about the factory, the local bar . . . a place where I can find prolos who are a bit aware of the exploitation we suffer, and who are looking for a way to solve the problem. The corporate group!" Pouget, "A roublard, roublard et demi!"

15. Here a debate, which raged at the very heart of the revolutionary union movement, points to the fact that the general consensus rejected individual acts of violence or activist propaganda, as soon as it became estranged from violence that was properly social. This war of words, waged between the review entitled *La guerre social* and *La bataille syndicale* (of Jouhaux, Griffeulhes, etc.), was presented in an article entitled "Insurrectionalisme, socialisme et syndicalisme" in *La vie ouvrière* (September 20, 1912), pp. 806–16.

*La bataille syndicale* explains its simultaneous drift away from the party and its rejection of violence: "These people wanted to replace organized union actions with individual acts, which they described histrionically or evoked through some insolent and often coarse expression. They wave their "Browning" [guns] and "Mademoiselle Cisaille" [wire-cutters] like banners, whereas both are but the most extreme means by which to resolve . . ."

*La guerre sociale* responded with an article in its August 21, 1912, issue: "*La guerre sociale* has never sought to pit individual action against the actions organized by the unions. Furthermore, it has never marched under the banners of the "browning" or of "mademoiselle cisaille." Nor has it ever constituted a program of action around them. *La guerre sociale* has always favored the organization and mass actions, and if it has at times suggested and exalted certain individual actions—as it will continue to do—it is because such actions are necessary, and because the large organizations are incapable of carrying them out. They are a final recourse, in matters of defense or retaliation, against both police brutality and governmental arm-twisting. But such are, of course, merely means to an end . . . to which one resigns oneself, and not matters of policy."

16. Gaucher, *Terrorists*, p. 118.

17. Touraine, *Voice and the Eye*, p. 20.

18. On March 4, 1976, winegrowers blocked the road and rail link to Montredon and, for the first time, used their guns against the forces of order. The shooting ended with the death of one of their own, as well as that of a member of the French CRS (Compagnies Republicaines de Sécurité) police force. Following this incident, the movement lost momentum and weakened. See Touraine, Dubet, Hegedus, and Wieviorka, *Pays contre l'Etat*.

19. The FLQ (Front de Libération du Quebec), founded in February 1963, combined independentist, socialist, and revolutionary ideals. It denounced the twofold national domination (American colonialism as the "natural ally" of English Canadian colonialism, according to its vocabulary) and supported social actions and strikes which it punctuated with symbolic (and sometimes lethal) attacks, before a sudden decline following "October"—i.e., following the kidnapping (on October 5, 1970) of James Cross, a British diplomat and, when the authorities took a hard line and rejected the exchange of Cross for the emancipation of political prisoners, that of Pierre Laporte, the vice prime minister of the Quebec government, on October 10. The latter was assassinated on October 17, and the FLQ, which had up to that time enjoyed strong support, found itself isolated and fell apart, as much by its own doing as by the effects of police repression. Among the several works devoted to the FLQ, the most complete and best informed is that of Fournier, *FLQ: Histoire d'un mouvement clandestin*. Several FLQ militants have published books, some at the time of the affair (see especially the important work of Vallières, *White Niggers of America*), and others following it (see especially Simard, *Pour en finir avec octobre*).

20. Apter and Sawa, *Against the State*.

21. See especially Festinger, *Theory of Cognitive Dissonance;* and Bremm and Cohen, *Explorations in Cognitive Dissonance*.

22. Festinger and Aronson, "Arousal and Reduction of Dissonance," p. 125.

23. Festinger, *Conflict, Decision, and Dissonance*, p. 3.

24. Dubet, *Galère*.

25. Here, I am referring to Steiner, *Fraction armée rouge*, who clearly shows the gulf that separated the Red Army Faction from the Revolutionary Cells and the Second of June movement.

26. This statement is reproduced *in extenso* in Baynac, *Socialistes révolutionnaires*, pp. 209–15.

27. Simmel, *Conflict*, especially pp. 27–28. See also Lewis Coser's discussion in *Functions of Social Conflict*.

CHAPTER SIX

1. Braudel, "Histoire et sociologie," p. 88

PART TWO

1. Della Porta and Rossi, *Cifre crudeli*. This short book offers an intelligent synthesis of the available statistics on Italian terrorism. The original data are found in Galleni, *Rapporto sul terrorismo*.

2. Bocca, *Noi terroristi*; Calvi, *Camarade P 38*; Stajano, *L'Italia nichilista*; and Della Porta, *Terrorismi in Italia*.

3. For Red Brigade texts, see Tessandori, *BR imputazioni*; Bocca, *Moro, una tragedia italiana*; Peci, *Io, l'infame*; and Giorgio, *Profession: terroriste*.

CHAPTER SEVEN

1. See for example the chapter concerning Sit-Siemens in Cavallini, *Terrorismo in fabbrica*.

2. Extract from a 1971 BR document cited by Della Porta and Casselli, "Storia delle Brigate Rosse," p. 163.

3. See Silj, *Maï più senza fucile!* p. 162.

4. See Ventura, "Terrorismo di sinistra."

5. Peci, *Io, l'infame*, pp. 49–50.

6. Cited by Bocca, *Noi terroristi*, p. 69.

7. See Peci, *Io, l'infame*, pp. 56–58. Similar descriptions are found in other works.

8. Raynaud, "Origines intellectuelles du terrorisme." This analysis of German and Italian terrorist ideologies does not avoid, on the subject of Italy, a fundamental weakness: it presents as a simple and relatively stable whole an ideology that had, over about a decade, undergone a number of transformations and had been a matter of some conflict, even within the Red Brigades themselves.

9. See Dalla Chiesa, "Terrorismo di sinistra."

10. In Della Porta and Caselli, "Storia delle Brigate Rosse." Here, it should be made clear that Giancarlo Caselli, the examining magistrate at Turin, played a leading role in the legal response to Italian terrorism.

11. Padovani, *Vivre avec le terrorisme*. This book, which has much in common with the interpretations offered by the Italian Communist party, and which is mainly based on well-informed police and legal sources, borrows its title from Luigi Manconi's excellent *Vivere con il terrorismo*. We should add that extreme caution should be exercised in taking up this theme of bureaucratic organization. When a terrorist movement is on the rise, the media often project the image of a highly rational terrorist universe; whereas when it is declining, it is a reverse image that is applied to the entire history of the movement.

12. Giorgio, *Profession: terroriste*. Both in this work and that of Marcelle Padovani, we may doubt the pertinence and the validity of the descriptions given, and leave the question of "disinformation," as put forward by the Italian Communist party, an open one.

13. On this affair, see Bocca, *Moro, una tragedia italiana*, or Katz, *I giorni*

*nell'Ira* and, less journalistic and more profound, Sciascia, *L'affaire Moro.* On the way in which Aldo Moro was, quite practically, abandoned by his party, see Wagner-Pacifici, "Aldo Moro Affair."

14. Girardi, *Coscienza operaia oggi.* See also "Le Brigate Rosse e la fabbrica: una discussione operaia," in Marchetti, Santina, and Rolli, *Violenza e la politica,* pp. 97–120.

15. See *Esperienze Sindicali-Periodico dei delegati FML di Torino e Provincia,* no. 2 (n.d.), devoted to the 1979 conference, and the October 1982 edition of the same document, devoted to the 1982 conference.

16. For an analysis that is at once political, legal and social, see Ghezzi, *Processo al sindacato.*

17. See Schimel, "Face au terrorisme."

18. Bocca, *Noi terroristi,* pp. 279–82.

19. Ibid., p. 232.

CHAPTER EIGHT

1. On national crisis, see Solé, *Défi terroriste;* and Graziano and Tarrow, *Crisi italiana.* On the relationship between the Italian intellectuals and the nation in crisis, see Mazzei, *Utopia e terrore;* and Ferrarotti, *L'ipnosi della violenza.* On social and cultural crisis, idem, *Alle radici della violenza;* Acquaviva, *Guerriglia e guerra revoluzionaria* and *Seme religioso della rivolta.* On the crisis in the family, see the highly journalistic account of Ferri, *Dov'era il padre.* On the crisis in the political system and the impasse that the "historical compromise" represented, see especially Pasquino, *Crisi dei partiti e governabilità.* On the theme of manipulation, see Galli, *Storia del partito armato.*

2. Melucci, "New Movements"; Pasquino, "Differenze e somiglianze."

3. Ferrajoli, "Critica della violenza."

4. Silj, *Maï più senza fucile!* p. 33. On the University of Trent, see also Tessandori, *BR imputazioni.*

5. Pizzorno, Reyneri, Regini, and Regalia, *Lotte Operaia e sindacato* (this volume concludes a series of six works of which the first five monographs are devoted to the sectors of automobile production, electrical appliances, electromechanics, telecommunications, and steel).

6. See Regini, *Dilemmi del sindacato,* p. 47.

7. Ibid., p. 49. One should be very cautious here: a good number of "workers' councils" were but the continuation, under a new name, of classical forms of union-controlled organization.

8. Cherki and Wieviorka, "Luttes sociales en Italie"; idem, "Luttes sociales en Italie: magistrats et autoréducteurs." This latter article shows the point to which the Italian judicial system had fallen into turmoil, shaken by the protest of the "Red judges" who were affiliated with the Magistratura Democratica and often leftist in their ideology.

9. Calvi, *Italie 1977.*

10. Ferrarotti, *L'ipnosi della violenza,* and *Alle radici della violenza;* Acquaviva, *Guerriglia e guerra,* and *Seme religioso della rivolta.*

11. Ventura, "Terrorismo di sinistra."

12. Silj, *Maï piu senza fucile!,* pp. 20–21.

13. Ibid., p. 22.

14. Raynaud, "Origines intellectuelles du terrorisme."

15. "To know how to lead the masses into revolutionary positions, such that these masses themselves become convinced by their own experience of the correctness of the line followed by the Party." Failure to observe this rule fatally leads to the estrangement of the masses, to putschism and to the ideological degeneration of communism into a leftist doctrinairism, or a "petit-bourgeois" revolutionary "adventurism."

16. Dalla Chiesa, "Terrorismo di sinistra."

17. Cf. Lerner, Manconi, and Sinibaldi, *Strano movimento di strani studenti* for an analysis which stresses the theme of marginality. See also on this theme the functionalist analysis proposed by Statera in *Violenza sociale e violenza politica*. This author offers the following as indications of marginality: a precarious social role, a lack or inadequate internalization of cultural or subcultural norms, etc.

18. Wieviorka, "Luttes étudiantes en Italie." Much of this article will be reproduced in this chapter.

19. Touraine, Dubet, Hegedus, and Wieviorka, *Lutte étudiante.* This work, which might have been entitled "The End of Leftist Politics," offers an analysis which I have for the most part used to interpret the Italian phenomena of the same period.

20. See Negri, *Dall'operaio massa;* and *Dominio e il sabottagio.*

21. Berardi ("Bifo"), *Ciel est enfin tombé,* pp. 121 and 150. This book is a French translation of articles which mainly appeared in the review *A traverso,* one of the most important organs of the movement.

22. Taken from his preface to Collectif A Traverso, *Radio Alice, radio libre,* p. 7. This work offers an excellent picture of this pirate radio station which sought to make itself a source of counterinformation and cultural production. See also, for texts translated into French, "Les Untorelli," *Recherches,* no. 30.

23. See for example Ferrarotti, *Alle radici della violenza.*

24. See above, note 21. See also Calvi's excellent anthology, *Italie 77.*

25. On Autonomia Operaia, see the documents brought together by the Comitate Autonomi Operai di Roma, *Autonomia Operaia.* See also Castellani, *Aut. Op.*

26. Cf. my "Luttes étudiantes en Italie."

27. Acquaviva, *Guerriglia e guerra,* who differentiates between three cultural rationales which became fused together into violence: a strongly Leninist neo-Marxism; a subjectivist individualism, which spoke in the name of basic human necessities; and a moralism inherited from a declining Catholic cultural matrix.

28. According to Galleni, *Rapporto sul terrorismo.* These figures give a clear indication of the qualitative and quantitative leap which occurred between 1977 and 1978.

29. See Della Porta, "Recruitment Process." This text is based in part on the categories of the sociology of mobilization and the rich literature devoted to *social networks.* It also makes use of empirical data concerning several hundred activists. It confirms our own observation that recruitment took place on a mass

level through networks of personal acquaintance, based on a common politico-cultural background.

CHAPTER NINE

1. On the method itself, see Touraine, *Voice and the Eye*. On its earliest applications, see Touraine, Dubet, Hegedus, and Wieviorka, *Lutte étudiante;* idem, *Antinuclear Protest;* idem, *Pays contre l'Etat;* Touraine, Dubet, Wieviorka, and Strzelecki, *Solidarity;* and Touraine, Wieviorka, and Dubet, *Workers' Movement*.

2. Federazione Metalmecanichi del Lavoro: Federation of Metallurgical Workers (CGIL, CISL, UIL).

3. See Touraine, Wieviorka, and Dubet, *Workers' Movement*.

4. On this process, see the chapters written by Mariella Berra, Marco Revelli, Silvia Belforte, Martino Ciatti, and Alberto Magnaghi in Gaudemar, *Usines et ouvriers*. There exists a considerable body of Italian literature on the subject, of which see especially Paci, *Struttura sociale italiana*. On the stakes involved in the restructuring program at Fiat, see Santilli, *L'autre usine*.

5. Does this imply that we should dismiss any approach that relates personality development and the transition to violence? The meeting of the first group with Mr. Stefano allows us to explore this question. This priest charms the group when he asserts that Marxist culture is instrumental and not fundamental to terrorism. Mario, who is personally working for a return to Marxism, goes a step further: "I have always said here that Marxism is not the pathway to terrorism." Mr. Stefano is a master of his craft, and knows how to make each of the group members speak, in turn, as if they were at confession. The personal trajectories of each member are reviewed, and we are ushered into the imaginations of these former activists, discovering all sorts of leads that had not previously been explored. Mario and Antimo acknowledge a close ideological affiliation with fascism and Paulo evokes his region's anarchist and anticlerical traditions. The group members stress the important place of the resistance in their intellectual development, the influence of the great valorization of partisans during the fascist period—or, conversely, a disgust or break with fascism, as had been the case in Antimo's family. Time and again, different members describe personal experiences. Mr. Stefano fairly stresses the presence of the theme of the resistance, seconded by a powerful anti-Americanism, in the language of the Red Brigades, which allows him to advance the hypothesis of a link between terrorism and frustrated nationalism. In the course of this meeting, however, his thesis falls apart. Mr. Stefano's conclusion is that terrorism is "metapolitical," seeing in its definitive form "the exclusion of democracy as a political arena . . . a pure step outward into the void, not on a political level, but on an existential one, a position in which there are no compromises."

His mode of intervention allowed us to glimpse the depth and complexity of the historical descriptions and layerings of experience, both collective and personal, which contributed to the formation of our former terrorists. It is clear that war, the nation, the resistance, and the relationship to the father occupy a significant place in the actor's worldview. But it is no less clear that one cannot go too far in this direction without losing sight of the social and political ideals which drove tens of thousands of Italians into violence. By the end of the meeting, the debate has returned to this level of discourse: politics, parties, labor struggles, and the state again become the subjects of conversation, and the categories become more classical.

A meeting such as this in no way authorizes us to reject explanations which perhaps derive more from psychology than from sociology. Quite the contrary, it suggests that one ought to draw a relationship between the impracticable or destructured nature of a social or political action and the important role played by individual perception and imagination in the commitment of the actor to violence. The group, ordinarily held in tow by its leader, enjoyed its dialogue with Mr. Stefano, and may have even felt the need to enter into his world. For Mr. Stefano, violence and armed struggle are things of the past. Behind the most overt meanings of his past activities, he has carried and laid up a great store of images which burst into view like plumes of steam when a valve has been opened. Rather than contrasting these images to others of a more immediately sociological sort, let us rather note that these are to be situated at another analytical level. And, if it is the case that they flare up in this way, it is because they once had their place in the great boiling cauldron of violence.

Is it possible to go any further in our research? We alternated the first group's meetings with a series of individual conversations, whose original function was to help this group, which was too often closed in on itself, to open up. A number of these discussions contributed a great quantity of details concerning the personal trajectories of our former terrorists, as well as their worldviews, their dreams, and their fears. We should be clear in stating here that these conversations indicated the possibilities of a path for which we lacked the analytical tools, and for which we had not set ourselves the task of exploring. It is Mario who went the furthest in his terrorist experience. He is tempted, from time to time, to talk about what that life was like, and the intensity with which he lived that period. He had known "self-destructive chains of events" as well as "moments in which I broke away completely, the feeling of an existential break that was triggered nearly in parallel with my political activities." He believes that "personal motives intertwine with more objective motives" and insists "in making people see that there are psychological voids" within terrorism. But at no time did anyone truly agree to commit himself to this line of discussion, and when our research came to an end, Mario recalled that the most personal themes, of family and the relationship to the father "enter into terrorism, but we said we wouldn't talk about that."

CHAPTER TEN

1. On Action Directe, see Hamon and Marchand, *Action directe;* Plenel, "Terrorisme à vocation révolutionnaire"; and idem, "France et le terrorisme."

2. On the Communist Combat Cells, see Offergeld and Souris, *Euroterrorisme;* and especially Francq, "Cellules communistes combattantes."

PART THREE

1. The spelling "Euskadi" is itself a subject of debate: the name is in fact written "Euzkadi" in certain traditionalist nationalist sectors. Because we had

to make a choice, we made one that was neither historical nor political, and opted for the most widely used spelling.

2. See Haupt, Löwy, and Weill, *Marxistes et la question nationale.*

CHAPTER ELEVEN

1. See Letamendia, *Basques;* and Garmendia and Elordi, *Resistancia vasca* (see especially, for the crisis of 1951, the epilogue to this latter work, pp. 249–66).

2. On this point, see the remarks of Javier de Landaburu, *Causa del pueblo vasco,* cited in Jaureguiberry, *Question nationale et mouvements sociaux,* pp. 160–61.

3. A comparable process again occurred in 1970, at a time when ETA had been dismantled and most of its militants sent into exile or imprisoned. At this time, the PNV's youth organization funneled itself piecemeal into ETA, breaking away from the PNV, which it judged very critically, both for its ideology and for its absence of effective reactions to the ongoing repression.

4. See for example, *La insurrección en Euskadi,* a long manifesto drawn up in 1963 and approved at ETA's Third Assembly in 1964. The text is greatly inspired by the ideas of one of ETA's first ideologues, Federico Krutwig, who was, under the pen name of Fernando Sarrailh de Ihartza, the author of the book *Vasconia.*

5. *Barro y asfalto.*

6. See Wieviorka, "Vie et mort de Pertur."

7. Letamendia, *Basques,* p. 182.

8. See Halimi, *Procès de Burgos.*

9. Letamendia, *Basques,* p. 195.

10. Aguire, *Operación Ogro.*

11. A spectacular example of this strategy was carried out in 1976, during the transition period: thirty prisoners, whom all knew would be released within a few months in any case, broke out of the Segovia prison and thus began to live an epic adventure. Under a heavy fog cover, some of the fugitives crossed the French border several times without even knowing it. Some of them were recaptured, and others killed by the Civil Guards. The Segovia breakout, masterminded by the Political-Military Front, would always be presented as yet another part of its fight to bring down the dictatorship.

12. Angel Amigo, *Pertur, ETA, 71–76,* p. 101.

13. For the first time in its history, the organization was rocked by the denunciations of "El Lobo" (the Wolf), a traitor who had reached a not insignificant level of responsibility within the organization. On this affair, see Unsurruxzada, *Infiltración.* This affair further hastened the crisis in the Political-Military Front. It is likely that the Military Wing would have acted more cautiously and quickly than did ETA-PM, which let "El Lobo" participate in undercover operations several weeks after doubts about the nature of his militancy had begun to arise.

14. Here, I am primarily basing my discussion on a letter Pertur wrote to his aunt a few days before his passing.

15. These figures correspond to the provinces of Alava, Guipuzcoa and Vizcaya alone. In Navarra, the PNV-EE coalition won 8.45 percent of the votes

cast, and HB 8.9 percent. For a very detailed analysis of the political system, party interactions, and the Euskadi election results in the final years of this decade, see Linz, *Conflicto en Euskadi.*

16. There is a wealth of literature on the subject of the origins of the PNV, and its ideologies which constituted the original Basque nationalism. See especially Larronde, *Nationalisme basque.* The history of the PNV remains to be written. See however, for their data, Roldo San Sebastián, *Historia del Partido Nacionalista Vasco;* Elórza, *Ideologias del nacionalismo vasco;* and Atienza, *Nacionalismo vasco.*

17. It should be noted here that Navarra was excluded from this statute. The specific theme of Navarra requires a great number of explanations, and poses a number of specific problems as regards the Basque movement.

18. Jaureguiberry, *Question nationale,* and Touraine, Dubet, Hegedus, and Wieviorka, *Antinuclear Protest.*

19. Having long since abandoned the armed struggle, Miquel Solaun was allegedly forced to collaborate in an ETA action (laying an explosive charge that was to have been detonated during the dedication ceremonies of a new building). ETA blamed the operation's failure on Solaun, who was accused, not of having left the ETA—many had done so without being troubled—but for having been a stool pigeon and traitor, and with having endangered the organization. Threatened with death in prison and mistreated by his fellow detainees, he was killed following his release, in a bar, in the presence of his wife and daughter. "Yoyès," a woman, was a former ETA leader who, having left the armed struggle, was put to death by ETA in 1986 for having participated in social reinsertion.

20. GAL is the organization which claimed responsibility for the Etarras killings, which were most often carried out on the French side of the border by assassins generally recruited from the "criminal milieu." There are a number of theories concerning the group: some believe GAL was financed by the Spanish oligarchy or by certain Basque businessmen. Others feel it was backed by the Spanish government or by military or police personnel who had more or less slipped out of state control. For still others, it was the manifestation of a strategy on the part of the French government—a highly improbable hypothesis.

CHAPTER TWELVE

1. Geertz, *Old Societies and New State.*

2. For a recent ethnological approach, see Goikoetxea, "Pays basque"; and Arpal, "País Vasco."

3. UGT, the General Union of Workers, was closely aligned with the Spanish Socialist Labor party, the PSOE.

4. For information concerning this organization as well as the PNV, the PSOE, and HB, which will be discussed shortly, see chapter 11.

5. This does not mean that it could ever fully satisfy each and every one: the veterans declared themselves to be safisfied, on the whole, with the text, whereas the separatist group, reduced to two members, reproached us, the researchers, for our partisanship, and for not having scientifically studied the climate of violence and oppression that reigns under the present regime.

6. The denunciation of repression was not proper to the separatist movement

alone. See, for example, Bandres (an EE legislator), "Situaciones de violencia," who explains, in terms close to those with which HB discourse is peppered, that the repression orchestrated by the central government lies at the source of political violence in Euskadi.

CHAPTER THIRTEEN

1. Fraga is the leader of the conservative right, Carrillo that of the Communist party; Onaindia is a former Burgos trial defendant who had been sentenced to death and is now a leader of EE, and Vizcaíno a major Basque business leader.

CHAPTER FOURTEEN

1. ZEN: Zona Especial Norte; the Special Northern Zone (of Spain); HASI: Herriko Alderdi Sozialista Iraultzalea (the Popular Revolutionary Socialist party, a party belonging to the HB coalition).

2. The problem of the relationship between HB and political institutions, as well as with the game of politics itself, was illustrated, in the late 1970s, by the writings of Ortzi (Francisco Letamendia Belzunce), who was a representative in the Spanish Parliament until his resignation on November 8, 1978. See Letamendia, *El no vasco;* and idem, *Denuncia en el parlamento.*

PART FOUR

1. Lewis, *Assassins.*

CHAPTER SIXTEEN

1. The brochure entitled *OLP, maintenant on sait* (The PLO, Now We Know) and distributed by the CIDIP (Center for Information and Documentation on Israel and the Middle East) develops this viewpoint to the point of caricature: the PLO "is composed of a variety of terrorist groups" (p. 8) and has a "foreign legion" (p. 11). Its "chartered killers," trained in the USSR and Eastern Europe, teach children "to kill at the age of twelve," going so far as to giving them drugs and screening, "as a reward for the completion of their training," pornographic movies for them (p. 15). It is "the wealthiest terrorist organization in history" (p. 25), etc.

2. In this line, the work by Friedrich Hacker is by far the best. See especially his *Crusaders, Criminals, Crazies,* and *Aggression et violence.*

3. See for example, among many other works of this sort, Laurent, *L'Internationale terroriste démasquée.*

4. Kriegel, *Réflexions sur les questions juives,* p. 224.

5. See for example Lewis, *Le retour de l'islam* (a French reworking of a collection of articles written in English over the past twenty-five years), who writes (p. 205): "When the situation calls for it, they [the PLO] can take on the look of quite conservative patriots. On the other hand, they have found the means to maintain close ties with radical international guerilla and terrorist movements. Their spokesmen can harangue the UN General Assembly, visit Castro, be received in audience by the Pope, and engage in informal conversations with Moscow, Paris, and even Washington. The one method they have used to arrive at this result has been to simultaneously maintain several levels of

discourse." See also Roland Jacquard, *Dossiers secrets du terrorisme* (this author is one and the same as Roland Laurent, cited above), who writes, "It would be naive to think that the quite natural disagreements which ripple through the various Palestinian factions—disagreements due either to personal quarrels or to more-or-less extreme approaches—constitute a major handicap for the task Yasser Arafat has assigned himself. Whether it be Ahmad Jibril's PFLP-GC, Abu Nidal's Fatah Revolutionary Council, the Wadi Hadad (a dissident from Habash's PFLP) Front, Mahmud Saidan's Palestine Liberation Front, or the Black September organization that strikes, the 'profits' always go to the PLO and its leader" (p. 109).

6. Gresh, *PLO.*

7. O'Neil, *Armed Struggle in Palestine,* p. 9.

8. Ibid., p. 107.

9. Our analysis stops with the 1982 siege of West Beirut by the Israeli forces and the PLO's departure from that city. Of course, it in no way claims to give a comprehensive account of the Palestinian question, but rather concentrates on those elements which contribute to an analysis of international Palestinian terrorism.

10. Sanbar, *Palestine 1948.*

11. Ben Jelloun-Ollivier, *Palestine.*

12. Ahmed Hamzé, in *Revue d'études palestiniennes,* 15:7.

13. See his interview in *Revue des études palestiniennes,* 14:5.

14. On this and a great number of other points, see Cobban, *Palestinian Liberation Organization.*

15. The PLA is not an organized army, but rather a group of militias, each of which falls under the leadership of the general staff of an Arab nation: Syria, Jordan, Egypt, etc.

16. Gresh, *PLO,* p. 9.

17. See, among others, the excellent analyses of Quandt, Jabber, and Lesch, *Politics of Palestinian Nationalism:* "Fatah could not fail to observe that its continued existence throughout 1965–1967 had been a function of Arab dissension, and was therefore careful to cultivate relationships in both conservative and progressive camps" (p. 174).

18. Cobban, *Palestinian Liberation Organization,* estimates that several tens of thousands of youth were trained in Fatah camps between 1967 and 1970.

19. *Revue d'études palestiniennes* 14:4.

20. Rouleau, *Palestiniens,* p. 2.

21. *Journal of Palestine Studies* 14, no. 2 (Winter 1985), p. 11.

22. All of the fifteen members elected to the central committee in the spring of 1980 had been active in the movement well before 1965: Cobban, *Palestinian Liberation Organization,* p. 10.

23. These proceedings of a meeting held in Moscow on November 13, 1979, were seized by the Israeli army in June 1982. They were published in Israeli, *PLO in Lebanon,* pp. 33–35.

24. The ANM was organized into militias, all more-or-less linked to Moscow. One of these took power in South Yemen.

25. In the newspaper *Al Ahrar,* March 22, 1970, cited in Gresh, *PLO,* p. 36.

26. For an analysis of PDFLP and PFLP ideologies (as well as that of Fatah) in the late 1960s, see Carré, *L'idéologie palestinienne de résistance,* a valuable book for the compendium of the movement's basic texts found in it. See also Chaliand, *Palestinian Resistance,* a book in which a certain sympathy for the PDFLP prevails.

27. In Quandt, Jabbar, and Lesch, *Politics of Palestinian Nationalism,* p. 109.

28. The PDFLP (Popular Democratic Front for the Liberation of Palestine) would later become the DFLP (Democratic Front for the Liberation of Palestine).

29. Its most sustained contacts are with a Trotskyist group called the Matzpen.

30. Cited by Gresh, *PLO,* p. 40, who also reproduces Hawatmah's contemporary statement in favor of a Arab socialist state "with no trace of national oppression."

31. Lewis, *Retour de l'islam,* p. 175.

32. Jihad, *Palestiniens sans patrie.*

33. Sayigh, *Palestinians;* Smith, *Palestine and the Palestinians.*

34. Sayigh, *Palestinians,* p. 6.

35. There exists a voluminous literature, often sensationalist in nature, on this theme. See for example Jacquard, *Dossiers secrets du terrorisme.*

CHAPTER SEVENTEEN

1. Habash, interviewed in *Revue d'études palestiniennes* 14:16.

2. On this, see Quandt, Jabber, and Lesch, *Politics of Palestinian Nationalism.*

3. On this point, see Lewis, *Retour de l'islam,* p. 381.

4. For a useful (although unfortunately partisan) analysis of the PLO's internal wranglings, see Gresh, *PLO.* Let us indicate in passing that our analyses will hardly dwell at all upon the existence of the communist movements. These were basically active in the occupied territories and had but little impact, as far as we are concerned, on PLO political strategy, and even less upon international terrorist activities. For a clear and exact chronology, see Baron, "L'OLP."

5. Interviews conducted in 1977 by a Lebanese researcher (who preferred not to commit her findings to writing) clearly show that in 1970 the PFLP leaders knew absolutely nothing about the Jordanian army. For them, a Marxist jargon took the place of hard facts, and they were convinced that Hussein's troops would revolt at their simple instigation. See also Khalil, "Internal Contradictions in the PFLP."

6. Vergès, *Pour les fidayine.*

7. July 1968: hijacking of an El Al Boeing at Algiers. Israel reacts with intense diplomatic pressure, obtaining from the International Federation of Airline Pilots' Associations a threat to boycott Algeria. The hostages are freed by the Algerian authorities and, two days later, in accordance with a quiet agreement between the two countries, Israel frees sixteen Arab prisoners.

December 1968: Attack on an El Al jet at the Athens airport. On the ground at Beirut airport, Israel destroys thirteen planes belonging to Arab companies, to make it clear to the Arab states that they must not facilitate aviational terrorism.

February 1969: Attack on an El Al Boeing at the Zurich airport, followed by attacks on El Al offices in Greece, Belgium, Germany, Iran, and Turkey, a bomb scare on a Swissair flight, etc.

8. Ann M. Lesch, review of *Palestine: The Arab-Israeli Conflict*, ed. Russen Stetler, *Journal of Palestine Studies* 11 (Spring 1974), pp. 131–36.

9. Leïla Khaled would subsequently publish her autobiography, *My People Shall Live*.

10. On this, see his memoir *The White House Years* (Boston: Little, Brown, 1979). On American Mideast policy, see also, for 1967–76, Quandt, *Decade of Decisions*.

11. Bar-Zohar and Haber, *Prince rouge*, p. 14.

12. According to Quandt (*Decade of decisions*), the members of Black September were originally Fatah dissidents who were close to Abu Jihad, a Fatah leader based in Jordan. Abu Jihad (*Palestiniens sans Patrie*) speaks of a spontaneous reaction by rank-and-file militants and a number of leaders. Other sources, mentioned by Cobban (*Palestinian Liberation Organization*), speak in terms of an initiative originating from the PLO's highest levels.

13. Bar-Zohar and Haber, *Prince rouge*.

14. O'Neil, "Toward a Typology," p. 43. The article by Schultz to which O'Neil refers appears in the same issue under the title "Conceptualizing Political Terrorism: A Typology," pp. 7–16.

15. The more terroristic a group becomes, the more difficult it is to gain reliable information on it. The departure of Wadi Hadad is a good illustration of this point. For some, this was the result of a split, while for others it was a maneuver orchestrated by George Habash, who wished to pursue terrorist activities without them being imputable to his organization. As weak as this latter interpretation might be, it cannot be rejected out of hand.

16. Arafat, interviewed in *Revue d'études palestiniennes* 14:7.

17. On this and a number of other points, see Hirst, *Gun and the Olive Branch*.

18. For the highly probable details, see Bar-Zohar and Haber, *Prince rouge*, pp. 234–38.

19. Klein, *Mort mercenaire*, p. 253.

20. Ibid., p. 112.

21. Here we quickly review these events, which received a great deal of commentary in their time. In July 1976, an Air France Airbus was hijacked over Entebbe by German skyjackers. The affair, organized by Wadi Hadad with the support of Idi Amin Dada, ended with a spectacular raid by the Israelis, who gunned the skyjackers down. For an account of the operation as viewed from the Israeli side, see Williams, "Entebbe Diary."

In October 1977, a mixed team of Germans and Palestinians hijacked a Lufthansa flight and demanded the liberation of Andreas Baader and Ulrike Meinhof together with a high ransom—the sinews of war never being absent from this sort of practice. The plane landed at Mogadishu, where an elite German army commando took it by assault, freed the passengers, and killed or captured all the terrorists.

22. For a sensationalist presentation of the Badawi Pact, see Sablier, *Fil rouge*, pp. 119–31.

23. Baudis, *Mort en keffieh*.

24. For higher-quality analyses, which differ with the usual psychological portraits given of Qaddafi, see Ibrahim, "Libye"; Bleuchot and Monastiri, "Logique unitaire libyenne"; and Dowes, "Qu'est-ce qu'un Etat terroriste?" See also Bessis, *Libye contemporaine*.

25. Gérard Michaud, "Terrorisme d'Etat." See also Carré and Michaud, *Frères musulmans*.

26. In 1980, the Rue Copernic attack was often interpreted as a manifestation of anti-Semitism carried out by a neofascist French far Right. Annie Kriegel was one of the first commentators to put forward a different interpretation, which we know today to have been the correct one. See Kriegel, *Refléxions sur les questions juives*, pp. 190–238, which redevelops and expands on a number of her articles. We should note that there are a number of hypotheses concerning the instigators of this attack, attributed by some to Abu Nidal, others to Wadi Hadad's successor Selim Abu Salem. It is likely that the Armenians of ASALA took part in the attack itself. The killings in the Rue des Rosiers were apparently directed by the Abu Nidal group. On the other hand, the October 9, 1982, attack on the synagogue in Rome was apparently carried out by a group which, led by Ibrahim El Amri, had split off from Abu Nidal's "Revolutionary Fatah" (this according to Villeneuve and Péret, *Histoire secrète du terrorisme*).

27. See Derogy, *Resistance and Revenge*.

28. Kurz and Merari, *ASALA,* p. 16. See also the writings of Bonnie Cordes, most especially "Armenian Terrorism."

29. Marian, "Terrorisme arménien après l'âge d'or." This article provides a relatively wide-ranging bibliography.

30. See especially the articles written by Georges Marion, Edwy Plenel, and J.-P. Péroncel-Hugoz in the November 21, 1986, issue of *Le Monde*. See also Bernières, "Terrorisme: pourquoi, qui et comment?"

31. The CSPPA (Comité de solidarité avec les prisonniers politiques arabes et du Proche-Orient [Committee for Solidarity with Arab and Middle Eastern Political Prisoners]) acronym appeared in Beirut in September 1986. It was first thought that LARF was using this as a cover. Later, other hypotheses favored the notion that the CSPPA was more closely linked to pro-Iranian groups.

32. Abdallah, *Pouvoir politique à Kobayat*

CHAPTER EIGHTEEN

1. See for example Meney, *Même les tueurs*.

2. See Muir, "Lebanon," p. 208. One finds a comparable set of arguments in Khalidi, "Conflict and Violence in Lebanon," who distinguishes between what he calls external and internal factors. See especially his chapter 4, "The Interplay between External and Internal Factors."

3. A few figures will give an idea of the complexity of the Lebanese communities. There are 1,300,000 Christians, of which 900,000 are Maronite, 250,000 Greek Orthodox, and 150,000 Greek Catholics. There are 175,000 Armenians, divided into Orthodox or Syriac Orthodox, Chaldean, and Protestant groups. There are 2,050,000 Muslims, of which 750,000 are Sunnites, 1,100,000 Shiites, and 200,000 Druzes. Lastly, there are 6,000 Israelis. These figures follow the

estimates given in MacDowall, "Lebanon." These estimates, which date from 1983, are approximate; the last census was taken in 1932.

4. For such an approach, see Corm, "Maronites et le pouvoir." This article offers an interesting analysis of the Maronites as well as of Shiites, Sunnites, and Druzes.

We ourselves have, in a much longer version of this chapter, used our general model to further analyze the Christian, Sunnite, and Druze denominations. See Wieviorka, *Dérives internationales.*

5. Seurat, "Quartier de Bâb Tebbâné."

## CHAPTER NINETEEN

1. Nasr, "Transition des chiites vers Beyrouth." See also Picard, "Enjeux politiques au Proche-Orient"; and idem, "De la communauté classe."

2. According to Nasr, in "Transition des chiites vers Beyrouth."

3. Here we use the term movement, as a means to distance ourselves from typologies that draw a distinction between various Shiite elites by way of promulgating a sociography of the Shiite community. See for example the classification into five categories that Deeb ("Lebanon") offers.

4. Rabinovich, *War for Lebanon,* p. 39.

5. In the August 18–19 issue of the *Daily Star.*

6. If we follow the March 11, 1986, issue of the bimonthly *Libanoscopie, Quelques points de repère sur le Liban* (published out of Paris by the Liban Moderne association), always meticulous and well-documented in its presentation, we may consider that "Hizbollah came from Iran at the time of the Israeli invasion (June 1982), by virtue of an agreement reached between Damascus and Tehran . . . They set up their headquarters in Baalbek . . . before gradually infiltrating the suburbs of south Beirut, where they consolidated their presence following the defeat of the Lebanese army and the multinational force, in February 1984." We should add that this "infiltration" was facilitated by a prior movement in the opposite direction: under the Shah, hundreds of Iranian dissenters came to Lebanon, where many received their military training, notably in the Palestinian camps, and were able to weave, both in Shiite and Sunnite milieus, political relations which served as the base for the infiltration of Khomeinism into Lebanon after 1979.

7. Shayegan, *Qu'est-ce qu'une révolution religieuse?*

8. The Amal movement's social policies are generally much more visible in the south than in Beirut. See Nab, " 'Happies' on the March," p. 4.

9. We should recall that it was such suicide-truck attacks that demolished the American embassy in Beirut in April; as well as the command headquarters of the multinational forces' French contingent, and the American marines' command headquarters, both in October.

10. Interview dated December 3, 1983, and cited in Wright, *Sacred Rage,* p. 82.

11. See "Israeli Experts Discuss Terrorism."

12. Kemp and Kfoury, "Terrorisme du troisième type."

13. Leba, "Chiisme," p. 109. A comparable viewpoint may be found in Raufer, "Révolution islamique et terrorisme," pp. 161–70.

14. "The Ayatollah's Outpost," in the July 1985 issue of the *Economist*. We should also point out that the leader of the commando which attempted, in France, to assassinate Shapour Bakhtiar, whose death warrant had been issued by Ayatollah Khomeini, was himself a Sunnite and not a Shiite.

15. Arkoun, "L'islam dans l'histoire," p. 22. See idem, *Lectures du Coran*.

CHAPTER TWENTY

1. See, for an illustration of this idea, Raufer's well-documented *Terrorisme au Moyen-Orient*.

2. On this point, see Villeneuve and Péret, *Histoire secrète du terrorisme*, which mentions Hagop Hagopian, Wadi Hadad, Carlos, Selim Abu Salem, and George Ibrahim Abdallah as early "playmates."

GENERAL CONCLUSION

1. See for example Madelin, *Galaxie terroriste;* and Raufer, *Terrorisme au Moyen-Orient*.

2. Lefort, *Democracy and Political Theory*.

3. From Carl Schmitt, *Der Begriff des Politischen,* cited by William Gueyden de Roussel in his introduction to *Légalité, légimité* (p. 21), the French translation of Schmitt's *Legalität und Legitimität*.

4. Furet, Liniers, and Raynaud, *Terrorisme et démocratie,* p. 10.

5. Villeneuve and Péret, *Histoire secrète du terrorisme*. See also Wieviorka and Wolton, *Terrorisme à la une*.

APPENDIX

1. Touraine, Dubet, Hegedus, and Wieviorka, *Lutte étudiante;* idem, *Antinuclear Protest*.

2. Touraine, Wieviorka, and Dubet, *Workers' Movement*.

3. Touraine, Dubet, Hegedus, and Wieviorka, *Pays contre l'Etat;* Touraine, Wieviorka, Dubet, and Strzelecki, *Solidarity*.

# Bibliography

Abdallah, Joseph. *Rapport du pouvoir politique à Kobayat*. Thèse de 3ᵉ cycle, Université de Paris—VII, 1983.

Acquaviva, Sabino. *Guerriglia e guerra revoluzionaria in Italia*. Milan: Rizzoli, 1979.

———. *Il seme religioso della rivolta*. Milan: Rusconi, 1979.

*Actes du colloque Frantz Fanon (31 mars–3 avril 1982)*. Paris: Présence africaine, 1984.

Aguire, Julien. *Operación Ogro: como y por que ejecutamos a Carrero Blanco*. San Sebastián: Hordago, 1977.

Alzueta, Joseba Goñi, and Erdozain, Jose M. Rodriguez. *Euskadi, la paz es posible*. Bilbao: Desclée de Brouwer, 1984.

Amigo, Angel. *Pertur, ETA, 71–76*. San Sebastián: Hordago, 1978.

———. *Operación Poncho: las fugas de Segovia*. San Sebastián: Hordago, 1978.

*Annual of Power and Conflict*. London: Institute for the Study of Conflict, 1985.

Apter, David A., and Sawa, Nagayo. *Against the State: Politics and Social Protest in Japan*. Cambridge, Mass.: Harvard University Press, 1984.

Arafat, Yasser. Interview in *Revue d'études palestiniennes* 14 (Winter 1984):3–9.

Aranguren, José Luis L. "El terrorismo como secularización de la violencia religiosa." In *Terrorismo y sociedad democratica*, ed. by Fernando Reinares-Nestares, Salvador Giner, et al., 71–78. Madrid: Akal, 1982.

Aranzadi, Juan. *Milenarismo vasco*. Madrid: Taurus, 1982.

Arendt, Hannah. *Crisis of the Republic*. New York: Harcourt Brace Jovanovich, 1972.

———. *The Origins of Totalitarianism*. 3d ed. London: Allen & Unwin, 1967.

Arkoun, Mohammed. "L'islam dans l'histoire." *Maghreb-Machreq* 102 (October–December 1983):5–24.

———. *Lectures du Coran: Islam d'hier et d'aujourd'hui*. Paris: Maisonneuve et Larose, 1982.

Aron, Raymond. *History and the Dialectic of Violence: An Analysis of Sartre's*

*"Critique de la raison dialectique."* Trans. Barry Cooper. London: Harper & Row, 1975.

————. *The Opium of the Intellectuals.* Trans. Terence Kilmartin. New York: Norton & Co., 1962.

Arpal, Jesus. "Solidaridades elementales y organizaciones colectivas en el País Vasco (cuadrillas, txokos, asociaciones)." In *Processus sociaux, idéologies, et pratiques culturelles dans la société basque,* ed. Pierre Bidart, 119–28 and 129–54. Publications de l'Université de Pau et des pays de l'Adour, 1985.

Asad, Talal, and Roger Owen, eds. *Sociology of "Developing Societies": The Middle East.* New York: Monthly Review Press, 1983.

Atienza, Javier Corcuera. *Origines, ideologia, y organización del nacionalismo vasco: 1876–1904.* Madrid: Siglo Veintiuno, 1979.

"Ayatollah's Outpost." *The Economist* (July 1985).

Ayçoberry, Pierre. *La question nazie.* Paris: Seuil, 1979.

Bandres, Juan Maria. "Las situaciones de violencia como realidad politica." In *Terrorismo y sociedad democratica,* ed. by Fernando Reinares, Salvador Giner, et al., 61–69. Madrid: Akal, 1982.

Baroja, Julio Caro. *El laberinto vasco.* San Sebastián: Txertoa, 1984.

Baron, Xavier. "L'OLP: 20 ans d'histoire." *Revue d'études palestiniennes* 14 (Winter 1984):155–65.

*Barro y asfalto.* Cuaderno Borrokan: Euskaldunak Derrok Bak, n.d.

Barrué, Jean. "Bakounine et Netchaïev." *Spartacus* 43 (November–December 1971).

Bar-Zohar, Michel, and Eitan Haber. *Le prince rouge.* Paris: Fayard, 1984.

Baudis, Dominique. *La mort en keffieh.* Paris: France-Empire, 1980.

Baumann, "Bommi." *Tupamaros Berlin-Ouest.* Paris: Les Presses d'Aujourd'hui, 1976.

Bawab, Dalal Bizri. *Introduction à l'étude des mouvements islamistes sunnites au Liban.* Thèse de 3ᵉ cycle, Paris, EHESS, 1984.

Baynac, Jacques. *Les socialistes révolutionnaires.* Paris: Robert Laffont, 1979.

Beaubernard, R. *Un "laboratoire sociale" au XIXe siècle.* Avallon: Editions de Civry, 1981.

Becker, Howard S. *Outsiders: Studies in the Sociology of Deviance.* New York: Free Press, 1963.

Becker, Jillian. *Hitler's Children.* London: Michael Joseph, 1977.

Ben-Jelloun-Ollivier, Nadia. *La Palestine. Un enjeu. Des stratégies. Un destin.* Paris: FNSP, 1984.

Ben Rafael, Eliezer. "Le conflit de guérilla: une approche sociologique." *Sociologie du travail* 4 (1986):426–42.

Bentivegna, Sara. "Violenza politica e quotidiani di partito." In *Violenza sociale e violenza politica nell'Italia degli anni 70,* ed. G. Statera, 195–213. Milan: Franco Angeli, 1983.

Berardi, Franco ("Bifo"). *Le ciel est enfin tombé sur la terre.* Paris: Seuil, 1978.

Beraud, Bernard. *La gauche révolutionnaire au Japon.* Paris: Seuil, 1970.

Berelson, B. R., and G. K. Steiner. *Human Behavior: An Inventory of Scientific Findings.* New York: Harcourt, Brace & World, 1964.

Beristain, Antonio. "Los terrorismos en el País Vasco y en España." In *Violencia y política en Euskadi*, ed. Fernando Reinares, 169–95. Bilbao: Desclée de Brouwer, 1984.

Bernières, Jean de. "Terrorisme: pourquoi, qui et comment?" *Les cahiers de l'Orient* 3 (1986):145–60.

Besançon, Alain. *Histoire et expérience du moi*. Paris: Flammarion, 1967.

———. *Les origines intellectuelles du léninisme*. Paris: Callmann-Lévy, 1977.

———. *Le tsarevitch immolé*. Paris: Plon, 1967.

Bessis, Juliette. *La Libye contemporaine*. Paris: L'Harmattan, 1986.

Bidart, Pierre, ed. *Processus sociaux, idéologies et pratiques culturelles dans la société basque*. Publications de l'Université de Pau et des pays de l'Adour, 1985.

Bigo, Didier, and Daniel Hermant. "La relation terroriste." *Etudes polémologiques* 30 (1984):45–61, 31 (1984):75–100.

———. "Simulation et dissimulation: les politiques de la lutte contre le terrorisme en France." *Sociologie du travail* 4 (1986):507–27.

Binder, L., ed. *Politics in Lebanon*. New York: John Wiley & Sons, 1966.

Birnbaum, Pierre. "Mobilisations, structures sociales, et types d'Etat." *Revue française de sociologie* 24 (1983):421–39.

Blackmer, D. L. M., and Sydney Tarrow, eds. *Il communismo in Italia e Francia*. Milan: Etas Libris, 1976.

Bleuchot, Hervé, and Taoufik Monastiri. "La logique unitaire libyenne et les modèles du colonel Kadhafi." *Hérodote* 36 (1985):83–104.

Bocca, Giorgio. *Moro, una tragedia italiana: le lettere, i documenti, le polemiche*. Milan: Tascabili Bompiani, 1978.

———. *Noi terroristi, 12 anni di lotta armata recostruiti e discussi con i protagonisti*. Milan: Garzanti: 1985.

Bonanate, Luigi, ed. *Dimensioni del terrorismo politico*. Milan: Franco Angeli, 1979.

Bonnell, Victoria. *Roots of Rebellion: Workers' Politics and Organization in Saint Petersburg and Moscow, 1900–1914*. Berkeley: University of California Press, 1983.

Bourricaud, François. *Le bricolage idéologique*. Paris: Presses Universitaires de France, 1980.

Braudel, Fernand. "Histoire et sociologie." In *Traité de sociologie*, ed. Georges Gurvitch, vol. 1. Paris: Armand Colin, 1958.

Bremm, Jack W., and Arthur R. Cohen. *Explorations in Cognitive Dissonance*. New York: John Wiley & Sons, 1962.

Broehl, Wayne G. *The Molly Maguires*. Cambridge, Mass.: Harvard University Press, 1964.

Busquet, Patrick, and Claude Vidal. *Le pays basque et sa liberté*. Paris: Le Sycomore, 1980.

Caciagli, Mario. "Il resistibile declino della Democrazia Cristiana." In *Il sistema politico italiano*, ed. Gianfranco Pasquino, 101–27. Rome: Laterza, 1985.

Calvi, Fabrizio. *Camarade P 38*. Paris: Grasset, 1982.

———. *Italie 77. Le "mouvement". Les intellectuels*. Paris: Seuil, 1977.

Camus, Albert. *The Rebel*. Trans. Anthony Bower. New York: Knopf, 1954.

Canovan, Margaret. *Populism.* New York: Harcourt Brace Jovanovich, 1981.

Carré, Olivier. *L'idéologie palestinienne de résistance.* Paris: FNSP-Armand Colin, 1972.

Carré, Olivier, and Gérard Michaud. *Les Frères musulmans.* Paris: Gallimard, 1983.

Cartwright, Dorwin, and Alvin Zander. *Group Dynamics: Research and Theory,* 3d ed. London: Tavistock Publications, 1968.

Castellani, Lucio, ed. *Aut. Op.* Rome: Savelli, 1980.

Cavallini, Massimo. *Il terrorismo in fabbrica.* Rome: Editori Riuniti, 1978.

Chaliand, Gérard. *The Palestinian Resistance.* Harmondsworth: Penguin, 1972.

————. *Terrorismes et guérillas.* Paris: Flammarion, 1985.

————, ed. *Guerilla Strategies: An Historical Anthology from the Long March to Afghanistan.* Berkeley: University of California Press, 1982.

Charnay, Jean-Pierre. "L'homme est un zoon politikon: il tue pour des idées." In *Terrorisme et culture,* ed. Jean-Paul Charnay as a supplement to *Cahiers de la FEDN* 11 (1981).

————. "Théorie stratégique de la praxis terroriste." In *Terrorisme et culture,* ed. Jean-Paul Charnay, as a supplement to *Cahiers de la FEDN* 11 (1981).

Chazel, François. "La mobilization politique: problèmes et dimensions." *Revue française de sciences politiques* 25 (1975):502–16.

————. "Les ruptures révolutionnaires." In *Traité de science politique,* ed. Madeleine Grawitz and Jean Leca, vol. 2. 635–84. Paris: Presses Universitaires de France, 1985.

Chbarou, Bachbar, and Waddah Charara. "Une mosquée de Beyrouth aujourd'hui: unité de la communauté et diversité des croyants." In *Mouvements communautaires et espaces urbains au Machreq,* 21–43. CERMOC: Sindbad, 1985.

Cherki, Eddy, and Michel Wieviorka. "Luttes sociales en Italie: magistrats et autoréducteurs." *Les temps modernes* (November 1976):635–73.

————. "Luttes sociales en Italie: les mouvements d'autoréduction à Turin. *Les temps modernes* (June 1975):1793–1831.

Chesnais, Jean-Claude. *Histoire de la violence.* Paris: Rabert Laffont, 1981.

Chevalier, Louis. *Laboring Classes and Dangerous Classes in Paris During the First Half of the 19th Century.* Trans. by Frank Jellinek. Princeton, N.J.: Princeton University Press, 1973.

Clark, Robert P. *The Basque Insurgents: ETA 1952–1980.* Madison: University of Wisconsin Press, 1984.

Cline, Ray S., and Yonah Alexander. *Terrorism as State-Sponsored Covert Warfare.* Fairfax, Va.: Hero Books, 1986.

Clutterbuck, Richard. *Living with Terrorism.* London: Faber & Faber, 1975.

Cobban, Helena. *The Palestinian Liberation Organization: People, Power and Politics.* Cambridge: Cambridge University Press, 1984.

Cohn, Norman. *Pursuit of the Millennium.* London: Oxford University Press, 1970.

Collectif A Traverso. *Radio Alice, radio libre.* Paris: Jean-Pierre Delarge, 1977.

Collectivo Prigioneri Comunisti delle Brigate Rosse. *L'ape e il comunista,* special issue of *Correspondenza Internazionale* 16–17 (Oct.–Dec. 1980).

Comitate Autonomi Operai di Roma, ed. *Autonomia Operaia*. Rome: Savelli, 1976.

Comitato 7 aprile e Colegio di difesa. *Processo all'Autonomia*. Rome: Lerici, 1979.

Commission internationale d'enquête. *La mort d'Ulrike Meinhof*. Paris: Maspero, 1979.

Confino, Michel. *Violence dans la violence, le débat Boukharine-Netchaïëv*. Paris: Maspero, 1973.

Cordes, Bonnie. "Armenian Terrorism." In *Trends in International Terrorism, 1982–1983*, 19–25. Santa Monica: Rand Corporation, 1984.

Corm, Georges G. *Collapse in the Middle East: From Suez to the Invasion of Lebanon*. Cambridge: Cambridge University Press, 1984.

――――. *Géopolitique du conflit libanais*. Paris: La Découverte, 1986.

――――. "Les maronites et le pouvoir économique au Liban." *Esprit* (May 1985):77–88.

Coser, Lewis. *Functions of Social Conflict*. New York: Free Press, 1964.

――――. *Men of Ideas: A Sociologist's View*. New York: Free Press, 1965.

Crenshaw, Martha. "The Causes of Terrorism." *Comparative Politics* 139 (July 4, 1981):379–400.

――――, ed. *Terrorism, Legitimacy, and Power*. Middletown: Wesleyan University Press, 1983.

Crouch, Colin, and Alessandro Pizzorno. *The Resurgence of Class Conflict in Western Europe since 1968*. 2 vols. London: Macmillan, 1978.

Dalla Chiesa, Nando. "Il terrorismo di sinistra." In *Terrorismi in Italia*, ed. Donatella Della Porta, 293–330. Bologna: Il Mulino, 1984.

Debray, Régis. *La critique des armes*, 2 vols. Paris: Seuil, 1974.

――――. *Teachers, Writers, Celebrities: The Intellectuals of Modern France*. Trans. David Macey. London: Routledge, Chapman & Hall, 1985.

Deeb, M. K. "Lebanon: Prospects for National Reconciliation in the Mid-1980's." *The Middle East Journal* 38, No. 2 (Spring 1984):267–83.

Della Porta, Donatella. "Recruitment Process in Clandestine Political Organizations: Italian Leftwing Terrorism." Paper read at international colloquium *Transformation of Structure into Action*. Amsterdam, June 1986.

――――. ed. *Terrorismi in Italia*. Bologna: Il Mulino, 1984.

Della Porta, Donatella, and Giancarlo Caselli. "La storia delle Brigate Rosse: strutture organizzative e strategie d'azione." In *Terrorismi in Italia*, ed. Donatella Della Porta, 153–221. Bologna: Il Mulino, 1984.

Della Porta, Donatella, and Gianfranco Pasquino. *Terrorismo e violenza politica*. Bologna: Il Mulino, 1983.

Della Porta, Donatella, and Maurizio Rossi. *Cifre crudeli: bilancio dei terrorismi italiani*. Bologna: Istituto Carlo Cattaneo, 1984.

Derogy, Jacques. *Resistance and Revenge: The Armenian Assassination of Turkish Leaders Responsible for the 1915 Massacres and Deportations*. New Brunswick, N.J.: Transaction Publications, 1990.

Dispot, Laurent. *La machine à Terreur*. Paris: Grasset et Fasquelle, 1978.

Dobson, Christopher, and Ronald Payne. *The Carlos Complex*. New York: Putnam, 1977.

Dowes, Allan. "Qu'est-ce qu'un État terroriste?" *Les Cahiers de l'Orient* 3 (1986):171–94.

Dowling, Joseph A. "Prolegomena to a Psychohistorical Study of Terrorism." In *International Terrorism in the Contemporary World,* ed. Maurice H. Livingstone, 223–30. Westport, Conn.: Greenwood Press, 1978.

Dror, Yehezkel. "Terrorism as a Challenge to Governments." In *Terrorism, Legitimacy and Power,* ed. Martha Crenshaw, 65–90. Middletown: Wesleyan University Press, 1983.

Dubet, François. *La galère: jeunes en survie.* Paris: Fayard, 1987.

Dubois, Pierre. *Travail et conflit dans l'industrie.* Thèse de doctorat ès lettres, Paris, 1979.

Dufour, Roger. "Les ressorts psychologiques de l'efficacité publicitaire du terrorisme." *Etudes polémologiques* 38 (February 1986):35–37.

Dumont, Louis. "L'Allemagne répond à la France: le peuple et la nation chez Herder et Fichte." *Libre* 6 (1979):233–50.

Durand, Claude. *Chômage et violence.* Paris: Galilée, 1981.

Eckstein, Harry. "Explaining Collective Violence." In *Handbook of Political Conflict,* ed. Ted Robert Gurr, 135–66. New York: Free Press, 1980.

———. "On the Etiology of Internal Wars." *History and Theory* 4, No. 2(1965):133–63.

Elórza, Antonio. *Ideologias del nacionalismo vasco.* San Sebastián: Txertoa, 1978.

Fanon, Frantz. *The Wretched of the Earth,* with a foreword by Jean-Paul Sartre. Translated by Constance Farrington. New York: Grove Press, 1963.

Fauré, Christine. *Quatre femmes terroristes contre le tzar.* Paris: Maspero, 1978.

———. *Terre, terreur, liberté.* Paris: Maspero, 1979.

Ferrajoli, Luigi. "Critica della violenza come critica della politica." In *Quaderni di Ombre Rosse* 2, 39–69. Rome: Savelli, 1979.

Ferraresi, Franco. "La destra eversiva." In *Terrorismi in Italia,* ed. Donatella Della Porta, 227–32. Bologna: Il Mulino, 1984.

Ferrarotti, Franco. *Alle radici della violenza.* Milan: Rizzoli, 1979.

———. *L'ipnosi della violenza.* Milan: Rizzoli, 1980.

Ferri, Edgarda. *Dov'era il padre.* Milan: Rizzoli, 1982.

Festinger, Leon. *Conflict, Decision, and Dissonance.* London: Tavistock Publications, 1959.

———. *Theory of Cognitive Dissonance.* Evanston, Ill.: Row, Peterson, 1957.

Festinger, Leon, and Elliot T. Aronson. "Arousal and Reduction of Dissonance in Social Contexts." In *Group Dynamics,* ed. Cartwright and Zander, 125–36. London: Tavistock Publications, 1968.

Fetscher, Irving, and Günther Rohrmoser. *Ideologien und Strategien.* Analysen zum Terrorismus, vol. 1. Opladen: Westdeutscher Verlag, 1981.

Flamini, Gianni. *Il partito del golpe.* 2 vols. Ferrare: Italo Bovolenta, 1981–1982.

Foss, Daniel A., and Ralph Larkin. *Beyond Revolution.* South Hadley, Mass.: Bergin & Garvey, 1986.

Fournier, Louis. *FLQ: Histoire d'un mouvement clandestin.* Montreal: Québec-Amérique, 1982.

Fowler, W. Warner. *Terrorism, Data Bases: A Comparison of Missions, Methods and Systems.* Santa Monica: Rand Corporation, 1981.

Francq, Bernard. "Les Cellules communistes combattantes: les deux figures d'une inversion." *Sociologie du travail* 4 (1986):458–83.

Friedlander, Saül. *L'antisémitisme nazi.* Paris: Seuil, 1971.

Furet, François, Antoine Liniers, and Philippe Raynaud. *Terrorisme et démocratie.* Paris: Fayard/Fondation Saint-Simon, 1985.

Gabeira, Fernando. *Les guérilleros sont fatigués.* Paris: A.-M. Métailié, 1980.

Galleni, Mauro, ed. *Rapporto sul terrorismo: le stragi, gli agguati, i sequestri, le sigle 1969–1980.* Milan: Saggi Rizzoli, 1981.

Galli, Giorgio. *Storia del partito armato.* Milan: Rizzoli, 1986.

Garmendia, Jose Mari. *Historia de ETA.* 2 vols. San Sebastián: Haranburu, 1980.

Garmendia, Jose Mari, and Alberto Elordi. *La resistancia Vasca.* San Sebastián: Haranburu, 1982.

Gaucher, Roland. *The Terrorists, from Tsarist Russia to the O.A.S.* Trans. Paula Sperlin. London: Secker and Warburg, 1968.

Gaudemar, Jean-Paul de. *Usines et ouvriers, figures du nouvel ordre productif.* Paris: Maspero, 1980.

Gavi, Philippe, Jean-Paul Sartre, and Pierre Victor. *On a raison de se revolter.* Paris: Gallimard, 1974.

Geertz, Clifford. *Old Societies and New State.* Glencoe, Ill.: Free Press, 1963.

Geismar, Alain. *L'engrenage terroriste.* Paris: Fayard, 1981.

Gellner, Ernest. *Nations and Nationalism.* Ithaca, N.Y.: Cornell University Press, 1983.

Gerlach, L. P., and V. H. Hine. *People, Power, Change: Movements of Social Transformation.* New York: Bobbs-Merrill, 1970.

Ghezzi, Giorgio. *Processo al sindacato.* Bari: De Donato, 1981.

Giorgio [pseud]. *Profession: terroriste.* Paris: Mazarine, 1982.

Girardi, Giulio. *Coscienza operaia oggi.* Bari: De Donato, 1980.

Gitlin, Todd. *The Whole World Is Watching: Mass Media in the Making and Unmaking of the New Left.* Berkeley: University of California Press, 1980.

Goikoetxea, Eugenia Ramirez. "Associations collectives et relations interprofessionnelles au Pays basque: ethnicité et revendication culturelle." In *Processus sociaux, idéologies, et pratiques culturelles dans la société basque,* ed. Pierre Bidart, 119–28. Publications de l'Université de Pau et des pays de l'Adour, 1985.

Goleman, Daniel. "The Making of a Terrorist Could Begin in Childhood." *International Herald Tribune,* 12 September 1986.

Graham, Hugh Davis, and Ted Robert Gurr, eds. *Violence in America.* 2d ed. Beverly Hills, Calif.: Sage Publications, 1979.

Gramsci, Antonio. *Il materialismo storico e la filosofia di Benedetto Croce,* ed. Franco De Felice and Valentino Parlato. Turin: Einaudi 1966.

Graziano, Luigi, and Sydney Tarrow, eds. *La crisi italiana,* 2 vols. Turin: Einaudi, 1979.

Gresh, Alain. *The PLO—The Struggle Within: Towards an Independent Palestinian State.* 2d ed. Trans. A. M. Berrett. London: Zed Books, 1988.

Guérin, Daniel. *Anarchism: From Theory to Practice.* Trans. Mary Klopper. New York: Monthly Review Press, 1970.

Gurr, Ted Robert. *Why Men Rebel.* Princeton: Princeton University Press, 1970.

————, ed. *Handbook of Political Conflict.* New York: Free Press, 1980.

Habash, George. Interview in *Revue d'études palestiniennes* 14 (Winter 1984):10–16.

Hacker, Friedrich. *Aggression et violence dans le monde moderne.* Paris: Calmann-Lévy, 1972.

————. *Crusaders, Criminals, Crazies: Terror and Terrorism in Our Time.* New York: N. W. Horton & Co., 1976.

Halimi, Gisèle. *Le procès de Burgos,* with a foreword by Jean-Paul Sartre. Paris: Gallimard, 1971.

Hamon, Alain, and Jean-Charles Marchand. *Action directe: du terrorisme français à l'euro-terrorisme.* Paris: Seuil, 1986.

Hamzé, Ahmed. Interview in *Revue d'études palestiniennes* 15 (Spring 1985):6–8.

Hardman, J. B. S. "Terrorism." In *Encyclopedia of the Social Sciences,* ed. Edwin R. A. Seligman, 14:575–79. New York: Macmillan, 1967.

Haupt, Georges, Michael Löwy, and Claudie Weill. *Les marxistes et la question nationale, 1848–1914.* Paris: Maspero, 1974.

Haynal, André, Miklos Molnar, and Gérard de Puymège. *Le fanatisme.* Paris: Stock, 1980.

Herman, Edward. *The Real Terror Network.* Boston: South End Press, 1982.

Hirst, David. *The Gun and the Olive Branch.* London: Faber, 1977.

Hobsbawm, Eric. *Primitive Rebels.* Manchester: Manchester University Press, 1959.

Hoffman, Bruce. *Rightwing Terrorism in West Germany.* Santa Monica: Rand Corporation, 1986.

Horowitz, Irving Louis. "The Rationalization of Terrorism and Its Unanticipated Consequences." In *Terrorism, Legitimacy, and Power,* ed. Martha Crenshaw, 38–51. Middletown: Wesleyan University Press, 1983.

Hourani, Albert. "Ideologies of the Mountain and the City." In *Essays on Crisis in Lebanon,* ed. R. Owen, 33–41. London: Ithaca Press, 1976.

Hudson, Michael. "The Breakdown of Democracy in Lebanon." *Journal of International Affairs,* 38, No. 2 (Winter 1985):277–92.

Huntington, Samuel. *Political Order in Changing Societies.* New Haven: Yale University Press, 1968.

Ibrahim, Amr. "L'effervescence minoritaire: la guerre au Liban et ses dialectiques minoritaires." *Esprit* 77–78 (May–June 1983):115–43.

————. "La Libye ou l'institution politique du terrorisme." *Esprit* 94–95 (October–November 1989):205–16.

Ionescu, Gheta, and Ernest Gellner, eds. *Populism: Its Meanings and National Characteristics.* London: Weidenfeld and Nicolson, 1972.

"Israeli Experts Discuss Terrorism and the Motivation of Terrorists with the IDF Journal." *IDF Journal* 2, No. 3 (May 1985):86–89.

Israeli, Raphael. *PLO in Lebanon: Selected Documents.* London: Weidenfeld and Nicolson, n.d.

Jacquard, Roland. *Les dossiers secrets du terrorisme.* Paris: Albin Michel, 1985.

Janke, Peter. *Guerillas and Terrorist Organizations: A World Directory and Bibliography.* Brighton (G. B.): Harvester Press, 1985.

Jaureguiberry, Francis. *Question nationale et mouvements sociaux au Pays basque Sud.* Thèse de 3e cycle, Paris, EHESS, 1983.

Jihad, Abu. Interview in *Journal of Palestine Studies* 14, No. 2 (Winter 1985):3–12.

———. *Palestiniens sans patrie.* Paris: Fayolle, 1978.

Johnson, Michael. "Popular Movements and Primordial Loyalties in Beirut." In *Sociology of "Developing Societies": The Middle East,* ed. Talal Asad and Roger Owen, 178–94. New York: Monthly Review Press, 1983.

Julliard, Jacques. *Clemenceau, briseur de grèves.* Paris: Julliard, 1965.

———. *Fernand Pelloutier et les origines du syndicalisme d'action directe.* Paris: Seuil, 1971.

Kaplan, A. "The Psychodynamics of Terrorism." *Terrorism* 1 (1978):237–54.

Katz, Robert. *I giorni nell'Ira.* Rome: Adn Kronos, 1982.

Kawahara, Hiroshi. "L'intreccio tradizionalismo-modernismo nel terrorismo giapponese." In *Terrorismo e violenza politica,* ed. Donatella Della Porta and Gianfranco Pasquini, 207–34. Bologna: Il Mulino, 1983.

Kedourie, Elie. *Nationalism.* London: Hutchinson and Co., 1960.

Kemp, Percy, and Assaf Kfoury. "Un terrorisme du troisième type." *Esprit* 10–11 (October 1984):175–79.

Keniston, K. *Young Radicals.* New York: Harcourt, Brace and World, 1968.

Kepel, Gilles. *Muslim Extremism in Egypt: The Prophet & Pharaoh.* Trans. Jon Rothschild. Berkeley: University of California Press, 1985.

Khaled, Leïla. *My People Shall Live: The Autobiography of a Revolutionary.* London: Hodder & Stoughton, 1973.

Khalidi, Walid. "Conflict and Violence in Lebanon: Confrontation in the Middle East." *Harvard Studies in International Affairs* 38 (1979).

Khalil, As'ad Abu. "International Contradictions in the PFLP: Decision-Making and Policy Orientations." *The Middle East Journal* 41, no. 3 (Summer 1987):361–78.

Klein, Hans-Joachim. *La mort mercenaire.* Paris: Seuil, 1980.

Konrad, Gyorzy and Ivan Szelenyi. *La marche au pouvoir des intellectuels.* Paris: Seuil, 1979.

Kornhauser, William. *The Politics of Mass Society.* London: Routledge & Kegan Paul, 1960.

Kriegel, Annie. *Reflexions sur les questions juives.* Paris: Hachette, 1984.

Krutwig, Federico [Fernando Sarrailh de Ihartza, pseu.]. *Vasconia.* Buenos Aires: Norbait, 1962.

Kurz, Anat, and Ariel Merari. *ASALA: International Terror or Political Tool.* Jerusalem: Jerusalem Post, 1985.

Lacoste, Yves. "Les embrouillements gèopolitiques des centres de l'islam." *Hérodote* 36 (January–March 1985):3–48.

Landaburu, Javier de. *La causa del pueblo vasco.* Paris: n.p., 1956.

Lange, Peter. "Il PCI e i possibili esiti della crisi italiana." In *La crisi italiana,* ed. Luigi Graziano and Sydney Tarrow, 657–718. Turin: Einaudi, 1979.

Lanternari, Vittorio. *Les mouvements religieux de liberté et de salut des peuples opprimés*. Paris: Maspero, 1962.

Laqueur, Walter. *Terrorism*. 2d ed. London: Weidenfeld and Nicolson, 1987.

Laroui, Abdallah. *The Crisis of the Arab Intellectual: Traditionalism or Historicism?* Trans. Diarmid Cammell. Berkeley: University of California Press, 1977.

Larronde, J.-C. *Le nationalisme basque: Son origine et son idéologie dans l'oeuvre de Sabino de Arana*. Thèse de doctorat en droit, Université de Bordeaux-I, 1972.

Lasswell, Harold. *Psychopathology and Politics*. New York: Viking, 1960.

Laurent, Anne, and Antoine Basbous. *Guerres secrètes au Liban*. Paris: Gallimard, 1987.

Laurent, Roland. *L'Internationale terroriste démasqué*. Paris: Alain Lefeuvre, 1981.

Leba, Assemaani. "Le chiisme et le renouveau islamique contemporain." *Hérodote* 36 (January 1985):105–9.

Lefort, Claude. *Democracy and Political Theory*. Trans. David Macey. Minneapolis: University of Minnesota Press, 1989.

———. *Les formes de l'histoire*. Paris: Gallimard, 1978.

Lequin, Yves. *Les ouvriers de la région lyonnaise*. 2 vols. Lyon: Presses Universitaires de Lyon, 1977.

Lerner, Daniel, and Lucille W. Pevsner. *The Passing of Traditional Society: Modernizing the Middle East*. Glencoe, Ill.: Free Press, 1958.

Lerner, G., L. Manconi, and M. Sinibaldi. *Un strano movimento di strani studenti*. Milan: Feltrinelli, 1978.

Letamendia, Francisco ("Ortzi"). *Les Basques: un peuple contre les Etats*. Paris: Seuil, 1977.

———. *Denuncia en el Parlamento*. San Sebastián: Txertoa, 1978.

———. *El no vasco a la reforma*. 2 vols. San Sebastián: Txertoa, 1979.

———. *Historia de Euskadi: el nacionalismo vasco y ETA*. Barcelona: Iberica de Ediciones y Publicaciones, 1971.

Lewis, Bernard. *The Assassins: A Radical Sect in Islam*. London: Weidenfeld and Nicolson, 1967.

———. *Le retour de l'islam*. Paris: Gallimard, 1985.

Liniers, Antoine. "Objections contre une prise d'armes." In *Terrorisme et démocratie*, ed. François Furet, Antoine Liniers, and Philippe Raynaud, 137–224. Paris: Fayard/Fondation Saint-Simon, 1985.

Linz, Juan J. "An Authoritarian Regime: Spain." *Cleavages, Ideologies and Party Systems*, ed. Eric Allardt et al., 291–341. Helsinki: The Academic Bookstore, 1964.

———. *Conflicto en Euskadi*. Madrid: Espasa Calpe, 1986.

Losito, Gianni. "La violenza politica della stampa quotidiana italiana: principali resultati di una ricerca; analisi del contenuto." In *Violenza sociale e violenza politica nell'Italia degli anni 70*, ed. G. Statera, 107–54. Milan: Franco Angeli, 1983.

MacDowall, D. "Lebanon, a Conflict of Minorities." In *Minority Rights Group*, 61. London: 1986.

Madelin, Philippe. *La galaxie terroriste.* Paris: Plon, 1986.

Maitron, Jean. *Le mouvement anarchiste en France.* 2 vols. Paris: Maspero, 1975.

———. *Ravachol et les anarchistes.* Paris: Julliard, 1964.

Manconi, Luigi. *Vivere con il terrorismo.* Milan: Arnoldo Mondadori, 1980.

Manconi, Luigi, Santina Mobiglia, and Andrea Rolli. *La violenza e la politica.* Rome: Savelli, 1979.

Mander, Jerry. *Four Arguments for the Elimination of Television.* New York: Quill, 1977.

Manoukian, Paul. *Le fruit de la patience.* Paris: Centurion, 1983.

Marcus, Joseph. *Social and Political History of the Jews in Poland, 1919–1939.* Amsterdam: Mouton, 1983.

Marian, Michel. "Le terrorisme arménien après l'âge d'or." *Esprit,* special "Terrorisme" issue (October–November 1984):47–64.

Marx, Gary T. "Issueless Riots." In *Collective Violence,* ed. James F. Short, Jr., and Marwin E. Wolfgang. Chicago: Aldins Atherton, 1972.

———. *Protest and Prejudice: A Study of Belief in a Black Community.* New York: Harper, 1969.

———. *Racial Conflict.* Boston: Little Brown, 1971.

Maxwell Brown, Richard. "Historical Patterns of American Violence." In *Violence in America,* ed. Hugh Davis Graham and Ted Robert Gurr, 19–48. Beverly Hills, Calif.: Sage Publications, 1979.

Mazzei, Giuseppe. *Utopia e terrore: Le radici ideologiche della violenza politica.* Florence: Le Monnier, 1981.

Melucci, Alberto. "New Movements, Terrorism, and the Political System." *Socialist Review* 56 (1981):97–136.

Meney, Patrick. *Même les tueurs ont une mère.* Paris: Table ronde, 1986.

Michaud, Gérard. "L'Etat de barbarie: Syrie 1979–1982." *Esprit* 94–95 [1984]. 2d ed. (1986):156–70.

———. "Terrorisme d'Etat, terrorisme contre l'Etat: le cas syrien." *Esprit,* special "Terrorisme" issue (October–November 1984); 2d ed. (1986): 171–84.

Michaud, Yves. *Violence et politique.* Paris: Gallimard, 1978.

Mickolus, Edward. *Transnational Terrorism: A Chronology of Events, 1968–1979.* Westport: Greenwood Press, 1981.

Minna, Rosario. "Il terrorismo di destra." In *Terrorismi in Italia,* ed. Donatella Della Porta, 21–72. Bologna: Il Mulino, 1989.

Mongin, Olivier. "Les métamorphoses de la violence." *Esprit* 94–95, 2d ed. (1986):235–44.

———. "Terrorismes: aspects conjoncturels et facteurs structurels." *Esprit* 94–95, 2d ed. (1986):1–7.

Morel, Jean-Pierre. *Le roman insupportable: l'Internationale littéraire et la France.* Paris: Gallimard, 1985.

Moscovici, Serge. *Psychologie des minorités actives.* Paris: Presses Universitaires de France, 1979.

———. *Psychologie sociale.* Paris: Presses Universitaires de France, 1984.

Muir, Jim. "Lebanon: Arena of Conflict, Crucible of Peace." *Middle East Journal* 38, No. 2 (Spring 1984):208.

Muller, Edward N. "The Psychology of Political Protest and Violence." In *Handbook of Political Conflict,* ed. Ted Robert Gurr, 69–99. New York: Free Press, 1980.

Nab, Ibrahim Abu. " 'Happies' on the March." *Middle East International* 213 (November 1983):4.

Nacacche, Georges. *Un rêve libanais, 1943–1983.* Beirut: FMA, 1983.

Nasr, Salim. "L'islam politique et l'Etat libanais (1920–1975)." In *L'islam et l'Etat dans le monde d'aujourd'hui,* ed. by Olivier Carré. Paris: Presses Universitaires de France, 1982.

———. "La transition des chiites vers Beyrouth: mutations sociales et mobilisations communautaires à la veille de 1975." In *Mouvements communautaires et espaces urbains au Machreq,* 86–116. CER-MOC: Sindbad, 1985.

Nasri Messara, Antoine. *Le modèle politique libanais et sa survie: essai sur la classification et l'aménagement d'un système consociatif.* Beirut: Publications de l'Université libanaise, 1983.

Naville, Pierre. *La révolution et les intellectuels.* Paris: Gallimard, 1985.

Negri, Toni. *Dall'operaio massa all'operaio sociale.* Milan: Multhiphia Edizioni, 1979.

———. *Il dominio e il sabottagio.* Milan: Feltrinelli, 1978.

———. *Italie rouge et noire,* with a preface by Bernard Henri-Lévy. Paris: Hachette, 1985.

Netanyahu, Benjamin, ed. *Terrorism: How the West Can Win.* New York: Farrar, Straus & Giroux, 1986.

Newman, Graeme. *Understanding Violence.* New York: Harper & Row, 1979.

Niebuhr, Reinhold. *Moral Man and Immoral Society.* New York: Charles Scribner's Sons, 1932.

Nisbet, Robert. *Social Change and History: Aspects of the Western Theory of Development.* London: Oxford University Press, 1969.

Nizan, Paul. *Les chiens de garde.* 1932. Reprint. Paris: Maspero, 1960.

Noakes, Jeremy. "The Origins, Structure and Functions of Nawi Terror." In *Terrorism, Ideology and Revolution,* ed. Noël O'Sullivan, 67–87. Brighton: Whitesheaf Books, 1986.

Notarnicola, Sante. *La révolte à perpétuité.* Lausanne: Les Editions d'En Bas, 1977.

Nuñez, Luis C. *Clases sociales en Euskadi.* San Sebastián: Txertoa, 1977.

———. *Opresión y defensa del Euskera.* San Sebastián: Txertoa, 1976.

Offegeld, Jacques, and Christian Souris. *Euro-terrorisme: La Belgique étranglée.* Montigny-le-Tilleul: Scaillet, 1985.

Onaindia, Mario. *La lucha de clases en Euskadi (1939–1980).* San Sebastián: Hordago, n.d.

O'Neil, Bard E. *Armed Struggle in Palestine: A Political Military Analysis.* Boulder, Colorado: Westview Press, 1978.

———. "Toward a Typology of Political Terrorism: The Palestinian Resistance Movement." *Journal of International Affairs* 32, No. 1 (Spring–Summer 1978):17–42.

O'Sullivan, Noël, ed. *Terrorism, Ideology, and Revolution.* Brighton: Whitesheaf Books, 1986.

Owen, Roger, ed. *Essays on Crisis in Lebanon.* London: Ithaca Press, 1976.

Paci, Massimo. *La struttura sociale italiana.* Bologna: Il Mulino, 1982.

Padovani, Marcelle. *Vivre avec le terrorisme.* Paris: Calmann-Lévy, 1982.

Pasquino, Gianfranco. *Crisi dei partiti e governabilità.* Bologna: Il Mulino, 1980.

———. "Differenze e somiglianze: per una ricerca sul terrorismo italiano." In *Terrorismo e violenza politica,* ed. Donatella Della Porta and Gianfranco Pasquino, 237–63. Bologna: Il Mulino, 1983.

———, ed. *Il sistema politico italiano.* Rome: Laterza, 1985.

Pécaut, Daniel. "Guérillas et violence: le cas de la Colombie." *Sociologie du travail* 4 (1986):484–505.

———. *L'ordre et la violence.* Paris: Editions de l'EHESS, 1987.

Peci, Patrizio. *Io, l'infame.* Milan: Arnoldo Mondadori, 1983.

Pereira de Queiroz, Maria Isaura. *Réforme et révolution dans les sociétés traditionnelles: histoire et ethnologie des mouvements messianiques.* Paris: Anthropos, 1968.

Pérez-Agote, Alfonso. *La reproducción de nacionalismo: el caso vasco.* Madrid: Siglo Veintiuno, 1984.

Perrot, Michèle. *Les ouvriers en grève.* 2 vols. Amsterdam: Mouton, 1974.

Picard, Elizabeth. "De la communauté classe à la résistance nationale: pour une analyse du rôle des chiites dans le système politique libanais (1970–1985)." *Revue française de science politique* (1986):999–1028.

———. "Les enjeux politiques au Proche-Orient: entre la crise sociale et la crise confessionnelle." *Recherches internationales* 18 (October–November 1985):24–42.

Pinard, M. *The Rise of a Third Party: A Study in Crisis Politics.* Englewood Cliffs, N.J.: Prentice Hall, 1971.

Pizzorno, Alessandro. *I soggetti del pluralismo.* Bologna: Il Mulino, 1980.

Pizzorno, Alessandro, Emilio Reyneri, Marino Regini, and Ida Regalia. *Lotte Operaia e sindacato: il ciclo 1968–1972 in Italia.* Bologna: Il Mulino, 1978.

Plenel, Edwy. "La France et le terrorisme: la tentation du sanctuaire." *Politique étrangère* 4 (1986):919–26.

———. "Le terrorisme à vocation révolutionnaire." *Etudes polémologiques* 38 (February 1986):7–26.

Portelli, Hughes. *Le socialisme français tel qu'il est.* Paris: Presses Universitaires de France, 1980.

Pouget, Emile. "A roublard, roublard et demi!" *Le Père Peinard* (London), 16–31, October 1894.

Quandt, William. *Decade of Decisions: American Policy toward the Arab-Israeli Conflict 1967–1976.* Berkeley: University of California Press, 1977.

Quandt, William B., Fuad Jabber, and Ann Mosely Lesch. *The Politics of Palestinian Nationalism.* Berkeley: University of California Press, 1973.

*Quelques points de repère sur le Liban.* Paris, bimonthly journal published by the Liban Moderne association.

Quéré, Louis. *Jeux interdits à la frontière.* Paris: Anthropos, 1978.

Rabinovich, Itamar. *The War for Lebanon*. Ithaca, N.Y.: Cornell University Press, 1984.

Randall, Jonathan. *Going All the Way: Christian Warlords, Israeli Adventurers and the War in Lebanon*. New York: Viking, 1983.

Rapoport, David C. "Fear and Trembling: Terrorism in Three Religious Traditions." *The American Political Science Review* 78, No. 3 (September 1984):658–77.

*Rapport du Sénat sur le terrorisme*. Paris: Imprimerie du Sénat, 1984.

Raufer, Xavier. *La nébuleuse: le terrorisme au Moyen-Orient*. Paris: Fayard, 1987.

———. "Révolution islamique et terrorisme: le poids des traditions," *Les Cahiers de l'Orient* 3, No. 3 (September–December 1986):16–70.

———. *Terrorisme: maintenant la France?* Paris: Garnier, 1982.

Raynaud, Philippe. "Les origines intellectuelles du terrorisme." In *Terrorisme et démocratie*, ed. François Furet, Antoine Liniers, and Philippe Raynaud, 35–135. Paris: Fayard, 1985.

Regini, Marino. *I dilemmi del sindacato*. Bologna: Il Mulino, 1981.

*Report of the International Task Force on Prevention of Nuclear Terrorism*. Washington: Nuclear Control Institute, 1986.

Rodinson, Maxime. *Marxism and the Muslim World*. Rev. and abridged ed. Trans. Jean Matthews. New York: Monthly Review Press, 1981.

Rodriguez-Ibanez, Jose Enrique. "Fragmentos sobre el terrorismo." In *Terrorismo y sociedad democratica*, ed. Fernando Reinares-Nestares, Salvador Giner, et al., 37–69. Madrid: Akal, 1982.

Rose, Sir Clive, Pr Franco Ferracuti, Peter Janke, and Pr Jacques Léauté. *Informe de la Comisión Internacional sobre la violencia en el País Vasco*. March 1986.

Rossanda, Rossana. "Il terrorismo italiano: spunti per un'analisi e una riposta isituzionale." In *La magistratura di fronte al terrorismo e all'eversione de sinistra*, pp. 83–90. Milan: Franco Angeli, 1982.

Rouleau, Eric. *Les Palestiniens*. Paris: La Découverte, 1984.

Roy, Olivier. "Iran: de l'incantation à l'expansion nationaliste." *Esprit* 94–95 (1986):185–90.

Rutenberg, Charyl A. "The Civilian Infrastructure of the PLO." *Journal of Palestinian Studies* 12, 3d series (Spring 1983):54–78.

———. *The PLO, Its Institutional Infrastructure*. IAS Monograph Series, No. 1. Belmont, Calif (May 1983).

Sablier, Edouard. *Le fil rouge*. Paris: Plon, 1983.

Saïd, Edward. *Covering Islam: How the Media and the Experts Determine How We See the Rest of the World*. London: Routledge & Kegan Paul, 1981.

Salomon, Ernst von. *Fragebogen: The questionnaire*. Trans. Constantine FitzGibbon. Garden City, N.Y.: Doubleday, 1955.

———. *The Outlaws*. Trans. Ian F. D. Morrow. London: Jonathan Cape, 1931.

Samin, Ahmet. "The Tragedy of the Turkish Left." *New Left Review* 126 (April 1981):60–85.

Sanbar, Elie. *Palestine 1948: L'expulsion*. Paris: Les Livres de la Revue d'études palestiniennes, 1984.

Sanguinetti, Gianfranco. *On Terrorism and the State*. Trans. Jean-François Martos and Lucy Forsythe. London:Left Bank, 1983.

San Sebastián, Roldo. *Historia del Partido Nacionalista Vasco*. San Sebastián: Txertoa, 1984.

Santilli, Giancarlo. *L'autre usine*. Thèse du 3e cycle, Université de Paris-VII, January 1985.

Sayigh, Rosemary. *Palestinians: From Peasants to Revolutionaries*. London: Zed Press, 1981.

Scarpari, Giarncarlo. "La vicenda del '7 aprile'." In *La magistratura di fronte al terrorismo e all'eversione de sinistra*, 37–63. Milan: Franco Angeli, 1982.

Schelling, Thomas. *The Strategy of Conflict*. Cambridge, Mass.: Harvard University Press, 1960.

Schiff, Ze'ev, and Ehud Ya'ari. *Israel's Lebanon War*. New York: Simon & Schuster, 1984.

Schimel, Anne. "Face au terrorisme: les lois spéciales à l'italienne." *Sociologie du travail* 4 (1986):528–47.

Schmid, Alex P. *Political Terrorism: A Research Guide to Concepts, Theories, Data Bases and Literature*. Amsterdam: Swidoc, 1984.

Schmid, Alex P., and Jenny De Graaf. *Insurgent Terrorism and the Western News Media*. Leiden: C.O.M.T., 1980.

Schmitt, Carl. *The Concept of the Political*. Trans. George Schwab. New Brunswick, N.J.: Rutgers University Press, 1976.

——. *Legalität und Legitimität*. 2d ed. Berlin: Duncker und Humblot, 1968.

Sciascia, Leonardo. *L'affaire Moro*. Paris: Grasset, 1978.

——. *Petites chroniques*. Paris: Fayard, 1986.

Seurat, Michel. "Le quartier de Bâb Tebbâné, à Tripoli (Liban): étude d'une assabiya urbaine." In *Mouvements communautaires et espaces urbains au Machreq*, 45–86. CER-MOC: Sindbad, 1985.

Severino, Emanuele. *Techne, le radici della violenza*. Milan: Rusconi, 1979.

Shayegan, Daryush. *Qu'est-ce qu'une révolution religieuse?* Paris: Les Presses d'Aujourd'hui, 1982.

Shils, Edward. *The Intellecuals and the Power and Other Essays*. Chicago: University of Chicago Press, 1972.

Shultz, Richard. "Conceptualizing Political Terrorism: A typology." *Journal of International Affairs* 32 (1978):7–16.

Sigal, Silvia, and Eliseo Veron. *Perón o muerte*. Buenos Aires: Legasa, 1986.

Silj, Alessandro. *Maï più senza fucile! Alle origini dei NAP e delle BR*. Florence: Vallechi, 1977.

Simard, Francis, Bernard Lortie, Jacques Rose, and Paul Rose. *Pour en finir avec Octobre*. Montreal: Stanké, 1982.

Simmel, Georg. *Conflict*. Glencoe, Ill.: Free Press, 1955.

Skocpol, Theda. *States and Social Revolutions*. Cambridge: Cambridge University Press, 1979.

Smith, Anthony. *Theories of Nationalism*. London: Duckworth, 1971.

Smith, Pamela Ann. *Palestine and the Palestinians, 1876–1983*. New York: Saint Martin's Press, 1984.

Solé, Robert. *Le défi terroriste.* Paris: Seuil, 1979.

Solzhenitsyn, Alexandr. *August Nineteen Fourteen: The Red Wheel—I.* Trans. Harry T. Willetts. New York: Farrar, Straus & Giroux, 1989.

Sorel, Georges. *Reflections on Violence.* Trans. T. E. Hulme and J. Roth. London: Macmillan, 1969.

Sprinzak, Ehud. "The Psychopathological Formation of Ideological Terrorism in a Democracy: The Case of the Weathermen." Paper read at Wilson Center Colloquium, March 1987.

Stajano, Corrado. *L'Italia nichilista: il caso di Marco Donat-Cattin, la rivolta, il potere.* Milan: Arnoldo Mondadori, 1982.

Statera, Gianni. *Violenza sociale e violenza politica nell'Italia degli anni 70.* Milan: Franco Angeli, 1983.

Steiner, Anne. *La Fraction armée rouge.* Paris: Méridiens-Klincksieck, 1987.

Sterling, Claire. *The Terror Network.* New York: Holt, Reinhart & Winston, 1981.

Sternhell, Zeev. *Neither Right nor Left: Fascist Ideology in France.* Trans. David Maisel. Berkeley: University of California Press, 1986.

Stetler, Russen, ed. *Palestine: The Arab-Israeli Conflict.* San Francisco: Ramparts Press, 1972.

Suleiman, Michael W. *Political Parties in Lebanon: The Challenge of a Fragmented Political Culture.* Ithaca, N.Y.: Cornell University Press, 1967.

Tessandori, Vincenzo. *BR imputazioni: banda armata, Cronaca e documenti delle Brigate Rosse.* Milan: Garzanti, 1977.

Tilly, Charles. *From Mobilization to Revolution.* Reading, Mass.: Addison Wesley, 1978.

Tocqueville, Alexis de. *Old Regime and the French Revolution.* Trans. Gilbert Stuart. Garden City, N.Y.: Doubleday Anchor, 1955.

Touraine, Alain. *La conscience ouvrière.* Paris: Seuil, 1966.

———. *La méthode de l'intervention sociologique.* Paris: ADIS, 1984.

———. *Return of the Actor.* Minneapolis: University of Minnesota Press, 1985.

———. *The Self-Production of Society.* Trans. Derek Coltman. Chicago: University of Chicago Press, 1977.

———. *Les sociétés dépendantes.* Paris: Duculot, 1976.

———. *The Voice and the Eye: The Analysis of Social Movements.* Trans. Alan Duff. Cambridge: Cambridge University Press, 1981.

Touraine, Alain, François Dubet, Zsuzsa Hegedus, and Michel Wieviorka. *Antinuclear Protest: The Opposition to Nuclear Energy in France.* Abridged trans. Peter Fawcett. Cambridge: Cambridge University Press, 1983.

———. *Lutte étudiante.* Paris: Seuil, 1978.

———. *Le pays contre l'Etat.* Paris: Seuil, 1981.

Touraine, Alain, Michel Wieviorka, and François Dubet. *The Workers' Movement.* Trans. Ian Patterson. Cambridge: Cambridge University Press, 1987.

Touraine, Alain, Michel Wieviorka, François Dubet, and Jan Strzelecki. *Solidarity.* Trans. David Denby. Cambridge: Cambridge University Press, 1983.

Tranfaglia, Nicola. "La crisi italiana e il problema storico del terrorismo." In *Rapporto sul terrorismo: le stragi, gli agguati, i sequestri, le sigle 1969–1980,* ed. Mauro Galleni, 477–544. Milan: Saggi Rizzoli, 1981.

——. ¿ *Una historia de incomprehension exige negociar?* Maidagan: Herria 2000 Eliza, 183.

——. "Les Untorelli." *Recherches* 30 (November 1977).

Unzueta, Mitxel. "Claves para comprender una situación." In *Violencia y politica en Euskadi,* ed. Fernando Reinares. Bilbao: Desclée de Brouwer, 1984.

Unzurruxada, Juan Cruz. *Infiltración.* San Sebastián: Hordago, 1979.

Vallières, Pierre. *White Niggers of America: The Precocious Autobiography of a Quebec Terrorist.* Trans. Joan Pinkham. New York: Monthly Review Press, 1971.

Ventura, Angelo. "Il problema delle origini del terrorismo di sinistra." In *Terrorismi in Italia,* ed. Donatella Della Porta, 75–149. Bologna: Il Mulino, 1984.

Venturi, Franco. *Il populismo russo.* 3 vols. Turin: Einaudi, 1952.

Vergès, Jacques. *Pour les fidayine.* Paris: Editions de Minuit, 1969.

Vidal, Daniel. *Le malheur et son prophète: inspirés et sectaires en Languedoc calviniste (1685–1725).* Paris: Payot, 1983.

Villeneuve, Charles, and Jean-Pierre Péret. *Histoire secrète du terrorisme.* Paris: Plon, 1987.

Violante, Lucciano. "Il terrorismo tra interpretazione e repressione." In *La magistratura di fronte al terrorismo e all'eversione de sinistra,* 116–22. Milan: Franco Angeli, 1982.

Wagner-Pacifici, Robin. "Negotiation in the Aldo Moro Affair: The Suppressed Alternative in a Case of Symbolic Politics." *Politics and Society* 12, No. 4 (1983):487–517.

Walter, Eugene Victor. *Terror and Resistance.* New York: Oxford University Press, 1969.

Wardlaw, Grant. *Political Terrorism.* London: Cambridge University Press, 1982.

Weber, Eugen. *Action Française: Royalism and Reaction in Twentieth-Century France.* Palo Alto: Stanford University Press, 1962.

Weinberg, L. *The Violent Life: An Analysis of Left and Right-Wing Terrorism in Italy.* Paper read at Twelfth Congress of the International Association of Political Sciences, Rio de Janeiro, August 1982.

Wieviorka, Michel. *Les dérives internationales du terrorisme: du mouvement palestinien à la question libanaise.* Paris: CADIS, for the FEDN, typed report, 1987.

——. *Les Juifs, la Pologne et Solidarnosc.* Paris: Denoel, 1984.

——. "Luttes étudiantes en Italie." *Les temps modernes* (June 1977):2252–77.

——. "Le miroir basque." *Esprit* 96 (December 1984):9–15.

——. "Terrorisme et media occidentaux." *Combat pour le diaspora* 20 (1987):9–23.

——. "Vie et mort de Pertur, militant basque." *Passée-Présent* 3 (1984): 183–99.

Wieviorka, Michel, and Dominique Wolton. *Terrorisme à la une: Média, terrorisme, et démocratie.* Paris: Gallimard, 1987.

Wilkinson, Paul. *Political Terrorism.* London: Macmillan, 1974.

Williams, Louis. "Entebbe Diary." *IDF Journal* (Tel Aviv) 2, No. 3 (May 1985):42–61.

Wolfenstein, E. *Revolutionary Personality: Lenin, Trotsky, Gandhi.* Princeton: Princeton University Press, 1967.

Wright, Robin. *Sacred Rage: The Wrath of Militant Islam.* New York: Linden Press/Simon & Schuster, 1985.

# Index

Abdallah, George Ibrahim, 257, 287, 338n.2 (chap. 20)
Acquaviva, Sabino, 103, 120, 327n.27
Action Directe, 37, 144, 146
Action Française, 18, 32
Alberoni, Francesco, 98
Amal movement, 273–74, 277, 278, 337n.8
Analysis vs. synthesis, 78–79
Anarchism: in Euskadi, 173; in France (1890s), 66–68, 323n.14, 323–24n.15; and subjectivism, 146
Angel (Basque separatist), 204
ANM (Arab Nationalist Movement), 229, 333n.24
Antenne 2, 47
Antimo (Italian terrorist), 328n.5
Antimovement. *See* Social antimovements
Antinuclear movements: in Euskadi, 167–68, 174, 210; in France, 118
Antiterrorism: by Antiterrorist Liberation Group (GAL), 169–70, 198, 331n.20; by Israelis, 244
Antonio (Basque separatist), 200, 204, 205, 206
Apter, David A., 71
Arab High Commission, 223
Arab League, 223, 224, 228
Arab Liberation Front, 236, 250
Arab Nationalist Movement (ANM), 229, 333n.24

Arafat, Yasser: in Palestinian movement, 224, 226, 227–28, 229; in Palestinian terrorism, 239, 240–41, 246, 251, 254
Arana, Sabino, 149
Arendt, Hannah, 6, 9, 31, 107, 294
Arias, 159
Arkoun, Mohammed, 283
Armed Proletarian Nuclei (NAP), 88, 110
Armenian Revolutionary Federation (Dachnak party), 255
Armenian terrorism, 254–55. *See also* ASALA (Armenian Secret Army for the Liberation of Armenia)
Aron, Raymond, 28, 31, 321n.9
ASALA (Armenian Secret Army for the Liberation of Armenia): decline of, 256; factionalization in, 256, 257; formation of, 255; fusion in, 71; ideology of, 65, 256, 259, 260; inversion in, 65–66, 256; nationalism in, 259; terrorist acts of, 255–56, 336n.26
Assad, Hafiz al-, 236, 253
*A traverso*, 116
Autonomia (movement): ideology of, 119; influence in other countries, 144, 163; inversion in, 65, 96, 133, 134–37; and Italian student movements, 114, 120; and Red Brigades, 88, 90–91, 141; relationship to armed struggle in general, 141–43; and subjectivism, 146
*Autonomia* (periodical), 90

357